HARVARD STUDIES IN BUSINESS HISTORY

1. JOHN JACOB ASTOR, BUSINESS MAN
BY KENNETH WIGGINS PORTER

2. JAY COOKE, PRIVATE BANKER
BY HENRIETTA M. LARSON

3. THE JACKSONS AND THE LEES: TWO GENERATIONS OF MASSACHUSETTS MERCHANTS, 1765–1844
BY KENNETH WIGGINS PORTER

4. THE MASSACHUSETTS–FIRST NATIONAL BANK OF BOSTON, 1784–1934
BY N. S. B. GRAS

5. THE HISTORY OF AN ADVERTISING AGENCY: N. W. AYER & SON AT WORK, 1869–1939
BY RALPH M. HOWER

6. MARKETING LIFE INSURANCE: ITS HISTORY IN AMERICA
BY J. OWEN STALSON

7. HISTORY OF MACY'S OF NEW YORK, 1858–1919: CHAPTERS IN THE EVOLUTION OF THE DEPARTMENT STORE
BY RALPH M. HOWER

8. THE WHITESMITHS OF TAUNTON: A HISTORY OF REED & BARTON, 1824–1943
BY GEORGE SWEET GIBB

9. DEVELOPMENT OF TWO BANK GROUPS IN THE CENTRAL NORTHWEST: A STUDY IN BANK POLICY AND ORGANIZATION
BY CHARLES STERLING POPPLE

10. THE HOUSE OF HANCOCK: BUSINESS IN BOSTON, 1724–1775
BY W. T. BAXTER

11. TIMING A CENTURY: HISTORY OF THE WALTHAM WATCH COMPANY
BY C. W. MOORE

HARVARD STUDIES IN BUSINESS HISTORY
XI

EDITED BY N. S. B. GRAS

STRAUS PROFESSOR OF BUSINESS HISTORY
GRADUATE SCHOOL OF BUSINESS ADMINISTRATION
GEORGE F. BAKER FOUNDATION
HARVARD UNIVERSITY

LONDON: GEOFFREY CUMBERLEGE
OXFORD UNIVERSITY PRESS

THE WALTHAM PLANT VIEWED FROM ACROSS THE CHARLES RIVER, 1944

Timing a Century

HISTORY OF THE WALTHAM WATCH COMPANY

CHARLES W. MOORE D.C.S.

Cambridge, Massachusetts
HARVARD UNIVERSITY PRESS
1945

PRINTED IN THE UNITED STATES OF AMERICA

To

N. S. B. GRAS

whose alchemy transmutes
the dust of history
into the bright coin of business policy

CONTENTS

ILLUSTRATIONS

TABLES

age, and finally is revivified for new service and perhaps new conquests.

This Company has belonged chiefly to that form of business known as industrial capitalism — the large-scale specialization in one job, the making of watches. Nevertheless, through one of its early executives, R. E. Robbins, it reflected some of the ways and methods of an earlier system — mercantile capitalism — and, through its recent president, Mr. F. C. Dumaine, Sr., it has exhibited many characteristics of financial capitalism.

The Industrial Revolution did much *for* society and it did much *to* society. Scholars have not yet attained an understanding of its effects. They have emphasized its influence on workers and on the tariff. But other conditions flowed from the movement. Certainly it gave a great opportunity to petty capitalists who had long been submerged by mercantile capitalism. Many of these petty capitalists (artisans, storekeepers, farmers) seized the new opportunity and became industrial capitalists. They became masters of the new techniques of production and distribution. For a long time the chief task of the industrial capitalists was to provide new services or old services hitherto supplied by handwork. For about two generations, normally, they had an easy time. Then, one industrial capitalist came to compete with another who had about the same technical equipment. Conditions were all the harder when a downward secular trend came along such as that of 1866–97. The result was commonly a loss of profits, unethical conduct, monopolistic efforts, and bankruptcy. The history of the Waltham Watch Company illustrates the transmutation of petty capitalists into industrial capitalists and their subsequent distress through competition, domestic and foreign.

The major contributions of this history of the Waltham Watch Company lie in the uncovering of policies adopted to meet the needs and necessities of the times. On the whole, the Company's experiences have been typical of American business. Pioneering, successful operation, and then distress have constituted the usual round of industrial capitalism.

There is no divine intervention in business affairs, no god charged with the duty of making affairs over so as to serve current needs more effectively. In the past the government could do little for business, except strike back by legislation: it had no positive plans. Indeed, the widespread existence of the *laissez-faire* policy of governments and of the classical economic theory of scholars would hardly allow any constructive formulation on the part of the public.

The only hope for progressive change lay in business itself. The reform actually came from investment bankers who were interested in keeping a wholesome condition in the investment field and in earning fees for handling securities. Their selfish interest led them to serve a great public purpose. The much-maligned J. Pierpont Morgan was the leader in the period chiefly 1893–1913. I do not imply that Morgan had any clear-cut general or public purpose in mind, but I do maintain that he started one of the most socially desirable developments in modern history in trying to introduce orderly competition and able management in business situations which had become badly demoralized and chaotic. That this is not a common view does not detract from its validity. The leading opponents of financial capitalism have been journalists and newspaper owners who have fattened on the false stories they have sold to a public that has been very willing to find a victim that could be accused of causing its distress. It mattered not whether this was in an upward secular trend (1897–1920), when the high cost of living was oppressing so many, or in a downward trend (1920–   ), when lower prices and lower wages were bringing distress. Politicians, social economists, socialists, and communists could join in the attack (witch-hunt, as it is sometimes called).

The banking firm which came to the rescue of the Waltham Watch Company in distress was not J. P. Morgan & Company but Kidder, Peabody & Company. So successful was this investment banking firm that the finances, management, and general operation of the Waltham Company have been regarded as on a greatly improved basis ever since the reorganization. This success was dependent upon the discovery of an able executive — Mr. F. C. Dumaine — whom the author of this history calls a "financial industrialist." This category of business men should be compared with the industrial banker who helps industrial capitalists, while he himself remains within the ranks of investment bankers.

It was Mr. Dumaine who proposed that a study should be made of his Company's history, since he wished to have a frank report for his own use. In order to facilitate such an investigation Mr. Dumaine made an unrestricted gift of the early records of his Company to the

Baker Library of Harvard University. Dr. C. W. Moore then undertook the study and therein used the records so deposited and others made available by Mr. Dumaine. When the private report to Mr. Dumaine had been finished, Dr. Moore then embarked upon a larger and independent research project of his own which resulted in a thesis submitted in part fulfillment of the requirements for the degree of D.C.S. at Harvard University. This thesis is substantially the present volume.

The Waltham Watch Company (Mr. F. C. Dumaine, Mr. Boucher, now vice-president and manager, and the other officers of the Company) have been interested in the *History* and have supplied information when requested. Moreover, Mr. Dumaine has criticized the manuscript and corrected some errors of statement. It is our ideal in business history to get facts from inside records and to get criticism from inside men who know facts and situations. No other history of business can have more than propaganda value. But, of course, the final statement of facts and of judgments based thereon are the author's and his alone.

The manuscript was ready to go to press in May, 1941, but publication was held up because of a lawsuit, which was not settled till February, 1944. This delay necessitated adding fresh information to sundry parts of the manuscript and a final chapter to bring the story down to date. At this point Mr. Ira Guilden took Mr. Dumaine's place as president and treasurer and at once put new life into the Company. Mr. Guilden has read the manuscript critically and has been able to make valuable suggestions, particularly concerning those parts of the text dealing with the watch trade. Although the Waltham Watch Company has not aided in the research and writing, it has provided financial assistance in publication so that the work could be sold at a reasonable price. To Mr. Guilden it appeared that the story was worthy of permanent record and that the publication would be a fitting tribute to those individuals who over the years have contributed to make Waltham Watch history. Mr. Leo Kamion, vice-president in charge of sales, of long experience in the watch trade, has given generously of his time and advice in selecting the illustrations.

In the writing and publication of this volume, as of all others in the Series, the responsibility for facts, generalizations, and opinions rests with the author alone. The editor seeks to provide the author with materials for study, criticisms of his work, and alternatives of method, approach, and interpretation. The editor's job is to stand in between the author, the sponsoring individual or company, and the public. Neither Harvard University nor the Harvard School of Business assumes responsibilities for the contents of any volumes that are published under its aegis because neither the University nor the School has any unity of opinion or view, except that of scholarly detachment.

The author has had a broad training for the task at hand. His education in engineering began at the Carnegie Institute of Technology. Then ensued about a decade of experience in business, in both production and distribution. Fortunately or unfortunately, this experience was not in the watch industry itself. Finally, several years of the formal study of business administration at the Harvard Graduate School of Business Administration led to the awarding of the degrees of M.B.A. and D.C.S. This broad background has given the author insight into significant situations and enabled him to interpret fragmentary bits of evidence beyond the power of the scholar who has not had such a variety of experience.

N. S. B. Gras

February, 1945

AUTHOR'S PREFACE

THE CHIEF VALUE of a history of the Waltham Watch Company lies in the fact that it is typical of American manufacturing experience. The enterprise was founded in a period that is famous for basic invention and fundamental progress in the mechanization of industry. It had its greatest growth in the era of expansion that followed the Civil War. It suffered, along with other domestic corporations, from increasing competition and sought to escape by a succession of measures, each one popular in its day. It became a part of the structure of financial capitalism, prospered mightily, and fell into deep depression, all in conformity with the general pattern. At the present time the Company is still faced with the problems that are the common concern of American business and industry.

Although the problems of the Waltham Company were and are typical, the ways in which they arose and were solved are far from commonplace. The voluminous records, covering a period of approximately a hundred years, disclose a series of oscillations between the extremes of failure and prosperity. The story is featured by a succession of striking and colorful personalities who provide a rich and varied human interest. But most important, from the historian's point of view, is the fact that the events trace the main issues of business development with remarkable clarity and dramatic emphasis.

* * *

This history has been written primarily for the business executive and the student, both of whom demand the greatest amount of useful information in the least possible space. For this reason the text has been devoted to those aspects of policy and action that are the immediate concern of the chief executive. Those details that were of potential interest to the scholar and the critic have been segregated in the footnotes and appendices. This arrangement was dictated in part by necessity — the older records are lacking in detail, the current policies and practice of the Company are not available for publication, and the

CHRONOLOGY

*c.*1500 The watch industry began in Nuremberg, Germany.
*c.*1695 Leadership of the watch industry was acquired by the English.
*c.*1840 The Swiss took the leadership of the industry from the English.
1843 The Dennison family was hard pressed by competition in the handicraft industries, by the stagnation of business activity, and by the secular decline in prices.
1844 The Dennison Manufacturing Company was founded in order to provide employment for the Dennison family (p. 7).
1850 The Waltham Watch Company, as it was later called, was founded at Roxbury, Massachusetts, by Aaron Dennison (p. 14).
1854 The Watch Company expanded and moved to Waltham, Massachusetts (p. 17).
1854 Capital was raised by promoting the Waltham Improvement Company (p. 18).
1857 The Watch Company made an assignment in bankruptcy (p. 20).
1857 The plant was purchased at auction by R. E. Robbins, of New York (p. 20).
1857 Less than 5,000 movements had been made.
1858 A recovery in general business occurred.
1858 Robbins sold a large minority interest in the Watch Company to the Improvement Company (p. 36).
1858 A new charter was obtained with a capitalization of $200,000.
1858 Employees numbered 110.
1859 Two hundred employees produced 50 movements per day.
1859 The Nashua Watch Company was founded (p. 67).
1859 The average daily wage was $1.57; the minimum, 33⅓ cents.
1860 First dividend of 3⅛ per cent in cash was paid (p. 63).
1860 The capitalization was increased to $300,000.
1862 Dennison severed his connection with the Company (p. 44).
1862 The Company purchased the bankrupt Nashua Watch Company.
1862 Three hundred employees produced 100 movements per day.
1863 The Civil War created a demand for inexpensive watches (p. 45).
1863 Prices were raised 15 per cent and then 10 per cent (p. 51).
1864 The first effective competition was begun by founding the Elgin National Watch Company (p. 68).

1913 A laboratory was built and a chemist installed.
1914 War was declared in Europe; this created a demand for time fuses.
1915 The manufacture of mechanical time fuses was begun (pp. 105–109).
1915 Total liabilities had increased to $15,716,000.
1915 The ratio of total liabilities to sales was 3.94; it had been 1.18 in 1890.
1916 A note issue of $2,000,000 was sold to provide working capital.
1916 Inventory had a book value of $5,314,000.
1916 The ratio of inventory to sales was 1.05 in 1916; it had been 0.70 in 1890.
1917 The United States declared war and threatened to commandeer the Waltham plant for the manufacture of time fuses. This work was pushed to the detriment of watch production.
1917 Wages were increased 10 per cent.
1919 The note issue was increased to $3,000,000.
1919 Wages were increased 8–10 per cent.
1919 Sales reached a peak of $8,666,000, but profits were overvalued on the balance sheet at $870,000 (Table 13, p. 110).
1920 Inventory had a book value of $10,000,000; total liabilities were $22,000,000.
1920 The net loss for the year was $500,000; notes payable amounted to $8,000,000.
1921 The postwar boom collapsed (pp. 116–117).
1921 H. L. Brown replaced Conover Fitch as general manager (p. 115).
1921 A firm of consulting engineers was retained to reorganize production (p. 115).
1921 G. K. Simonds, representing the banks, replaced Brown as general manager.
1921 The accounting practice was revised.
1921 Net loss for the year was $2,500,000.
1921 Wages were cut 10 per cent (p. 180).
1922 Simonds became president (pp. 118–127).
1922 His attempt to reorganize operations was only partially successful (pp. 126–127).
1922 Efforts of the directors to obtain new capital and management were, after much difficulty, finally successful.
1923 New capital and management were provided by Kidder, Peabody & Company (pp. 144–150).
1923 F. C. Dumaine became president and treasurer (p. 160).

1923 An attempt to cut wages precipitated a strike which was settled by an increase in wages of about 10 per cent (pp. 184–185).

1923 Drastic reductions in personnel were accomplished; strict discipline enforced; sweeping economies inaugurated (pp. 162–164).

1923 Deflation of the capital structure was begun (p. 192).

1924 A wage cut of 10 per cent was the immediate cause of a strike involving almost all the employees (p. 171).

1925 The strike was broken after a bitter struggle which lasted five months (pp. 188–190).

1926 The books showed a profit for the first time since 1919; earnings were $1,246,000.

1926 Companies alleged to be assembling Swiss watch parts in the United States provided sharp competition (pp. 213–216).

1928 Earnings decreased 32 per cent.

1929 Panic and growing competition further decreased earnings.

1930 The Tariff Act of 1930 increased the duty on Swiss watches, which in turn led to smuggling (pp. 210–213).

1932 Operations were unprofitable; deficit, $580,000.

1932 Wages were cut about 30 per cent (p. 208).

1933 The National Industrial Recovery Act was passed, and wage rates were increased 28 per cent; employment, 19 per cent.

1934 Wage rates were increased 10 per cent to bring the Company in line with competitors (p. 221).

1934 Employment was the highest since 1928 — 2,500 persons (p. 221).

1936 A profit of $313,000 was earned.

1936 The tariff on watches was reduced about 35 per cent by invoking the flexible provision in the Tariff Act of 1930, in connection with a reciprocal agreement with Switzerland.

1939 * The control of retail prices under the Fair Trade Acts was begun.

1940 * The policy of casing and timing all movements at the factory was adopted.

1940 An "educational" order for time fuses was placed with the Company by the United States government in anticipation of war.

1941 Waltham employees were organized by the A. F. of L. (p. 278).

1941 Suit was filed against the Company by several stockholders, under the leadership of a single broker, for payment of dividends on class A common and 6 per cent preferred. Decision was that the Company should pay these dividends for 1939, 1940, and 1941 (p. 282).

* Detailed information on recent operations was not made available for use in this study.

CHAPTER I

SOURCES OF A NEW AMERICAN INDUSTRY 1850

Aaron Dennison, Founder of the Waltham Watch Company

In the archives of the Waltham Watch Company is an old photograph, somewhat faded, but still clear in its detail. It shows a family gathering on the terrace before a spacious English home. Ivy almost conceals the old brick walls and shades the tall French windows. From the costumes we may guess that the picture was taken in the late 'eighties. The dominant figure in the group is a large, loosely knit man with a white beard, a patriarchal beard, long and full. We recognize him — from the portrait in oil which hangs in the lobby at the Waltham plant — as Aaron Lufkin Dennison, the founder of the Company. The painting shows Dennison some twenty years earlier, when he was still active in Waltham affairs, but his expression is the same in both portraits. The directness and strength give a sense of calm conviction, of patient tolerance, of confidence and power. His features are rugged and well formed; his bearing, judicial. We can easily understand that those who knew him, even though they thought his schemes preposterous and called him the "Boston Lunatic," still could not doubt the keen quality of his mind and the integrity of his purpose.

Aaron Dennison was not the first of his tribe to show the pioneer spirit. The family is supposed to have originated in the north of France, moving to England in the sixteenth century at the time of the Huguenot persecutions. The first records show that in 1567 the Dennisons were in Hertfordshire, England. In 1631 they went to Ireland, which had recently become a fairly safe residence for Englishmen, and in 1695 George Dennison was born in Dublin. When George was seventeen years old he left Ireland in a sudden and unexpected manner. This was the year 1712, and the long War of the Spanish Succession (1702–14) was working toward a close; recruits for the navy were hard to find. Young George was then in college at Dublin but had the ill fortune to meet a press-gang from a British man-of-war and promptly found himself aboard ship. Service in Her Majesty's navy apparently did not please him, for upon the arrival of the ship at Newfoundland he took occasion to return to civilian life. The records do not disclose the manner of his going, but I suspect that he was quite as informal in his departure as Her Majesty's officers had been about his "enlistment."

George Dennison had no intention of remaining in so bleak a spot as Newfoundland, and accordingly made his way to Boston. After serving as clerk for a Boston mercantile firm, he went to Annisquam, near Gloucester, Massachusetts, became a shipowner, and engaged in the fish business. At his death he left an estate valued at £1,532, including a parcel of "wild land" at Freeport, Maine. His sons Abner and David settled on this wild land and built a sawmill and a ship for the coastwise trade in lumber. They prospered and multiplied, and at the turn of the century the fifth American generation was arriving to claim a place in Freeport. Aaron Dennison, of this fifth generation, was born there on March 6, 1812.[1]

By this time there were too many Dennisons in Freeport, for the town offered little in the way of opportunity. Uncle Cornelius had left for the frontier in Illinois, and when Aaron was six years old his parents decided that it was time to look for greener pastures. With that decision there began a series of moves from smaller to greater things that became the outstanding feature of Aaron Dennison's long and varied career. Freeport was a small rural town of thirteen hundred inhabitants, depending for its prosperity on lumber and shipbuilding. Twenty-five miles away to the southwest was the trading center at Portland; seven miles to the northeast lay the thriving manufacturing town of Brunswick. Of the two, Brunswick seemed more attractive. The manufacturing activities included a cotton mill of 4,000 spindles; more than that, Brunswick was a seat of learning. The town is described in Jedediah Morse's *Gazetteer of the Western Continent* (Boston, 1810), as follows:

> Brunswick, a post town in Cumberland Co. Maine, contains 1809 inhabitants. . . . A College is in this town in a flourishing state, under a president, a professor of languages, a professor of philosophy, and two tutors. . . . The funds are increasing with the value of the land in

this district. The legislature has given six townships, and the Hon. James Bowdoin, lands and money to the amount of 10,000 dollars. It is called after him *Bowdoin College.*

If we include the village of Topsham on the opposite bank of the Androscoggin River, Brunswick was half again as large as Freeport; more important than size, however, was the atmosphere of industrial activity and speculative interest that Brunswick afforded. It was a good town for a craftsman, and Aaron's father, Andrew Dennison, was a shoemaker by trade. In 1818 Andrew Dennison with his wife and four children left Freeport for Brunswick, settling in Topsham on the north bank of the river.[2] Six years later, 1824, the Dennisons moved into Brunswick proper.

Aaron's father, as we have said, was a shoemaker; but he was no mere cobbler. Shoemaking machinery was not developed until some thirty years later, and in 1818 a shoemaker was literally a maker of shoes. Although undoubtedly a competent craftsman, Andrew Dennison was not particularly famous for his workmanship. His restless spirit and varied interests made it difficult for him to remain long at his bench.[3] In addition to his shoemaking, he found time for many other activities. He was a colonel in the Maine militia, a farmer, a zealous churchman, a lover of music, and the father of nine children. In his later years he aspired to the position of postmaster; he was an inventor, a shrewd factory manager on a small scale, and his letters show him as a homely philosopher, sound in logic and temperate in his views. The following paragraph is from one of his letters written to his son Aaron, who was at that time (1837) in Boston:[4]

> I am afraid that you do not have exercise enough to keep you in good health and spirits & and to remedy that difficulty as much as possible I should like to have you retire to rest by 9 and rise certainly by 5 in the morning and take a good long walk in the morning air at least one hour every morning when it is suitable weather. Don't neglect this for I think it is important.

Aaron Dennison had come to Boston in 1833, after serving three years as an apprentice to a jeweler in Brunswick. It was during his apprenticeship that he began to develop his ideas about watchmaking and at that early date he invented an automatic cutter for making the wheels which, with the pinions, form the gear train of a watch.[5] For

Corporate Names Used by the Predecessors of the Waltham Watch Company and Approximate Dates on Which They Were Adopted

1850 Dennison, Howard & Davis (also known as Howard, Davis & Dennison)
1850 American Horologe Company
1853 Warren Manufacturing Company
1853 Boston Watch Company
1853 The Waltham Improvement Company was founded as a financing subsidiary and land company
1857 Tracy, Baker & Company
1857 Appleton, Tracy & Company
1858 Waltham Improvement Company was merged with Appleton, Tracy & Company, using the W. I. Co. name
1859 American Watch Company
1885 American Waltham Watch Company
1906 Waltham Watch Company
1923 Waltham Watch and Clock Company
1925 Waltham Watch Company

him about various details of the work and closed by saying, "Don't forget to learn all about hair springs, main springs, dials, hands, Gilding &C — as it is a good way acrost the pond —."[29]

Dennison was encouraged by what he saw in England. The Industrial Revolution had not yet touched the trade of watchmaking; handicraft methods were the rule. His report on conditions in the trade was in part as follows:[30]

> I found that the party setting up as manufacturer of watches bought his Lancashire movements — a conglomeration of rough materials — and gave them to A, B, and C, and D, to have them finished; and that A, B, C, and D gave out the different jobs of pivoting certain wheels of the train to E, certain other parts to F, and the fusee-cutting to G — dial making, jeweling, gilding, motioning, etc., to others, down almost the entire length of the alphabet. And how that, taking these various pieces of work to outside work people, who if sober enough, to be at their places, were likely to be engaged in someone's work who had been ahead of them, and how, under such circumstances they would take the occasion to drop into a "Pub" to drink and gossip and perhaps unfit themselves for work for the remainder of the day! Finding things in this condition, as a matter of course, my theory of Americans not finding any difficulty in competing with the English, especially if the interchangeable system and the manufacturing in large quantities was adopted, may be accepted as reasonable.

The construction of the watch factory was not undertaken lightly. Edward Howard had met Dennison in 1842, and they had begun to talk about the new method of watchmaking in 1845. About 1849, they took hold of the thing in a serious way; before undertaking to organize the Company, however, they built some of the essential machine tools and tested them. The experiment was a success, and the tools were laid aside for future use.[31]

PERSONNEL

While Dennison was in Europe, matters in Boston were progressing. A room was partitioned off in a corner of the Howard & Davis plant, and, on Dennison's return, work was commenced on a model watch and the additional equipment necessary to produce it.[32] But more important, perhaps, than the product or the equipment was the group of men recruited for the work. At the very beginning of the enterprise and throughout the early years, the Company built up a staff of thoroughly able men possessing, as a group, a wide range of skill and experience. N. P. Stratton had helped Pitkin Brothers to build their watch factory in East Hartford in 1837, and he had worked for Dennison as repair man for a short time in 1849.[33] James T. Shepard, Stratton's brother-in-law, had worked at the Springfield Armory for a number of years.[34] Charles S. Moseley, who joined the group in 1852, later became famous as an inventor and machine designer of remarkable skill. A Scottish dial-maker, an English jewel-maker, and two jewel-setters from New York also contributed to the varied assortment of techniques that were required by the new enterprise. The success of the new firm in getting under way is especially noteworthy in view of the many handicaps. There was no other watch factory in the country at that date, no machine tools having the necessary precision, nor were there any allied industries to furnish the finer parts and materials. Besides, there was no assurance that it would be possible to market the prodigious volume of seven watches per day even if the factory could produce them at that rate!

THE ROXBURY PLANT

In spite of all obstacles, the partners felt confident that the experiments — which were conducted with much secrecy — pointed to ultimate success. Shortly after Dennison's return from England, the proposed watch factory took on the substance of reality — the announcement is contained in a letter from Eliphalet to his father dated October 11, 1850. He wrote, "There is a new building going up on Howard & Davis premises of substantial brick 100 ft. long. I guess what it is for and you have the same privilege." [35] Dennison moved his family to Roxbury in December, and the building was completed in January.[36] The Waltham Watch Company was, at last, well under way.

CHAPTER II

SUCCESS AND FAILURE

Demand for Quick Profits

The watch company was organized with a view to large immediate profits. This objective was a necessary evil imposed by the conditions of the capital market. In the period from 1848 to 1850, when Dennison was looking for financial backing for his plans, the demand for capital so far exceeded the supply that lenders could obtain from 6¾ to 18 per cent interest on prime security.[1] Speculators anticipated much higher returns and occasionally received them. As a result, promoters were forced to promise great things in the way of earnings and they had to lay plans that would show a profit at the earliest possible date.

Technological Difficulties

Dennison was quite ready to promise all that was expected of him and to set forth figures to prove his point. He was thoroughly optimistic, his optimism being founded on a sound knowledge of the industry. The difficulties to be overcome did not seem to be great. The design of the watch mechanism was already well standardized; the output of the new factory would meet no competition except from handicraft producers; the principles of Dennison's method of manufacture were already well established in other industries. The only real problems were those of detail in the design of the necessary machinery and the development of a normally efficient business organization. Some of the machines had been built and tested before the Company had been launched, and that took care of the most serious difficulty. As for business organization, all the partners had been successful business men and there appeared to be no cause for worry on this score. The new enterprise was really a very simple matter if one took the pains to give it a careful, unprejudiced examination.

There were, however, many critics who ridiculed the whole project.

So much for the theory — the practice proved to be quite different. Immediate profits were not forthcoming, and difficulties were encountered in almost every department of the work. But the critics were no better forecasters than Dennison and his supporters. The project was successful in many respects, in spite of serious shortcomings in the plan of action.

The first step was an error. Dennison tried to design an 8-day pocket watch and the model was completed during the summer of 1850, but it did not keep good time. The watch was equipped with two mainsprings, but this expedient did not provide the necessary uniformity of action. It ran too fast at the beginning of the week when the springs were tightly wound, and too slowly at the end of the week when they had nearly lost their power. A few watches were made from the 8-day model, but the rate was so variable that the type was dropped and the work was started on a standard 36-hour watch of the English lever type.[2] This model resembled the standard English pattern except that the fusee and chain were discarded. The incident of the 8-day watch illustrates a feature of Dennison's character that is often encountered. He was prone to attempt more than was prudent and he failed to discriminate between ideas which were immediately feasible and those which possessed deferred or remote possibilities.

The second stumbling block lay in the problems of machine design. The experiments with the machines built by Dennison in 1849 had not been exhaustive, and many difficulties were encountered in continuous service that had not been apparent in the tests. Extreme accuracy was required. On some of the parts it was necessary to work to $\frac{1}{5000}$ of an inch. The need for precision and the microscopic size of some of the finished parts imposed conditions that the makers of standard machine tools of that day were not prepared to meet. The Company had no choice but to redesign Dennison's original equipment and build the new machines in their own shops. "Attempts were made," according to Howard, "to have them executed outside but it was impossible to get them constructed carefully."[3]

PLANNING FOR THE LONG PULL

Another difficulty lay in determining the most suitable scale of operations. Dennison was attempting to inaugurate a mass-production industry. He had no background of experience in this new technique except what could be gleaned from the manufacturers of firearms and from the few tentative steps in the direction which had been taken by the clock industry. There was no adequate information on which to base an estimate of the output necessary for the efficient use of mass-production methods. The plant at Roxbury was so much larger than the usual watchmaker's workshop that it seemed to be entirely adequate, but experience proved otherwise. Howard's account continues, "It was more than three years before the establishment had fairly and fully started in the business of making watches, and then it was found that it would require ten times as much room as had been provided, and we set about building a very much larger factory. . . ."[4]

THE MOVE TO WALTHAM

Other versions of the story state that the dust from Hampden Street filtered into the plant to the detriment of the accuracy and appearance of the watches. And it is probable that Dennison's love of rural surroundings and village life also influenced the decision. He visualized an industrial community surrounding the new factory—a community which would combine the best features of the city and the country. With this ideal in mind, he obtained an option on the Bemis Farm. Marsh tells the story in this fashion:[5]

> The "Bemis Farm" [was] situated on the south side of the Charles River about threequarters of a mile from the center of the village of Waltham, and only ten miles from the city of Boston.
>
> Having found a satisfactory location for the factory, the next thing was to make it evident to the employees that country life was a thing greatly to be desired. Accordingly, Mr. Dennison used to plan excursions into the country, the objective point, of course, being a certain pasture on the south bank of the Charles River. And then he would endeavor to awaken in his companions a little of the enthusiasm which always seemed to have possessed him by pointing out to them some of the very charming locations on which to build houses. It is related that on one of these outing days, Mr. Dennison mounted a stone wall, and waving his long arms toward the adjoining field, he exclaimed to his companions, "Somewhere about there, gentlemen, there is going to be a watch factory."

The factory was subsequently built on the spot then designated.

ORGANIZATION OF THE BUSINESS

The purchase of the Bemis Farm was accomplished by organizing a new company, the Waltham Improvement Company, which we shall hereafter call "the Land Company." Money for the construction of the new plant was borrowed from the Land Company, which consisted largely of Waltham residents. The Watch Company owned 25 per cent of the stock of the Land Company, and both Howard and Curtis were on the board of directors of the new organization. Dennison, with other members of his family, owned 7 per cent of the stock; David P. Davis, Howard's partner, owned one per cent. Although the partners in the Watch Company controlled 33 per cent of the Land Company stock, they did not hold office; both president and treasurer were stockholders from the village of Waltham.

The enterprise at this stage of development consisted of three closely related parts: the Watch Company proper; the Land Company, which owned the Bemis Farm; and the community of watchmakers that grew up around the plant. This community was a part of the project as conceived by Dennison, and it was carefully fostered by his successors, often at considerable expense to the Company. Accommodations for single men and women were provided, but the central idea was that employees should own their own homes.

The Waltham Watch community was a great success. It was not only a financial success for the stockholders, but it was also one of the outstanding accomplishments of American industry in the field of social experiment. The community developed a remarkable degree of solidarity and a notable *esprit de corps* of which Waltham officials and employees were inordinately proud and which helped to maintain unbroken peace and coöperation between management and labor for a period of seventy years. When the new plant was built in 1854, Dennison moved to Waltham and occupied the Bemis homestead, living among his workers in true patriarchal style.

The new plant was ready to operate in October, 1854. The payroll was increased to 90 hands and production rose to 30 watches per week. The outlook for the new industry was promising. Success seemed to hinge on the efficiency of the business organization.

Business organization at Waltham was very simple. Dennison managed the plant; Edward Howard looked after the finances. Each man

Drawn from nature by A. C. WARREN, Waltham. Reproduced by Grace E. Marsh, West Newton. L. H. Bradford and Co.'s Lith., Boston

WORKS OF THE BOSTON WATCH COMPANY AT WALTHAM, MASS.

had an established clientele among retail jewelers, and the two combined were large enough to absorb the output of the plant — at least so long as business was good. Every effort was made to increase production and thereby reduce costs. There were two considerations, however, that detracted seriously from the earning power of the Company. One was the continual need for designing, building, and repairing machinery. Another was Dennison's love of experiment and invention. He had never before had the means for extensive experimental work at his disposal, and it is possible — as Tracy intimates[6] — that extravagance in such matters was a major cause of the troubles that followed. This much is certain, that Dennison's passion for new developments was in direct conflict with his responsibility for economical factory management.

FINANCIAL STRAITS AND BANKRUPTCY

The first indication of financial trouble was a loan of $600 given by the Land Company to the Watch Company, October 6, 1855. This sum might have been borrowed to finance the manufacture of goods for the Christmas season, but there is no suggestion in the records that the Land Company proposed to furnish working capital for the watch factory. The loan is a suspicious circumstance. Doubt as to the soundness of the Watch Company's finances is confirmed by the tardy payment of the seventh assessment on Land Company stock owned by the Watch Company. The seventh assessment was due on October 1, 1855, but it was not paid until April 3, 1856. A year later the Watch Company was in serious straits, and borrowed $6,000 on notes which were guaranteed by the Land Company. These notes were executed in September and October, 1856.

In the fall of 1856 the decline in general business that had begun in May took a sharp turn downward. Sales fell off and there was an urgent need for funds. Dennison went on the road himself to secure new retail outlets for the product and was fairly successful, but the depression grew rapidly worse. Income dwindled and every possible source of funds was tapped. The partners contributed all they could. The Land Company extended further credits. The Watch Company's inventory and movable assets were pledged as security for loans.[7] The exclusive agency for the product was sold to Fellows & Shell, a firm of watch wholesalers in New York, for $20,000. Even that was not

troubled, I asked him what was the matter. He replied that he had been going up and down through the street trying to find someone who would buy the Waltham watch works which were to be sold at auction by the Sheriff in a few days. I said to him "Come and spend the night with me at my home on Staten Island; — we have just time to reach the last boat, — and we will talk the matter over," I had not before heard of the coming sale but I had for some time had in mind that my firm should get control of that business whenever there should come an opportunity. The business of our firm had heretofore been exclusively that of importing watches.

Accordingly, Mr. Baker went home with me and told me about the situation and the plans of his firm. The next morning I saw Mr. R. E. Robbins and urged him to look into the matter, and if he should find it practicable, to acquire the property, for I felt sure that they were making a good watch movement, and that we could certainly make the business of manufacturing them and selling them profitable.

Both these accounts were written nearly thirty years after the event and are subject to minor errors, but the gist of the tale should be reliable. Tracy emphasizes the weak financial position of the old Watch Company and the extreme measures taken by Dennison and his partners to raise money. There is also evidence of the maneuvering of various parties for control of the Company. Howard wanted the plant to fall into the hands of his friend Rice, who held the chattel mortgage on the Company's movable property. Dennison wanted it to go to Tracy and Baker, who showed a more speculative temper and had offered Dennison a liberal contract for his services as superintendent. Robbins and Appleton were sitting in the background waiting for a chance to apply their shrewd business judgment and financial skill to this project of Dennison's, after it had proved to be a mechanical success. In the end, the prize went to the mercantile men — Robbins and Appleton.

The difficulties in the old Company and the frictions in the new are also set forth in a letter from Dennison to his brother Benjamin, dated Liverpool, July 4, 1857. It reads in part:

You are aware that my start from home was quite sudden although not wholly unexpected by me as there had existed a necessity for someone to make the journey for many months previous for the purpose of stocking up a little or obtain some help or both. And since the sale and there appeared to be a show for a new establishment [operated by Howard and

Rice] depriving the old of a portion of even their short supply of help and materials the necessity for the journey and promptness in movement became more pressing still.

The prospect of remaining in Europe was pleasing to Dennison. The letter continues:

To me this would be a change much to be desired — as it would relieve me from the befogged position in which I have been placed for a number of years or perhaps I should say the consequences of such a position, as it is not to be presumed that the present owners are to *repeat* the folly of the old concern of trying to keep the machine going without at least — *oil* enough to grease the wheels.

In addition, Dennison was glad to remain at a distance from the new owners.

Up to my leaving, perhaps you are aware, my position in the new concern had not been fairly settled. There was indeed a distinct understanding with the parties Tracy & Baker with whom I conferred as to the purchase that I was to have the general superintendence of the business and to have 5 pr ct. on the manufacture with a guarantee that the same should not fall below 3000$ a year and there was a dead certainty in my mind that with any decent management of financial matters, I should realize from 4 to 5,000$. This is just what I felt was my just proportion of the business.

It turned out however, after the sale, that the parties whom I had the understanding with took in two other partners who I fancy were not made acquainted with the nature of my claims or expectations, and for that reason I have been preparing myself for a disclaimer from the new partners. . . . I know but one of the partners who came in subsequently (he the money man [Robbins]) and of him only enough to discover that under all the circumstances, if he was to have much to say about the business, the sooner I could make it convenient to leave the better.

These letters allow us to piece together some of the inside story of this early period. Dennison anticipated the inevitable collapse as early as November, 1856, for his sister Matilda wrote to him on the twenty-fifth about her own business affairs, adding, "By the way you talk quite strongly of a bust up at the Watch Factory. . . ." Not only were times hard and the Company's treasury empty but we have seen also that Dennison was severely critical of Howard's financial management, and a general internal quarrel is implied. Here are the first clues to what later proved to be Dennison's most serious weakness — a pronounced tendency to work at cross purposes with his financial supporters and to develop violent mutual antagonisms. In Howard's case any differences of opinion that existed at the time were soon forgotten, and Dennison's later correspondence bears witness to the enduring friendship between the two men.

SELECTION OF MANAGEMENT BY TRIAL AND ERROR

There was also friction between the *new* partners. The original plan gave the management of the Watch Company to Baker — Tracy and Robbins to remain inactive. The new firm was called Tracy Baker & Company.

Tracy's account continues:

Baker came home to get his traps to return [to Waltham] at once, and our partnership articles were made in triplicate to be signed. But instead I received a letter from him demanding a change in our articles of copartnership. . . . [But] we were all in equal interest, pro rata to our cash paid in, and there seemed nothing further to demand. After a brief correspondence Baker would not do anything, and never again came to Waltham.

Stratton completes the picture in a letter written to Dennison in July. Stratton was temporarily in charge of the factory and he kept his friend Dennison informed of current events and Company gossip at Waltham. He reported the sequel to Baker's defection as follows:[2]

You are aware before this of the dissolution of Tracy Baker & Co. and the organization of the new firm of Appleton Tracy & Co. Mr. [James] Appleton is to be resident partner, while Mr. Tracy remains in Philadelphia for the present as matters look a little squally in that direction. No doubt in the end, it will result in the dissolution of Tracy & Baker [of Philadelphia], as the quarrel has gone so far.

It is possible that Baker was incensed that no compensation for his services as manager was included in the articles of partnership. Or Robbins may not have had any higher regard for Baker's executive ability than Tracy expressed when he said of him, "Bear in mind here that Baker was only a clerical man, a fine writer and bookkeeper."[3] Or perhaps Baker was induced to resign so that a place could be made for James W. Appleton, Jr., older brother of Robbins' partner, D. F. Appleton. Or Baker may have been so hard pressed by the depression that he was forced to liquidate his more speculative ventures. This much we know, that Robbins bought up Baker's interest in the firm for $6,000[4] and he also purchased from him on the same date (June 30, 1857) two parcels of land — 10 acres near Philadelphia and 24,000 acres in the State of Arkansas.

During these changes in ownership and management the plant was operating under difficulties. Dennison was in England trying to get materials and skilled craftsmen. On July 12 Stratton wrote to Dennison:

> In all probability you will be sent for to return by the middle of Aug. I cannot get along without you much longer. I have everything to do myself. Neither Mr. Tracy Appleton or Robbins have been here for eight or ten days.

Dennison returned to Boston as scheduled and took up his duties as factory superintendent.

This trip to Europe — Dennison's second — had been a great adventure. He had watched the preparations for laying the transatlantic telegraph cable and was highly enthusiastic. He wrote in his letter of July 4:

> There are many *croakers* as there always must be where a bold and unheard of enterprise of this kind is started, predicting a failure but to me the thing is as feasible, so far as laying the wire is concerned, as it would be to stretch a rope from the Brunswick shore to Cow Island, — but there is a possibility of the electric currents not passing so readily for such a distance with the wire all immersed in Water but this *possibility* is hardly to be taken into acct.

He also commented at length on the construction of the *Great Eastern*, a steamship 680 feet in length and of 22,000 tons displacement, adding, "And I think if you and I live 10 years more we may see steamers of 50,000 tons burthen." These lines reveal most clearly the cast of Dennison's genius, as well as one of his faults. They show the scope of his vision, the extent of his confidence, and his contempt for minor obstacles. They also illustrate the major flaw in his thought and action — he was prone to pursue matters of great principle so closely that he neglected consideration of essential details. He did not adequately provide for the future expenditure of time and money required in perfecting a commercial process and in refining a commercial product.

Dennison's absence in England proved to Robbins that he was still needed at Waltham, but his control of business policy and management ended when Robbins took the reins. From that time until 1883, a period of twenty-six years, the Waltham enterprise was dominated by the Robbins and Appleton group. The change was radical and complete. Its effect on the business was phenomenal. It will be worth while to leave the Waltham story for a moment and discover who these men were and what sort of talent they brought to the new venture.

Royal Elisha Robbins was born in the village of Kensington, Connecticut, in 1824, son of a Congregational clergyman and author. This circumstance assures us that his early training taught him the wise use of money and the proper deportment for a man much in the public eye. At the age of seventeen he accepted a position with his uncle, Chauncey Robbins, in the firm of Robbins & Martin of Birmingham, England. There he learned the fundamentals of the general export trade and eventually took charge of the watch department. When the firm was dissolved five years later, he returned to New York and established his own business importing watches for the American market. At that date, 1846, there were very few watches made in this country and those produced by Swiss and English craftsmen were much in demand.

Robbins' venture in New York was timely. The year 1846 was mildly prosperous — it was the first year of real prosperity since the collapse of the cotton boom in 1839. The following year brought a boom in the wake of the Mexican War which continued with only minor recessions for a period of ten years. Robbins' business expanded. In 1850 he took his brother Henry into partnership and the firm was called Robbins & Brother. Somewhat later, D. F. Appleton became a junior partner and the firm was called Robbins Bros. & Company.

By 1857, after eleven years as a merchant in New York, Robbins was rich, a bachelor, and in poor health.[5] On February 1, 1857, the firm of Robbins Bros. & Company was liquidated, and a new firm

ROYAL ELISHA ROBBINS

Treasurer of the Company, 1859–1902

of Robbins & Appleton was formed. R. E. Robbins put $50,000 into the new firm as a "special" or silent partner.[6] About four months later he invested $35,000, a large part of his liquid assets, in Tracy Baker & Company, the purchasers of the watch plant at Waltham. This transaction gave Robbins a controlling interest in two firms, one producing watches and the other marketing them.[7] He was in a position to act as the presiding genius and responsible authority in both concerns, leaving the burden of executive routine to subordinates. If that was his intention, he was only partially successful, for he found it necessary to take an active part in both making and selling the product.

Daniel Fuller Appleton was born in Portland, Maine, in 1826, of a distinguished New England family. He learned watchmaking in a jewelry store in Portland operated by his older brother, James W. Appleton, Jr. At the age of twenty-one, Daniel went to New York where he found employment that proved to be only temporary. Seeking a new opening, he answered an advertisement for a clerk and secured the position. His new employer was R. E. Robbins. Young Appleton progressed rapidly to a position of responsibility, and mention has been made of the part that he played in the negotiations with Tracy and Baker. He was not active, however, in the Watch Company during the first years, but his brother James was a member of the Waltham staff.

Here in brief is the background of the new management. On the Robbins side it was literary, ecclesiastical, and mercantile on an international scale. On the Appleton side there were wide connections in politics, law, and diplomacy, as well as the army and the Church. On both sides there was a wealth of experience in watches and an intimate acquaintance with the jewelry trade. There was also a knowledge of finance and speculation, for Robbins, at least, was interested in railroads, the transatlantic cable, marine insurance, and western land. These varied and sophisticated talents were especially useful at Waltham. The enterprise had been conceived and started as a mass-production industry, and from the first it required a degree of skill in marketing, finance, and business organization that did not become common until some fifty years later. Men like Howard, Curtis, and Dennison — typical industrial capitalists of that day — had narrowly specialized talents and were ill equipped to solve the complex problems which attended the manufacture and distribution of watches on a mass-production scale. The requisite skill was not a matter of genius nor could it be acquired on short notice. There was at that date only one dependable source of business executives of the type required at Waltham, and that was in the ranks of men trained in the school of mercantile experience. The best of these men had behind them the accumulated precedent of centuries of international trade. They knew the business difficulties of manufacturing; they had mastered the intricacies of coördinating the specialized activities of production, distribution, and finance even when spread over half the globe; they had a capacity for detail born of experience in dealing in many articles of trade; and they possessed an understanding of men and management acquired by trial and error in the markets of the world. They also had wealth, social position, and political influence. Both Robbins and Appleton were splendid examples of this class. Their talents, added to the genius of Dennison and the technical skill of his assistants, were outstanding factors in producing the deluge of profits which soon began at Waltham.

When Robbins bought the Watch Company, it could hardly have been called a going concern. The assets consisted of the factory buildings and the ground on which they stood, the few fixtures and materials that Rice had left after taking away the collateral for his chattel mortgage, and the employees who chose to remain at Waltham rather than join Howard and Rice at their watch plant in Roxbury. Cash in the till on June 1 amounted to $3,592.33. The intangible resources were a substantial amount of goodwill and the questionable asset of Aaron Dennison's services. On the liability side there were two mortgages, amounting to $14,380. A list of the assets, totaling $50,000.35, is given in the opening entries in the Company's books.[8] Robbins took these fragments and set about building a business organization.

The first problem was that of securing factory personnel. A trial proved that Robbins could not get along without Dennison and he recalled the latter from Europe, giving him a contract as factory superintendent. I am sure that Robbins expected trouble with Dennison — the friction between them must have been evident from the start — but there was no alternative. Stratton and Moseley were competent technicians and supervisors, but they had not yet reached the point where they could serve in Dennison's place. The need for factory

DANIEL FULLER APPLETON

Partner, 1857–1911

hands was also a matter of concern, but the attempt to recruit craftsmen in England was not successful. Dennison wrote from Liverpool:

> But as to help we can hardly offer any inducement for an Englishman to emigrate, as workmen in our line, as well as most trades similar such as jewelry manufacture &c &c, are getting quite as good pay and have every reason to be as happy here as they could with us.

Dennison's failure to recruit English workers was not crucial. Probably the number of workers who left Waltham to join Howard's new organization was smaller than anticipated. At any rate, there is no record of serious difficulty from a lack of skilled labor during this period.

A more important personnel problem lay in the danger that Dennison and his men, Stratton and Moseley, might unduly dominate factory operations and fail to enforce the policies that Robbins laid down. This contingency was guarded against by appointing men of other sympathies to key positions at Waltham. W. H. Keith, clerk of the new corporation and former treasurer of the Land Company, was active in affairs at Waltham and very critical of Dennison's methods.[9] C. G. Robbins[10] was also a member of the staff, but the records do not disclose whether he was connected with manufacturing or with sales. In general, we may say of Robbins' organization that there was much emphasis placed on specialized talent and that weakness on the part of one specialist was offset by strength among his associates. The organization was well balanced, and no one, except possibly Robbins himself, was allowed to become indispensable to the Company.

PROBLEMS OF DEPRESSION AND PANIC

Robbins had heretofore been either lucky or shrewd in timing his ventures, but in 1857 the trend of the times was against him. The depression which had begun in the spring grew worse during the summer months, and the failure of the Ohio Life Insurance and Trust Company precipitated the panic of 1857. The crash came in September, and the trials of the following months were severe indeed. Robbins gave an account of them many years later at a banquet for the Foremen's Association:[11]

> Then conditions became serious. I had used up all my money and was well in debt. We had produced but few goods, and there was absolutely

no sale for those. The Firm had advanced all it was convenient or possible to do. Their customers were failing in every direction, money was 2% a month — when it could be had at all. It was a time of general panic, never equalled before or since in this country. I remember one cold night, — I think late in November — I called a meeting of all hands at the factory and explained to them the situation. I told them I was almost at the end of my resources, but rather than shut down I would make an effort to run through the Spring if they would *accept half pay*. It was a cold cut of 50%, but every one accepted my proposal.

DEVELOPMENT OF A STABLE BUSINESS ORGANIZATION

The success of Robbins' proposal for a voluntary reduction in wages may be traced to a variety of causes, particularly to Robbins' skill in his contacts with labor, to his personnel and wage policy, and to the economic security which his workers apparently enjoyed. These factors not merely contributed to this particular *coup,* but they also promoted the general prosperity of the Company. So important is the part they play in Waltham history that we shall discuss them in some detail.

Robbins, like Dennison, was a natural leader of remarkable talents, but his manner and methods were entirely different. Dennison was tall and rangy. A powerful man both physically and emotionally, he bore a general resemblance to his contemporary, Abraham Lincoln. Robbins, on the contrary, was built to a smaller scale and a finer proportion, all more in keeping with his sedentary calling. His portrait, hanging in the lobby of the factory at Waltham, depicts a man of physical repose and a calm, judicial mind. He seems to stand apart from all prejudice and bias, somewhat detached and impersonal. Other facets of his character appear in his reports to the stockholders. There we find evidence of a shrewd, analytical mind in his clear and colorful statements of policy, and a reserve of force which comes to light in the completeness and finality of his decisions. One might expect such a man to be cold and aloof, but this was not true of Robbins. He looked out upon the world with keen understanding and warm sympathy. There is a well-established tradition that he was always accessible to any of his employees, and they trusted the honesty of his motives and the wisdom of his decisions.

The second factor that assisted in the adjustment of the new Company to the trying conditions of 1857 was the personnel policy. When the Company was founded by Dennison, it was recognized that the mechanical problems were difficult and every effort was made to hire the best craftsmen that could be found. Under Robbins this policy was amplified and extended. Premium wages were paid, and workers from old New England families were given preference when new jobs were filled.[12] As a result, the Waltham personnel was of high character and remarkably homogeneous. Both management and labor had the same New England background and subscribed to the same general economic and social philosophy. The problems of leadership were much simplified by these conditions.

The third factor that helped to relieve the shock of panic was the high degree of economic independence enjoyed by the Company's employees. A considerable number of the factory hands were unskilled workers, many of them young women who lived at home and were not dependent on wages for the essentials of life. The remainder were largely skilled craftsmen who often had other sources of income or some savings available for emergency use. Since Waltham was a small town of about 6,000 population, it is probable that many workers were drawn from the surrounding farms. The Company stimulated home-ownership by employees in the village which grew up on the land surrounding the factory, and subsistence farming was possible for those who wished to practise it. In general, the Company took measures to prevent the exploitation of workers by local landlords and endeavored to keep the cost of living at a minimum.

The combined result of these three factors was the development of a body of employees possessing a great deal of solidarity and a keen interest in the Company's problems. The extent to which these factors contributed to the earnings of the Company cannot be precisely determined, but the Waltham records reflect the opinion that they were all highly important. According to John Swinton:[13]

> Mr. Robbins thought that the chief value of agreeable and wholesome surroundings was in their moral influence upon the work-people, and that, leaving out of consideration the obligation as well as the delight an employer should feel in providing for his employes the best practical conditions of labor, it is clearly his best interest so to do. Anything that lightens the strain of labor upon the mind, or serves to promote cheerfulness and contentment, is an economical advantage.

It will be quite proper to discount Swinton's glowing description on the ground that his zeal as a labor reformer had made him overcredulous. There still remains, however, much circumstantial evidence that confirms the general tenor of his report. Waltham history in times of success, as well as in periods of failure, tends to support the opinion that the carefully integrated program for recruiting personnel, for maintaining cordial labor relations, and for improving the economic security of employees was a source of increased earning power for the Company. This program was very expensive, but the opinion was widely held among employees and officials that it was profitable. The directors and stockholders also gave their support to the policy. Unfortunately, the subject is too involved and our knowledge of it too fragmentary to permit any rigorous deductions.

This story of the panic of 1857 has been pieced together from a variety of sources, most of them subject to bias in favor of Robbins. In spite of the possibility of my being prejudiced, I maintain that this interpretation is the correct one; but a jaundiced eye might easily see in these events the maneuvers of an unscrupulous management. This derogatory interpretation might conceivably run in the following fashion.

The factory at Waltham operated at a normal rate during the summer of 1857, but panic developed in September and the plant was practically closed throughout October. After a month of idleness, Robbins offered the employees half-pay if they would return to work, and they were forced to accept this or face the prospect of a prolonged period of idleness.

Robbins then reopened the plant and operated at full production until the following September, accumulating an inventory of watches having a value of about $84,000. He sold about two-thirds of this inventory to the trade during the last four months of 1858 and the balance to the newly formed American Watch Company. The proceeds from the sale of the watches, which had been produced at subnormal wages, went into Robbins' own pocket. Speaking of wages and output, he said:[14]

Many of them [the workers] were already working "by the piece," and very soon by making extra exertions, they made fair wages, while the cost of goods was of course largely reduced. The pay roll was getting heavy and still there were no sales. . . . Mr. Appleton reminds me today that in order to assist me at that time he took boxes of watches to Portland and Providence and sold them at auction. Thus, by all sorts of efforts we kept going. We not only did not stop a day, but we drove the works to the utmost. I felt certain of the result.

It would be possible to use these facts in connection with the sale of the watch plant, which will be discussed later, in an attempt to prove that Robbins indulged in a shameless exploitation of labor, of his partner, Eliashib Tracy, and of his fellow-townsmen at Waltham. Some such opinion was held by a few of his contemporaries. We have already seen that Aaron Dennison disliked Robbins heartily, and Aaron's brother Eliphalet had an even poorer opinion of him. Eliphalet's testimony is frankly prejudiced, but it is not without weight. He wrote in a letter to Aaron, who was then (1874) trying to gain a foothold in England:

As to your project of importing American goods [watches] in the rough, and finishing them I hardly see why it could not be done to great advantage, but after what has passed between you and Robbins I should as soon think of approaching the man in the moon.

He loves money, but at the same time he loves fame, and would be careful not to aid any project by which you would reach success. He is a very narrow man.

Eliphalet Dennison was wrong in this specific criticism, for Robbins did give Dennison real assistance in getting started in business in England. The fact remains, however, that Robbins was severely criticized by those who felt the keen edge of his shrewdness. He believed in the basic Yankee tenet that a hard bargain was good business and good ethics. He drew a clear line between business and philanthropy, and he made a huge success of both.

CENTRALIZATION OF MANAGEMENT

The management of the Watch Company under Dennison had been a coöperative effort. Dennison had operated the factory, while Howard attended to the financial administration. Howard probably also supervised the sales work, except in emergencies when it became advisable for Dennison to leave the factory and infuse the customers with his contagious optimism. When it came to the last ditch, Dennison took a hand in both sales and finance. The results of this loose form of organization were unsatisfactory, and Dennison expressed his objections to the arrangement in his letter of July 4, 1857:

> What I would like to do the next time is to have no partnership business but begin at the bottom — single handed — and work up by degrees. I have all my life been trusting financial matters to others and thereby suffering very considerably in reputation as a manager in that respect — while my *nature is* to be close in my expenditures even to meanness, however present *appearances* may be to the contrary.

The confusion of policy and authority that had existed in the old Company was soon clarified by Robbins. He put the technical details of factory operation in Dennison's hands, but all final authority he reserved for himself. He moved his residence from New York to Waltham and gave his whole attention to the watch business. Except for Tracy's minority interest of 15 per cent, Robbins was sole owner. Tracy concentrated his efforts on his own business in Philadelphia and there was no one to dispute Robbins' policies — no one, that is, but Dennison, who found it difficult to confine himself to the management of factory operations. He chafed under the restraint, but Robbins held him in check, refusing to give rein to his restless ingenuity.

The general policy that Robbins followed at Waltham is characteristic of the mercantile capitalist. The keynote has already been given in Appleton's statement that the intention was to *control* the business and make profits from the individual functions of manufacturing and selling. Robbins acted on this principle and entirely divorced the two branches of the work. The factory was operated by Dennison under general instructions from Robbins, but the selling was carried on as an independent enterprise, also under Robbins as selling agent.[15] Although the segregation of selling from manufacturing took place gradually, it was effective in principle as early as April, 1858. A few sales, however, were made at the factory until 1871.

The new policy brought a gradual reorganization of the salesforce that developed in the usual mercantile pattern. Robbins, in the rôle of merchant prince, kept his headquarters in Boston, where he could supervise the domestic and foreign trade in watches and at the same time be near the point of manufacture. When he first took up the active management of the enterprise, Robbins lived at Waltham, but he soon established himself in Boston and traveled the ten miles to the factory only when his presence there was necessary. The work in Waltham and New York, and later in London, was placed in the hands of competent and trusted junior executives. In this fashion the Waltham Company, which had been born of spontaneous enthusiasm and specialized genius, became a sophisticated business organization. At the top was the chief executive with a sound knowledge of finance, men, and business methods. Acting under him were subordinates, each a specialist in his particular field of effort. These subordinates were chosen not merely for specialized skill but also because of an understanding of the complex relationships which govern the flow of trade and the accumulation of profit. In the course of a very few years — less than five — Robbins had accomplished the transition from the primitive organization of industrial capitalism, characterized by Dennison's objectives and methods, to a full-fledged, highly developed business structure which was far ahead of his time. Robbins took a business devoted primarily to the *production* of watches and developed it into a balanced mercantile enterprise by the application of conservative financial judgment and a superb knowledge of men of every rank and calling. Judging by the performance of the Waltham staff, we must conclude that Robbins knew the capacity of the men he selected and that he knew the conditions required to call that capacity into play. This transition which Robbins accomplished so quickly is still in the process of fulfillment for a large segment of American business. Phenomenal skill in production and finance is common, but our knowledge of men and the motives which lead them to work is still rudimentary. Much progress has been made, to be sure, in the development of a scientific basis for labor relations, but the application of this science to practice is proceeding very slowly. Many firms depend chiefly on the natural capacity for leadership possessed by their executives, few of whom have the skill in human relations that Robbins consistently displayed.

SALES DURING PANIC AND RECOVERY

The reorganization of the Company brought excellent results. The sales for the first month, June, 1857, were $789.20; the cash outlay, $6,690.19. But by September sales had increased to $5,286.27, and outlay stood at $5,057.67.[16] Cash in the till at the end of the month was down to $243.32. At that point the depression in general business turned into panic.

The situation at Waltham was very serious. Robbins put nearly $6,000 in cash into the business in October. About $2,000 was obtained by dumping watches on the New York market,[17] but in spite of this effort sales for October declined to $3,084.35. In November sales practically ceased, the total for the month being $167.90. At this juncture Robbins appealed to his workers, as related above, and a wage cut of 50 per cent was agreed upon, but Robbins still had to supply working capital out of his own pocket. Further measures were taken to stimulate sales. Robbins & Appleton secured a preferential discount of 10 per cent above the usual 20 per cent, and a new and cheaper model, the *Parker* movement, was introduced.[18] Then the frenzy of panic subsided.

In December the gloom began to lift and sales rose to $3,515.69. January and February brought a further relapse, but March showed a strong upward movement which produced record sales of $7,894.28. During late spring and summer the trend continued upward, to the great satisfaction of Robbins and the envy of some of the stockholders in the Land Company.[19]

THE WALTHAM MERGER

According to the official documents, Robbins sold the watch factory to the Land Company for $125,000. When the deal had been completed, however, and a new charter issued in the name of the American Watch Company, Robbins was manager of the new Company and owner of 62 per cent of the stock. The story behind the facts is told by W. H. Keith, a member of the committee representing the directors of the Land Company in the transaction:[20]

> There was evidence . . . that the chief owner and manager of the new watch company [Robbins] was not satisfied with the location of his works. Waltham was a clever little town, with a population [6,000] not quite large enough to form a city, and to him it was very dull. He would change his temporary home from there to other places often and finally to the Parker House in Boston. But it seemed to him there was no resting place, excepting as he said, in going to and from the factory by sail.

Keith goes on to say that he feared that Robbins would move the business to the New York area and leave the Land Company with the difficult problem of finding a new tenant for the factory building. In order to protect the interests of the Land speculators, Keith proposed that the Land Company purchase the Watch Company.

Robbins' version of the story is told by Marsh:[21]

> The future began to look very promising, but more capital was needed. In these circumstances Mr. Robbins proposed to the Waltham Improvement Company [the Land Company] that inasmuch as the prosperity of that Company was in a great measure dependent upon the success of the Watch firm, their mutual interests would be best promoted by a union of properties in one Company, whose capital should be made large enough for their objects.

A comment by Dennison indicates, however, that Robbins was scheming to get control of the Land Company. He wrote in a letter some sixteen years later:[22]

> The talk, and threat of winding up [the affairs of the Anglo-American Watch Company, of Birmingham, England] which has been going on now for a whole year had about as much meaning as R E R's cold water which he used to throw before he got full control of the business.

Although this comment is not of great significance when it is interpreted in the light of the rivalry between the two men, it seems quite safe to say that the motives that gave rise to the transaction were mixed. The business was thriving and it appeared to be a highly promising speculation. On the other hand, Howard was expected to provide some stiff competition, and Dennison was contemplating a new plant of his own.[23] Added to the fear of competition was the conservative attitude that is the common aftermath of a severe business disturbance, together with the growing uncertainty arising from the political tension between the North and the South. Under these conditions many investors were seeking to convert their speculative holdings into cash, while others were anxious to participate in returning prosperity. Robbins did both; he extended and diversified his speculative holdings and at the same time fortified his cash position. The consolidation of the two companies produced an immediate profit for Robbins and substantially reduced his financial risks.

The terms of sale offered by Robbins were accepted by the directors of the Land Company at a meeting on June 14, 1858. The terms were as follows:[24] a total of $125,000, of which $100,000 was payable in stock of the American Watch Company and $25,000 in notes of the Land Company. The offer was accompanied with an appraisal of the property as follows:

APPRAISAL BY R. E. ROBBINS

Paid by Mr. Robbins for Real Estate over incumbrances . .	$ 8,500
Real Estate Mortgage thereon	7,380
Mortgage on personal estate by Cook in dispute	7,000
Paid for personal property over said mortgage	35,250
Parts of watches finished and unfinished	25,000
Imported stock material	4,000
Expenses in alteration, fixtures & repairs of real estate . . .	5,000
Expense of manufacturing of tools and machinery necessary for manufacturing watches	25,000
Advertising extensively in United States	2,500
	$119,630
Deduct Mortgages	14,380
	$105,250
Price for the physical assets	$105,000
Bonus for the "risk and labor consequent upon the establishment of the business"	20,000
Total Sale Price	$125,000

It would appear from the above appraisal that Robbins sold the watch plant for cost plus a bonus of $20,000. To the casual observer this bonus represented a blanket payment which covered wages of management, interest on the investment, and compensation for risk; but the bonus was not the extent of his profits. Robbins explained the transaction in these words:[25]

I took payment in shares of the corporation [American Watch Company], reserving my stock of watches to be sold by myself. By degrees all these were withdrawn and marketed, my debts were paid off and I found on settling my accounts that, estimating my shares at par, I had not only saved my capital, but, as the miners say, "Cleaned up" a moderate profit for the two years work.

The consolidation of the Land Company and the Watch Company was completed on January 1, 1859, and this date marks the end of the formative period in Waltham history. When the Company was founded, questions of organization and policy were decided in whatever way seemed expedient. The Company lacked a strong executive possessed of sufficient capital to support his administration. The business had been too small and too highly speculative to attract a man of requisite wealth and ability. Under these circumstances the organization did not crystallize into an orderly, stable business structure but remained formless and irregular like a pool of quicksilver, yielding to every external pressure. After the consolidation, however, the organization retained its basic structure for a period of sixty-four years. There were many significant changes in the Waltham Company during that period of development, but they came about slowly as the result of well-matured policies. The organization of the Company in those years was stronger than the economic forces that impinged upon it.

CHAPTER IV

THE GOLDEN AGE, 1859–1882

Sources of Prosperity

THE GOLDEN AGE of the Waltham Watch Company dates from the consolidation in 1859 to the appointment of Ezra Fitch as general manager in 1883. During those twenty-four years Robbins was the sole authority in matters of policy, and he kept a close personal supervision over the details of administration. The remarkable prosperity which the Company enjoyed in this period must be credited largely to Robbins' skillful management, but other factors outside the business and beyond his control were also of major importance. Many of the fundamental economic trends of the day were clearly in his favor, and, although we must give him credit for keen analysis and timely action, the fact remains that he was lucky.

The best piece of good fortune that befell Robbins was the rapid increase in the use of machinery that began with the Civil War. At this date the fundamental principles of machine design had been developed, the technique of mass production had been established, and the means of accelerating and extending transportation had been worked out. In brief, the Industrial Revolution had been demonstrated in principle, and American entrepreneurs were about to reap a rich harvest from the general application of those principles to practice.

About seventy years before the Civil War, Samuel Slater had evaded the prohibitions of English law and brought spinning machinery to New England cotton mills. In the ensuing seventy years the use of machinery had extended into almost every industry in the country, and the advantages of the new production methods were apparent to everyone. The new system was much more than a source of profits for business men; it appealed to all classes of the country. Tradesmen, craftsmen, and farmers — each one saw in this marvelous modern improvement an opportunity to raise his own standard of living in a very substantial way. This was especially true of the farmer, who found here an opportunity to turn from hard labor on the land to less arduous work in the factory. He might also trade the isolation of farm life for the stimulating contacts of the factory town. Even the consumer profited handsomely from an ever increasing diversity of products available at ever lower prices.

This new order of affairs, which we shall call *industrial capitalism*, was not simply an accelerated process of production and distribution, nor was it merely a new economic order based on the factory system. It was, in fact, a national philosophy and a way of life. It was the accepted ideology of the public from top to bottom (except in the South), and there were no apparent defects in the system that could not be attributed to individual abuses. Confidence in the principles of the new order was practically universal, and an unlimited field of application for those principles awaited exploitation.

Robbins was lucky, too, in that he had the leading place in a new industry. Dennison's contribution to watchmaking had been unique and fundamental. Ten years of work in perfecting Dennison's theories and in building up a production staff had given the Company a substantial advantage, and Robbins pursued that advantage with characteristic vigor. He made every effort to maintain and improve the position of leadership that Dennison had established for the Company.

Other fundamental trends favored Robbins' venture in the watch business. In the period from 1860 to 1880 the population of the United States increased by 11,500,000, and the per capita wealth rose almost 70 per cent. The Civil War created a temporary demand for watches that was large and insistent; and the postwar industrial development promoted a respect for speed and punctual performance which greatly stimulated the normal demand. Only the secular trend was unfavorable, and its influence was overcome by the stronger positive forces. In spite of the long and rapid fall of prices from 1864 to 1879, the Waltham Company made a profit in every year of the decline.

These, in brief, were the underlying factors that formed the background for the events and policies of the period. The manufacture of watches was a new industry in the young and vigorous structure of industrial capitalism. The popular faith in the principles of industrial capitalism was firmly established. The pressure of population and the accumulation of wealth were favorable factors. And finally there was the growing emphasis on the old adage, "Time is money." In response to these forces the succession of events was swift and dramatic.

THE SECESSION DEPRESSION

A wholesome prosperity followed the consolidation at Waltham, and the first dividend — 3⅛ per cent — was declared on March 21, 1859.[1] In the spring of the following year there was a second dividend of 8 per cent in cash and 10 per cent in script. Another dividend of 5 per cent was voted in August, 1860, and then prosperity waned. Lincoln's election to the presidency, the secession of South Carolina, and the occupation of Fort Moultrie followed before the close of the year. Sales fell off rapidly and the February dividend was passed. Fort Sumter was attacked on April 12, 1861, and the Civil War had begun. Robbins' own account of these events continues:[2]

During that year, came the outburst of the Civil War which brought the business to a standstill and threatened to again bankrupt the enterprise. There was little hope of finding a market for the factory product, unless it should be so reduced in quantity as to be manufactured at a loss. It was therefore decided to reduce expenditures to the lowest point, but to keep the factory in operation to such an extent as to hold the leading operatives. The hours of labor were therefore reduced, and some of the machinists were employed in the manufacture of small lathes, for which a market was found. Some of the workmen enlisted in the Volunteer Army, others were discharged, and a very few kept at work on movements and cases. Nothing was thought of but preparation for war. Our men dispersed, many of them enlisted. Robbins & Appleton and I, finding our occupation gone, took a contract to feed troops on Staten Island. Dan Sickles' Brigade and Billy Wilson's Zouaves were among the soldiers to whom we dealt out our beef and bean soup.

The change in tactics, as compared with Robbins' plan of action in the panic of 1857, is noteworthy. In 1857 the factory was pushed to capacity, but in 1861 operations were reduced to a minimum. In both cases, however, wage rates were reduced in a drastic fashion. Robbins' report to the directors, dated March 27, 1862, outlines the policy followed in the Secession Depression:

The object this year has not been to make money, which with about one third of the usual sales was clearly impossible, but rather so to conduct the factory as not to create new debt, to keep in employ the principal hands and to lose by such contracted operations as little as might be.

The loss as proved by the accounts has been $4010.85, that it is not larger, is owing in a great degree to the extreme generosity of the contract hands, who with but one or two exceptions in recognition of the extraordinary

FIRING THE DIALS, 1884

ONE OF THE WORKING ROOMS, 1870

state of things, allowed their contracts to be suspended during the entire year and accepted from one quarter to one half less pay than that to which the Company was legally bound. At least ten thousand dollars have been saved to the Company by these worthy unselfish men. The officers also voluntarily abated a similar proportion of the salaries to which they were entitled.

These formal statements, published after the crisis had passed, are probably accurate, but a better understanding of the situation may be obtained from contemporary documents. On May 9, 1861, about a month after the attack on Fort Sumter, Robbins took decisive action to meet the war emergency. His letter of that date to W. H. Keith reads:

With this exception [the ladies' model] there is not a watch of which we have not several months supply in ordinary times, so there is none of which we should be in need before we could produce it, supposing the war were brought suddenly to a close. I cannot therefore resist the conclusion that it is my duty as it is in the interest of the company to reduce the force of the factory to its *very minimum*. That minimum should be about wholly devoted to the small watch. . . .

I wish all this done in the most kind and considerate manner, and every word of interest and sympathy spoken that can alleviate at all so sad a business.

All my feelings are with our people; and it is my duty to the company that compels me to request you will see this done, and done at once.

Under these circumstances it is not surprising that the contract hands and officers were willing to accept drastic reductions in wages. Resistance on their part would have been decidedly imprudent. In fact, no criticism of the wage policy appears in the records. There was, however, considerable resentment against the management for the policy of adjusting employment to the fluctuations in demand. Keith reports:[3]

Fickleness has been char[ged] on us as a company; "Take in hands today and discharge tomorrow" is said to be our practice. . . . We had better run as we do to a disadvantage than to increase and back down again.

Even in this early period of industrial capitalism there was a disposition on the part of the workers to hold the Company responsible for continuity of employment. This attitude is not only evident in Keith's report of criticism of the Company's policy, but it also is implied in the solicitude which Robbins expressed for "our people." The concept of mutual dependence and responsibility existed, and it was particularly strong at Waltham, but the survival of the Company was the paramount consideration in the eyes of both management and labor.

DENNISON'S DEPARTURE

The year 1861 also brought open hostilities between Dennison and the Waltham management, and, in December, Dennison's connection with the Company was severed. At a special meeting of the board, January 3, 1862, the following resolution was passed:

> Whereas it appears to the Board that A. L. Dennison an employe of this Company as Superintendent of the Mechanical Department of the Factory, has at sundry times and in various ways, omitted and neglected to perform the various duties incumbent on him under an agreement dated Sept 1st. 1860, and has otherwise discharged his duties in an unsatisfactory and disagreeable manner, and whereas the said Dennison has offensively intermeddled with other departments of our business which are in no way under his care or control and has made unfounded statements and unjust complaints to some or all of our Directors and Stockholders to the discredit of its constituted Officers, to the depression of its Stock, and to the detriment of the Company's credit and reputation, therefore,
>
> Resolved by this Board, that the said A. L. Dennison has violated and rendered void the aforesaid existing agreement between this Company and himself and we hereby discharge him from our service and forbid his admission to the workshops of the Factory.

Relations between Dennison and Robbins had never been good. There was a fundamental conflict between the two men: Robbins, the shrewd, sophisticated merchant with a sharp eye for profits on the quick turn; Dennison, the industrial capitalist, bold and strong, striving actively in the present for some distant accomplishment, some ill-defined return. The gulf between them was great and there is frequent evidence of the difficulties that it caused. For example, the records of the directors' meetings show a succession of bickerings over the terms of his employment,[4] and, even after an agreement had been reached, the directors insisted that Dennison post a bond of $5,000 for fulfillment of the contract.[5] In spite of the strained relations, Dennison continued to serve as superintendent as long as Robbins remained on duty at Waltham; unfortunately for Dennison, Robbins had occasion to leave for a period of some months.

Robbins' temporary absence from the factory came about in this fashion. After his long residence in New York, Waltham seemed dull, and his bachelor's apartments at the Parker House in Boston not entirely satisfactory. In his search for recreation and congenial social environment he went as far afield as Gloucester, where he was a frequent guest of the Hortons. According to family tradition it was customary for him to make the journey, a distance of some twenty miles, on horseback. As these journeys became more frequent, it was apparent that Mary Elizabeth Horton was the object of his attentions. The details of the romance are not mentioned in the records, but we know that Robbins' suit was successful and that they were married on October 2, 1861, leaving on the following day for a honeymoon in Europe.

Robbins and his bride remained in Europe about three months, and during this period Keith was in charge at Waltham. Dennison was difficult to handle. He had strong convictions in regard to Company policy; he was impatient of delay and scorned timidity; in particular, he was overly fond of the precipitate use of direct action whenever and wherever opportunity beckoned. An open rupture soon developed; the immediate causes were two: a quarrel between Dennison and one of his foremen, and Dennison's irrepressible urge to assist in building up a wartime market for cheap watches. Keith recounts the details of the departmental fracas with some asperity and gives the impression that Dennison was despotic in his use of authority.[6] That episode, however, was of minor importance compared to the issue raised in regard to the soldier's watch. That issue was crucial to the future of the Company and will bear a closer inspection.

Among Dennison's personal acquaintances in the retail trade was I. P. Libbey, whose jewelry store was at 340 Pennsylvania Avenue, Washington, D. C. It is not clear whether the idea of a cheap watch for soldiers originated with Dennison or with Libbey, but the correspondence clearly defines the situation which existed. Libbey wrote to Dennison on November 3, 1861, discussing the war situation as applied to watches, and stated that in his opinion watches sold to soldiers would average from $12 to $18, very few being sold for a higher price. He added that about two months previously there had

were in conflict with similar plans laid by his business colleagues to develop Dennison's work to their own advantage. In this instance Dennison wished to act as sales agent in England, as well as purchasing agent for foreign materials. His proposal to act as sales agent did not meet with Robbins' approval, and negotiations were "broken off rather suddenly."[10] Dennison did go to England at about this time, taking his family with him, but apparently not as a representative of the Waltham Company.[11] Dennison spent the following eleven years in various unsuccessful attempts to capitalize on his experience in the watch industry, but he did not figure again in Waltham history until 1874.

The difficult situation which existed between Aaron Dennison and Robbins is neatly summed up in a bit of advice that Aaron received from his brother Eliphalet who was then — in 1874 — president of the tag and box business that Aaron himself had started. Eliphalet wrote, "I do hope you will not try to embark in any new enterprise on the capital of others or where you will be amenable in any way to others as to how you shall think or act."[12] This comment indicates that Eliphalet had given up hope that the characteristics which hampered Aaron's success as a member of the business community could ever be brought under control. Aaron's genius was great, but his faults from a business point of view were equally conspicuous. He lacked emotional stability. He exhibited an intolerant impatience with the forms and conventions of mercantile business methods. His philosophy was too much influenced by an all-embracing altruism, and yet his instinctive reactions were strongly egocentric. Speaking of Aaron's reputation as a business man, Eliphalet said:

> In addition to this there will be plenty of conscientious testimony that you are a schemer, without personal success, and that while your connections lasted with these enterprises in this way, they were not successful.[13]
>
> Your difficulty seems to me to be that your self-consciousness of right, purity of motives, and fine sense of justice is so sensitive to the contact of the opposite character shown in the slightest degree so horrified you that an immediate and impassable barrier is created — a negative atmosphere, that seems to make compromise out of the question.
>
> This firm sense of justice and strict integrity unfits you to cope with the artifices of the wiley, and crafty men of the world or even to suspect what stretches of conscience they will submit to, to accomplish their ends.[14]

The conflict between Dennison and Robbins has been described in detail because it illustrates a divergence in philosophy which lies at the core of a number of problems in business administration. It is an old issue, at least as old as the conflict between business and the medieval Church over usury and a just price. It is a modern issue, rising to great importance at Waltham in later years. A few examples may clarify the point. Other valued members of the research staff, like Dennison, have proved intractable. Labor and management took opposite sides of the issue in the long strike of 1924. The political aspects of the question were of paramount importance to the Company during Theodore Roosevelt's "trust-busting" campaign of 1907. Methods of allaying strife from this source are major considerations in the fields of advertising and public relations. In Dennison's case a solution was reached by removing him from the payroll, but in general this is not a satisfactory answer. As political and economic power shifts from "big business" to the dependent elements in the economic structure, it becomes increasingly desirable to solve such problems by education and compromise.

WAR AND MERCHANDISING POLICY

In the treasurer's report of 1862 Robbins congratulated the stockholders on the small loss incurred in the previous year — $4,010. The report continues:

> It was hardly to have been expected that a business so sensitive to the touch of hard times as ours, should have escaped without a serious diminution of Capital the unparalleled troubles of this memorable year. And now fortunately the tide seems to have turned in our favor. The high tariff, high rates of exchange and insurance affecting the prices of foreign watches, the growing reputation of our goods, and the more general feeling of favor towards all home production which our foreign complications have induced, begin now that the public confidence is somewhat restored to tell sensibly to our advantage. . . . The demand as yet is for low priced goods as in such circumstances is always the case, consequently we are paying special attention to the manufacture of such on which the profit will be small but I have no fear that unless we are met by some overwhelming public disaster, trade will not soon demand the better and even the best goods we produce.

Robbins' prophecy was fulfilled. By 1865 the soldier's watch — the *Ellery* — accounted for 44.7 per cent of unit sales and 30.4 per cent of the dollar volume. The standard models were in good demand and there was a small market for especially high-priced goods. Details are given in Table 1.

TABLE 1

ANALYSIS OF SALES FOR AUGUST, 1865
WALTHAM WATCH COMPANY

Model	List Price [a]	Percentage Unit Sales	Percentage Dollar Sales
Ellery	$13	44.7	30.4
P. S. Bartlett	16	42.8	41.0
Appleton Tracy & Co.	38	7.5	19.6
A. T. & Co., Ladies'	40	0.7	1.7
Bartlett, Ladies'	30	4.2	6.6
American Watch Co.	175	0.1	0.7

[a] Minimum list price of movement only. Some specially fitted models were listed as high as double the minimum for the "plain" movement. Discount to Robbins & Appleton, 15.43%.

SOURCE: Sales book, 1865–76.

Earnings for the period of the war were remarkably high, as shown in the figures in Table 2. Earnings include the appreciation of inventories resulting from inflation of the currency, and this factor may somewhat distort the picture.[15]

TABLE 2

SALES AND EARNINGS, 1860–1865
WALTHAM WATCH COMPANY

Year Ending Jan. 31	Sales	Earnings	Earnings as Per Cent of Sales	Earnings as Per Cent of Capital [a]
1860	$180,583	$49,837	28	25
1861	164,546	33,100	20	11
1862	61,465	— 4,010 [b]	..	..
1863	242,778	36,050	15	12
1864	576,885	124,557	22	42
1865	838,534	491,573	58	164

[a] Capital = $200,000 for 1860; other years, $300,000.
[b] Deficit.

SOURCE: Annual reports.

Detailed records for the period of the war are missing, but the annual reports of the treasurer provide us with a summary of the situation. Since these reports were given to the stockholders orally and were not intended for general publication, they are probably more accurate than corresponding records would be today. They were not, however, a frank and full discussion of events, as Robbins made clear in the report of 1879 by saying:

> It will not be expected that we should give you any detail of our plans of manufacture for the future. It would not be prudent as respects our competition who, as it is, in some way learn them earlier than they should.

The increase in the volume of sales was in part a result of the war, for the original impetus came from the military demand, but much of the subsequent increase was inherent in the normal growth of the new industry. The two forces acting together produced a meteoric rise from $180,583 in 1859 to $3,340,479 in 1883. Robbins stated in the report of 1864:

> I have the pleasure to say the demand for our production continues not only unabated but in quantities we find ourselves wholly unable to supply. Indeed the trouble for the last year has been so to divide the watches amongst our very numerous customers as to produce the least dissatisfaction.

As the volume of sales increased, costs and prices also rose. The index of wholesale commodity prices climbed from 100 in the spring of 1862 to 220 in the closing quarter of 1864. The price of watches followed the general trend. In the annual report of 1863, covering the preceding year, Robbins said:

> During the year we were enabled to establish an advance of our prices of about fifteen per cent and lately another ten per cent has been added, to which the trade has responded with as much readiness as we could expect.

And the following year he added:

> The several advances in price we have been partly compelled and partly invited to make, have been paid with entire readiness, and although these prices have now reached a very high point the demand continues as brisk as ever.

A part of the rise in prices must be charged against the depreciation of the currency and the general rise in costs. Part of it might be considered war profiteering. Some of it, on the other hand, was excusable on the grounds that the product was better. New models offered better dollar value to particular types of consumers, notably the small watch for women and the *de luxe* model for the ultra-prosperous. There was also a substantial improvement in quality, which resulted from better methods and equipment and from greater skill in their use. The treasurer's report for 1863 reads in part:

> And as to quality the advance has been so notable that there are now left probably but very few unprejudiced judges who will not give us the credit of making — everything considered — the best watches of the world. . . . And the cheaper article of today is in fact as good as the dearer one of 1859.

DEVELOPMENT OF ADVERTISING

That the expenditures for advertising Waltham watches mounted rapidly as the Company grew is evidenced by the figures in Table 3.

TABLE 3

ADVERTISING EXPENSE, 1865–1877[a]
WALTHAM WATCH COMPANY

1865	$ 7,347.17	1872	$63,562.69
1866	12,818.48	1873	27,211.11
1867	17,598.26	1874	27,842.56
1868	38,685.60	1875	17,131.25
1869	40,339.35	1876	24,079.94
1870	60,556.07	1877	30,388.24
1871	44,886.15	1877[b]	15,054.27

[a] Years ending Jan. 31.
[b] Centennial Exposition.

SOURCE: Ledger B.

The earliest advertisements in the available records are two full-page insertions in De Bow's *Review* for 1859. The print is very fine and the copy consists of a recital of the awards received by Waltham watches, followed by testimonial letters praising the accuracy and beauty of the product. It was claimed that Waltham timepieces were "equal in regularity to the best Marine Chronometer," and figures were given showing a rate of gain from four to twelve seconds per month. The author of one testimonial, assuming an air of professional authority, praised the mechanical design and compared the reliability of Waltham watches to that of the sun. Such extravagance was quite in keeping with the advertising practice of the period.

An advertisement, appearing in 1868 in the *State Journal* of Springfield, Illinois, showed interesting changes in technique. The reckless hyperbole of 1859 had been replaced by a style of copy which used more restraint in its literal claims, but indulged in poetic raptures. To support the emotional appeal there were quotations from press notices appearing in such famous publications as the *Times, Herald,* and *World* of New York, and *Harper's Weekly*. In 1876 still further changes in advertising copy were evident. The style then was sophisticated, the treatment highly technical, and the major topic was the Waltham display at the International Exposition at Philadelphia.

The use of displays at fairs and expositions had been a part of Waltham's advertising program since 1856.[16] Success at local and national fairs had been so complete that the Company decided to plunge heavily into the International Exposition in Philadelphia in 1876, and $15,000 was appropriated for the purpose. Interest in the exhibit was enhanced by including operating machinery as well as 2,200 completed movements, most of them in gold or silver cases. The judges gave Waltham the first award in its field, and the public showed a keen interest in the exhibit.

The combined showing of machinery and watches effectively illustrated two ideas which were new to the general public: first, that semiautomatic machinery could largely replace the use of skilled craftsmen even in the most delicate operations; and second, that the products of these machines were better and cheaper than goods produced by hand. This was news of the first order to producers and consumers alike, and the name Waltham became a part of the folklore of the country — a synonym for miraculous achievement. Robbins wrote in his annual report of 1877, "Our triumph at Philadelphia was undoubtedly the most conspicuous of all American successes."

The proposal to display Waltham machinery and methods to the general public caused so much captious criticism that Robbins felt it necessary to reply. His comments on this subject in the report of 1876 show an unusual breadth of vision:

Many questions have been asked as to the prudence of exhibiting machinery, where doubtless it will attract the attention of foreign manufacturers. In reply it is to be said, that only sixteen machines will be showed out of some thousands we make use of and which are necessary in any watch factory conducted upon our system. In fact we shall show only the process of making wheels and pinions, and it will be bound to be of interest rather to the public than to the trade. Besides it is not by exhibition of our tools and processes even if it were large and complete that the establishment of new factories is promoted. On the contrary, no greater discouragement to such enterprises could possibly be given than by the free exhibition of the factory itself and all it contains. In every case that I know of, it has been by misrepresentation of the facts that capital has been attracted to new concerns, and not by any true statement of the case, and this the capitalists, who have been attracted are now quite ready to admit.

The policy outlined above was carried to its logical conclusion when the plant at Waltham was opened to visitors. Many persons of national and international renown visited the Waltham plant, and the Company derived a great deal of excellent publicity from this source. Notable visitors included the Hon. Anson Burlingame with members of the Chinese Embassy in 1864, General Grant in 1876, the mayor of Boston with a delegation from Siam in 1884, and royalty more than once, including the King and Queen of the Sandwich Islands and Princess Liliuokalani.[17]

COMPETING FOR THE WORLD MARKET

The first attempt to develop the foreign market for Waltham watches was made by Robbins while on his honeymoon in Europe, late in 1861. He tried to secure a satisfactory agent in London, but was unable to do so. The war boom followed soon after, and there was no surplus product available for the export market. The lively state of domestic trade continued after the war, although somewhat abated, and there was no cause to develop the export trade until 1873. The panic of that year resulted in a decision to close the plant for a period of four months, and this time was devoted to the design of goods for the foreign trade.

The annual report for the following year was a gloomy one with respect to the domestic situation, but good progress in foreign markets was recorded. The report read:

The considerable and growing trade with foreign countries developed within the year has obliged us to make goods especially suited to the tastes of foreign markets and some extra outlay in new tools and machinery has been necessary in consequence of these efforts to extend our business. We are very much encouraged by the favor with which our goods are being received outside of the United States. It now really appears as if we should at no distant time compete successfully for the watch trade in the markets of all nations. With these large objects we have established a selling agency in London conducted for our own account which is being devoted with great energy to the introduction of our goods to this general trade of the world.

The report continued with a list of the countries buying Waltham watches: "the leading States of South America, the West Indies, Great Britain and her principal colonies, China, Japan and some of the countries of Europe." The enthusiasm of this section of the report is probably in part the result of a desire to divert the attention of the stockholders from domestic reverses, but the statistics of later years justified Robbins' optimism.

Our knowledge of the management of the London office during this period is limited, but some of the personalities involved are worth recording. The London office was first opened by Robbins & Appleton but was soon placed in the hands of Dennison's old friend, N. P. Stratton, who was directly responsible to the factory at Waltham. Stratton visited Dennison at Birmingham with the hope that he would travel for the Company in England, and Stratton wrote to Robbins for approval of Dennison's terms. Robbins apparently did not like the idea, and with good reason, for Dennison himself was lukewarm in the matter. Failing to make satisfactory arrangements with Dennison, who was then over sixty years old, Stratton hired the son, Edward B. Dennison. It was Edward's first job, other than working for his father, and he took to it with youthful enthusiasm. He wrote to his father shortly after his arrival in London:[18]

I sometimes feel like *hugging* Stratton, he looks so jolly and fat and has done so much for us. He is as kind to me, as if I were some particular friend of his, and with this in view we get on so well together.

Although Robbins apparently did not wish to employ Dennison directly, he did not harbor any ill will against him. On the contrary, he gave substantial assistance in Dennison's final and successful effort to establish a business of his own. After many heartbreaking failures in the manufacture of watch movements, Dennison turned to the production of cases by methods similar to those he had developed at Waltham. This project was just getting under way at the time that Stratton was opening the London office. Dennison's cases were of superior quality and attractively priced, and he succeeded in getting orders from Waltham for nearly all the silver cases required by their English trade. Edward Dennison wrote to his father on December 10, 1874:

I am so glad that you have got this work, & to have Mr. R. E. R. [Robbins] & his brother speak so favorably of your undertaking is very agreeable for me to hear.

The combination of Waltham movements and Dennison cases became a popular one in England, and the London office prospered, as shown in Table 4.

TABLE 4

LONDON OFFICE SALES, 1876–1884[a]

WALTHAM WATCH COMPANY

1876	£30,606	7s	1d[b]	1881	£ 23,066	6s	11d
1877	52,580	3	5	1882	100,785	1	4
1878	50,571	2	2	1883	107,189	6	3
1879	48,223	8	9	1884	56,795	7	1[c]
1880	64,127	7	3				

[a] Calendar years.
[b] 11 months.
[c] 5 months.
SOURCE: Ledger B.

EXPANSION OF THE PLANT

In the year 1859 the plant at Waltham was still a small enterprise. Approximately 200 factory hands were employed to produce 50 watches per day. The simpler operations were performed with manually operated machine tools — punch presses, drills, lathes, et cetera, while the more delicate branches of production were accomplished by the same handicraft methods that had been used for generations in England and Switzerland. In 1883 there were approximately 2,000 employees producing over 1,200 movements per day in a new plant using vastly improved equipment and methods. These revolutionary changes were accomplished in a period of fifteen years without undue strain on the Company's resources and without any trace of the objectionable social by-products that frequently attend an industrial boom.

One of the difficult decisions of the war period was to determine the amount of expansion which the circumstances justified. The profit possibilities inherent in a large wartime demand at high prices were a great temptation to overexpansion, but the inequalities between the economic resources of the North and South pointed toward an early end to hostilities. In 1864 Robbins' report to the stockholders contained this summary statement:

> Last year you will remember I expressed the purpose of the Directors not to make during the then coming year any enlargement of the works, but rather to employ to the best advantage possible the room we then occupied. That purpose has been substantially adhered to, the only new buildings being one absolutely necessary for the better accommodation of Mr. Hastings, a new boiler house, which was equally necessary for our security, and a small addition to the north wing.
>
> Entertaining now the same conservative views I then expressed, but taking into account the great change in our financial position, the more established and general preference given to our goods, the immense actual demand for them, and other obvious considerations such as that if we don't supply the demand others will attempt it in competition with us, after a good deal of reflection I have recommended to the Directors a considerable addition to our works and they have authorized its immediate commencement.

The proposed increase in capacity was from 150 movements per day to 250 movements and an increase of about 200 hands.[19] The estimated cost of the project was $60,000 to $70,000. The report continues:

> If the present state of things continues the outlay would be reimbursed in a single year, while on the other hand if the war should cease and foreign goods should come in on better terms than now to compete with us, we should be so much the better able to meet competition. The more watches we manufacture the less they cost and it is only a question of cost which we need fear the decision of.

It was difficult, however, to determine the proper rate of expansion. If plant capacity was increased too rapidly, the burden of fixed charges would endanger the financial standing of the Company in times of depression. If expansion was too slow, the excess of demand over supply in times of prosperity would attract new capital to the industry. A middle course would result in trouble from both directions. Robbins chose the conservative policy and refused to borrow money for new construction, but he did extend his building program as rapidly as venture capital became available. Part of the building fund came from undivided profits and part from the sale of new issues of common stock. This conservative policy obviated all financial embarrassment, but left the field open to new producers. It is doubtful, however, that any practical rate of expansion could have prevented the growth of competition in the manufacture of watches. The industry seemed to retain some of the romantic atmosphere with which Dennison had endowed it at birth, and many competitors entered the field without the necessary prerequisites for success.

The financial statements for the beginning and end of the period give a record of the expansion in terms of investment. (See Table 5.)

TABLE 5

COMPARISON OF FIXED ASSETS, 1860 AND 1884[a]

WALTHAM WATCH COMPANY

	1860	1884
Watch Factory Estate		
(Land and buildings)	$ 35,485.62	$400,000.00
Machinery	66,668.48	320,378.17
Real Estate, unsold land	33,560.51	13,758.67
Housing and Store for Workers	8,203.94	85,747.69
Total	$143,918.55	$819,884.53

[a] Years ending Jan. 31.

SOURCE: Treasurer's reports.

The nature and extent of the changes that occurred in the factory are indicated in the following excerpt from the Annual Report of 1883:

With the exception of that small building [the north wing] there will remain at the close of the present year nothing at all of the factory as it existed five years ago. . . . We shall at last have a factory large enough, substantial handsome comfortable convenient and yet not too fine for our very nice purposes. It is even now a true Palace of industry of which you may well be proud.

The advantages of such a sweeping program of reconstruction and expansion were alluring, but the risk was very great. Let us consider the advantages in detail.

The larger plant made it possible further to increase the economies derived from mass-production methods, and this was a crucial issue in the competitive situation. The producer who manufactured the largest number of watches with the most modern machinery might hope to dominate the market. But Waltham was not the only producer to aspire to leadership of the industry, and the resulting competition was depressing to prices and profits. The Annual Report of 1879 gave a clear description of the situation and a forceful definition of policy, which has been summarized in these paragraphs:

The root of the trouble [price-cutting] is the present inability of the public to take so many goods as are now annually manufactured. . . . You will naturally ask why then do we propose to increase our production. The hard and ungenerous answer is that as it is impracticable to bring all the makers to an agreement to curtail, the weaker ones must be forced to it by those who have the power.

The process is by large production to effect cheap production and thus to undersell.

That party who can make watches the cheapest will have them to make. We have the lead so far in all the world in this particular — that we are able to give the best watch for the money asked in all grades, and that money is now little enough in the case of the cheapest watch [$2.54] to command every market.

Volume of production was not the only factor affecting costs. The development of new labor-saving machinery and the simplification of watch design were of primary importance. Automatic machinery was being rapidly developed, although in the early days there was strong opposition to this trend. Abbott tells us:[20]

Anything approaching an automatic machine was frowned upon. In spite of this fact, Mr. Webster may be credited with forcing automatic machinery to the front as he constructed a machine to run half-automatically against the positive orders of management.

Parallel to the development of machinery, and achieving similar economies, was the simplification of the design of the watch movement. On this score, Orra Stone reports:[21]

> The first and most important task of Mr. Robbins and his associates was to develop new machines and processes for the manufacture of various parts that enter into the fabrication of a watch. Simplification of the mechanism was the great desideratum. Many parts were found to be superfluous and were eliminated and by the time the Centennial Exposition in 1876 rolled around experts testified that fully three fourths of the parts which at that time were employed by English watchmakers had disappeared from American watch construction.

The net result of the use of automatic machinery and the development of simplified designs was to reduce labor costs. Not only was less labor required, but workers of relatively little skill could be substituted for many of the craftsmen previously employed. Under ordinary conditions this shift from skilled to unskilled labor would have resulted in serious technological unemployment, but the growth of the payroll was so rapid that labor of all degrees of skill was in good demand throughout this period except in times of depression.

The rapid increase in the number of employees at the watch factory did create a shortage of housing facilities in the community, but Robbins took care that it did not become acute. In 1864 he reported to the stockholders:

> One of the greatest embarrassments under which we labor is the want of houses for our workpeople. Reluctant heretofore to invest the Company's means which were so much needed in the factory itself, in such houses, we have been in hopes that individual effort or speculation would increase the number of houses in our neighborhood as fast as we should need them, but the extension of our business has been so considerable in the last two years we find all at once that we have outgrown the town. We have therefore been compelled ourselves to commence the erection of buildings which are so much needed. Eight new tenements are about completed and more will be put up during the summer provided men can be found to build them.

In the following year the housing conditions were even worse, and the report of 1865 reads:

> About 32,000$ has been expended the last year in the erection of cottages, tenement houses, and a boarding house. We regret to add to our invest-

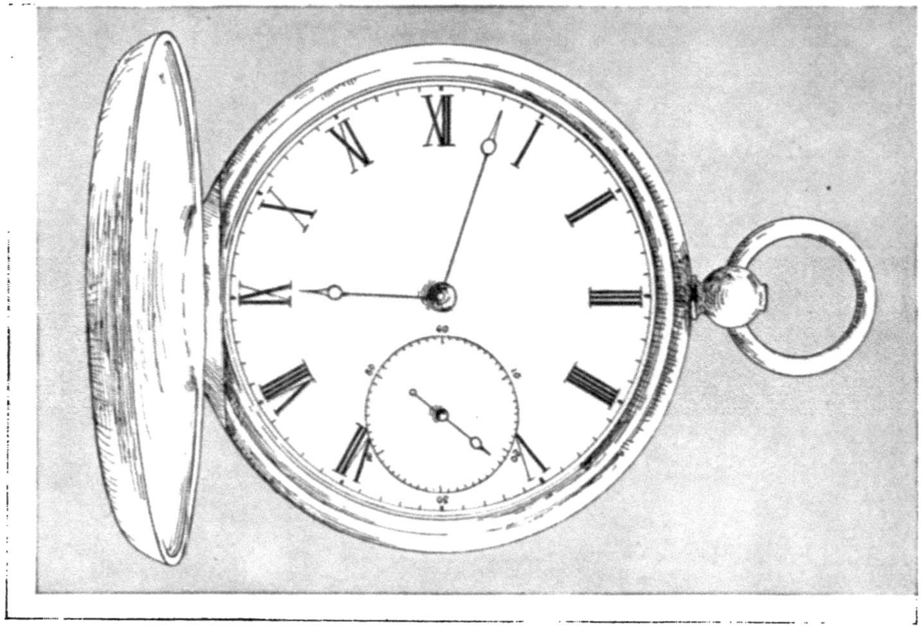

A WALTHAM WATCH OWNED BY ABRAHAM LINCOLN

ments in this species of property but it has been unavoidable and if private enterprise does not provide more such accommodation we shall be forced ourselves to expend more money for the purpose. Our people must live somewhere.

The emergency continued after the end of the war and $33,000 was spent for housing in the following year. "We trust," said Robbins, "there will not be occasion to make much more such investment,"[22] but by 1884 the total was over $85,000.

Another addition to the capital assets was the purchase in 1878 of a shop in New York for the manufacture of gold cases. Additions to the Waltham plant also provided for increased production of silver cases. Robbins' comments in the report of 1879 were:

The purchase of the New York gold case shop [from Robbins & Appleton] . . . is a transaction we have long wished to make. We now have control, freed from the conflicting interests of our Agents of a watch business complete in all its branches of gold and silver casemaking.

This move was a part of the response to changing market conditions which Robbins discussed in the report two years later, saying:

Our manufacture is increasing not only in volume but in variety and attractiveness. We are better able than ever before to meet the demands of the public as to sizes shapes and appearance. Even the most fastidious buyers may now be satisfied. . . . Our movements are presented in gold cases of the greatest excellence and beauty and at the lowest cost.

The relation of case-making to marketing was stressed in the report of 1873 by the remark that:

The Case department has been the object of a good deal of attention with a view to a permanent increase in its product. The goods now turned out from that department have been very much improved in quality and certainly have the preference in the market. Unfortunately, a sharp competition in that branch of our trade keeps the profit of it at a low rate. Indeed except for the control it gives us of the price of a complete watch, a control it is important we should not abandon, it would be easy to find more profitable employment for our capital.

The advantages of the program of expansion and modernization have been outlined in some detail — the complementary risk of obsolescence will be mentioned briefly. The rapid development of new machinery, the adoption of more efficient methods, and changes in the taste of consumers, all combined to produce rapid obsolescence in certain large areas of the factory. It was difficult, if not impossible, to predict when and where the major burden of obsolescence would fall. As a consequence, it was necessary to prepare for sudden major changes throughout the factory. In fact, preparation was necessary in all departments of the business — finance, production, engineering research, and marketing — and this condition has continued to the present. Rapid change has always been an outstanding characteristic of the American watch industry.

DIVIDENDS AND FINANCIAL POLICY

The chief financial problem of the period from 1859 to 1883 was the procurement of capital for the expansion program. The total requirement in terms of capitalization was $1,300,000. Of this amount $350,000 was obtained by the sale of new issues of common stock, and $950,000 was derived from earnings re-invested in the business.[23] This left sufficient earnings to provide for substantial dividends, thereby maintaining a strong market for the stock.

Robbins set forth this dividend policy in the report for 1863:

> The Directors therefore propose to make the most and best of what we have got, believing it capable of earning steady and if not large, at least satisfactory dividends. It must be borne in mind that the war is not over, that the monetary condition of the country[24] is most extraordinary, and that we are liable now to fluctuations in trade on these accounts while we are not less liable perhaps to be injuriously affected by the return to the normal condition of public finances. I insist then that our true policy [is] to occupy as strong a financial position as possible, that any profits if we have any over and above what is sufficient for small and regular dividends should after the extinguishment of our debt be allowed to accumulate with this object. They should be allowed to form indeed by their accumulation a permanent increase of capital which the Company now in its enlarged operations really needs and which will enable it to face with confidence whatever vicissitudes these anomalous times may have in store for us.

As the war boom grew and Waltham profits rose to unexpected heights, this policy was relaxed, but the figures for surplus indicate that the conservative point of view was not abandoned.

The results of the conservative financial policy were highly satis-

TABLE 6

DIVIDENDS AND SURPLUS, 1860–1884
WALTHAM WATCH COMPANY

Year ending January 31	Dividends	Surplus
1860	3⅛% cash [a]	$ 56,976
1861	13% cash, 10% script	33,100
1862	Passed	29,089
1863	4% cash [b]	43,772
1864	11% cash	134,648
1865	22% "	610,221
1866	60% cash, 150% stock	234,198
1867	28% "	265,128
1868	5% "	456,151
1869	11% "	496,985
1870	20% "	616,067
1871	20% cash, 66⅔% stock [c]	245,741
1872	20% "	188,953
1873	12% "	309,760
1874	12% "	311,322
1875	5% "	336,200
1876	6% "	360,458
1877	3% "	391,417
1878	7½% cash	417,049
1879	4% cash	441,545
1880	5% "	497,393
1881	9% "	632,630
1882	8% "	886,759
1883	8% "	1,103,053
1884	9% "	1,431,111

[a] "In pursuance of agreements to which I need not now refer." Treasurer's Report, 1860.
[b] Paid out of surplus.
[c] See note 23.

factory. The Company had greatly expanded its productive facilities and had paid for the additions to the plant, largely out of the earnings of the period. In his annual report following the close of the war — 1865 — Robbins felt justified in saying:

I think gentlemen I may safely congratulate you not only on the past but on the prospects of the future for our works. We have now so much capital, so much reputation and popularity in fact so solid and broad a basis that I dismiss for my part all apprehension for the future come what will financially and politically to the general public. And while I do not allow that we can remit anything of watchfulness, prudence and care in the management of the factory I think we may at least permit ourselves to feel certain of the great value of our property as a permanent and reliable source of income.

Such was the beginning of the golden age at Waltham — a period of prosperity and security, an era of proud supremacy, of technological improvements, and of market expansion. This state of affairs continued so long that the name *Waltham* became a by-word for mechanical perfection, finish, and precision. During this period the development of the technique of mass production was rapid. Manufacturing costs fell sharply with increasing production, and distribution costs also declined, but in smaller proportion. Lower costs brought lower prices and a wider market for the products. The rising standard of living, the increasing interest in mechanical contrivances, the development of the railroads and acceptance of the philosophy of speed and progress — all these factors contributed to the expansion of the market for watches and changed the status of the watch from that of a luxury to a necessity. But all such movements run their course, and competition eventually brings an end to the period of smooth sailing. So it was at Waltham.

COMPETITION AND ADMINISTRATIVE POLICY

Administrative policies at Waltham were gradually modified to conform to changes in the competitive situation. These changes developed rapidly and exerted so much pressure on the Company that it was considered necessary at various times to alter the basic plans for sales, production, and finance. In cases where the management responded promptly and decisively to the new conditions, the Company prospered. When the management would not or could not institute the necessary revisions of policy, there were difficulties which led sooner or later to the appointment of new executives. The story of Waltham's recurring successes and failures turns chiefly on the one issue — that of prompt and adequate adjustment to new conditions in the industry.

Foreign competition dominated the American watch industry from its earliest beginnings until the panic of 1873. Luther Goddard opened a watch shop in Shrewsbury, Massachusetts, in 1809, but he was forced to close when the protection of President Jefferson's embargo on foreign goods was removed. In 1837 the Pitkin Brothers made some use of machinery in producing watches at their plant at East Hartford, Connecticut, but they were still unable to compete successfully with imported watches. Dennison suffered the same fate, but Robbins succeeded in establishing lower prices and higher standards of performance than those of foreign producers. These superior standards increased the prestige of American watches and began to undermine the foreign control of the United States market, but the importation of watches continued to increase until 1872. After that date the control of the market passed from foreign to domestic producers.

The dominant foreign producers of watches were the Swiss. Beginning about 1840, they had taken the supremacy from the English by virtue of their technical skill, the low scale of wages, and the use of child labor.[25] In 1870 it was said "that half the watchmakers tools in England were in pawn."[26] But Swiss supremacy in our market was brief; by 1876 it had passed to the American manufacturers. The rise and decline of the Swiss control is shown in Table 7.

TABLE 7

WATCH MOVEMENTS, 1864–1876

Year[a]	Swiss Exports to U. S.	Waltham Company Production
1864	169,000	38,103
1865	226,000	44,632
1866	262,000	52,168
1867	207,000	72,831
1868	209,000	64,482
1869	206,000	42,089
1870	330,000	55,042
1871	342,000	66,655
1872	366,000	74,530
1873	204,000	79,346
1874	187,000	64,847
1875	134,000	49,243
1876	75,000	84,737

[a] Waltham figures are for the fiscal year ending Jan. 31.

SOURCES: Waltham Watch Company annual reports; *La Nationale Suisse*, Chaux-de-Fond, Switzerland, Nov. 17, 1876.

When the Swiss realized the extent of the American competition, they began to remedy the defects in their methods and to adopt the American system. They did not merely copy the mass-production method, but they also grafted the American ideas on the Swiss practice of cottage manufacture. In this manner they were able to obtain the increased efficiency and precision made possible by semiautomatic machinery, and at the same time they retained the economies of household industry on operations which still had to be performed by hand.

Since the Swiss are excellent craftsmen and technicians, they soon made rapid progress in adopting the American system. In this process of industrial education they were assisted by Aaron Dennison himself. We cannot determine how much Dennison contributed to the transfer of the American system of watch manufacture to Switzerland, but we know that he operated a plant in Zurich for the Tremont Watch Company from 1864 to about 1866.[27] Rapid assimilation of the new methods was facilitated also by the Swiss capacity for collective action. The Commission de Commerce and the government schools of watchmaking provided means for disseminating the technical information brought from the United States. As a result of these various efforts, the decline of the Swiss watch industry was arrested and exports to the United States increased rapidly to a total of more than $2,000,000 for each of the years 1881 to 1884. But the Swiss did not regain their dominant position until much later. Comparative figures for this period are given in Table 8.

Robbins' success in meeting foreign competition had been clearly established by the earnings record for 1859. Profits for that year were 28 per cent of sales, totaling just short of $50,000. Reports to that effect circulated rapidly, and new capital began to flow into the industry at once. As foreign competition weakened, domestic producers grew and flourished.

The earliest competition in the domestic industry was that of E. Howard & Company, founded in 1857. Howard had possession of the original watch plant that he and Dennison had built in Roxbury. Charles Rice had the movable equipment taken from the Waltham plant before it was sold to Robbins. They joined forces after the sale and began the manufacture of watches in the original plant. The Howard Company "practically failed"[28] in 1863 and was reorganized.

TABLE 8

VALUE OF WATCHES, MOVEMENTS, AND MATERIALS, 1876–1884

Year [a]	U. S. Imports [b]	Waltham Watch Company Sales
1876	$1,456,809	$ 974,925
1877	772,432	844,509
1878	812,582	1,033,000 [c]
1879	920,599	995,000 [c]
1880	1,529,948	1,619,737
1881	2,086,296	2,109,967
1882	2,584,475	3,005,809
1883	2,522,111	3,340,479
1884	2,062,804	3,545,054

[a] Year ending June 30 for imports; Jan. 31 for Waltham Company sales.

[b] Imports of watches into the United States came chiefly from Switzerland; in 1884, 83% were from that country. Before 1884, imports from Switzerland were not segregated in the American statistics.

[c] Estimated from sales in number of movements.

SOURCES: *Foreign Commerce and Navigation of the United States;* Waltham Watch Company records.

A second reorganization occurred in 1881, and Howard retired in the following year. The extent of the competition offered by the Howard organization is somewhat in doubt—perhaps it was not very great. We may form some hazy estimate from a paragraph in a letter from Eliphalet Dennison to his brother Aaron, dated February 11, 1874:

> As to what you owe Howard, I don't care a fig—He boasts of his quarter million, much of which is from the seed planted by you.
>
> To be sure he has cultivated [it] well (besides I don't believe the quarter million story).

The next competitive enterprise was the Nashua Watch Company, established at Nashua, New Hampshire, in 1859. The Nashua project was promoted by Waltham employees, and Stratton was the moving spirit of the venture, assisted by Bingham (formerly of Nashua), Moseley, Vander Woerd, and others.[29] Capital amounting to $100,000 was obtained from Nashua residents.

The Nashua venture soon came to grief; the business failed in 1862. The high-grade watch which Stratton produced met a poor demand in the depressed markets of the early days of the Civil War, and the available capital was not sufficient to carry the company along until the beginning of the wartime boom. Robbins bought the business, including the stock of about 1,000 finished watches,[30] the buildings, and the equipment, for $23,000.[31] The machinery was moved to Waltham where it was operated as a separate department until 1878. Stratton, Moseley, and Vander Woerd were taken back on the Waltham payroll.

Three other concerns attempted to enter the industry in 1863 and all of them failed. The difficulties of entering a mass-production industry were underestimated. The amount of capital required and the high standard of performance demanded of both management and labor were not fully understood. The task of creating a large demand in a national market was regarded too lightly. But these lessons were quickly learned and put to use by the founders of the Elgin enterprise. This concern was organized in 1864, and three years later was producing an 18-size, 15-jewel watch in sufficient quantity to justify sales at competitive prices.

There are two versions of the origin of the Elgin enterprise. The one formerly posted in the lobby of the Elgin factory stated simply that the business was founded by Benjamin W. Raymond, a former mayor of Chicago, John C. Adams, and his brother, George B. Adams, a jeweler in Elgin. A more circumstantial report appeared in the *Keystone* for August, 1890. It reads in part as follows:

> Twenty-six years ago, Patton S. Bartlett and Ira G. Blake, employees of the American Watch Co., of Waltham, paid a visit to Chicago, and while there conceived the idea of starting a great watch factory in the inviting fields of the growing west. They formed the acquaintance of J. C. Adams, of Elgin, a practical watchmaker, who became enthused with the idea. After some effort, a Company was formed August 27, 1864, under the name of "The National Watch Company," of Chicago, Illinois, with a capital stock of $100,000. . . . The location of the factory was offered to Elgin, on condition that a tract of thirty-one acres of land be deeded to the Company, and $25000 worth of stock be subscribed by the city. After efforts to comply with these conditions had failed, four of Elgin's citizens stepped to the front and fulfilled the requirements.

The founders of the Elgin Company were particularly alive to the necessity of securing experienced men for key positions in the plant.

The *Keystone* account reports, "In September, 1864, Mr. Wheeler and Mr. Adams went east to secure competent men to help start the factory on a practical basis." But Abbott relates that the task of recruiting personnel was given to Bartlett and adds, "He [Bartlett] was one of the half dozen who was paid a bonus of $5000 and $5000 a year for five years to go to Elgin and start a factory."[32] Whatever the exact procedure seven supervisory positions at Elgin were filled by men from the Waltham plant, namely Charles S. Moseley (superintendent), George Hunter, John K. Bigelow, Otis Hoyt, Charles E. Mason, D. R. Hartwell, and P. S. Bartlett. In addition to other inducements, the men from Waltham were each given an acre of land from the plot donated by Elgin citizens.[33]

The development of the Elgin Company was rapid. Operations were barely under way when the company applied for a special charter with an authorized capitalization of $500,000. The three-story wooden factory building erected in January, 1865, was abandoned in the following year, and operations were transferred to a new factory having approximately 23,000 square feet of floor space. The first Elgin watches were finished in this plant in 1867, and thereafter the line of movements was rapidly increased. By January, 1868, there were six 18-size models, and other grades and sizes were added in rapid succession. The volume of production continued to increase, the rise being accelerated by the demand for models designed to sell at "popular prices"—this policy, which was adopted in May, 1876,[34] proved so successful that the competition of the Elgin plant became a major threat to the Waltham Company.

Although Elgin competition was the source of the most concern, there were many other producers. In his report of 1886, Robbins gave a list of seventeen domestic watch manufacturers.[35] The growth of this competition can be readily traced from references to Robbins' annual reports. In 1865 he spoke of "having a monopoly of Waltham watches which have vastly increased their hold on the public preference in the last few years." In 1871 he wrote proudly of profits earned in spite of depression "and of all competition whether foreign or domestic." Six years later, in 1877, he confessed to the smallest profits in many years, "due, principally to the great reduction in prices, which we were . . . forced to accept before we had effected corresponding economies." The following year he sadly refers to "the very bad condition of things in this unhappy country . . . and the reckless and needless competition from our brother manufacturers." The report (of 1879) contains a frank and full account of the competitive situation, which was calculated to quiet the alarm that had seized the stockholders.

Robbins was temporarily relieved of any necessity for further explanations by the return of prosperity. The resumption of specie payment in 1879 brought a three years' respite, but the pressure of competition was soon renewed and a definite reversal of policy was made. Robbins announced the change in the Annual Report of 1884:

> We are consequently turning our force upon the cheaper grades which for the present are most in demand. To produce these in large enough quantities to make them by themselves profitable is a new experience for us, and one which will give our manufacturing skill a sharp trial. Economy in all directions will be necessary and every screw must be turned home.

The execution of the new policy required a new man as chief operating executive of the Company, a man who would subordinate the exigencies of the factory and of production to the demands of the market. Such a man was found in Ezra Fitch, trained as a salesman and sales manager for Robbins & Appleton. The year of his appointment as general manager — 1883 — may be taken as the end of Waltham's golden age and the beginning of the fight for the control of prices and markets. The year 1883 was the turning point in policy and management, but Robbins had recognized the inevitable nature of the change some years before. He had said in his Report of 1879:

> In years gone by our main anxiety has been in regard to quality. In the days of inflated money, inflated prices and a partial monopoly it was easy to pay high wages, to use unperfected machinery and yet with ready sales to make money. Now that . . . the inevitable competition has come, with depressed and exacting markets our task now partly before and partly behind us has become a very different one and much more difficult.

CHAPTER V

COMPETITION IN THE WATCH INDUSTRY 1864–1907

Competition and the Secular Trend

A business does not exist alone. It is part of an industry — a group of similar business units. It is also a part of a general trend in so far as its fortunes are bound up with those of practically all other units, particularly in the matter of demand for products and profits from production.

Let us consider first the general trend or the long-time or "secular trend" of business. This is a movement of prices and profits, first upward for about a generation, then downward for about the same time. Whether this behavior is inherent in business or not, at least it seems to have been the pattern of performance since the eighteenth century. Of course, the prices and profits experience brief deviations within the general movement. In a general way, indeed, there is a rather standard pattern of behavior. In the secular trend upward the set-backs or depressions are of relatively short duration. In the secular trend downward, however, the depressions last longer and are of greater social consequence. Such is the theory of the secular trend which seems to have great significance in business history.[1]

The secular trends that have to do with the Waltham Watch Company's history are roughly as follows:

Secular Trends in American Business

Of course, the pattern, as here displayed, is greatly oversimplified. We are interested at this point only in the over-all picture. We cannot escape the observation that the high point in prices and profits has occurred at the end of a great war or just following a great war. Because of the control of prices (and wages), however, we may escape a comparable downtrend following the second World War.

The Waltham Watch was born and experienced its early growth in the upward trend of 1843–66, during which there were a mighty move westward, the opening up of the California gold mines, and the heavy demands of the Civil War. In other words, the general trend of business was distinctly favorable to new products and new ventures.

We might expect that the downtrend of 1866–97 would have at once affected the business of the Waltham Watch Company unfavorably. Actually, however, we see little serious effect of the general decline in prices until about 1883. We are perhaps the more surprised when we remember that competition in the watch industry had begun in 1864 with the establishment of the Elgin Watch Company. Clearly we have to explain why the Waltham Company escaped hard times during the period 1866–83. There are two explanations. First, the demand for the new American watch was so great that men would buy it at the expense of other commodities. And, second, the great western market was opening up as people flocked in from Europe and elsewhere. A study of the behavior of business in the downward secular trend shows that the company making a new product of wide use experiences relatively less difficulty than do concerns in older and well-established industries.

Even the Waltham Watch, however, was ultimately in line to experience difficulties — those that came from distress in general business and those that are inherent in competition. Solutions were proposed and efforts made to stave off the worst effects. All this is normal — not peculiar either to the Waltham Watch Company or to the watch industry.

It is in the downtrend that things happen — in both business and social affairs. In the period 1815–43 mercantile capitalism decayed and industrial capitalism took its start. In the period 1866–97 industrial capitalism suffered severely from over-competition as well as from declining prices, and financial capitalism (control of production by investment bankers) made its initial bid for power and control. And then, to complete the picture, during the period that began in 1920 financial capitalism declined and the new system of national capitalism (political control of private business) took its place. But it is the downtrend of 1866–97 that concerns us most here. During this period the watch industry tried to solve its problems by means of agreements and associations; the bankers did not enter to create a financial capitalistic régime.

During the period 1897–1920 public opposition to agreements, associations, and trusts joined with opposition to financial capitalism or the control of business by investment bankers (spoken of as the Money Trust). Although neither Waltham nor the watch industry was at this time involved in financial capitalism, both made herculean efforts to stave off the disasters that threatened, including the use of agreements and associations, as was common among many industries at the time. Nevertheless, the public opposition to financial capitalism became part of the movement from which the watch industry, like many other industries, suffered. More about these situations will appear below.

GROWTH OF COMPETITION, 1864–1885

The Waltham Company was virtually immune to competition for a period of about twenty years. Early difficulties at Waltham were essentially of an engineering nature, relating chiefly to the development of machine tools of radically new design. No serious competition was encountered until the Elgin Company was founded in 1864, but after that date new capital came into the industry rapidly. In all, approximately sixty enterprises for the manufacture of watches were established in the United States, and only three of them have survived.[2]

By 1874 the effects of competition on the Company's affairs were clearly discernible. In his Annual Report dated February, 1875, Robbins mentioned "the depression of almost all industrial commercial and financial interests which has universally prevailed," and then summarized the measures which he had undertaken to meet the situation. He wrote:[3]

> Great improvements in many respects have been effected in the direction both of economy and quality of goods while the variety of our manufactures has been largely increased.
>
> The considerable and growing trade with foreign countries developed within the year has obliged us to make goods specially suited to the tastes of foreign markets. . . . We have established a selling agency in London. . . .
>
> The consolidation of the two general departments [the machinery bought

from the defunct Nashua Watch Company had been operated as a separate department] under which the administration of the factory was until lately carried on, which was effected in the course of the year has proved to be of very great advantage. . . .

Important reductions have recently been made not only in the day pay and piece work prices but also in the salaries of all the officers and clerks of the Company as well as in those of the Superintendents and some of the foremen. These reductions have been cheerfully submitted to on the part of every one concerned.

The preceding quotation describes the first sequence in the downward spiral of prices, profits, and wages that characterize the declining secular trend. It illustrates the process by which the pressure of competition on prices is transmitted throughout the entire business structure. It emphasizes the fact that the pressure of competition determines the ultimate level of wages. Once set in motion, the downward spiral tends to continue until its accumulating evils become unbearable.

Although Robbins did not hesitate to cut wages when it was expedient, he did not depend on wage reductions as his major competitive weapon. His policy on this score is clearly defined in the Annual Report for the following year, 1876, in which he said:

We have also still further reduced the prices of all qualities of goods from ten to fifteen per cent, but as the cost has been proportionately reduced by means of reduced rate of wages, cheaper raw materials, improved and extended machinery, enlarged shop space, and a greater force at work, we are still able to show a living profit. . . .

We have in obedience to the demand of the times, devoted ourselves to making the lower and less costly grades of goods. . . . This policy of making cheap goods to meet the times and a great many of them, so as to secure a low cost . . . has been so far successful. . . . We have in this otherwise distressful year first begun to realize our early and late dreams of really cheap goods and successful competition with the great producers of Switzerland. The years business has been fought for and won on the basis of the intrinsic values of the goods, against all other foreign and domestic.

It is a fact that this years selling price is the cost of last year and so it has been these three years. And these reductions have been largely due to improvements in mechanical means and methods, the end of which we have not even approached.

When the declining secular trend carried prices to dangerously low levels, Robbins reduced his costs by using mass production on an even larger scale. By this means he recovered a satisfactory share of the market, but only for a brief period. The policy of increasing output had one fatal drawback — it was easily copied. The net result was a large increase in the productive capacity of the industry and further weakness in the price structure. In spite of its faults the policy of expansion was followed for a period of approximately ten years, but by 1883 it was apparent that more effective methods of meeting competition were required. Robbins reported to the stockholders:[4]

> It seems clear that our business although larger has not been quite so profitable as that of the year preceding. Severe competition has lessened our returns perceptibly while obstruction and detention occasioned by our large and embarrassing building works have interfered still more with the profit and loss account.

At this juncture, 1883, Ezra Fitch was brought to Waltham in the capacity of general manager and was entrusted with the task of developing new lines of effort in the attempt to prevent the continued encroachment of competitors.

Before Fitch could inaugurate a new program for cutting costs, he found it necessary to improve the morale and secure the coöperation of the factory staff. These craftsmen had been trained under conditions of virtual monopoly, and the advent of competition found them unprepared for the new conditions. They were governed in their work by arbitrary rules and precedents that had acquired, in a third of a century, the unquestioned authority of common law. To make matters worse, the factory executives were incompetent and obdurate. Faced with new conditions to which they could not successfully adapt themselves, the factory personnel became alarmed and developed the symptoms of unrest which go by the collective term of low morale.

The reorganization of the factory was begun at the top. Charles Vander Woerd[5] had been general superintendent since 1876, but his skill as a manager had fallen far short of the genius which he displayed in mechanical matters. Shortly after Fitch arrived at Waltham, Vander Woerd resigned and left the way clear for a general change of policy and practice.

The general policy that Fitch wished to enforce was that of coöperation between the craftsmen of the factory and the salesmen of the firm of Robbins & Appleton, exclusive agents for Waltham watches. Until 1883 the factory had dominated the whole enterprise; factory

cases to one jobber at a material reduction from the prices at which he had stocked up the other jobbers. This great block of goods then came on the market at a figure lower than the other wholesalers had been able to buy their goods. The result was that every wholesaler had to dispose of his stock of cases at an actual loss. Such demoralization was fatal to trade. The jobbers thought that the remedy was that the manufacturers should be induced to agree to sell to all jobbers at a uniform price. To administer that remedy the association was formed.

For the next seven years the association led a stormy career. Self-preservation demanded unity, but the divergent interests of various groups prevented the achievement of any permanent solidarity. Small jobbers were in conflict with large ones and new producers were at odds with the old-line companies. The modest measure of success attained by the association brought forth a barrage of invective from retailers, politicians, and the press. Internal intrigue and dissension created gaps in the ranks of the association, and the threat of punitive action under the State antitrust laws finally resulted in voluntary dissolution.

What the association actually accomplished is difficult to determine. It is quite probable that it helped to stabilize the market for watches in the latter part of the depression of 1884–85, but Table 10 shows that it did not result in abnormally high profits for the Waltham Company during the prosperous years that followed.[12] The association may have postponed the drastic liquidation of small producers and jobbers which eventually overtook the industry, but it failed to effect any permanent solution of the problem of overcapacity.

The history of the National Association of Jobbers in American Watches was typical of the period. The Standard Oil Company, the Whisky Trust, and the oatmeal millers each employed a loose confederation as a preliminary step to a more effective form of combination.

The record of the Oatmeal Millers' Association roughly parallels the developments in the watch industry.[13] The watch manufacturers began to organize in 1885; the Oatmeal Millers' Association was founded one year later. The first organization of the oatmeal millers was a very loose confederation of twenty concerns, which lasted but a few months. The second attempt was made by a group of twelve millers and took the form of a chartered company, the Consolidated

TABLE 10

SALES AND PROFITS, 1883–1911
WALTHAM WATCH COMPANY

Year Ending Jan. 31	Sales	Profits	Profits (Per cent of sales)
1883	$3,340,479	$ 336,293	10.0
1884	3,545,054	348,058	9.8
1885	3,105,615	247,029	7.9
1886	2,981,321	156,711	5.2
1887	3,376,159	186,532	5.5
1888	4,030,823	264,559	6.5
1889	4,167,496	390,595	9.4
1890	4,132,018	349,548	8.5
1891	4,277,487	403,582	9.4
1892	3,396,539	282,987	8.3
1893	missing	249,827	missing
1894	2,001,494	246,830	12.3
1895	1,653,776	211,199	12.8
1896	2,085,893	225,116	10.8
1897	1,743,055	222,962	12.8
1898	1,899,779	243,935	12.8
1899	2,479,087	272,182	11.0
1900	3,107,566	517,913	16.7
1901	3,248,474	1,006,400	31.0
1902	3,522,582	1,011,110	28.7
1903 [a]	4,427,365	1,121,001	25.3
1904	4,001,263	938,704	23.5
1905	3,660,689	868,387	23.7
1906	3,941,844	731,803	18.6
1907	4,320,138	755,621	17.5
1908	3,985,527	608,296	15.3
1909	3,149,662	458,536	14.5
1910	3,673,241	441,517	12.0
1911	3,427,796	150,478	4.4

[a] Fourteen months; i.e., beginning with 1903, figures are in each case for year ending Mar. 31.

SOURCE: Treasurer's reports.

Oatmeal Company. The third organization of the oatmeal millers was a holding company, the American Cereal Company, founded in 1888. The holding company structure and a reduction of the group to seven constituent companies gave the American Cereal Company a strong centralized control over operations. This third venture in the field of combination survived the attacks of the government and the debilitating effects of internal friction, and it continues today under the name of the Quaker Oats Company. The watch industry also attempted to strengthen its position by horizontal combination, but with a low degree of success.

CONTINUATION OF COMPETITION

When the jobbers' association collapsed, price-cutting began with a vengeance. In September, 1891, the Waltham Company cut prices 20 per cent, and wages also were reduced, but the amount of the wage cut was not published.[14] The Rockford Watch Company cut wages 2½ to 15 per cent and offered to meet Waltham and Elgin prices.[15] In 1892 goods were sold by Waltham at such low figures that the sum of $348,000 was deducted from surplus to cover the resulting loss and other nonrecurring items of depreciation. In speaking of this deduction, Robbins said:[16]

> Referring to the charge against Surplus & Reserve account in the foregoing statement I have to say that in the year 1885 we set apart a portion of our accumulated profits as a reserve for contingent or possible losses or depreciations. The Reserve was about $286,000. . . . This year unfortunately, we have need to use it in the way originally contemplated as possible. That sum and about $64,000 more have been required to cover the diminution of our assets occasioned by a serious break in prices last April making necessary large allowances of rebates to our customers upon their stocks bought in the preceding year, and also by the sale of some goods below cost. We have thought best at the same time to write off a large sum for depreciation in value of machinery which has been thrown out of use by changes in our manufacture and the introduction of many automatic tools. . . .
>
> The business of the year has in fact resulted better than might be expected considering the great cut in prices for which as it was not of our initiation but forced upon us by our competitors, we were not at all well prepared. We regarded that reduction as a misfortune and in a great part needless but we have come to think somewhat differently about it. It has been the means of widening our market & strengthening our position in it. Naturally too, it has stimulated our endeavors to lower the cost of manufacture thro' improvements in machinery and methods.

The above report is clearly colored by a desire to present a favorable picture to the stockholders, and it fails to give a proper realization of the critical emergency that confronted the industry. Competition within the industry was the basic cause of business and economic difficulties, but other, secondary factors require consideration, particularly those relating to the political situation and the downward secular trend.

The political situation was distinctly unfavorable to the keenly competitive industries. The long downward swing of prices that extended from the close of the Civil War to 1896 had revived a bitter political schism in the United States. The Democrats of the South and West, representing agriculture, the cattle industry, and mining, were attempting to wrest the control of the federal government from the financial and industrial interests of the North and East, and to substitute inflation for the Republican policy of adhering to the gold standard. The attack of the inflationary forces reached its height in Bryan's campaign for the presidency, in 1896, on a platform advocating the free and unlimited coinage of silver. The power of Bryan's oratory and the obvious strength of his following so threatened the financial structure — already undermined by heavy withdrawals of gold — that the depression of 1896 resulted.

Bryan's campaign also marks the low point of the postwar secular trend. After his defeat at the polls in November, 1896, there was a strong recovery in both the business cycle and the trend. The conservative victory relieved the business community of the danger of currency inflation, but it did not end the political attacks on business. The fight was continued in all industrial sections of the country somewhat as a class struggle — a contest between the consuming public and organized finance and industry.

The political attacks on business combinations were of a purely partisan nature, the objective being to obtain the lowest possible prices for consumers. The idea that competition could ever be destructive or that the great mass-production industries needed an organized market does not seem to have occurred to the public or the press. Their attitude was one of rebellion against the extortion of an industrial and financial plutocracy. The spirit of the times is shown in the following incident: [17]

Springfield, Ill., Feb. 14 [1889] — The Merritt Anti-Trust bill went through the House Judiciary Committee this afternoon, although some of its members thought its friends were imprudent in pushing it into the House without having received more extended consideration. It was evident, though, from the temper of the committee meeting, which was the largest and most interesting of the session, that the people were clamoring for some legislation of the sort, and when Mr. Merritt and some of the Chicago jewelers who seem to have been the victims of the jewelers' trust had given their testimony the members were ready to pass anything that had been organized "to prohibit the restriction of trade."

Even the conservative New York *Tribune* applauded the attempts to restrain the action of trusts, but the editors did emphasize the fact that current legislation was falling short of its objective and injuring the small business men who were making common cause with the consumer against the trusts. The *Tribune's* editorial position is given in this comment on the Missouri antitrust law:[18]

There seems to be a concurrence of opinion that the law fails to reach some of the very offenders whose conduct caused its enactment, while it strikes a multitude of people who were not aimed at. In this particular it illustrates the fate of much hasty legislation designed to protect the public against abuses. Quite too often such legislation fails to do the good intended, but does do a great deal of mischief unintentionally.

The political agitation of this period was a by-product of the downward secular trend in prices which followed the Civil War. The decline was so great[19] that it produced a number of serious maladjustments in business, politics, and the monetary system.[20] The movement reached its low point in 1896, but the entire period from 1891 to 1899, inclusive, was one of exceptional economic stress and political agitation.

The bottom of the secular trend was marked by three depressions which followed each other in rapid succession. The first was a repercussion of the financial prostration in England that followed the failure of Baring Brothers (1890). The reaction in America was brief, and in a few months the speculative excesses connected with the rapid expansion of the railroads were resumed. Two years after the Baring crisis the failure of the Philadelphia & Reading Railroad touched off a similar panic in the United States. The two years of acute distress that followed were featured by the Pullman strike in Chicago and the march of Coxey's Army of the unemployed. Business had barely returned to normal when Bryan's silver campaign produced another depression comparable to the panic of 1893. These three depressions had their immediate causes in monetary and political factors, but they were all expressions of the maladjustments arising from the secular decline in prices.

The deadlock between the advocates of unrestricted competition and the forces of organized industry and finance was broken by the defeat of Bryan in 1896. The carefully considered verdict of the country placed the control of industry and the currency in the hands of the conservative Republicans — that is to say, in the hands of the financial capitalists — with the reservation that the public interest, which had often been flouted, should thereafter be well served. Under this charter from the electorate the financial capitalists accelerated the process of organizing the facilities of production and distribution into large units, using any methods that promised to conform with the letter of the antitrust legislation. From this point — the defeat of Bryan in 1896 — the movement of the secular trend was upward.

In the period from 1892 to 1898, the Waltham Company returned to its old policy of increasing the scale of its operations and improving the efficiency of equipment and methods. New capital for such expenditures was not available on attractive terms, and it became necessary to squeeze a million dollars out of the liquid assets of the Company for this purpose. About half of this sum was invested in new machinery, and the remainder was devoted to building up the inventory of goods in process.[21] Robbins' Annual Report of 1894 makes this comment:

> The immediate effect of the great panic which set in about the middle of June [1893] was a large falling off of business. Not to dwell on the dreary history I will only say we at once set about to minimize its effects upon ourselves as much as possible. By means of reductions in wages, by the consolidation of departments, by the more general use of automatic machinery which fortunately we were able to bring into effective play in large quantity, and by the curtailment of expenses in every direction we not only offset the great disadvantage of our reduced working force but were able to run at a profit.
>
> As for the future it is for us far from discouraging, and altho' great depression still exists in the watch trade there are visible many signs of improvement. The economical basis upon which the factory is now established and the lowered cost of our products give assurance of most gratifying prosperity when the general revival comes which in my opinion can-

not be long deferred. Our watches were never so popular never so cheap and never so good as now.

The Annual Report of 1894 is the last that we have from Robbins' pen. At that date he had served as the Company's treasurer for thirty-seven years and had passed his seventieth birthday. He had been seriously ill in 1889, and his son Royal had temporarily taken over his post as treasurer.[22] In 1896 Mrs. R. E. Robbins died, and in 1898 R. E. Robbins suffered a stroke. He retained the office of treasurer until his death in 1902, but he gradually relinquished his duties to Ezra Fitch and to his son Royal.

The hope of prosperity expressed by Robbins in his report of 1894 was promptly dashed by the slow and irregular recovery of that year and by the silver depression of 1896. This period of renewed disappointment must have weighed very heavily on Waltham officials, but unfortunately we have no record of their opinions on current conditions. The small profits which were earned each year in 1892–99[23] tend to conceal the desperate character of the competition which undoubtedly existed at this period. In fact, this new competition was so severe that it drove the Company to new experiments in organized marketing, in spite of the unsatisfactory experience with the jobbers' association.

RECOVERY AND ATTACK, 1897–1907

The year 1897 brought cyclical recovery and the upward movement of the secular trend. Gold was discovered in Alaska in 1898. There was also a rush to apply the methods of financial capitalism as broadly as possible: conspicuous examples are the formation of the International Harvester Company and the International Mercantile Marine in 1902, and the growth of the railroad empires of Morgan, Hill, and Harriman. Under the influence of the new prosperity the old monetary and political problems were forgotten. *The Commercial and Financial Chronicle* reported:[24]

Undoubtedly the two events of most importance during the year [1900], both bearing on the present and the future, were the passage by Congress of the Gold Standard and Refunding Bill and the defeat for the second time of William J. Bryan as an aspirant for the presidency.

The net result of these favorable factors was a boom of unusual strength and long life. The stock market, taking its cue from industry, indulged in "the wildest kind of speculation." [25]

The affairs of the Waltham Company, always susceptible to changes in general business, entered a phase of unparalleled prosperity. Sales for the calendar year 1901 were double the figure for 1896, and profits increased more than fourfold.[26] These profits arose in part from the increased volume of production and the higher efficiency of the plant, but it was popularly believed that they were the result of price-fixing by members of the watch industry.

TABLE 11

SALES AND PRICES, 1890–1905
WALTHAM WATCH COMPANY

Year ending Jan. 31	Total Sales (Dollars)	Sales in Movements	Nominal Unit Price [a] (Dollars)
1890	4,132,018	409,413	10.09
1891	4,277,487	433,645	9.86
1892	3,396,539	466,648	7.28
1893	[b]	[b]	[b]
1894	2,001,494	392,097	5.10
1895	1,653,776	330,381	5.01
1896	2,085,893	431,025	4.84
1897	1,743,055	363,302	4.80
1898	1,899,779	370,978	5.12
1899	2,479,087	552,139	4.49
1905	3,660,689	752,941	4.86

[a] The nominal unit price is total sales in dollars divided by sales in movements. It varies with the manufacturing cost, the character of the demand (for higher or lower quality), and the amount of competition. Total sales include watch cases and materials.
[b] Data for 1893 missing.

SOURCE: Treasurer's reports.

During the years 1906 and 1907 charges were brought against the manufacturers of watches and cases that they had formed a Watch Trust. It was said that they were selling watches abroad for less than they sold them for at home, that they were selling watches of the same grade at the same prices through collusion of one company with another, and that they were using undue influence to force railroad employees to buy their watches. The companies concerned denied the accusations as presented. Clearly some of the accusers did not have clean hands. In a study of the watch industry and trade, however, the charges and replies would repay careful study.

In any consideration of the part played by Waltham in coöperative action within the industry, we should have to give considerable attention to Fitch. The qualities for which he was admired at Waltham were equally appreciated in the industry at large. In one sense, at least, he was a great man, for he acquired wealth and high standing without losing the plain and direct manner that was appropriate to him as the son of a sea captain. Although he was shrewd enough to accumulate a large fortune in an era of avid speculation, he wore an air of ingenuous simplicity that was thoroughly disarming. F. C. Beckwith, president of the Hamilton Watch Company, said of him, "His mild manners and sterling character endeared him to all who knew him."[27] The extent of the influence that Fitch exerted in the industry cannot be accurately appraised, but it is safe to say that he inclined toward coöperative action and that his abilities were well suited to his purpose. It is conceivable that he may have accomplished much in the way of parallel action by individual members of the industry without resorting to anything in the nature of an agreement.

The case against the watch industry was not tried in court, because the Department of Justice did not consider the evidence strong enough to warrant an indictment and trial. Nevertheless the industry was attacked in the press and from the political rostrum with unparalleled vigor and vindictiveness. President Theodore Roosevelt took a personal interest in the affair,[28] and lesser political lights found in this much belabored issue a favorable vehicle for their forensic talents. The watch industry was one among many that were made the target of concentrated political attack. The rise of these attacks and their effect may be traced in the financial journals of the period.

These were the years of unhampered control of the country's industry and finance by the forces of financial capitalism. The national administration was favorable, and even the Supreme Court displayed a benevolent attitude.[29] Given a free hand, the efficiency of financial capitalism was nothing short of miraculous. *The Chronicle* commented:[30]

Perhaps the most noteworthy characteristic of 1902 is the fact that it marked a further very distinct advance in that unexampled era of prosperity which found its inception in the result of the presidential election of 1896. We think there can be no question that in volume of business 1902 excelled all of its predecessors.

The prosperity was general — everybody shared in it — but serious discord immediately arose over the fraction that accrued to labor. *The Chronicle* reported:[31]

Labor troubles have been a feature of the history of all recent years — 1901 having been marked by the steel workers' strike and 1902 by the anthracite miners' strike — but it remained for 1903 to disclose what trouble it was possible for labor unions to create when they are in unchecked control of affairs. The year was marked by an extraordinary series of labor disturbances.

The discontent spread to consumers and to small business; like the steel workers and the coal miners, the former group had ample grounds for complaint against the less scrupulous leaders of financial capitalism. This new discontent manifested itself in political attacks on financial capitalism in general and on the "trusts" in particular. One result was the passage of the Knox bill to facilitate prosecutions under the Sherman Antitrust Act and the Interstate Commerce Act. *The Chronicle* goes on to say:[32]

The outcome of the trust agitation proved in a similar manner disturbing. . . . Being a wholly new contrivance [the Knox bill], there is doubt and uncertainty as to the outcome, and fear and uncertainty everyone knows is always detrimental to business interests.

In 1903, also, the attitude of the Supreme Court shifted to the left, and the Court handed down a decision in favor of the government in the Northern Securities case in 1904.

The discord in the economic system checked the speculative fervor and produced the rich man's panic of 1903–04. Waltham profits reflect this turn of affairs, and we note a decline from the peak of the three preceding years. After 1904 the political pressure continued and increased; as it increased, Waltham profits declined in spite of the return of general prosperity.[33]

By 1906 the political agitation against the trusts had become a major issue, and Theodore Roosevelt was staking his political fortunes on the success of this revolt against the leadership of financial capitalism. *The Chronicle* reports:[34]

The spirit of hostility which developed against corporations and corporate interests and against capital and wealth was one of the distinctive characteristics of the year. This hostility found expression in various ways — in the utterances of public officials, in legislative enactments and indictments and prosecutions in the courts. So far as those prosecutions sought to enforce the laws and punish those who had been transgressing them, only praise can be spoken of the endeavors. But, unfortunately, this does not seem always to have been the purpose in mind. Often it looked as if the object were to hold up to opprobrium men who had held a position of high esteem in the community and to make it appear that these men, because of their wealth, must be and were detestable creatures. In and out of the public halls there were frequent references to "capitalistic wealth" and swollen fortunes.

Although freed from imminent prosecution in 1907, the watch industry, like many other industries, was still in a difficult position. There was always the danger of new investigations. The antitrust legislation was continually being strengthened, the platforms of all the leading political parties were hostile to combinations, the Supreme Court was less favorably inclined than in the early 1900's, and the public was inflamed by popular writings.

CHAPTER VI

THE DECAY OF MANAGEMENT, 1910–1921

Form and Substance of Control under Robbins

THE PRINCIPLES of democratic government are outwardly followed in almost all formal organization in the United States. The governing bodies of the Church, the state, and of business corporations are theoretically representative of their membership, but *in practice* the active control and the constructive management do not follow the democratic pattern. The administrative organization of our government is bureaucratic, that of the Church is a hierarchy, while the management of war and business is normally conducted along purely autocratic lines.

Business corporations, in particular, are careful to employ democratic forms of organization, but ordinarily the democratic processes do not extend to the control of policy or management.[1] Parliamentary procedure is rigorously followed in the meetings of the stockholders and directors, but action at these meetings is limited, as a rule, to ratification of the policies and acts of the chief executive. This was the state of affairs that existed at Waltham under the management of Royal E. Robbins.

The relations between Robbins and his associates — employees, directors, and stockholders — reflected the political equality, the economic freedom, and the mutual respect that were a prominent part of New England tradition. But these relationships were matters of form and courtesy; they did not hamper Robbins in the unqualified exercise of his authority over the conduct of the business. He was, in fact, a benevolent despot, but his rule was not based on the extent of his ownership of stock in the Company. His exercise of control was dependent on the support of his stockholders; he was a dictator only by virtue of their unfailing confidence in his ability.

CONTEST FOR AUTHORITY IN THE SECOND GENERATION

After R. E. Robbins' death, there was a contest for control of the Company between his son Royal, who succeeded him as treasurer, and Ezra Fitch, the president. The two contestants held widely different opinions and supported diametrically opposite policies. The younger Robbins, like his father, was a shrewd conservative, while Fitch believed in taking full advantage of every opportunity for expansion. Unfortunately for the future of the Company, young Robbins was not able to win the support of the stockholders. Fitch, however, was in no better position; he also failed to obtain a clear-cut victory. The stockholders, unable to make a choice between the two executives, gave them equal authority and left their responsibilities undefined. Under these circumstances the actual control of the Company's affairs depended largely upon precedent, intrigue, and political maneuvering among the stockholders and directors.

DECLINE OF PROFITS

In the absence of a well-organized management, the earnings of the Company began to decline. During the panic of 1907 the fall was rapid, and it continued at an accelerated pace during the recovery of 1908 and 1909.[2] This was a plain warning that a serious disaster lay ahead, and Robbins' sons took prompt action to liquidate their interest in the Company with as little publicity as possible.

Royal Robbins' first move in severing his connection with the Waltham enterprise was to sell his interest in the firm of Robbins & Appleton. At that time the firm had a contract with the Company to sell the entire product of the factory for a commission of 6 per cent. Robbins & Appleton apparently was reaping a handsome harvest by selling Waltham watches at prices that did not yield a profit to the Company. This state of affairs had attracted unfavorable comment,[3] and Royal Robbins apparently anticipated that it would not long continue. Accordingly he sold his interest in the firm of Robbins & Appleton to the remaining partners, receiving his share of the assets plus a bonus of $15,000 yer year payable over the life of the sales contract with the Waltham Company.

In the same year (1909) both of Robbins' sons, Royal and R. C., sold nearly all of the Waltham stock which they had inherited from their father. Having transferred their capital to other uses, they retained their offices of treasurer and vice-treasurer, respectively, and awaited the development of the storm of criticism that was brewing among the disappointed stockholders.

THE STOCKHOLDERS' REVOLT

Stockholder revolts are not unknown, but it is little wonder that they are headlined on the financial pages when they do occur, and it is worth noting, also, that these occasional revolts are almost always led by some important stockholder interest; an uprising of small rank-and-file stockholders is almost unknown.[4]

DENNISON AND GALBRAITH

The moving spirit in the uprising of stockholders at Waltham was Cornelius C. Buckley. Buckley was a newcomer among Waltham stockholders and apparently something of a speculator. He had taken advantage of the panic of 1907 to purchase Waltham common stock in the amount of $70,000 par value. When the Waltham Company failed to participate in the recovery of 1908–09, he became alarmed and vociferous. He appeared at the 1909 stockholders' meeting in an indignant and critical mood.

Buckley's real grievance was the precipitate drop in profits, but he chose to make a special issue of the renewal of the contract with Robbins & Appleton. The content of Buckley's complaint has not come to light, but the grounds for objection on the part of the stockholders are not hard to surmise. The chief partners in the firm of Robbins & Appleton were also the managers of the Waltham Watch Company. Under the commission agreement between the firm and the Company, it was possible for the management to divert into their own pockets the profits of the business of making and selling watches, up to a maximum of 6 per cent of sales less selling expenses. As a matter of fact, the commission of 6 per cent was not exorbitant. It cost the Company an average of 8.8 per cent to operate its own Sales Department from 1911 to 1922, inclusive, and the lowest cost for the period was 7 per cent. At the time, however, it appeared to some of the stockholders that the profits taken by Robbins & Appleton were inordinate.

The Buckley incident is described by H. P. Robbins,[5] who was present at the stockholders' meeting of 1909. His account opens with a summary of the history of the firm of Robbins & Appleton and then continues:[6]

When the contract expired in 1909, Robbins & Appleton submitted, for the approval of the Board of Directors a new contract reducing the commission 2% making it 6%. I strongly objected to the ten year term of this contract, but realizing that I was in the minority, I merely refused to attend the Meeting at which this contract was approved. This contract was subsequently ratified at the stockholders annual meeting, which, in view of the large holdings of Mr. Fitch and the other members of the firm of Robbins & Appleton, was to be expected.

At that Meeting Mr. C. C. Buckley appeared protesting against the ratification of this contract and also protesting against certain other details of management of the Company. Mr. Buckley was treated with scant courtesy and practically no consideration. I had never seen him before and was inclined to regard him, as any director would in such a situation, as a trouble maker. The result, however, of Mr. Buckley's agitation of a year ago is the new Board of Directors which was elected Friday. Mr. Putnam, Mr. Burr and I have struggled almost continually for the past two months to prevent Mr. Buckley doing something which would be likely to injure the Company [he threatened to sue the directors], nevertheless, the fact that Mr. Buckley was making an agitation of this sort, made possible the election of the new Board and the outlining of the plan for the abrogation of the contract with Robbins & Appleton.

After the stockholders' meeting of 1909, Buckley became more importunate and finally insisted on examining the Company's stock and transfer books. After much delay the directors granted him permission, and Buckley was able to obtain from these records a list of stockholders who might help him to overthrow the management. Permission to examine the books was granted on April 21, 1910, and the next annual meeting was scheduled for May 20. During the intervening month, Buckley succeeded in thoroughly undermining the confidence of the stockholders in the Fitch régime.

The day of the meeting came, and Fitch was desperate. The annual report showed a further decline in profits, and Fitch apparently had no program of improvement that he dared to offer to the stockholders. There was danger that the management would be completely ousted, for the large shareholders — the Appletons and Fitches, the Robbins group, and J. P. Morgan — owned only 27.2 per cent of the total stock outstanding. Delay was advisable in order to prevent the management of the Company from falling into new, and possibly incompetent, hands.

The situation on the day of the meeting was beyond any control that Fitch could exert. In this emergency he called in R. S. Gorham, attorney, of Ropes, Gray & Gorham, and retained him "as special counsel in such matters as may arise concerning the relations of the Company and its selling agents."[7] This action was approved at a meeting of the directors at noon on May 20, 1910.

The stockholders convened at 2:30 P.M. of the same day, ready for a hand-to-hand encounter with the management, but instead they found themselves listening to Attorney Gorham. His address must have been a masterpiece of bland persuasion, but we can only guess at his eloquence from the guarded report of the Minutes:

> The President in the Chair.
>
> Mr. Robert S. Gorham moved that after the reading of the Treasurer's Report the meeting stand adjourned for three weeks.
>
> Voted: That the Treasurer's Report be laid on the table and that the meeting stand adjourned until Friday June 10, 1910, at 2.30 P.M.

The stockholders dispersed, and Fitch had another opportunity to set his house in order.

Under the guidance of Robert Gorham, things began to happen at Waltham:[8]

1. Robbins & Appleton offered to terminate the sales contract, provided that proper compensation was offered by the Company. In the event of disagreement, the amount of compensation was to be determined by arbitration.
2. The directors accepted the offer and voted to terminate the selling contract as of June 30, 1910.
3. The directors appointed a special advisory committee "with powers to fill vacancies, to make an audit and examination of the affairs of the Company, and to make a confidential report thereon to the Board of Directors." Two directors and one stockholder were appointed to the committee.
4. R. C. Robbins, James W. Appleton, A. K. Sloan, and E. A. Marsh resigned from the board, and a committee was appointed to confer with leading stockholders on the selection of four new directors.

This program was accepted by the stockholders at their meeting on June 10, 1910. Four new directors were elected to represent the small stockholders, the "outsiders." These four, added to the two directors elected in previous years for the same purpose, gave the small stockholders a majority on the board of directors. The majority block consisted of the following men:

Augustus Peabody Loring
William Lowell Putnam
I. Tucker Burr
Arthur Lyman
Charles W. Leonard
Horace E. Hildreth

ELECTION OF A REPRESENTATIVE DIRECTORATE

When Gorham sent the bill for his services to the board of directors, he was suffused with a justifiable pride, for he had saved the day at Waltham with a swiftness and precision that was truly Napoleonic. The feat was so remarkable that it seems easy to forgive a touch of braggadocio but Arthur Lyman insisted that more modesty and less candor were advisable. The reproof was contained in a letter from Loring to Gorham dated January 26, 1911:

> Mr. Lyman objects to your putting in that you elected Messrs. Loring, Lyman, Leonard and Hildreth a Board of Directors in place of James Appleton etc.
>
> He thinks that the stockholders ought to get the credit of the election and that the Company ought not to pay the expense of electing any of its directors.
>
> Will you kindly revise the wording of your bill.

The methods employed by Gorham in selecting the new directors and in securing their election are not disclosed by the records. It is probable that he followed the simple rules of social and political behavior that were the accepted practice of the time and place. There is no evidence of any deep intrigue or devious machinations. Gorham was assigned the task of nominating a group of men who would be acceptable to the small stockholders of the Waltham Company as directors, that is, as trustees of the responsibilities and equities of the stockholders. Although Gorham's methods are not precisely known, his standards of judgment are evident from the qualifications of the directors whom he nominated. Some of those qualifications are given in Table 12.

TABLE 12

ATTORNEY AND DIRECTORS, 1910[a]

WALTHAM WATCH COMPANY

Name	College	Boston Business Address	Director of Banks	Director of Mills	Total Directorships Held
R. Stetson Gorham	Harvard Law	60 State St.	......	......	1
A. Peabody Loring	Harvard Law	40 State St.	State St. Tr. Suffolk Sav.	Plymouth Cordage Co. Mass. Mills	15
Wm. Lowell Putnam	Harvard Law	60 State St.	State St. Tr. Suffolk Sav.	Plymouth Cordage Co.	16
I. Tucker Burr	Harvard Law	53 State St.	Parkinson & Burr	Nashawena Mills	5
Arthur Lyman	Harvard Law	60 State St.	Old Colony Tr. Suffolk Sav.	Mass. Mills Nashawena Mills	28
Charles W. Leonard	......	232 Summer St.	Home Sav.	Nashawena Mills	9
Horace C. Hildreth	Harvard M. I. T.	Harvard, Mass.	......	Hildreth Bros.	..

[a] Gorham was special counsel retained to make peace between the management and the stockholders. Putnam and Burr were elected to the board to represent the outside stockholders in 1906 and 1907, respectively. Loring, Lyman, Leonard, and Hildreth were added by Gorham in 1910. The remaining directors — E. C. Fitch, Conover Fitch, Francis R. Appleton, Royal Robbins, and H. P. Robbins — represented the inside stockholders, that is, the large stockholders and the management.

A casual examination of the table easily discloses the cloven hoof of financial capitalism. We see the alliance with State Street, the New England equivalent of Wall Street. We note the interlocking directorates and the concentration of economic power, especially in the case of Arthur Lyman, who was a director or trustee in twenty-eight organizations. At this point we might hastily jump to the conclusion that the financial disaster which followed at Waltham was a result of the abuses of monopolistic financial power, of the sinister influence of the "money trust," but any such conclusion would be very far from the facts.

Although the new directors had been selected by Gorham, they actually represented the small stockholders. If the new directors acted together as a block, they constituted a majority of the board. This arrangement was a potential curb on the exercise of discretion by management, but it was the best bargain that Gorham could drive with the stockholders. They had control, through ownership of a majority of the common stock,[9] and they went to the stockholders' meeting of 1910 prepared to use it.[10]

The symptoms of indirect control by organized finance or by persons of great wealth were deceptive. The banks were not a power in the situation, for there was a good market for Waltham notes and borrowings were light.[11] The new directors were not large shareholders themselves[12] — Lyman and Loring owned no Waltham stock at all — neither were they the tools of the "financial interests." The force that put these men in office as directors was the confidence of the small stockholders, who were largely residents of Metropolitan Boston and had some knowledge of the candidates.

The attitude of the small shareholders towards their representatives was the result of two factors — a distrust of business management in general and a lack of confidence in the particular men who were in control at Waltham. The general distrust had been fostered by the political attacks on Wall Street made by Bryan in 1896 and revived by Theodore Roosevelt in the period from 1904 to 1908. The election of peace-loving Taft had not settled the issue, and Woodrow Wilson brought the conflict into the foreground again in his campaign for the "New Freedom" — a return to the methods and ideals of petty capitalism. Under these circumstances any evidence of mismanagement brought a reaction against the financial interests and entrenched wealth, against the large stockholder and the inner circle of management. Many of the small stockholders at Waltham had bought their shares from insiders following the stock-watering operation of 1906,[13] and the decline of Waltham earnings and stock prices since that date had brought a sharp sense of loss to the little fellows.[14] In their resentment they turned for leadership to local men of prominence whom they felt they could trust.

The search for new leadership in industry was not peculiar to Waltham. There existed in New England, at the beginning of the century, a large number of persons who held small blocks of stock in the industries of the region. These small stockholders were of various types. Some were the relatives and descendants of the early industrial pioneers; others belonged to the prosperous professional groups. There were also a liberal sprinkling of industrial wage-earners and a large number of widows, orphans, and charitable organizations. After the death of each successful industrial capitalist, there was an additional group of small stockholders searching for new leadership.

The small stockholders did not usually find leadership in the sons of the deceased captains of industry. They did not find it in the banks. It was not to be had from a government that was sometimes bitterly critical of business management and at other times shamelessly indifferent to brazen abuses. But the small stockholder *did* find leadership among the solid, conservative men of their own communities — neighbors, whose shrewd New England judgment of risk and profit had kept them modestly affluent through succeeding generations. As these leaders grew in number, they came to constitute a separate profession; part lawyer, part industrialist, and part banker, they were known simply as *trustees.*

The ideal trustee in Boston in 1910 was a lawyer by training, preferably a graduate of the Harvard Law School. His ancestors had been prosperous merchants or professional men in Boston, or its vicinity, for several generations. His office was on State Street; his residence was along the shore between Cohasset and Marblehead. He had at least one conspicuous connection, either in banking or in industry. If he had held public office, but was not a professional politician, so much the better. In brief, his name carried a connotation of stability and security, enduring through generations of risk and change.

These trustees constituted the vanguard of financial capitalism.[15]

In the succeeding years the system has been developed to a point of great scope and intricacy. It has been exploited by greedy and unscrupulous operators, and it has been soundly pilloried by politicians, the public, and the press. Fundamentally, however, financial capitalism is an elaboration of the trustee system, and it will continue to be a vital element in our economic structure as long as it provides more competent and socially responsible leadership than is found in the ranks of industry or politics.

THE NEW LEADER — AUGUSTUS P. LORING

The official records of the Waltham Company merely state that Augustus P. Loring was a director and member of the executive committee from 1910 to 1921, but he was also the *de facto* leader of the majority block of directors. Fitch gave him credit for even greater responsibility, saying, "He really acted as chairman of the board. I don't remember that he was ever elected to that office, but he did the work at any rate."[16]

Loring gravitated to a position of leadership because he possessed the peculiar qualifications required by the circumstances — he was an ideal trustee. To begin with, he was part and parcel of the Boston scene. He had been born there in 1856. He had attended Harvard College and graduated from Harvard Law School, exactly as his father had done before him. In 1884, he had married Ellen Gardner — also of Boston. He had chosen for his career the management of industrial property in New England, as his father had done, and he had his office on State Street, the headquarters of Boston business and finance.

By temperament Loring was also well suited to his position at Waltham. He was a conservative and followed the business principles of his ancestors — principles that had remained fixed over a period of many generations. Caleb Loring was a sedentary merchant in Boston in the early nineteenth century. In 1824 he further diversified his interests by subscribing to 19 per cent of the stock of the newly formed Plymouth Cordage Company, and became its first treasurer.[17] Succeeding generations of Lorings have maintained a close supervision of the cordage plant, and its success is a monument to their managerial skill — but they cannot properly be termed industrial capitalists. They have clung tenaciously to the principles of the sedentary merchant:

the diversification of risk, the delegation of administrative routine to associates, the formulation of policy from a background of wide experience and intimate current knowledge, and a control of management which is based on the confidence of the many who share with them the risks of ownership. While the rest of the country was engaged chiefly in the hazardous specialization of industrial development, the Lorings pursued their customary policy of diversifying risks and integrating specialized functions. As the years passed they added commercial and investment banking[18] to their other interests, thereby passing directly from mercantile into financial capitalism and avoiding the dangers of the intermediate industrial stage.

When Loring was made a director of the Waltham Watch Company in 1910, he was in the full tide of his varied career. He was serving as director or trustee in fourteen other organizations, including banks, cotton mills, an insurance company, a hotel company, and the Plymouth Cordage Company, of which he was president. In addition to these duties, he had a considerable volume of professional business as attorney and trustee. He was also the author of a small volume, *A Trustee Handbook*, which was in its third edition in 1907.

LORING'S PROGRAM OF REORGANIZATION

The new directors gave the stockholders action, and plenty of it. They met on June 16—six days after their election by the stockholders—and transacted the following business:

1. The old management was confirmed in office by the election of E. C. Fitch and F. R. Appleton as president and vice-president, respectively.
2. Three majority directors, Lyman, Loring, and Hildreth, were appointed a committee to conclude the negotiations with Robbins & Appleton for cancellation of the selling contract.
3. The treasurer and Burr were appointed to make the financial arrangements for setting up a sales department at Waltham.
4. A committee composed of two majority and two minority directors was appointed to select a sales manager.
5. A committee of majority directors was appointed to consider a downward revision of officers' salaries.

On June 23 the directors met again and promoted I. L. Lake of the Chicago office to the position of manager of the New York sales office. They appointed a committee "to keep in touch with the selling end [and] to take up the problems and questions of policy which are bound to arise." They voted a small but reassuring dividend of one-half of one per cent on the common stock.

Further meetings followed at intervals of about a month. Royal Robbins tendered his resignation,[19] and Harry L. Brown was elected to succeed him as treasurer. The Federal Advertising Agency was employed to spend a $30,000 advertising appropriation; in addition, there were expenditures for the usual catalogues and circulars. A new salary schedule was adopted, and the position of vice-president was temporarily abolished. An executive committee consisting entirely of majority directors — Putnam, Loring, and Leonard — was formed. Putnam, who was the chairman of the executive committee, was given a salary of $5,000 per year.

Sweeping authority was held by the majority directors, but the records disclose that they did not have things entirely their own way. For example, Conover Fitch had his salary raised from $5,000, the amount voted on October 18, to $10,000, beginning November 1. This hasty retreat from a stand in favor of economy suggests an inner weakness in what was ostensibly a rule of the majority. Loring explained this weakness in his letter of October 31, 1911, addressed to his fellow-director of the majority party, C. W. Leonard. The letter reads in part as follows:

> Mr. Pearson told me that at the Chelsea Clock Co. after trying every other way, he found it absolutely necessary to break up the entire old organization, and go through a terrible period of wasteful production and poor business before he got his new organization successfully running, but the result was a complete success. In his opinion that was the only possible course to pursue at Waltham. . . .
>
> I have recognized from the beginning that the large holdings of stock by Mr. Fitch, Mr. Appleton and others would make it impossible to bring about a complete reorganization. Therefore, I early came to the conclusion that we had to get along with Mr. Fitch, but that we had got to improve the organization somehow or another. Frankly I think we would be better off without any of the three men that you mention . . . as they keep up the old traditions and hold the Company in the ruts.

The difficulties of effecting a revolutionary reorganization without changing the top management were considerable, but Loring was willing to make the attempt. His letter to Leonard outlined his criticism of the old management and his plan of reorganization by the infiltration of new subordinates:[20]

> Frankly, I do not think that we can leave the management of the Company to Mr. Fitch with the assistance of . . ., . . ., and . . . . I think that the old management had shown itself unequal to modern conditions, and that new men such as Brown, Olney, and Folsom were absolute necessities. I fully appreciate the ingenuity and knowledge of the old management in designing watch movements: but I think they failed in economical and systematic manufacture; that they had no cost system from which intelligent selling prices could be derived, and that selling methods were weak and poor.
>
> As it looks to me, we have got to use the good qualities of all the men that we have but to *limit* their activities to the sphere of their *successful* operation, and we must get more young blood into the Company.

Loring's scheme for reorganization by introducing new men in subordinate positions had serious disadvantages. Good men were hard to find, and incompetents successfully posed as men of ability. Furthermore, there was no guarantee that new subordinates would remain faithful to the directors, in opposition to their immediate superiors. Loring's letter continues:[21]

> Mr. Putnam has done very good work in shaking up the machine and getting in some new blood and modern ideas: but that this might be done more tactfully I am inclined to concede.

The difficulty may have been Putnam's lack of tact, or perhaps it was lack of coöperation from Fitch, for Loring wrote:[22]

> Two recent [about 1911] instances of the sort of management that has run the Company down are the putting out of a chronometer at a ridiculously low price . . . and the concession of the large commission on the "Equity Watch,". . . . In both cases Mr. Fitch took matters entirely in his own hands and ignored the new men. . . .
>
> Folsom is doing good work; although he irritates Mr. Fitch by showing him figures to *prove* to him that he is losing money where he *thought* he was *making* it.
>
> The cost department should be developed still further and the selling is in serious need of thorough overhauling and should in some way be taken out of Fitch's hands.

The program outlined by Loring in this letter was apparently in reply to Leonard's suggestion that the new directors turn the management back to Fitch, since the majority directors had not been able to obtain the good results for which they had hoped. Loring was opposed to any such action, and closed his letter by saying:[23]

Perhaps these results can be arrived at in a better way than we are now working on: possibly through the Executive Committee itself: but I do not believe that any of these reforms can be brought to pass by throwing the whole control back into the old organization, which I also think is quite important to retain, but to limit in its activities.

The details of Loring's plan of reorganization show a good grasp of the practical problems involved. He was indignant at the "enormous overhead charges" and critical of the obscure accounting methods. He cautioned Harry Brown about the practice of allowing unsalable goods to accumulate in the inventory. He objected to the use of full-page advertisements, saying, "It seems to me that we get very little for our money," and he advised smaller advertisements in greater number.[24] He suggested a change in the style of advertising copy, saying, "In other words I would get out of generalities and into particulars as much as you can."[25]

Loring was also an advocate of economy. He wrote to Conover Fitch on June 8, 1915, "I think that as we are cutting the rest of the organization so much, it would be wise to make a cut here [in the clerical and selling force] also."

When it came to sales policy, Loring was a hard-headed realist. For purely practical reasons he was against price-fixing. He said:[26]

I have received the article, which is careful and conscientious, setting forth the argument on the side of price regulation: but unfortunately I do not think it is popular with the general public: nor do they care a cuss for the argument.

It is against modern sentiment: and you are not a good merchant unless you are sticking the knife into somebody and selling goods at less than cost.

Loring also believed in free competition between the retailer and the mail-order house. He wrote to E. C. Fitch on January 6, 1911:

I have received the copy of "Dry Goods Economy." It seems to me that we are extending too much protection to the retailer.

That is to say that his margin of profit, and the margin of profit to the jobber, are both entirely disproportionate to the cost of the goods, and this being the case that we are fighting a losing case against the department store and the catalog house.

To my mind, we shall have to make some adjustments of the matter or be driven to it.

The present situation is not in a state of equilibrium and therefore cannot continue to stand.

Although Loring did not believe in protecting retailers against competition from mail-order houses, he was willing to help them by supporting installment selling. In a letter to Conover Fitch on January 10, 1913, he wrote:

It does seem as if our great object should be to increase our sales in every legitimate way: and there is no doubt that the installment plan of selling goods is one of the modern ways of doing so, and we might as well get onto the wagon somehow or another.

DIVERSIFICATION OF OUTPUT

From 1850 to 1916 it was the policy of the Waltham Company to limit manufacturing activities to the production of jeweled watches. There had been, however, some exceptions to that rule. Dennison had experimented with a variety of products from sewing machines to concrete, but none of them was put into actual production. Robbins had manufactured small lathes for a brief period during the depression that preceded the Civil War. There had also been a departure from the policy of specialization in the manufacture of watch cases, which was carried on from 1860 (perhaps earlier) until 1872. The poor results obtained from these experiments in diversification had effectually discouraged further efforts of this sort, and the Waltham Company manufactured nothing but watch movements from 1873 to 1910.

Diversification was adopted as a policy at Waltham about 1911. The new products and the years of their appearance are as follows:

	Product	*Year*
1.	Eight-day clocks, for travelers and for use in automobiles	1911
2.	Banjo clocks, through the purchase of the Waltham Clock Company *	1915
3.	Mechanical time fuses for controlling the burst of shrapnel	1915

	Product	*Year*
4.	Automobile speedometers	1916
5.	Blood-pressure gauges	about 1917
6.	Phonograph motors. At least one order was filled, but subsequent orders were refused	about 1920

The possible reasons for adopting the policy of diversification are numerous, but the records mention only one. The minutes of the directors' meeting of December 3, 1917, show an opportunist attitude toward diversification:

As this [speedometer] business was taken up as a variety to be used in times of depression we would not recommend going out to seek new business at present because the factory is so very busy on the out put of watch movements, but we believe that in normal times . . . the business will be of great value to help keep the factory going when the watch business is poor.

The turn toward diversification was undoubtedly influenced by the example set in the high places of financial capitalism. From these quarters came the stimulating news of great accomplishments through the use of three devices—integration, horizontal combination, and diversification.[27] Of these three only diversification seemed applicable at Waltham. Integration had been undertaken as far as seemed advisable by taking over the selling function from Robbins & Appleton. The attractiveness of horizontal combinations was spoiled by the recent display of public antipathy to anything resembling a trust or monopoly. Diversification, however, gave promise of excellent returns.

Conditions at Waltham were particularly favorable to diversification. Much of the machinery was adaptable to the manufacture of a variety of precision instruments. The engineering staff, under the supervision of the versatile inventor, Olof Ohlson, could be expected to carry the Waltham tradition of superlative performance into new lines of effort. There was no recent precedent to indicate that diversification was dangerous or unprofitable; furthermore, the practice of keeping several irons in the fire was consistent both with current financial methods and with the ancient precepts of Boston mercantile policy.

After 1910 there was a continuous drive at Waltham to develop entirely new products which presented opportunities substantially different from those encountered in the production of watches. Some of the new products were failures, and others became profitable only after a long period of trial and error. Frequent disappointments raised questions as to the advisability of diversification, and the program of development was often changed but the basic policy was continued in force. The difficulties in the way of obtaining profits from new and different products were certainly no greater than those encountered in a further development of the watch mechanism, and the expenditure of effort along both new and old lines seemed to promise the greatest returns.

WAR, PROSPERITY, AND RECKLESS EXPANSION

The direct effects of the World War on the Waltham Company appeared in 1915. In December of that year a new department was opened, the function of which was concealed by the title, Department #900. The purpose of the new department was the manufacture of time fuses for controlling the burst of artillery projectiles.

When the work on the time fuses started, the prospect of additional revenue from the manufacture of munitions was welcome, indeed. At that date the watch industry was still suffering from the depression which attended the opening of hostilities in Europe, and profits were at a low ebb.[28] The hope then arose that the time fuse would be comparable in its effect on earnings to the soldier's watch of the Civil War period. Eighteen months later this point of view was substantially changed. The difficulties of designing and building a precision timepiece that would withstand the shock of being fired from heavy artillery were greater than had been anticipated. Furthermore, because of the destruction of the fuse when the shell burst, it was almost impossible to trace the causes of inaccurate performance. As the difficulties became more formidable, the incentive to overcome them became less. The war boom was in full swing in 1917, and the Waltham Company no longer had any particular need for new markets; the domestic consumption of watches had increased with astounding rapidity, and the plant was operating at full capacity.

When the United States War Department approached the Company with a request for an increase in the production of fuses, Waltham officials made an effort to get other manufacturers of movements to share in the work. Since other watch producers had had no experience in making fuses, they declined and devoted their attention to satisfying the demand for watches. In the absence of other bidders, the burden of fuse production devolved upon Waltham. This burden was accepted by Waltham officials partly from a sense of patriotic duty, partly because the government showed an inclination to commandeer the plant if coöperation with the War Department was not freely given. As a result, experimental work was pressed with vigor, and a contract for 350,000 fuses of improved design was awarded to Waltham on March 27, 1918.[29]

The profitable character of the fuse-making venture is open to serious question. According to the income-tax reports for 1918–21, inclusive, Waltham derived a profit of $405,760, or 25.4 per cent of sales, from the fuse contract.[30] Offsetting this tangible gain was a large loss of potential sales volume which occurred during the war and postwar booms. So much space and attention was given to the manufacture of fuses that watch production was far less than the demand. The Sales Department tried to treat all jobbers fairly, and without discrimination, but the result was unsatisfactory. The situation is summarized by C. L. Depollier[31] in a letter to E. C. Fitch, written August 12, 1920, a date which marks the early stages of the primary postwar depression. He wrote:

> The trouble with the Waltham line today is that it is every dealer's watch with no special value for any, and for this reason when the demand drops off no dealer will concentrate on or even give the Waltham line a true and honest chance by properly presenting it; backing up its Quality and helping to sustain its price. No manufacturer can afford to sprinkle production, — satisfying no-one, antagonizing everybody, — and then expect Loyalty from all.

Although handicapped by the diversion of factory space and engineering talent to the manufacture of fuses, the Company made a strong effort to increase the production of watches. All the available space in the factory was put into service, including many of the passageways. When the limits of available space had been reached, the local supply of labor also was exhausted, and it became necessary to set up four branch plants in other Massachusetts communities: Quincy, Newburyport, Gardner, and Greenfield.

The rapid expansion of manufacturing operations,[32] combined with the high cost of materials and labor, created a necessity for a large amount of new working capital. This requirement was further increased by a shift in demand from less costly watches, which had been so popular before the World War, to the more expensive grades.[33] These expensive grades required a longer manufacturing interval between raw material and finished product, thus increasing the physical volume of goods in process as well as the unit cost. The natural results of these changes in demand and output were rapid increases in inventories, accounts receivable, and bank loans. The treasurer's report of May 20, 1920, explained these phenomena in a soothing and convincing way:

> The demand for the Company's product continued to exceed the supply through the year, and every effort has been made to restore watch production to a prewar basis. The year's earnings have been distributed as follows: — $300,000 has been paid in dividends on the preferred stock, and $175,000 on the common stock. The regular rate of depreciation allowed by the Government on machinery and plant has been taken amounting to $275,000. Any items of doubtful value in the merchandise account have been written off, and an appropriate reserve made to take care of Federal Taxes. In addition to this, approximately $400,000 has been added to surplus.
>
> The Company's loan during the year has increased nearly $2,000,000, which is balanced by corresponding increases in merchandise and accounts receivable. This necessary increase in working capital is caused by the wage increases granted during the year and reflected so heavily in the value of work in process and in the increased demand for the higher grades of the Company's product which in turn greatly increases the accounts receivable. This gratifying development seems to have already justified the extensive advertising of Waltham quality which the Company has carried on for the past two or three years.

The stockholder who preferred to use his own comparative figures would probably have reached the same optimistic conclusion from a compilation of sales and earnings such as the one in Table 13.

DEMOCRACY IN BUSINESS MANAGEMENT

When the directors began actually to exercise control over the Company's affairs, there was a distinct improvement in earnings.[34] This improvement reflected the advantages of democratic control over the chaos which had followed the death of Robbins, but it concealed

TABLE 13

SALES AND EARNINGS, 1915–1920
WALTHAM WATCH COMPANY

Year [a]	Sales	Earnings
1915	$3,104,895	$303,476
1916	3,981,956	216,686
1917	5,037,090	571,872
1918	6,062,660	778,270
1919	6,653,474	810,785
1920	8,665,500	869,976

[a] Ending Mar. 31.

SOURCE: Day & Zimmerman, Inc., *Report No. 1870 on Inventory of the Waltham Watch Company,* Aug. 10, 1922.

the cumulative drop in efficiency which is usually associated with democratic methods.

The use of democratic principles was not confined to matters of form, as had been the case under Robbins, but was extended to all matters of policy and to many of the major details of execution. The rule of the majority ceased to be a pleasant fiction and became an embarrassing reality. The democratic system spread through all the departments of the business, bringing in its wake a train of evils which are familiar to students of civil government.

There was a lavish expenditure of Company funds for the convenience, entertainment, and comfort of employees and officials. There was a drop of approximately 50 per cent in the efficiency of labor, together with a loss of effectiveness in management that defies estimate. The management became a bureaucracy, outwardly subservient to the directors, but actually devoted to personal advantage. The directors laid down the law with sage wisdom, but could not get it enforced. They attempted to supervise enforcement themselves, but could not overcome bureaucratic resistance. Among themselves the directors alternated between venomous quarrels and assiduous "backscratching" and busied themselves about appointments for their friends and relatives. As these abuses grew, the initial advantage of an active directorate was lost, and the Company was in a worse condition than in 1910.

The administration of the Company from 1910 to 1921 is a story of wanton extravagance, gross inefficiency, and a marked lack of business foresight. But before we condemn either the democratic system or the men who used it, it may be well to review the chief factors in the administrative situation at Waltham.

The program that Loring laid out for the reorganization of the Waltham Company was a good one. It was founded on wide experience and keen observation, it was sound and practical, but it did not achieve the desired results. The program itself was not at fault, and there is ample evidence that Loring was thoroughly competent. The failure of his administration was the result of a condition that he could not remedy, namely a lack of cohesion and solidarity among the small stockholders and the directors who represented them.

The weakness of Loring's position lay in the fact that he did not have the power to discharge the chief executive, and without that power he could not command the enforcement of his policies. He could debate and urge and compromise. He could demand, and get, compliance with the *letter* of his instructions. But he could not overcome the inertia and resistance of an administrative bureaucracy which was secure in its tenure of office. In spite of his best efforts, he could actually accomplish very little.

It might be argued that Loring did not display sufficient diplomatic skill in his dealings with the old guard at Waltham, but Loring was no novice in such matters. He was a seasoned politician — a member of the Massachusetts Senate for two terms — and had acquired the knack of cushioning the recoil of a command, or a criticism, by the use of well-chosen forms of expression. Although he was surrounded by urgent problems, he cautiously avoided the use of a brusque approach, which he said reminded him "of pulling a cat out of an ash barrel by the tail."[85]

In view of these qualities in the man and his program, I am forced to the conclusion that he attempted the impossible. The formulation of policy was vested in the directors who represented the outsiders, but the execution remained in the hands of the entrenched management block. As long as this cleavage existed, the possibility of maintaining profitable business operations was, I believe, extremely remote.

DISINTEGRATION OF EXECUTIVE CONTROL

The difficulties which have just been mentioned were not apparent in the spring of 1920. The flawless optimism expressed by the treasurer's report was shared by all groups connected with the Waltham Company. The directors, confident that the business would require more acreage, authorized the purchase of land adjacent to the plant "whenever it seems desirable in the opinion of the Management."[36] The stockholders, meeting on May 20, gave the directors — and, by implication, the management — a unanimous vote of confidence. The banks were liberal in providing working capital, and consumers continued to demand more Waltham watches than the factory could produce.

A year later, with the depression of 1921 at its lowest low, Waltham's illusion of prosperous security was completely blotted out. In its place was the solid bulk of impending bankruptcy. Not the comforting bankruptcy of legal subterfuge, but a Frankenstein creation of personal ruin, a catastrophe that was spiritual, physical, and financial. Conover Fitch, Ezra's son and general manager of the Company, was the first to crack under the strain. On February 21, 1921, the directors gave him a six months' leave of absence, in which to recover his health before facing again the almost hopeless task of salvaging some small fraction of the Company's assets. Others were not so sensitive and would not, or could not, believe that the whole structure of the Waltham organization was rotten to the core. But it was true, notwithstanding, and we shall go back a few years to spot the evidence of inner weakness that passed unnoticed at the time.

One of the most serious obstacles to thorough reorganization at Waltham was the lack of any party discipline among the directors of the majority block. They were individualists, some of them of the rugged and doggedly determined type. Loring mentions a controversy between Putnam and Leonard in a letter of March 12, 1912, addressed to E. C. Fitch; and a more picturesque clash of personalities was detailed by Loring in his evidence at the Abbot trial:[37]

Q. Do you know the reason for Mr. Arthur Lyman's resignation from the board?

A. Yes.

Q. What is your recollection as to that?

A. He got rusty.
Q. Got what?
A. Rusty.
Q. What do you mean by that?
A. Couldn't get along with anybody else. . . .
Q. What did he do at that time to show that he was getting rusty?
A. He objected to the Redmond plan because he said he had not been sufficiently consulted. He had been away canoeing, so he couldn't. And he didn't see me when I wanted to see him; and he wouldn't see the other directors, and he wouldn't discuss the merits of the plan, or any other plan.

The incompetence of the managing executives was marked. Ezra Fitch was a feeble administrator, lacking in force and directness, but much of the responsibility for inefficiency at Waltham rests upon the second officer. Putnam was chosen as managing director and vice-president in 1911, but Loring intimates that his methods or manner created friction. He was succeeded in 1912 by Conover Fitch, who seems to have shared his father's lack of managerial skill. H. L. Brown, treasurer and successor to Conover as general manager, was recommended by State Street interests, but "Silk Hat Harry," as he came to be known, did not succeed in averting the impending catastrophe. Appointments of less importance were influenced by family ties or friendship — considerations that were presumed to guarantee the ability of the candidate, but which often failed to do so.

While the management of the plant was growing worse, the directors were busy about such inconsequential matters as those contained in the following letter from a director to H. L. Brown:

Mrs. Morgan [manager of the cafeteria] came in to me about your lunch, as she is in the habit of doing when she gets puzzled about a thing. I told her what you wanted was an English lunch, with some nice cold salad, or cold dish on the sideboard, and your hot dish and vegetable on the table: and I suggested also that the dessert might be on the sideboard, except possibly ice cream in the season, and serve yourselves.

It is going to be difficult for her to get anybody who can do it during the summer: but in the fall I can get you a steward that I had and who is on my brother's boat this summer, who will be at liberty on the first of October. . . .

I told her that I thought the two courses would be sufficient, but if you had soup, to serve it in cups. I really do not think she has appreciated exactly what you wanted and I think she has had rather contradictory orders from you, Mr. Fitch, Conover and Olney, and she really did not know where she was at.

Poor Mrs. Morgan! Her confusion was no greater than that of her superiors, and the friendship and counsel of the director did not help her to balance the top-heavy budget of the cafeteria.

The absence of coördinated action at the top of the organization was attended by a lack of discipline among the workers. The employees were grateful for the kindly interest that Fitch took in their affairs and they responded to his benevolence with a very genuine loyalty, but it was a loyalty of a clannish sort. They were quick to rally against any outside attack on the organization or its people; they were devoted to their leaders; they labored with reasonable diligence for the common good. But mixed with this loyalty was an uncompromising independence. Authority was respected only where individual judgment ran along parallel lines. Custom was stronger than law, and infractions of discipline were ignored unless they ran counter to the ethical standards of the rank and file. Executive decisions were practically impossible of enforcement unless they enjoyed popular approval.

Factory supervision was not exempt from this influence. Foremen frequently produced two or three times as many parts as were ordered so that their departments would be kept busy.[38] Working hours and company materials were used for private purposes. Discipline was not merely lax, it was shamelessly loose, and the vice-president finally wrote a letter upbraiding his foremen:[39]

The Management feels the necessity of calling your attention to the fact that the Foremen of the Departments do not spend enough time actively supervising the work for which they are responsible. . . . Too much time is spent in the corridor, at the door, in the garage, visiting in other departments, and most of all sitting in your *own office*. . . . In too many instances Foremen show a tendency to occupy the position which should be filled by the head office girl.

Unbridled individualism also made its appearance in the executive ranks. Each officer operated in his own water-tight compartment, and coöperation was conspicuously absent. For example, Fitch excused his failure to provide detailed reports to the stockholders by saying, "Well, the way we managed was to divide the duties, and that was the treasurer's end of the business, . . . just as I claim to know more about manufacturing . . . I never had much of anything to do with the financial end."[40]

When Conover Fitch was given leave of absence in February, 1921, his duties as general manager were assigned to Harry Brown, the treasurer. Brown had been in the hotel business before coming to Waltham and knew that he could not master the details of a reorganization of the factory. In this emergency he followed the fashion of the day and called in a firm of consulting engineers.

The engineers were shocked at the conditions in the Waltham plant. Their testimony reads in part as follows:[41]

> We found some twenty-five departments, operating departments, in that plant without any coördination of the activities of each department. We found each foreman operating his department as though it were a plant in itself — he determined largely his own production; hired his own personnel; and he purchased his own materials, largely; with the result that he was considering himself more or less complete within himself, and failed utterly to coördinate the activities and results of his department with other departments. In many cases we found personnel in the departments very inefficient; we found two generations very often, sometimes, in one or two cases, three. We found family relationships playing a very important part, as far as morale was concerned; and about everything that would violate a good manufacturing condition was present.

The engineers further stated that 4,000 men were employed to do the work that 2,000 could have performed under conditions of reasonable efficiency.[42]

The office also was badly disorganized and heavily overstaffed: the Cost Department alone had 151 employees, and 41 persons were employed to operate the cafeteria. Delays and errors in office routine were common, and ruffled customers could not always be appeased by pointing to the labor shortage or the strictures of war conditions.

The whole situation was summed up by Loring at the Abbot trial when he said "that there was no one brain that was bringing the whole work together and seeing that it flowed smoothly in a continuous stream from one department to another."[43]

In financial matters the signs of faulty policy are apparent from the beginning of the Fitch régime. In spite of his disclaimer of responsibility for the financial management of the Company, there is strong evidence that Fitch, by imposing the Sales Department's point of view on Robbins, altered the traditional conservative basis on which Waltham finances had been built. The change may be illustrated by two extracts from the treasurer's reports. In 1881 Robbins, as treasurer and chief executive of the Company, told the stockholders, "The policy of making our money before we spend it will no doubt be pursued hereafter as it has been heretofore even if our dividends are continued at a moderate rate."[44] Speaking of business depressions, he added, "We propose therefore to strengthen the Company so materially in its capital and reserves that no ordinary revulsion will disturb us." The report of 1885, a year after the advent of Fitch, is in a very different tone. Prior to 1883 the Company had been practically free of debt, but the balance sheet of 1885 shows "Notes and Accounts Payable" amounting to $636,098. Robbins explained in his comments attached to the balance sheet that the management had deliberately avoided the retrenchment which had been practised in previous depressions. He continued, "We accordingly find ourselves with a heavy stock of goods and a considerable debt."

The reasons for this change of policy, permitting an accumulation of inventory and debt, are logical enough: operations for the year had been fairly profitable; the staff of skilled workers had been preserved intact; the popularity of Waltham watches was greater than ever; foreign business had been good. Although these explanations appear over Robbins' signature, they smack too strongly of the salesman's attitude to be purely his own. In subsequent reports the same optimism shines forth. Meanwhile the inventory rose from $2,000,000 to $11,000,000, the debt mounted to more than $8,000,000, and the burden of capitalization increased to $12,000,000. This was the state of Waltham's finances in 1921.

The top-heavy financial structure was preserved from collapse during the postwar boom by the liberal loan policy of the banks, but this policy changed with the drastic price deflation of 1921. In reëxamining their portfolios in the light of the lower price level, the banks discovered that the Waltham loans were not adequately covered by the Company's current assets. The confidence of the banks in the ability of the management at Waltham was also damaged by the circulation of reports exposing the inefficiency of Waltham labor.[45] In the fall of 1921 the Company needed still more working capital. The banks dared not withdraw their support and force the Company into liquidation, for fear that their loans would not be fully covered by the proceeds of a forced sale. After much negotiation a further extension of credit was granted, on condition that the banks should control the management of the Company.

By this time the Company was an inheritance of doubtful value. It consisted of a good name, somewhat tarnished; a plant ill equipped to fill the new requirements of the postwar market; an intractable personnel, long accustomed to flout industrial discipline; and an organization bogged down in the accumulated precedent of many years of mismanagement. At this point the banks were faced with the task of securing an executive who was competent to take this mass of error and confusion and rebuild it into an efficient industrial organization.

CHAPTER VII

CONTROL BY COMMERCIAL BANKS

Creditor Banks Choose Gifford K. Simonds President

Late in 1921 the First National Bank of Boston, coöperating with other creditor banks, took over the control of the Waltham Watch Company. The bankers had reached the conclusion that the Waltham executives were incompetent and cast about for an able and reliable executive. They selected one of their own directors, Gifford K. Simonds, who was treasurer of the Simonds Saw and Steel Company, of Fitchburg, Massachusetts.[1]

The qualities that recommended Simonds for the position of chief executive at Waltham were apparent when he discussed the affair with the author in 1939. His stimulating personality and poised animation reflected a capacity for strong and active leadership. A stocky frame of medium height gave him an air of rugged vitality; his full features, boldly outlined and firmly set, gave promise of effective organization and timely, purposeful action. His expression, on meeting a stranger, was keen and appraising, but not unpleasantly critical. His manner was friendly and informal and seemed to recognize a bond of mutual respect, but it did not tempt one to essay any hasty familiarity.

Simonds talked rapidly with an emphasis and conviction that displayed the driving enthusiasm of the pioneer. He used a wealth of picturesque idiom, and his speech was clear and forceful — except for an occasional cryptic phrase. He was very frank and open in conversation, but the sharp edge of his comments on men and affairs was softened by a tolerant discretion. By nature, he was neither suspicious nor vindictive, but he was in no sense gullible. His interests were warmly human, but his judgments were impersonal and objective.

The duties and responsibilities of Simonds' varied business ventures did not oppress him. He carried them lightly with the full assurance of success expressed in word and gesture. He was obviously prosperous, and his confidence that the future would yield as good returns as the past led him to be generous in financial matters with his friends and his employees. It would appear, however, that his generosity was not mere philanthropy and that it was usually repaid in kind.

Simonds' impressive personality was backed by a good record. He had been general manager of the Simonds Saw and Steel Company, of Fitchburg, Massachusetts, for ten years (1912–22).[2] Under his direction the company had prospered handsomely. In the period from 1911 to 1921 the company's assets had risen from $2,400,000 to $6,300,000, and the debt in the same period had decreased from $800,000 to $250,000.[3] He had operated the four Simonds plants and had maintained a large selling organization, including three foreign offices. He was well known in Boston business circles and had been a director of the First National Bank for several years.

There was one feature of his industrial experience, however, that was a liability in the Waltham situation. His previous tasks had been easy by comparison with his new responsibilities. The accomplishment at Fitchburg had not been a single-handed exploit — the whole Simonds family, both men and women,[4] had taken part in it. They owned 80 per cent of the common stock;[5] and, up to the days of multiple vice-presidents, a majority of the officers had borne the Simonds name. This condition had existed ever since the foundation of the company by Abel Simonds in 1832; and from one generation to the next, they had grafted on the old policies the new ideas about business management. The company had passed smoothly and steadily through the various stages of industrial capitalism, from a simple village workshop to a complex industrial unit with national and international ramifications. And finally, with the shift in emphasis to financial management, the company had taken its place with other large enterprises in the structure of twentieth-century financial capitalism.

Under such circumstances the discipline and morale of the plant were good, and there was little to prepare Simonds for the deep-rooted resistance to control that had developed in the Waltham personnel. His description of Waltham morale, given on the witness stand in 1927, is characteristic of his vigorous manner. He said:[6]

For myself, in our plant, I wouldn't take a pencil that didn't belong to me. There they took home pencils and paper, pencils and paper for their kids to go to school with, and if anything went wrong at home, a chair found broken, or a table, they would bring it down to have it fixed up and sent back. The head men would do that, the foremen would do it. And I was not used to that, and it looked all wrong to me, because, I would go through the plant, and I would see something that had nothing to do with a watch, being repaired for somebody. It permeated all through the plant, so that it was something that I was not used to.

These actions on the part of employees required more than policing. They required more than the close supervision that Simonds gave to everything that went on in the Waltham plant. There was need for a formidable display of power in order to make it clear to everyone that the new standards of performance would be enforced.

Simonds recognized that the enforcement of discipline was a major issue, and he made careful preparations for the test of strength that he would face upon his arrival at Waltham. Before accepting the responsibility of reorganizing the Company, he demanded complete authority and required each director to present his resignation, subject to acceptance when and if Simonds might consider it desirable to make changes in the board. He also protected himself from interference by the officers of the banks. He agreed to ask the banks for no more funds, on condition that he be given an absolutely free hand in all other matters. "I wouldn't work for a bunch of bankers," he explained, "unless I had complete authority."[7]

In spite of the precautions taken by Simonds to ensure respect for his authority, it is doubtful that he ever really succeeded in gaining a working control over the organization. Real authority was spread among four factions in the organization, each faction holding its authority by virtue of some unique and indispensable service which it supplied. No formal waiver, no obsequious submission could alter the power of resistance held by each group. The bankers had a strangle hold on the Company by virtue of the fact that the bank loans exceeded the value of the assets. The directors had behind them the steadfast support of the small stockholders, which was virtually the force of public opinion. The members of the management group were entrenched in their positions by long tenure and by highly specialized experience in the intricacies of watchmaking, and this hold was strengthened by the ownership of substantial blocks of stock. Last, and perhaps most important, was the power of resistance that rested in the rank and file of Waltham employees.

The confusion of authority which actually existed at Waltham is illustrated by the following incident. Simonds criticized the executives for "looking out for themselves and their jobs ahead of the welfare of the Company." [8] Harry L. Brown, treasurer and erstwhile general manager at Waltham, had a conference with his fellow executives and addressed a suave explanation to A. P. Loring, ranking member of the board. The letter read in part: [9]

> These men all said that they thought the criticism was most unfair and while there may have been some of that feeling in the past it did not exist today and they were sure that there was not a single foreman or factory executive who was not on his toes, so to speak, and working for all he was worth. . . . They came back at me with such force that I could not help believing that any cases of lack of esprit de corps are few in number if they exist at all.

This letter only faintly suggests the stubborn and effective opposition that Simonds encountered. There was, in fact, little tangible evidence of the deep-rooted obstructions that were placed in his path. The conflict was thoroughly suppressed, and the amenities of business conduct concealed the bitter antipathy that existed. Harmony appeared to rule, and the staff was quick to resent any insinuation to the contrary.

The very enthusiasm of this lip-service was suspicious, and it was at variance, too, with the feeble attempts of the executives to improve the efficiency of the plant. The lack of practical results, however, is not necessarily an evidence of ill will. A great part of the inertia, which effectively prevented a rapid readjustment of the organization in line with Simonds' plans, was undoubtedly the result of an honest conviction that the old ways — with minor corrections — were the right ones. The fact remains that Simonds never received the full coöperation of the Waltham staff. He felt it keenly, and in the long run it was the thing that defeated him. Looking back on it three years later, he said, "I was a stranger all the time I was there." [10] And again, when asked why he had dropped out of the Company, "I had got tired of it, the business didn't interest me, had to break the hearts of too many families, to tell them that they had gone broke; and I had lived in it about as long as I could." [11]

The precise nature of Simonds' relations with the creditor banks does not appear in the records, but Simonds, himself, stated that the officers of the banks did not hamper him in his administration at

Waltham. In spite of these assurances, I am convinced that the cautious attitude of the banks had an unfavorable effect on policy and action during the year that Simonds was president. The banks were cautious and, therefore, opposed to drastic remedies that might further devaluate the inadequate assets that secured the Waltham bank loans. The banks had this characteristic in common with the other factions who shared control at Waltham — they sought the greatest protection for themselves rather than the good of the whole organization. As a result of this near-sighted, timid attitude, all Simonds' plans for reorganization were reduced to innocuous proportions. To be sure, everyone made concessions, and there was a great show of progress and improvement. The valuation of the inventory was written down by nearly $3,000,000. The payroll, which had previously been reduced by laying off a thousand hands, was maintained at the lower figure in spite of urgent recommendations that skilled workers be reëmployed. A few openly recalcitrant foremen were discharged, and the "efficiency expert" resigned. These measures were good as far as they went, but Simonds insisted that they were inadequate; subsequent events proved that he was right. Speaking particularly of his statement that inventories were still overvalued and should be carried on the books at a much lower figure, Simonds said:[12]

> It is pretty hard to convince your stockholders that they should throw away their money. It is hard to convince them of that, and no one could convince them, and no one would believe that my disposition towards the assets was correct, and therefore I thought that possibly I was wrong.

And again, in regard to the formulation of business policy in general, he said:[13]

> I will put it this way: I was among a lot of people who were critical of me — the banks, the directors, the officers, the help, the trade, wanted to see what was going to happen. I couldn't carry into that business what I might see as right as readily as I could in my own business until I had built up confidences around the different places.

SIMONDS' BUSINESS POLICIES

As a matter of fact, Simonds' plan for reorganizing Waltham affairs was worthy of every confidence, and his accomplishments in the execution of the program were considerable.

His first proposal was to revise the financial structure of the Company, reduce the inflated inventory to sound values, and pay off the debt. His second objective was to raise the efficiency of the plant and thereby make it possible to reduce the payroll. These two policies meant a heavy loss of capital to be accepted by the owners and the loss of their jobs to many employees, including some executives. Resistance to this program was inevitable but some progress was made, notwithstanding. On October 16, 1922, after a year of effort, the debt had been reduced by $800,000 through the expedient of forcing on the market some of the excess inventory.[14] Had there been ample time for deliberate action, this would have been quite satisfactory, but the banks were inconsistent in their attitude: they were cautious but at the same time impatient; they would not wait for a slow recovery.

"Economy" was kept continually before the staff. So strong was this campaign for reduced costs that on March 14, 1922, Brown complained in a letter to Loring, "We are making progress every day and if everybody will be patient and give us time, we can certainly get the plant into splendid shape eventually."[15] Production costs were cut, and such expensive luxuries as the cafeteria and swimming pool at the Riverside Club were disposed of. Pensions were curtailed. The attendance of a doctor and an optician was discontinued. Plans for an elaborate dental clinic were abandoned.

Efforts were made to speed up production. The workers threading hairsprings had worked 15 minutes and rested 6 minutes — the rest period was abolished. Loring reported, "There were some parts of the work that were done with a magnifying glass, on the eye. He [Simonds] said it was too quiddly to do the work in that way, and he took away the magnifying glass,"[16] thereby depriving these workmen of the insignia of their craft. There is some question about the wisdom of these particular actions, some doubt as to the advisability of devoting so much time to detail, but Simonds' plan was to correct the obvious errors of practice that had developed in every department and to provide factory executives with specific instructions that could easily be carried out.

The third feature of Simonds' plan of reorganization was his personnel policy. That was the critical issue at Waltham in 1922, just as it had been in the crisis under Dennison in 1857, and it remained a most important and difficult problem until the end of the Dumaine régime in 1944. Personnel problems are difficult because there is as yet no considerable body of scientific data for use in their solution, and executives rely very largely on their own experience for guidance in such matters.[17] Since skill in business administration is usually the result of long years of training in a particular business environment, most executives lack the breadth of experience necessary to obtain correct solutions to problems bearing on human relations. Dennison knew well the springs of action that motivate the New England yeomanry and the lures that guide the mechanic, the inventor, and the engineer to achievement. But it took him forty years to learn the simplest fundamentals of human conduct in the world of business and finance. Robbins, on the contrary, was a man of unusual scope. In his boyhood he had learned the ways of the plain people of New England in his father's rural parish. On this excellent foundation had been laid his years of experience with English merchants and manufacturers, and more years of schooling in the business and financial capital of his own country. He knew intimately and well men of every type and class, and he used that knowledge adroitly. With Simonds the situation was different. His experience was wide in many respects, but it was limited chiefly to a successful and well-disciplined business environment. He did not fully appreciate the universal inefficiency that twenty years of mismanagement can produce in an organization of 4,000 people.

The general lack of efficiency was evident, and Simonds knew that very many Waltham employees had not contributed and never would contribute effectively to the Company's prosperity. He knew that the inefficient employees were so numerous that, if they were all discharged, the Company could not carry on. He believed, however, that the organization contained enough men of ability to salvage the Company, if those men were given an opportunity to use their talents. Simonds was confident that the few able and efficient employees would rally to his support and form a nucleus of disciplined action, to which less competent members of the group might adhere like mussels to a rock. In this hope he was mistaken. The residue of executive ability remaining at Waltham was not adequate for the task of reorganization.

A major objective of Simonds' personnel policy was the development of initiative. Under the previous régime, initiative had been largely suppressed. Employee turnover had been practically nil, and promotions had depended almost entirely on seniority. Under these conditions, employees could achieve success merely by longevity; special effort was quite likely to go unrewarded. Simonds thought that he could induce the employees to work harder, and accordingly he kept wages and salaries at current levels and opened the channels of promotion to anyone who could show genuine ability. He also made it a policy to discharge no one, except for insubordination.

The results of the changes instituted by Simonds are difficult to determine, but in the aggregate they must have been fairly successful. On January 18, 1923, Brown, the treasurer, issued a report claiming remarkable improvement. He wrote, "An entire reorganization of the manufacturing end of the business was started in the spring of 1921, and is now in effect in all assembling departments with a resulting saving in manufacturing costs now estimated at about 25% of former operating costs." And he continued with an estimate that "the company today is making a monthly profit of over $75,000 before interest is deducted. . . ."[18]

These figures should be taken with a grain of salt, for they unquestionably represent window-dressing in an attempt to impress the investment bankers. Taken at face value, they would be equivalent to $900,000 profit per year, but Conover Fitch says, "That would be true if it [the monthly rate] could be maintained. . . . That was in a way a hope, and it remained to be seen whether that could be fulfilled or not."[19] Similar reservations are applicable to the statement credited to Simonds, "that he felt . . . he had accomplished all that he had set out to do; that the Company was in a very healthy condition; that they had turned the corner and he was satisfied that it was going to be a winner."[20]

Simonds' attitude toward the Company changed radically in the course of his fourteen months as general manager. At first, according to his own testimony, his only reasons for believing in the future of the Waltham business were that "They had a good reputation," and that "Elgin made money."[21] His confidence in his own ability to supply the missing elements of successful management was complete. On this theory he plunged into the work without reservation.

The agreement with the banks, as outlined by Simonds, stipulated that he should spend one day a week at Waltham but he actually was there "every day, ten or twelve hours"[22] a day, leaving his home "at Marblehead Neck at 6 o'clock in the morning, and getting his breakfast at a lunch cart on the way up."[23] He proceeded to learn at first hand everything he could about the Waltham Company's business. He went through every part of the plant thoroughly by daylight, but that was not enough. At four o'clock in the morning he sometimes visited the fireman in order to see what was going out in the rubbish. He stood on the street corners and in railroad stations asking passersby what time it was, so that he could engage them in conversation about Waltham watches. He stood behind a retail counter for three weeks learning what consumers expect of a watch. Simonds took no details for granted — he investigated for himself anything that a layman might properly judge. These activities kept him away from the office, and he was criticized by the directors for neglect of his duties. But Simonds had the whip hand, and the directors were forced to confine themselves to passive resistance and diplomatic pressure.

FAILURE OF LIBERAL POLICY

What the result of Simonds' policies might have been in the long run remains a matter of speculation. The banks, not content to wait for a clearer indication of their merit, demanded immediate repayment of their loans. This action by the banks was not unreasonable, for the future of the Company was highly uncertain. The banks apparently felt that their own ability to control the operations of the Company had proved to be inadequate. The diffusion of authority that had existed under the Fitch-Loring management continued in actual practice under Simonds. The wide gap between ownership and management was not reduced, but increased, by the intrusion of the banks into the contest for the balance of power. Operating efficiency could not be obtained when so much energy was devoted to playing the game of intramural business politics. Under these conditions one cannot form a fair appraisal of Simonds' executive ability on the basis of his performance at Waltham.

The difficulties encountered by Simonds and Loring were closely parallel. The fundamental problem was caused by the distribution of ownership among a number of powerful groups having divergent interests. No satisfactory solution was possible as long as this condition persisted.

Simonds was slow to abandon his hope of recovery at Waltham, for confidence and optimism were deeply ingrained in his nature. On June 30, 1922, after seven months' experience with the Company's problems, he was still willing to participate in a new reorganization and to contribute heavily of his own funds. This scheme was considered favorably by the directors and was developed into a formal proposition which was dubbed the "Simonds plan." It was to be presented for the approval of the directors on July 10, but before that date Simonds had changed his mind and withdrawn his financial support.[24] Nobody else was willing to take his place. As late as December, 1922, Brown and Conover Fitch seemed to think that Simonds wanted to remain as president, but about that time he said in regard to his own efforts to arrange for financing, "Well, I'm through. . . . I don't see anything in store now except a receivership. . . . I can't interest any bankers in this proposition."[25] After this conversation the Allyn plan was developed, with the understanding that Simonds would assume management of the reorganized company. He considered the proposal and, about the turn of the year, he refused to participate, saying, according to the testimony of the assistant treasurer, "I don't think I can be identified with this. The banks have got bigger things in mind for me. This is only a small proposition and I will have to pass it up."[26]

Simonds stated that the banks asked him to continue in charge at Waltham but that the difficulties of acting as their representative were more than he cared to undertake. "Several individuals" offered financial support for a reorganization, but they were strangers to Simonds and he refused to accept their assistance. He would not run the risk of interference from a new and unknown group of directors. At this juncture the banks succeeded in inducing Kidder, Peabody & Company to underwrite a reorganization. The new plan took effect on February 9, 1923, and ended Simonds' term of service with the Waltham Company.

CHAPTER VIII

REORGANIZATION, 1923

THE REORGANIZATION of the Waltham Watch Company was consummated on February 9, 1923, by F. C. Dumaine and Kidder, Peabody & Company, after nearly two years of debate and negotiation. It was a distinguished achievement, and the way in which it was brought to pass is typical of financial capitalism at its highest stage of development. The great difficulties that were overcome and the splendid results that were later achieved are evidence of the remarkable efficiency of organized financial power. The methods used in consolidating control and in distributing profits are less praiseworthy in theory, but they are defensible on the grounds of practical necessity. Experience may lead us to a better solution for such problems, but in 1923 an assignment in bankruptcy was the stockholders' only other recourse.

OPPOSITION TO REORGANIZATION

The reorganization was opposed throughout the entire course of negotiations by a small, but active, minority of the Waltham stockholders. The first proposal, by Redmond & Company, called for a thorough reorganization of the financial structure that entailed sharp reductions in the equity of stockholders. The militant minority fought the plan and proposed a less drastic refinancing scheme of their own, but they could not get financial support for it, nor could they find a competent executive to put it into effect. The Company was in a really desperate situation, and the financial world knew it. New capital could be obtained only in case the stockholders were willing to forfeit a large part of their equity.

When the plans of the minority failed to materialize, a second proposal was received, this time from Kidder, Peabody & Company. A small group of die-hards among the stockholders attempted to prevent the adoption of this plan, in the vain hope that some easier court for an injunction to prevent the stockholders' meeting of February 8, 1923, which was called to consider the Kidder, Peabody proposal. The petition was denied but the bitter-enders carried the fight into the meeting, heckling the presiding officer with embarrassing demands for information. A woman stockholder remarked:[1]

> I would like to move that a committee be appointed to report on a financial statement of the company. This is the first time we have not had a statement of the company within at least a month of a meeting; and if Kidder, Peabody & Company are doing this philanthropic thing I have an idea the million dollars they will make out of it will be the consideration, and naturally they will rush it through and those who are going to be taken care of by Kidder, Peabody & Company will help in rushing it through.

And then the chairman appears to have said:

> The motion is out of order. There is a motion now before the meeting to accept the [Kidder, Peabody & Company] offer.

The motion to adopt the plan was put to a vote and carried, and the reorganization went into effect.

Ratification of the plan did not close the issue by any means. Six months after the Kidder, Peabody reorganization had been adopted and put into operation, Edwin Hale Abbot brought suit in the Massachusetts Supreme Judicial Court of Equity, charging a long list of defendants with conspiracy, fraud, and the sale of the Old Waltham Watch Company at an unjust price.[2] We shall discuss these charges later in the chapter, but for the present they will indicate the atmosphere of tension, fear, and intrigue in which the plan of reorganization was developed and executed. They will serve to emphasize the wide differences of opinion entertained by various groups of stockholders, by directors and officials, and by investment bankers, concerning the real significance of the business conditions which followed the World War. Perhaps the reader should review those conditions and make his own analysis of the situation at Waltham.

INFLATION LEADS TO FINANCIAL CRISIS

The crisis at Waltham was the direct result of the inflation that culminated in the boom of 1920. Inflation in 1920 was not a fear, it was a reality. Both government and business had been contributing heavily to the excessive demand for all the factors of production:

raw materials, labor, and capital. The federal deficit of twenty-five billion dollars for war and rehabilitation in Europe was still circulating in the bloodstream of business. Capital issues involving new money exceeded two billion dollars a year.[3] Credit inflation was also going full blast, with an increase in the total deposits of all reporting banks in the country of almost 100 per cent in the period from 1915 to 1920.[4] Deficit financing by State and local governments added another four billion dollars in the interval from 1912 to 1922, and there was an increase of about a billion dollars in the stock of monetary gold from 1915 to 1920. These inflationary forces were gradually increasing over the period, and the effect was cumulative, reaching its peak in the spring and summer of 1920.

Prices had responded like a rocket. At the peak in 1920 the index of wholesale prices was more than double the 1913 average. Many commodities far exceeded that ratio, for example:[5]

	1913 — High	*1920 — High*
Cotton	14.50 cents per lb.	43.75 cents per lb.
Hides	19.75 cents per lb.	41.00 cents per lb.
Petroleum	$ 2.50 per bbl.	$6.10 per bbl.
Pig Iron	$18.50 per ton	$50.46 per ton

The speculative spirit of the times is illustrated by an article appearing in the *Annalist* for March 29, 1920. The headline runs, "Cotton's Spectacular Performance Had a Sound Basis," and it closes with the forecast that there "is no limit to the price to which good grades may climb."[6] Supreme confidence in the upward movement of prices is also shown in the high rate of interest paid by speculators for short-term funds. Call money rates rose to 25 per cent.

The feverish optimism of the postwar boom infected almost everyone, even conservative New England bankers. Under its influence the banks discarded the time-honored practice of restricting loans to seasonal requirements and advanced to the Waltham Company funds which became a part of the permanent capital of the business. Furthermore, the liquid assets of the Company were not large enough to cover the loan. To be sure, the books of the Company did show that the inventory was three million dollars larger than the debt;[7] but the book value was inflated and much of the inventory was not readily marketable.

The great size of the inventory was caused in part by the demand for prompt shipment of a wide variety of styles,[8] but other factors had even greater influence. The physical volume was increased by an excessive amount of work in process and by the manufacture of unsalable parts. The value was inflated above the normal market value by the use of an unsuitable method of accounting, as we shall see later.

The huge inventory consisted largely of work in process, and this was to some extent the result of delays in converting parts into finished watches. There was some dispute between Loring and Conover Fitch about the time required to produce a watch. Loring claimed "that there was six weeks labor on a watch, and that it loafed around the rest of the time . . . about a year." [9] Fitch, on the other hand, insisted that "the average production time . . . was somewhere between a year and eighteen months." [10] Part of this discrepancy is the result of a difference of emphasis as to the quality of watch produced. Fitch was thinking of high-grade timepieces, Loring of the more popular and less expensive watch. But Loring's point of view seems more reasonable and Fitch bears it out by saying, "I don't claim that we were as expeditious as we should have been." [11]

The inventory was swollen, too, with large stocks of material that could not be readily disposed of except as scrap. The plant did not follow any coördinated manufacturing schedule. Loring testified: [12]

> Each foreman of a room was running . . . at full capacity, irrespective of whether the parts were needed or not. . . . There was a great deal too much raw material; and I include in "raw material" finished watch cases. A great many too many jewels. . . . There was a great deal too much brass . . . too much oil . . . too much steel to repair the machinery with. I don't know of anything there wasn't too much of, except some parts of watches and they were in the minority.

Statements in regard to excess materials are seen repeatedly in the records with estimates that stocks of some items would last twenty, thirty, or forty [13] years. Outside appraisers positively identified materials, parts, and tools "of little or no value to the company" which were carried on the books at $1,163,432.[14] The actual total value of the inventory was never precisely determined, for too much work was involved in such a task, but these comments and figures indicate that the book value was far from realistic.

Accounting methods at Waltham gave full effect to the general inflation and added an extra fillip of their own. Inventory was entered on the books at the cost of materials and direct labor, plus a charge for overhead amounting to 100 per cent of direct labor. Materials and labor were charged at boom prices; and the overhead charge was also excessive, being even higher than the actual expense. This method would have been excusable if an adequate reserve for depreciation had been established, but, practically speaking, there was none.[15] Such negligence is especially striking when compared with the records of the previous administration, for in 1864 a reserve of 31.7 per cent had been established to allow for the fall in prices after the Civil War. Both precedent and caution were in the discard.

A large element in the prosperity of the period from 1914 to 1920 was the rapid development of machinery, engineering, and mass-production methods. Henry Ford gave the new technique its greatest publicity, but it was a national, not a personal, movement. The modern chemical industry, which took form under the stimulus of war requirements, was also essentially a mass-production industry. The new techniques resulted in a marked increase in manufacturing efficiency, and the consequent reduction in costs gave rise to a breath-taking acceleration of business activity. This phenomenon, perhaps more than any other single circumstance, contributed to the faith in a mythical new era in which deflation would no longer play a part.

Summing up the chief inflationary factors that contributed to the accumulation of an unmanageable inventory and debt at Waltham, we have:

1. Deficit financing by the government.
2. Large issues of new capital by business.
3. Credit inflation by the banks.
4. Increase in the stock of monetary gold.
5. Consumer demand for variety in merchandise.
6. Waste and inefficiency in manufacturing at Waltham.
7. Inflationary accounting methods.
8. Wide development of mass production.

The net result was an unbounded optimism. The leading headline in the annual review of the *New York Times Annalist* read:[16] BANKERS FORESEE CONTINUING ERA OF PROSPERITY IN AMERICA, but, in less than four months, the actual decline set in.

DEFLATION BRINGS INSOLVENCY

The first signs of deflation were the decline of the index of agricultural activity and the prices of hides and rubber. These early developments and a minor slump in the stock market occurred late in 1919, but the movement in the first months of 1920 had again turned upward.

The continuation of the inflationary rise was particularly conspicuous in the field of bank credit, which was already expanded far beyond normal limits. "The pyramid of credits was proceeding at an alarming rate and it was evident that if expansion continued to proceed at such a rapid rate, it would merely be a question of time until the credit structure of the country would explode."[17] The Federal Reserve agents had been preaching "the conservation of credit and the diversion of resources from unnecessary and extravagant uses," but, on February 2, stronger measures were applied by increasing the rediscount rate on commercial paper to 6 per cent. The New York City banks responded at once with retrenchment. Banks throughout the country reacted more slowly; by the time the movement was completed, in July, 1922, however, the contraction of bank credit, as indicated by the total earning assets of the Federal Reserve banks, amounted to 68 per cent of the 1920 peak.[18]

The next harbinger of deflation was the stock market, which broke in April, 1920, and touched bottom in August, 1921. The price index for 25 industrials fell from 129 to 68. The rise in the index of wholesale prices reached its peak in May and fell over 40 per cent, taking cotton from 43.75 cents per pound to a 1921 low of 11.2 cents per pound. Production, employment, and wages followed in turn, producing the greatest decline in business activity that had been recorded in this country—27.0 per cent below normal. The shock of the 1921 depression was severe and it was keenly felt in every walk of life, but the duration was brief—the resumption of normal activity followed in a few months.

The fact that Waltham did not take full advantage of the returning prosperity in 1922 indicates the presence of problems more serious than those connected with the business cycle. In the long run, it is these standing problems that present the greatest hazards. They lack the element of dramatic emergency, and frequently there is a great temptation to neglect them.

Prominent among these long-term problems was the prolonged downward trend of prices which normally follows a major war. This phenomenon, which made a belated appearance in 1920, caught the Waltham organization entirely unprepared. In May, 1921, after the movement was well under way, we find an entry of $1,000,000 for inventory depreciation. This was a futile gesture, inasmuch as that sum was only 8.9 per cent of the inventory and entirely inadequate in view of the magnitude of the recent upward swing of prices. At best it was merely a tardy recognition, in principle, of the deflation that was already an accomplished fact. It is not altogether strange that Waltham officials failed to anticipate this movement — the theory of the secular trend was not then considered, and it is not widely applied in business management even today. This apology does not bear close inspection, however, for the inevitable character of a drastic postwar deflation of prices had been clearly visualized by Robbins in 1864.

Another major source of difficulty was the advanced stage of development attained by the watch industry. Maturity brought the usual train of complications — the end of the rapid expansion of the market and a further increase in the intensity of competition.

The market for Waltham products fell off sharply, dropping 35 per cent in the two depression years, 1920 and 1921. In addition to the normal shrinkage of sales of a luxury product in times of depression, Waltham was faced with the loss of its market for war materials. The $1,600,000 contract for shrapnel fuses was completed with the close of 1920, and the demand for the specially designed army watches was reduced to peacetime proportions. The foreign market was very weak: exports of watches and parts from the United States in 1921 were less than 40 per cent of the 1919 peak. There was, however, a brisk market for Waltham automobile speedometers; but that product was a new development which had been neglected during the War, and the production was low both as to quality and as to quantity.

To make a bad situation worse, competing watch producers, domestic and foreign, had been flourishing during the War. While Waltham had been devoting much energy and attention to munitions, Elgin and Hamilton had been forging ahead on watch production. By 1920, Elgin had a capacity of three thousand watch movements per day and was planning an expansion program to cost a million dollars. Both Elgin and Hamilton increased their capitalization substantially in the period just after the War, presumably to reflect an increased productive capacity. Foreign competition was particularly alarming, for the imports of watches, chiefly from Switzerland, had risen from $2,615,744 in 1913 to $15,688,233 in 1920. But more serious still was the fact that the Swiss were excellent merchandisers. In the production of small wrist watches of attractive design, they claimed to be far ahead of American manufacturers.[19]

Competition was serious, but it was not the worst problem at Waltham. In spite of the drastically curtailed sales volume, the factory was quite unable to fill its orders. A letter dated October 16, 1920, from the office of the Superintendent of Time Service for a group of Eastern railroads reads:[20]

> Am simply swamped with orders for Riverside and 21 jewel Crescent Streets and 23 jewel Vanguards [all high-grade watches] with Vanguards far in the lead. If at all possible send at least one hundred, have at least fifty 23 jewel Vanguards. Will take one hundred and fifty if you will send them.

A pencil notation at the bottom of the letter bears witness to the desperate shortage of high-grade movements:

> Will ship 15 within a week
> 5 Vang.
> 5 Cres.
> 5 Riv.

At this date the nominal capacity of the factory was 2,500 watch movements per day, but this capacity was not in marketable types. The production of expensive timepieces was limited by a lack of skilled labor, while the cheaper fashionable watches could not be produced in volume for lack of suitable designs and equipment. The postwar market was demanding an overwhelming proportion of small wrist watches. It was finally necessary to curtail production to approximately 800 movements per day, and of this number about 500 were of the high-grade type. Two-thirds of the plant was idle.[21]

One of the most discouraging features of the situation was the age of the Waltham management. It was old in years of service — forty years old — when F. C. Dumaine came in and completely revamped it. It was old in terms of development, for it represented the early stages of industrial capitalism. Modern devices and systems had been adopted, to be sure, but the proper use of these aids had not been understood. They remained little more than a fungous growth, sapping the funds and energy of the business, without materially changing the basic structure of the organization. Until Dumaine took it over, the business remained a Gargantuan collection of small workshops, which had never been integrated into a watch factory at all. And, finally, the Fitch management was old because it was set in its ways. It had lost its flexibility and had crystallized in the pattern of an earlier, simpler age. There was no changing it, no salvaging the fine material of which it was composed without completely breaking it down and piecing it together again to form the mosaic of a modern industrial organization.

This completes the survey of the deflationary factors that led to insolvency. They include:[22]

1. The postwar depression.
2. The downward postwar secular trend.
3. The age of the watch industry and the increasing pressure of competition.
4. The low productivity of the Waltham plant.
5. The age and inflexibility of the Waltham management.

All these circumstances, except the temporary one of depression, not only led to insolvency but also prevented any satisfactory measure of recovery. Nothing short of complete reorganization offered any reasonable promise of success.

At this distance, and prompted by a knowledge of subsequent events, we should have no difficulty in forecasting insolvency for the Waltham Company. In 1920, such clarity of vision was not so easily attained. Recent events had overwhelmingly justified the spirit of optimism; anything less sanguine was considered both heresy and folly. As a nation we were victors in a War for Democracy, creditors and philanthropists to a prostrate world, undisputed leaders of modern material culture — all this honor and glory made it hard to visualize concretely the hazards of expansion or to estimate precisely the odds in favor of bankruptcy. Therefore, it is not surprising that many Waltham officials, directors, and stockholders failed to recognize the serious nature of the Company's position until the possibility of finding simple remedies no longer remained. Attempts at correction, prior to the final drastic reorganization, all failed to appraise adequately the critical state into which the Company had been allowed to drift.

SEARCH FOR NEW CAPITAL

The trouble began in April, 1921, when F. S. Moseley & Company were unable to sell more than half the volume of notes necessary to take care of maturing obligations. There were three good reasons for this cool reception accorded to Waltham paper by previously optimistic investors: the unsound condition of Waltham finances, the break in the stock market, and the weak financial condition of Robert H. Ingersoll & Brother.

The Ingersoll watch had been an experiment in mass distribution undertaken in 1892. The watches had originally been produced by the Waterbury Clock Company, but the business had prospered mightily and had soon demanded additional productive facilities. Ingersoll continued to buy from Waterbury but also operated two new plants of his own. The close of the postwar boom found Ingersoll's company in financial difficulties, and in April of 1920 an extension of credit was sought from the banks. This affair dragged on for a year and finally ended in the purchase of the Ingersoll assets by the Waterbury Clock Company, who marketed their product as the Ingersoll-Waterbury Company.

The combined effect of Waltham mismanagement, the depression, and the trouble with Ingersoll finances spoiled the general market for Waltham notes. The large banks, however, were ready to come to the rescue, and in July additional bank credits of $1,250,000 were obtained from a group of Boston banks. "The sale of paper, however, fell off still more, and in September it became evident that further financing would be required. An arrangement was made with the group of banks to supply further funds to the amount of $1,580,000 secured by a pledge of the company's receivables."[23] These additional credits were given not from choice, but because they were necessary in the protection of the large stake which the banks already had in the Company.

When the banks gave the first credit, they exacted a promise that permanent financing would be arranged as soon as possible. When they gave the second credit, they demanded additional security. At this point, the banks demanded delivery of the Waltham receivables as collateral, and they also took over the management of the Company. Augustus Loring, who represented the Company in dealing with the banks, explained to the court at great length that "the banks would no longer finance any company, applying it particularly to our company, [with] . . . permanent capital on which to do their business." Bank loans in the future were to be for seasonal requirements, and borrowing corporations "must go out of debt once a year."[24]

Sanity had returned to the banking community, but not the dollars that had been lent so rashly. For the return of their money they were dependent on Loring's promise to arrange for permanent financing. There appeared to be nothing more that the banks could do for Waltham, or for themselves.

Loring was as good as his word. He "raked the whole United States"[25] in search of permanent financing. The roster of the firms that he consulted includes both the familiar financial leaders and those of lesser standing. He approached the problem from several angles. He tried to get new firms to sell Waltham notes, but could find no one who would handle them. He asked the National City Bank of New York to float a bond issue, but without success. Mergers and consolidations were discussed with the South Bend Watch Company, owned by the Studebaker interests; with Miller of the Hamilton Watch Company; and with Elgin officials. These discussions began with promise, proceeded with vigor, and ended in smoke. Interest was keen, yet there was no real meeting of minds when it came to terms. Studebaker appeared on the scene first and stayed the longest, but Loring discovered that "all they wanted to do was to sell the South Bend Company to the Waltham, really, so that was that."[26] No agreement could be reached with Miller of Hamilton, even after prolonged and detailed negotiations. Hulburd, president of Elgin, might have taken Waltham at a price, but ideas on price were widely divergent.

The only alternative left was to turn to the investing public, using the good offices of an investment banker. Accordingly, proposals were requested from Lee Higginson & Company; Redmond & Company; Drexel, Morgan & Company; Merrill Lynch & Company; the Marshall Field, Glore, Ward Company; Tucker, Anthony & Company; Hayden, Stone & Company; A. C. Allyn & Company; Kidder, Peabody & Company. Kidder, Peabody and several others refused to submit plans.

Of those firms that gave the project active consideration, all failed on at least one of the three major prerequisites:

1. Guarantee of adequate capital.
2. Provision for competent management.
3. Approval of the Waltham stockholders.

A. C. Allyn failed to get sufficient capital. Hayden, Stone tried to get William B. Mayo, chief engineer for Henry Ford, to take the management, but there was not enough life left in the Waltham outfit to suit a man of his experience in Ford's hard-driven organization; after receiving the operating statement for April, 1922, he wired his refusal. Allyn tried to get Simonds to carry on; tried to get Dickinson of Elgin to take it; tried to get young Royal Robbins to go back into the harness and repeat his father's exploits at Waltham — all without success.

October 1, 1922, rolled around and the loans were due at the banks. A last appeal was made to the bank syndicate for an extension of the loans, but without avail.

Redmond & Company offered the only other alternative at that date. This firm, alone, of all the investment bankers consulted, had presented a fully developed plan for the consideration of the directors. Unfortunately, the plan was not well received; the debate between Loring and Lyman was heated.[27]

Loring: "I think that, taking the market price of the stock . . . into consideration . . . the plan is an exceedingly fair one."
Lyman: "I think that a better plan can be devised."
Loring: "Mr. Lyman, for God's sake, get that plan going! We have got to do something."
Lyman: "Oh, no; the banks are in there, and they can't go out; they can't get their money; they have got to stay in."

But the banks did *not* stay in; perhaps Loring was not a good poker player. Perhaps there was more than bluff in the implied threat of the banks to close the plant and liquidate the Company. In any case the real importance of the debate over the Redmond plan lies in the recalcitrant attitude of the stockholders, which it illustrates.

An attitude of resistance might be expected from the stockholders towards *any* plan that would greatly reduce the value of their holdings. The Waltham officials and directors had learned this lesson well from the Redmond debate. Thereafter, they regarded the problem of reorganization from political as well as financial angles. Arthur Lyman's resignation from the board was the first of a number of astute political moves that are a prominent feature of subsequent negotiations. It seems reasonable to suppose that no plan could have been adopted without the display of some political genius. In business, as in government, the will of the majority responds more readily to the suggestions of propaganda than to the logic of debate.

The Redmond plan had been rejected in May, and five months later (October, 1922) the bank loans were overdue. The banks became really worried, and Philip Stockton of the Old Colony Trust Company took a hand in the matter. He requested Kidder, Peabody & Company to consider underwriting the Waltham reorganization, and asked Loring to supply Kidder, Peabody with information on the Waltham Company's position. Loring did so.

You will recall that Kidder, Peabody had previously refused to submit a reorganization plan, but by this time conditions were different. General business had been on the mend for over a year. Industrial stocks were selling close to their 1920 highs. The volume of sales on the New York Stock Exchange was up 57 per cent; miscellaneous bond sales were up 109 per cent. New capital issues had increased 34 per cent. The primary postwar depression was over.

More important, perhaps, than recovery was rapid spread of stock ownership. The profits of both war and postwar prosperity had been large and widely distributed. These profits and the corresponding advance in stock prices had created a widespread desire to share in the speculative gains of the industrial stockholder. The heightened interest in industrial investments was stimulating the purchase of securities by a new and larger section of the public. Under the twin impetus of swift recovery and eagerness on the part of many small investors, the market for new capital issues flourished; and the caution of investment bankers relaxed. Kidder, Peabody & Company reversed its former position and offered to underwrite a plan of reorganization for the Waltham Company.

At that date, 1922, a new *gold rush* was getting under way. As far back as Civil War days, Jay Cooke had discovered and tapped the reservoir of wealth held by the small investor. Cooke's campaign for selling the government five-twenties "was the beginning of a development which in a large measure laid the foundations of the American system of security distribution."[28] This development had been orderly, even though at times over-rapid, but the World War changed the tempo of the movement. It took on the sharp edge of excitement. Tales of easy wealth came drifting in from widely separated fields of industry: tales of fortunes gleaned from a wide variety of small, inconspicuous projects; millions from motors, chemicals, oil, and steel; fabulous bonanzas from the sprawling networks of power and transportation. Beginning with a sober realization of the magnitude of American industrial achievement, postwar finance soon took on the color of flagrant speculation. The tempo of investment became frenzied as "the public"—the small investors—increased their commitments in industrial securities and contributed to the phenomenal expansion of productive capacity. After 1921 the acceleration of the flow of capital continued without major interruption until the financial delirium of 1929 was reached.

There is a temptation to regard the flow of capital during the years 1922 to 1929 as a mere speculative orgy and to charge the unpleasant aftermath to the baleful influence of investment bankers, but the logic which supports that view is specious. The high rate of business activity occasioned by World War I and the postwar boom resulted in a great increase in the national income. The American standard of living rose; it did not rise so rapidly as income, however, and a large surplus remained. Capital accumulated, especially throughout the middle class. The units were small, but the aggregate exceeded all previous experience. It was important to the stability of our economic system that these small units of capital be collected and put to work, and it was the function of the investment bankers to provide channels for the investment of these funds. The investment bankers did their job well, and conspicuous cases of bad judgment or poor ethics should not conceal the excellent average of their performance.

The reorganization of the Waltham Watch Company is a case in point. In this instance it was necessary for the investment bankers to secure both management and capital for the continuation of the business, and to safeguard as far as possible the interests of the old stockholders. The Kidder, Peabody plan of reorganization fulfilled these requirements in a remarkably efficient manner. The methods which they used and the extent of their success are shown in the following excerpts from the evidence in the Abbot suit and in the analysis of the plan given in the concluding paragraphs of this chapter.

THE TRIAL: *Abbot* v. *Waltham Watch Company, et al.*

Abbot brought suit in behalf of all the aggrieved stockholders for the recovery of losses occasioned by the reorganization.

The Bill of Complaint, consisting of 46 counts, describes the workings of a conspiracy by which the stockholders were supposedly defrauded. The complaint charges that the conspirators "combined and entered into a scheme to procure the dissolution of the defendant company and a sale of all its assets . . . upon terms unjust and inequitable . . . to the stockholders, and that the improved financial and manufacturing condition of the defendant company rendered such sale and dissolution unnecessary."[29] Subsequent paragraphs bristle with accusations. Glancing through hurriedly, we read: "inadequate, inaccurate, and misleading information . . . falsely and fraudulently pretending. . . . in many particulars untrue. . . . intended and designed to secure . . . unjust and inequitable terms." The complaint also charges that facts, figures, committees, and dates of meeting were jockeyed about in such a manner that there appeared to be no alternative to the Kidder, Peabody plan of reorganization, except the total loss of equity through foreclosure by the banks. That is the essence of the forty-six counts.

The trial brought a brilliant turnout of witnesses: the Fitches, father and son; Robert Winsor, a moving spirit of Kidder, Peabody & Company and bosom friend of F. C. Dumaine; Augustus P. Loring, executive director and chief legal adviser to the old Company; James A. Faust, consulting efficiency engineer; G. K. Simonds, interim president for the banks; and several others. Most of the witnesses testified with force and vigor, each one not merely defending his own good name and purse, but also upholding the accepted practices of his profession — explaining and justifying that part of the American system of business management to which he personally adhered.

Abbot himself represented the ordinary stockholder, "the outsider," who must rely on published material for his knowledge of the company of which he is a part-owner. Abbot's testimony describes his futile efforts to obtain comprehensive information on the Waltham Company's position, also his equally unsuccessful attempts to participate in the activities of the inner councils of management and finance. All such channels were closed to him, and the only opportunity for redress, in his opinion, lay in the courts.

At this point the question inevitably arises as to the part played by favoritism and personal concession in the acceptance of the Kidder, Peabody plan. It is not surprising to find from the evidence that many of the persons in positions of influence were worried chiefly by the impending blow to their own finances. This is only natural. It is true also that Kidder, Peabody & Company arranged loans to influential stockholders for which the recipients were very grateful; and they admitted to the inner circle of the distributing syndicate a few individuals who were prominent in Waltham affairs. The court in its decision did not find anything irregular in these circumstances, nor do we mean to imply here that there was any departure from the legal and ethical standards of the day. There is no evidence of intent to prejudice the judgment of anyone at Waltham. The worst comment that we seem justified in making is that Kidder, Peabody showed the marked disregard for public opinion that was characteristic of the times.

The attitude of business toward public relations has changed substantially since 1922, but there is still some doubt as to the amount of publicity which it is desirable to give to business affairs. Decisions of great moment are commonly made by small groups of leaders in private conferences; precise details are developed by specialists working in comparative seclusion. This is the common pattern of business and government even in the most democratic countries. It is characteristic of management of every type: public or private, successful or incompetent, philanthropic or piratical. In our own government — supposedly a model in such matters — democratic methods are confined to the ratification of plans which have been previously formulated by committees of the chosen few. The existence of an inner circle of business management, together with unofficial negotiations and limited publicity, does not necessarily imply unethical motives or harmful results. After nearly four years of litigation, the Abbot case was dismissed. No fraud was found.

By the use of inference and innuendo it would be possible, of course, to construct a scathing indictment of investment-banking practice from the testimony in the Abbot case. Such treatment of the subject might have been useful in 1929, when the machinery of investment banking often functioned not wisely but too well. Today, however, it would serve no constructive purpose. Having learned, in 1929, a hard lesson on the evils of autocracy in business and finance, we are still in the process of learning the limits of the successful application of democratic theory to business practice. Past prejudice will not assist us in the new task. Let us appraise the plan of the reorganization in the light of its results.

ANALYSIS OF KIDDER, PEABODY PLAN OF REORGANIZATION

The capitalization of the Company before and after reorganization is set forth in Table 14.

TABLE 14

CAPITAL STRUCTURE BEFORE AND AFTER FEBRUARY 9, 1923
WALTHAM WATCH COMPANY

Old Company	
50,000 shares of 6% Preferred Stock	$5,000,000
70,000 shares of Common Stock	$7,000,000
New Company	
17,000 shares of 7% Prior Preference Stock Sold for cash at $100 per share	$1,700,000
50,000 shares of 6% Preferred Stock [a]	
70,000 shares of Common Stock Class B [a]	
25,000 shares of Common Stock Class A Sold for cash at $10 per share	$250,000

[a] No par stock.

The Class A common stock was referred to as "management" stock, and in 1928 it was distributed as follows:

Kidder, Peabody & Company	10,480½	shares
F. C. Dumaine	10,480½	"
F. S. Moseley & Company	2,329	"
Waltham executives	1,710	"
	25,000	shares

The plan was designed to achieve the following ends:

1. Pay off the banks.
2. Provide additional working capital.
3. Reduce interest charges.
4. Set a just price on the stockholders' equity.
5. Provide ample incentive to management.
6. Pay a profit to the investment bankers.

As regards the first three objectives, there is no difference of opinion; they were attained in a satisfactory manner. The debt to the banks was paid, dollar for dollar. Ample funds were supplied for the current requirements of the business. Interest charges were reduced by 30 per cent. The remaining objectives were major points of debate in the Abbot trial, and we shall report on them more fully.

Abbot put a great deal of emphasis on the injustice of the plan; but what really constitutes a just price? The question has long been the source of much perplexity to governments, moralists, and business men — they have debated it for many centuries without even arriving at a satisfactory definition of the term. We shall not settle the issue here. We may, however, determine what the price actually was and what was the effect the reorganization had in the long run on the fortunes of those stockholders who gave it their support and confidence. New money was needed, and it was hoped that the stockholders would subscribe cash for the new issue of prior preferred stock — the plan dealt severely with them if they failed to do so. Ten dollars in cash was required for each share of old common stock owned; twenty dollars, for each share of old preferred stock owned. In return for the cash subscribed, the stockholder received an equivalent amount of the new 7 per cent prior preference stock.

The exchange of old for new common stock was on the basis of ten shares of old stock for nine of new. But this rate of exchange applied only to those stockholders who had subscribed cash for new 7 per cent prior preference stock. Common stockholders who would not, or could not, put up any cash exchanged their stock at the rate of ten shares of old for two and one-half of new. In other words, common stockholders who did not put up any new money lost about 75 per cent of their equity.

Similar terms of exchange applied to preferred stockholders, except that the rate of exchange for subscribing stockholders was ten shares of old 6 per cent preferred stock for eight shares of new. Preferred stockholders who did not subscribe also lost 75 per cent of their equity.

Stockholders who voted against the plan at the stockholders' meeting of February 8, 1923, were entitled to have their stock appraised by the courts and to receive the amount at which it was appraised. Stockholders who did not vote against the plan, but who failed to assent before the expiration of the time limit, had no rights whatever and their stock was worthless. Ample time was allowed, however, and the expiration date was set ahead to permit laggards to realize on their holdings.

It may easily be seen from these terms that stockholders who were willing to accept the plan, and able to raise the necessary funds, fared very well indeed. For the stockholder who could not get sufficient cash for the subscription the plan seems quite harsh, but the actual figures do not confirm this superficial analysis. The apparent loss of equity resulting from the low rate of exchange was greatly outweighed by the increased value of the stock after the reorganization had begun to show its effect on earning power.

Before we can estimate the loss or gain to the stockholders, we shall have to reach some decision as to the real value of the stock at the time the reorganization took place. Four methods of estimating are worth inspection: book value, value in liquidation, capitalization of earnings, and market value.

The book value of the stock has been calculated, using the values that appear on the Company's books and correcting for the inflation that was shown to exist. Since the corrections are only rough estimates, the result is merely approximate. By this method the value of the common stock is nothing, and that of the preferred stock is $68 per share.

The value in liquidation must also be purely an estimate, but the probability that any equity would have remained for the stockholders seems very remote. Tangible assets at book value, adjusted for inflation and for yield at sale in bankruptcy, amount to $7,064,000. Creditors' claims total $8,030,611. Recovery by the creditors on this basis would be 88 cents on the dollar, with nothing left for the stockholders.

A capitalization of past earnings would show a very high value for the stock, but the past was dead at Waltham and the operations for 1922 showed a loss of $30,964. Current indications in February,

1923, pointed to a value of zero for both common and preferred stock on the basis of earning power. George P. Gardner, Jr., answered a question as to the status of the Waltham Company as a going concern by saying: "Yes, it was still going, running downhill."[30]

Under these circumstances, the market value of the stock seems to be the best standard of appraisal. It represents the composite judgment of the financial community, and, while it is subject to the rise and fall of market optimism, it has the advantage of including in its evaluation the intangible elements which other calculations disregard.

In using market values as a basis of comparison, we have taken the median prices of the stocks on the Boston Stock Exchange. Prices for the old stock are for the period January 1 to February 9, 1923; for the new stock, prices for the year 1928 have been used. This comparison gives effect to the profit-making ability of the new management, which after all is the nub of the question. The prices are shown in Table 15.

TABLE 15

STOCK PRICES, 1923 AND 1928
WALTHAM WATCH COMPANY

Common Stock		Preferred Stock	
Median price, old stock, Jan. 1 to Feb. 9, 1923	$ 4	Median price, old stock Jan. 1 to Feb. 9, 1923	$14
Median price, new stock, for the year 1928	$75	Median price, new stock for the year 1928	$90.50

Using the prices shown in Table 15, we get the profits accrued to the stockholders according to the various options; see Table 16.

TABLE 16

PROFITS TO STOCKHOLDERS[a]
WALTHAM WATCH COMPANY

Common stockholder, subscribing cash, profits	400%	Preferred stockholder, subscribing cash, profits	174%
Common stockholder, not subscribing cash, profits	300%	Preferred stockholder, not subscribing cash, profits	61%

[a] Real or paper profits, according to the circumstances.

Part of this profit is chargeable to the general rise in the stock market. In the period 1923–28, the price index for 25 industrial stocks rose 151 per cent.[31] Preferred stocks, of course, did not appreciate in this proportion.

Conclusions on the question of a just price are likely to embroil us in fruitless argument. It seems safe to say, however, that the old Waltham stockholders who assented to the reorganization did very well. Their profits were much greater than those of the average stockholder over the same period.

The next specification on our list is that the plan of reorganization should attract management of adequate ability. This phase of the plan was, in part, specifically defined in the text of the plan, and to some extent it was a matter of informal understanding.

The chief attraction of the plan for management was the 25,000 shares of management stock, referred to as Class A Common stock. This stock was to receive 20 per cent of the yearly profits after payment of fixed charges and prior preferred dividends.

According to verbal reports, Robert Winsor originally offered to give the Class A Common stock to Dumaine as a bonus, in consideration for which Dumaine was to manage the business without compensation. At the last minute, however, it became evident that more cash was needed and Dumaine purchased approximately 42 per cent of the issue at $10 per share. Of the remainder about 7 per cent was sold to other Waltham employees, and the rest to the Kidder, Peabody and F. S. Moseley firms at the same price. Dumaine had no beneficial interest, directly or indirectly, in the underwriting syndicate.

F. C. Dumaine served as president of the new Waltham Company for a period of several years without compensation. The management stock did not pay any dividends until 1927, and on July 1, 1927, the directors awarded the president $75,000 in recognition of the splendid results of his work. This payment was for services from the time of the reorganization to July 1, 1927. After that date he received a yearly salary.[32] Dumaine took the job with full confidence that it could be done successfully. He put his own time and money into the project on a purely speculative basis. He took nothing out of the business, for himself, until it was in sound condition and yielding returns to all its stockholders. It would be an error, however, to suppose that Dumaine was poorly paid for his efforts. The salary which the directors voted him was a handsome one, and the dividends on his original holdings of management stock averaged $19,138 per year over the eighteen-year period, 1923–40. Dumaine seemed pleased with his bargain, and the stockholders, too, had good grounds for satisfaction.

The final objective of the reorganization was to show a profit to the investment bankers. Here also the plan was a marked success. Of course, we should remember that profits, as we figure them here, are gross profits; out of this profit must come the commissions of the security salesmen, the overhead charges of the distributing syndicate, charges to cover the risk of underwriting, the cost of negotiations leading to the formulation and acceptance of the plan, and other legitimate expenses. What the residue of net profit actually is will remain a matter of individual estimate. The gross profit, however, can be figured with reasonable accuracy.

The profits from the reorganization were approximately as shown in Table 17.[33]

TABLE 17

GROSS PROFIT CALCULATIONS
WALTHAM WATCH COMPANY

Total Gross Profit on the underwriting of senior securities	$ 437,945
Income and speculative profit	
Dividends on Class A Common Stock held by Kidder, Peabody & Company and associates, 1923–38	421,655
Value of 12,809½ shares of Class A Common stock held by Kidder, Peabody & Company and associates at $30.90 less cost of $10 per share	267,718
Dividends on 10,000 shares Preferred stock, 1923–28, 1 year at $6	60,000
Sale price of 10,000 shares of Preferred stock, 1928, at $85	850,000
Dividends on 7,000 shares of Class B Common stock, 1923–28	none
Sale price of 7,000 shares of Class B Common stock, 1928, at $60	420,000
Transactions in Prior Preference stock, profit estimated	30,050
Total Gross Return to the investment bankers, approximately	$2,487,368

A profit of $2,487,368 represents a magnificent return on the investment of money and effort that Kidder, Peabody & Company and their associates put into the Waltham reorganization. It is only fair to discriminate, however, between the underwriting profit on senior securities of $437,945 and the profit resulting from the speculation in stocks. This speculative profit was in reality a profit-sharing bonus on the accomplishments of management. From the stockholders' point of view, it was good business, for payments were made only when, as, and if profits accrued to the stockholders. It would be highly desirable if we could devise a cheaper method for salvaging enterprises which have come to serious disaster, and of collecting and allocating capital for speculative industrial ventures. It would appear that no cheaper method existed *then,* and current efforts to reduce the profits of speculative business are associated with a marked loss of business courage and a shrinkage of new capital issues. It would be too much to say that restricted profits are the sole cause of stagnation in capital markets, but the possibility remains that there may be a fixed relationship between risk and profit that cannot be altered by government fiat or the pressure of public opinion.

BY-PRODUCTS OF REORGANIZATION

In weighing the costs and profits of reorganization, there are some items to consider that do not appear on the books of account. There are the jobs and homes of two thousand workers. There is the effect of a two-million-dollar payroll on the business interests of a small community. There is the financial security of a large number of stockholders, many of them small stockholders. There is the effect on the business morale of New England manufacturers in their attempt to maintain both the vigor of their industries and a high standard of living for New England workers — maintain them in the face of bitter competition from cheap labor in this country and abroad.

The reorganized Waltham Company under the leadership of Dumaine made a vital contribution to New England industry. He developed and illustrated the business methods by which a manufacturing enterprise may be kept active and profitable — profitable to the men who put their money in the till, as well as to those who spend their lives at the desk or bench.

CHAPTER IX

MANAGEMENT AND INDUSTRIAL DEVELOPMENT

Summary of Industrial Development at Waltham

The qualities that characterize a good business administrator are too familiar to need much comment here. A keen mind having breadth of view and a shrewd sense of comparative values, a faculty for decisive and expedient action, and a personality that commands respect — these are the essential requirements for business leadership in any period or place, but the possession of these qualities does *not* constitute a blanket guarantee of success. On the contrary, the prerequisites for success include specific talents which vary with the nature of the business venture, with the stage of development of the national economy, with the growth of the industry, and with the age of the business itself.

The task that confronts the chief executive of a business enterprise is perpetually in a state of flux. Under some circumstances the changes are slow and the same policies and talents may be passed from one generation of administrators to the next, with excellent results. This happy state of affairs was quite common before the Industrial Revolution, and it is still to be found in countries that are experiencing a slow economic development. I say this is a happy state of affairs because in those so-called backward countries economic development is synchronized with the slower process of human adjustment. In modern industrial nations the situation is quite reversed. The task of managing a particular business usually changes too rapidly for individual adjustment. New conditions call for revisions of policy that violate the established principles of the executive. Previous experience, habit, and prejudice prevent a prompt response to the new conditions — administrative efficiency begins to wane.

If we review the careers of the Waltham Company's former chief executives, we find that each one was conspicuously successful at the beginning of his term of office. In each case, too, the success was qualified later either by outright failure or by tacit admission of the need for change. Dennison went into bankruptcy. Robbins began to relinquish command twenty years before the end of his active career. Fitch's brilliant success was followed by his spectacular failure. This rhythm of success and failure occurs too often in the ninety years of Waltham history to be purely accidental. There is, in fact, a clearly discernible pattern in the development of the watch industry that correlates with changes in management. This pattern is of interest in that it suggests the possibility of predicting the date at which a change of management may be desirable and of determining the qualities which the new executive should possess. A knowledge of the pattern may also be of value in maintaining executive efficiency by accelerating the process of individual adjustment to keep pace with greatly altered circumstances.

INDUSTRIAL DEVELOPMENT — CREATIVE STAGE

The inception of a new industry is preceded by a new idea or invention and a great deal of enthusiastic promotional effort. Genius is required, and it must be the sort of genius that can be sharply focused on a specific objective. This quality is rare, but Aaron Dennison had it in full measure.

If we review the history of the Waltham Company back to the conception of the idea in Aaron Dennison's mind, it will take us to about 1839. Dennison said, many years later:[1]

> The principal thinking up of the matter was done when I was in business at the corner of Bromfield and Washington Streets in Boston. Many a night after I had done a good day's work at the store, and a good evening's work at home repairing watches for personal friends, I used to stroll out upon the Common and give my mind full play upon this project and as far as I can recollect what my plans then were as to system and methods to be employed, they are identical with those in existence at the principal watch factories at the present time.

In the interval between the first planning and the active promotion of the project with Howard, Dennison found time to whittle out wooden models of equipment[2] and to construct a pasteboard model of the factory.[3] In all, this period of development covered approximately ten years, 1839–49.

The work of invention continued to be a vital part of the watch-factory activities after its incorporation. The first task was to design a watch that would lend itself readily to machine production. The second and more difficult job was to design the watchmaking machinery. Dennison did much of this work himself, but his major achievement as an executive was in building up a staff of thoroughly competent designers.

Dennison was much more than an inventor. He had that gift of prophecy that is the hallmark of the inspired promoter.[4] He was visionary in the breadth and scope of his outlook, but intensely practical in his basic notions about men and machines. He displayed these qualities to their best advantage in laying out the new factory at Waltham. He planned for the future, and he did it with a grand flourish.

The most remarkable characteristic of the Waltham plan, as laid out by Dennison, was that it was admirably suited to immediate execution and yet made adequate allowance for eighty years of expansion and change.

This brief comment covers only a small part of Aaron Dennison's achievements as an inventor and promotor, but it is enough to show him in his characteristic field of action. As a financier his record is decidedly checkered.

Dennison knew something about finance. He had been in Boston as a journeyman during the credit inflation and land boom of 1836 and the ensuing panic of 1837. He had seen the cotton boom that followed. Dennison may not have watched these movements as a financier, but at least he must have seen their effects on the jewelry business and on employment. When the severe depression of 1842 and 1843 arrived, he had been in business for himself for only three years, and the pinch of the times must have stuck in his memory. In spite of this experience, the panic of 1857 found him unprepared. "For some time after entering the new factory, about fifty hands were employed, but few, if any, watches were produced. This necessitated a continual draft upon the very limited capital of the Company, relieved by little, if any, income, so that it was but a question of time when financial trouble would be inevitable, and in less than two years matters had

Fitch was a specialist — a salesman — and he had made a remarkable record in his specialty. The development of competition suggested the advisability of giving the management of the Company to a sales specialist, and Fitch was the logical man for the job. He had one deficiency: he remained a specialist. He never mastered the technique of factory management, or sales management, or financial management — but he knew what kinds of watches would sell most quickly and he knew how to get along with his customers and his competitors.

The Sales Department had two fundamental policies. The first was to attract more business by aggressive merchandising which would give the customer a wide range of choice in making his purchases. The second policy was to keep prices at a profitable level by any legal means that could be devised. Both policies met with substantial success at first but it proved difficult to hold the advantages gained.

In the years immediately following the installation of Fitch as president, the market was held by an aggressive merchandising policy. The variety of styles and sizes was increased rapidly. By 1896 they were so numerous that the London office prepared a telegraphic codebook to reduce the cost of transmitting rush orders. The codebook lists thirty-five different watch movements of various qualities and of six sizes. There were thirty-two special features of construction or appearance that could be added. Plain cases were available in five metals, three styles, and three finishes. Fancy cases, not included in the codebook, were offered in profusion.

Fitch remained in control until 1921, and his influence was dominant at Waltham until Dumaine arrived in 1923; but the policies originated by the Sales Department were a failure after 1907. The directors were aware of this state of affairs as early as 1912, and they made three efforts to change the administration. These efforts failed largely because the directors thought of the change in terms of personalities, apparently not realizing that the entire basis of management at Waltham had become outmoded. The Company needed a complete revision of policy and a general stiffening of discipline and morale. The directors sensed the need of change — it was plain enough in every financial statement from 1912 to 1922 — but they lacked the courage and foresight to break with the president and establish a completely new administration.

In the meantime, both production and finance were neglected. The science of factory management as developed by Taylor and others did not receive any recognition at Waltham until 1921, when an over-rapid application of these theories was attempted. The new developments in corporation finance were also allowed to pass unheeded. Whereas other corporations were acquiring new capital by the sale of securities to the public via the investment bankers, Waltham relied on the market for commercial paper and on the commercial banks. Policies in both production and finance were determined on the basis of superficial analysis with an eye to Waltham's glorious past and a naïve disregard for the hazards of the future.

Another important change from the preceding stage of development is in the relation between ownership and management. After 1883, management was dissociated from ownership. Although in later years Ezra Fitch invested a large part of his estate in Waltham securities, he did not at any time own a majority of the stock. Control rested with R. E. Robbins up to the time of his death in 1902; his sons Royal and R. C. Robbins, treasurer and vice-treasurer, respectively, held the purse strings until 1910. In 1910 the Robbins brothers retired, and after that time the ownership became diffused. The board of directors was split by factional disputes. There was no strength or solidarity either in the board or in the management.

INDUSTRIAL DEVELOPMENT — FINANCIAL COÖRDINATION STAGE

The watch industry passed into the fourth stage of development about 1912. At this stage no single line of effort was sufficient to maintain the Waltham Company in a prosperous condition. Competition was not confined to any particular field; it extended to every phase of production, distribution, and finance. A working knowledge of each of these fields was essential to success as an industrial manager, but specialized knowledge was not enough. The primary task of the chief executive at Waltham after 1912 was the coördination of the various parts of the business into a well-integrated industrial unit. This approach to the problem was not used until Dumaine had taken up the work.

Dumaine, then, was an industrialist of the financial school. Like Dennison, he was interested in the mechanics of watch design and watch production. Like Robbins, he was unremitting in his efforts to obtain the greatest possible output at the lowest unit cost. He resembled Fitch in his careful attention to all the problems of distribution and in his attempts to maintain cordial relations within the industry. But Dumaine had a specific contribution of his own, a direct answer to the problems presented by a progressive lowering of profit margins. He had a faculty for closely coördinating all the activities of the business in terms of industrial finance. The problems were intricate and complex, but the method of solution was simple.

The Dumaine management was proud of the absence of any "system" of control. There were no charts, no voluminous reports, no bulky files of forms and records. But if one wished to know any of the essential figures (since 1923) of performance or cost, he could find them in a series of some half-dozen looseleaf books, indexed for easy reference. The entire set, covering twenty-one years of operation, would about fill the top drawer of a standard desk. The current data covered but a few sheets of paper. These were the bare essentials, the vital statistics of the business. Special reports were prepared as required, but no data were collected regularly unless they were of constant and important use. The records were simple, brief, and direct.

OWNERSHIP AND MANAGEMENT

The details of Dumaine's methods and policies will be discussed in subsequent chapters, but the relation of management to ownership may be mentioned at this point. At the time of the reorganization Dumaine purchased about 11,500 shares of Class "A" Common stock. The "A" stock carried equal voting rights with all other stock, giving Dumaine only a small minority interest.

In spite of this theoretically small ownership, Dumaine always functioned as an owner-manager. Subsequent purchases may have given him a majority of the voting strength, but that was hardly important. Regardless of the amount of stock which stood in his name, he held undisputed and sole authority over the Company's affairs. This authority was partly a tribute to his reputation as an executive of outstanding ability; it was partly a result of the support of his friends and associates in Boston financial circles; it was partly the effect of the indomitable force of his personality. Whatever the source of his authority may have been, there is no questioning its existence. It was evident at every turn.

General conclusions from the history of a single concern are not warranted, but it is interesting to note some of the distinguishing features that are common to two of the financially successful administrations at Waltham. In each case there was a strong, centralized management of a nonspecialized character, the chief executive being a man of broad experience in production, distribution, and finance. In each case, ownership and management were concentrated in the same hands. The authority of the senior officer was absolute and final — no record of opposition by the board of directors is in evidence.

CHAPTER X

THE DUMAINE MANAGEMENT IN ACTION

Organizing the Executive Staff

Dumaine and Boucher arrived at Waltham in February, 1923, and took over the management. There was nothing uncertain or tentative about that action. It was apparent to everyone who saw and talked with Dumaine and his associate that the transfer of authority was complete and final. This impression was created without fanfare or ostentation; it was simply the result of the bearing and manner of the two men. They wore the air of command as a blacksmith wears his apron — simply because it is a part of the business of shoeing horses, because he is used to it, and because he likes it.

The team of Dumaine and Boucher was held together by the bond of common principles, and it functioned by virtue of dissimilar talents and temperament. Dumaine is short, thick, and immovable in his tenacious grip on the essentials of business strategy. Boucher is tall, spare, and facile in his mastery of business tactics. Both men are justly proud that they have reached the top the hard way. Both men are fighters with this difference: Dumaine fights at the drop of a hat but always with regret that such means are necessary; Boucher swaps yarns or punches, as the circumstances demand, and enters into the spirit of either occasion with equal pleasure.

The new organization was laid down on very simple lines. Dumaine was president and treasurer with offices in Boston. Boucher was general manager; every phase of manufacturing and distribution came under his direct authority. His time was divided between his headquarters at Waltham and the various sales offices. Ezra Fitch was vice-president, acting in an advisory capacity, only, and supplying the executive staff with the essential element of specific watchmaking experience. Graves was continued as assistant treasurer. Freistadter, who had been master-watchmaker under the old dispensation, was made manufacturing superintendent. These five men made up the management. Authority and responsibility were highly centralized and clearly defined.

The incoming management included a new board of directors. This group also was a credit to Dumaine's régime. Charles Francis Adams gave it social distinction and political connections. Louis K. Liggett lent his much publicized name to the undertaking. Philip Dexter and Allan Forbes represented the commercial banks that had assisted in the distribution of the new securities. The Dumaines, father and son, represented management. Robert Winsor and George Peabody Gardner, Jr., looked after the interests of Kidder, Peabody & Company and of other investment bankers. James L. Richards added to the strength and prestige of the group. It is regrettable that the formal brevity of the directors' records leaves us no clue as to the precise part that they played in the Dumaine management. In the absence of direct evidence we may assume that relations between the president and the board were cordial, and there was probably little occasion for the directors to display the influence over management which they are supposed to exert.

The back leaf of the report to the stockholders, for the year 1923, bears the usual list of executive personnel:

OFFICERS

F. C. DUMAINE, *President and Treasurer*
E. C. FITCH, *Vice-President*
F. C. GRAVES, *Assistant Treasurer*
I. E. BOUCHER, *General Manager*
J. FREISTADTER, *Manufacturing Superintendent*

DIRECTORS

Charles F. Adams	F. C. Dumaine, Jr.	Louis K. Liggett
Philip Dexter	Allan Forbes	James L. Richards
F. C. Dumaine	George P. Gardner, Jr.	Robert Winsor

Dumaine was conspicuously successful in retaining and using most of the talent in the old organization. In going over the original records and correspondence, I find it very evident that he studiously avoided unnecessary changes in Waltham supervisory personnel and that, where changes were absolutely necessary, they were made with the least possible inconvenience to the men concerned. Efforts were made to find new work for those who could not be continued in their old positions, but the possibilities in this direction were not always acceptable to the employees. At best, such readjustments are inevitably painful, and it was particularly difficult at Waltham, for "the various departments [Dumaine said] . . . were, almost without exception, in need of improvement. Manufacturing, accounting, stores, and selling all required extensive rearrangement."[1]

The attempt to retain the old personnel did not involve any compromise with the old top management — that was eliminated, root and branch. Ezra Fitch, for example, remained with the Company, and Dumaine has paid frequent tribute to the value of his services and the splendid spirit in which he gave them. His part in the new régime was, however, purely advisory and not executive. Dumaine defined his policy on this point in a letter to an old stockholder, saying, "The new [Dumaine] management is entirely new, none of the old people who were responsible for its downfall are in control of the new company in any way."[2]

ENFORCING ECONOMY

There was need for economy at every turn, but the administration of the office needed immediate attention. There was an opportunity to make important savings and, more than that, it was necessary to simplify the office routine before it would be possible efficiently to supervise improvements in the factory.

Economy began at the top. Dumaine himself received no salary; Boucher's compensation was "very moderate,"[3] his incentive consisting of an option on a block of Class A stock. Ezra Fitch felt the edge of the economy measures, for Dumaine wrote him, "I am sending you herewith a check for your April salary, at the rate the incoming Board has authorized me to pay you. I regret that it was not possible to carry out your desire in this matter, and trust you to understand and appreciate the situation."[4] Under the old régime executive salaries had been lavish, totaling over a hundred thousand dollars a year for the four top men. The saving at this point was substantial.

Salary reductions for top executives and for certain members of the Sales Department were in order, but average salaries for office and

FREDERIC CHRISTOPHER DUMAINE

President of the Company, 1923–1944

factory workers were not excessive. No general reduction of salaries was attempted. A large reduction in office payroll was possible, however, because many employees were not needed at all. The jobs which they filled had been created in an attempt to substitute so-called "scientific management" for the good business judgment which the Fitch administration lacked. Many of these jobs were abolished at once.

The Accounts Payable Department had consisted of nine clerks, a chief clerk, and over half a million dollars' worth of bills, some of them long overdue. Instructions were given to pay all the bills. Some of the creditors were so delighted to get payment that "cash" discounts up to 10 per cent were allowed. When the bills had been paid, a single clerk could handle that phase of the accounting.

There was a department for cost accounting and production control, but the department, being two years behind in their work, did not know what it cost to make a watch. Originally the department had had 151 employees; Loring reduced it to 72; Simonds cut it down to 17; Boucher cut it to 1 person.

The Planning Department had 17 people getting out plans for a new 7¼ Ligne watch. Some parts for the new watch were not available in sufficient amounts; stocks of other parts exceeded reasonable requirements. The department was abolished and one man was kept.

Many minor executives had private offices and private secretaries. This practice was discontinued and a central stenographic division was established. And so it went through the whole office. In three weeks' time, ninety-two useless jobs were abolished.

The saving in money — about a thousand dollars a day — was important, but the effect on methods and morale was of greater consequence. This initial campaign demonstrated at once, and for all time, that direct and simple methods would be used; also that every employee must earn his wages, not merely in effort expended, but also in results accomplished. The threat of passive resistance, which had so greatly weakened Simonds' position, almost entirely disappeared. The air was cleared and the way opened for the revisions in other departments that would be more difficult to plan and to enforce.

The results of this action were not entirely favorable. The drastic changes naturally produced a strong feeling of insecurity throughout the plant. There were much gossip and some grumbling, a good deal

The first reduction was merely a step toward the ultimate goal of price equality in the domestic field of competition. As rapidly as circumstances would permit, prices were reduced to a parity with Elgin and Hamilton.

The value of the intermediate price drop lay in the fact that it did not change the established selling tactics. Waltham salesmen could still talk superior quality and demonstrate it by charging more than the market price. They could stoutly claim that Waltham traditions were respected and maintained by the new management, thus preserving in the sales organization that inner sense of confidence that is the sustaining force in any sales campaign.

Cutting prices was not the only measure required to maintain sales volume; the quality needed radical improvement. Complaints were coming in from all directions. The serious nature of the difficulties on this score is apparent from the following letter sent by one of the largest Philadelphia retailers to his wholesaler and transmitted to the Waltham factory:[9]

Dear Sir:

It is most unfortunate that with every shipment of 7-½ ligne watches that we receive from your factory, half of them have to be returned for one cause or another, notwithstanding our repeated efforts by mail calling your attention to test them out and see they are made right.

Of the four watches that we received as per your invoice #3742 . . . the mainspring in watch #88502 was broken. [Watches #91197 and #88500 stopped after running less than 12 hours.] All three of these watches we are returning for credit today. . . .

This gets neither you nor ourselves any merchandise to put before the public and if we were to put it before the public in the shape we receive it from your factory, the writer is certain that the Waltham Watch Company's reputation that they have been building up for three quarters of a century would be dashed to pieces.

A note on the margin of this letter indicates that these movements had been inspected both at Waltham and at the wholesaler's shop.

Quality is an elusive thing at best, and in a watch it is a hidden attribute that is fully tested only in service. Quality is designed into a watch by management, but it is actually created by the conscientious fingers of skilled craftsmen. There are only two men who know the true quality of a watch—the man who makes it and the man who wears it. As an actual fact, not one worker but hundreds contribute directly to the quality of an assembled movement. One clumsy, careless, or mischievous workman in the whole chain of production can spoil the finished article, and it is often impossible to locate the source of trouble.

Quality was Dumaine's most vexing problem. Improvement was made, but there were many reverses and Dumaine felt them keenly, as we may see in this letter to Ezra Fitch, written on January 21, 1924:

My dear Mr. Fitch:

In the ten or eleven months past since we joined you at Waltham, there have been many problems to solve but none which reasonable intelligence, time, and care could not settle.

The one exception is this question of the quality of the product which continually crops up . . . I almost never buy a watch or movement of any kind, the performance of which comes under my personal observation . . . without trouble or complaint for something.

Now comes this extraordinary letter from Detroit regarding the Speedometer being supplied the X—— people. Nothing ever happened to Waltham in the past, or could happen in the future, more disastrous to the welfare of the Company than the loss of this contract because of inferior workmanship, or incompetent workmanship, or whatever you may choose to call it.

The great difficulty with this particular question is, I feel (and I know Mr. Boucher must feel likewise) absolutely helpless to put my finger on the trouble or to make the necessary correction because of lack of knowledge of the technicalities involved in this particular thing.

We went to you in good faith, believing the workmanship in the factory at least justified the reputation Waltham has enjoyed all these years.

Continued and persistent criticism of quality of output are most disconcerting and unless discontinued must end in disaster.

I don't know why I am writing this letter to you particularly, except for the need of having someone to whom I may unburden myself.

This kind of experience with the speedometer is not unusual when the device is a radically new mechanical design, and the trouble, which pertained to a detail in the driving mechanism, was corrected. The question of quality, however, continued to occupy Dumaine's attention, and perfection was his goal.

Since perfection is impossible, Dumaine protected the Company's good name by giving prompt action to the replacement of defective goods. Serious complaints often received his personal attention, and he was careful to see that satisfaction was rendered. His courtesy under criticism was unfailing.

HOUSECLEANING IN THE SALES DEPARTMENT

In 1922 the Sales Department was badly demoralized. Sales expense for the year amounted to $879,459 on a sales volume of $5,459,905, or 16.1 per cent. This was almost double the average figure for the period from 1911 to 1922.[10] Drastic action was needed and it was immediately forthcoming.

The largest item in the sales budget was the advertising appropriation, which had been set by the old management at 3 per cent of sales. Actual expenditures, however, were higher. For the year ending March 31, 1920, they amounted to more than $300,000, and officials estimate that $450,000 in advertising contracts were canceled by the new management in 1923. Dumaine's advertising policy is succinctly stated in a letter to Hulburd of Elgin: "I can't help feeling strongly unless done with the greatest care the money spent for advertising is very largely wasted."[11]

Salaries were cut by the elimination of nonproductive members of the sales staff. The use of missionary salesmen was discontinued. The Montreal office, where expenses had been running 40 per cent of sales, was closed and the agency given to the Goldsmith's Stock Company. The joint subsidiary at London, operated by Waltham and the Dennison Watch Case Company, of Birmingham, was dissolved. These economies brought additional savings of well over two hundred thousand dollars.

The management of the Automotive Division was changed. There had previously been general dissatisfaction with affairs in that division. Nikola Tesla, whose patents were the basis of Waltham Speedometer designs, was dissatisfied with speedometer sales. The automotive sales manager was dissatisfied with factory production. Dumaine did not approve of the expenditure of $60,000 for the division, especially since $48,000 was in salaries and commissions alone. It was several months before a new manager could be secured, and in the meantime Boucher added the duties of division manager to his long list of responsibilities.

One phase of the reorganization deserves a word in passing. The discipline in the Sales Department was, in some few cases, very poorly maintained. This difficulty is so prevalent that it does not require detailed discussion. Suffice it to say that the few lapses of ethical conduct that were brought to light were dealt with in summary fashion. In general, however, resignations from the Sales Department resulted from the fact that fewer persons were needed to carry out the very simple sales campaign that had been adopted by the new management.

ENFORCING TERMS AND RESTRICTING CREDIT

Poor discipline in the Sales Department was evident in the failure to obtain standard terms of sale and prompt settlement of accounts. In spite of the advantages of distributing through a selected group of wholesalers, the Company had had a great deal of trouble with collections. Even where the ultimate credit risk was not excessive, the slow accounts represented a burden on the working capital of the Company. Dumaine reports that in 1923, "We found the credit methods at Waltham deplorable . . . and decided orders for watches carrying long credits or payable with notes were not worth having and we have discontinued the practice entirely."[12]

Dumaine also attempted to control carelessness in the adjustment of claims for the repair of defective goods. Unfair claims were occasionally presented by customers, sometimes with the connivance of salesmen who hoped to curry favor with the customer by supporting the claim. This practice apparently flourished at Waltham, and Dumaine ruled that, in cases where the responsibility clearly did not rest with the factory, the claims for adjustment should be denied. Rulings of this kind are difficult to enforce, particularly where it is also necessary to maintain a reputation for prompt replacement of unsatisfactory merchandise. It was possible, however, to stimulate an alert attitude in the adjustment department without creating customer ill will.

SUMMARY OF DUMAINE'S INITIAL MOVES AT WALTHAM

The success of a new management depends, to a very considerable extent, on the impression made upon the old personnel at the beginning of the relationship. There is always a preliminary test of strength between the old guard and the new leadership. The result of this test should be decisive, but at the same time it should end in an amicable understanding of the mutual advantages which the future offers. The major steps that Dumaine took to accomplish these ends were as follows:

1. A drastic rearrangement of executive personnel that completely destroyed the old system of management.
2. The elimination of excess personnel and elaborate methods from the management routine.
3. The prompt adjustment of factory production to the demands of the market as regards style, quality, and price.
4. A broad readjustment of Sales Department expenditures in the overhead and executive categories, but only minor changes in the rank and file of productive personnel or in the basic methods of selling.
5. A general effort (not always successful) to remove uncertainties, retain valuable personnel, raise morale, and promote respect and confidence in the management.

CHAPTER XI

THE STRIKE, 1924

The Outbreak

Seventy-five years of industrial peace at the Waltham Watch Company came to an end in 1924, eighteen months after Dumaine's arrival. The immediate causes of the hostilities were a general wage cut, ranging from 0 to 40 per cent, and the tactless manner in which the cut was announced. On August 11, 1924, two hundred workers walked out of the Finishing Department and stopped the flow of production. The spirit of defiance spread rapidly, and in three days the entire plant was involved.

Resentment grew into hatred and fed on the host of grievances, real and fancied, that had been accumulating since the World War. The wage cut was branded as outrageous; the working conditions were reviled as oppressive and intolerable; the loss of time-honored privileges was bewailed as a wanton and useless persecution.

As time passed, the hope of any early settlement faded and disappointment still further increased the tension. The picket line grew from an orderly group to a jeering throng of hundreds. Workers who remained on the job were escorted home by groups of strikers following ominously at their heels, in utter silence. The silence changed to taunts and insults, and soon a shower of over-ripe tomatoes and eggs gave special emphasis to the jibes.

The climax came on a warm night late in September. Conferences had been under way between Dumaine and leaders of the local watchmakers' union. They had reached an agreement, in principle, on a compromise offered by the Union. This compromise accepted the Company's reduced wage scale, but men receiving $40 per week, or less, and women receiving $20, or less, were to be exempt from the cut. The accountants had been working into the night to determine whether the Company could afford to accept the terms or not.

The announcement of peace was expected at any moment. The

workers and their friends had gathered in full force at the State Armory to celebrate the victory. There was music and dancing. The gaiety reached a pitch that had not been seen since the early days of the strike. Then there was a call for attention; the Conference Committee was reporting that the 40–20 offer of the Union had been rejected. The strikers, in turn, rejected the Company's counter proposal of a 7½ per cent cut, and it was announced that the committee would return to the plant and report to President Dumaine. A shout was heard, "Let's go with the Committee!" A roar of approval followed, and there was a rush from the hall.

When the tension broke, the mob spirit flared instantly. Women fainted; some were trampled. Outside, a mêlée of men, women, and cars surged down to Prospect Street and across the bridge, picking up the curious and the idle on the way. In a matter of seconds, they were at the gates of the plant in a howling frenzy — a thousand, two thousand, three thousand — as the excitement spread through the community. The Union leaders lost control, even of their own people, and the wildest labor demonstration in the history of Waltham was staged. There were jeers and calls for Dumaine and Boucher, and the possibility of an assault on the group of officials who had remained in the president's office seemed very real. The mob was in the hands of irresponsible, impromptu leadership, and the moment of complete hysteria was dangerously near.

Quick action was taken to prevent a catastrophe. A panicky citizen who saw the first wave of strikers sweeping up Crescent Street telephoned the police, who arrived on the scene with commendable dispatch. The first squad of police was soon followed by detachments from nearby communities, and the fury of the mob relaxed — the crisis passed. After more than two hours of bedlam, the crowd had yelled itself hoarse and began to disperse.[1]

The crisis passed, but not without irreparable damage. The spirit of compromise was dead.

After this episode, the lines of combat tightened, and the strikers realized that they had neither the power nor the financial resources to win the strike alone. They appealed to the American Federation of Labor, stating their case in an open letter under a December date line. The statement mentioned the drastic wage cut and "intolerable conditions." It referred bitterly to Dumaine as a "General" who was using the "Starvation Method" of breaking the strike, and it stated, "We think it better for Waltham to have this industry, of which we have so long been proud, perish from the face of the earth than to have these financial pirates [Dumaine and Kidder, Peabody] triumph and treat their workers like the serfs of old."[2]

The other side of the story is equally simple. To Dumaine the strike was a major battle in the war against competition. Business had been on the down grade for over a year, the recession beginning about five months after the Waltham reorganization. Competition was keen and Waltham wages were higher than those paid by competitors. If the business was to survive, it had to meet competition as regards both prices and wages. Dumaine did his best to explain, saying that Waltham employees must inevitably meet the competition of watchmakers in other parts of the country and that only in this way could the Waltham business continue. His explanations, however, failed to convince the strikers, and he turned to the enforcement of a competitive wage scale at Waltham by hiring any former employees who would return at reduced wages and by bringing in new workers as rapidly as they could be trained.

When the strike was called, the press and the public sympathized with the workers. "It must be conceded," said Ernest Faulkner, president of the Union, "that 2,800 unorganized intelligent workers who had been employed in a plant for long terms up to 45 years would not quit upon any slight provocation." This argument was popular, and it was often used in the early days of the strike. The general public apparently found it amply convincing, and the newspapers were willing to give plenty of space to copy which tended to support that point of view.

As the strike wore on, violence increased and the business men of the community suffered severely. At that stage of the proceedings the press was inclined to berate both parties roundly. The Waltham *News Tribune,* of October 24, carried an editorial that was distinctly impatient in tone:

For the strike the responsibility must rest upon the Company, not because it was forced to reduce its wages but because of the disregard of justice and equity and the crude manner in which men and women of character and intelligence were called on to accept the cut. . . . For the continuation of the strike, after it has become evident that the wages paid prior to August 11 will not be restored, the responsibility rests upon the strikers.

One thing stands out clearly both in the partisan statements and in the more or less neutral press comment — there existed at Waltham, prior to the strike, a very high tension in labor relations, a confirmed antagonism, an openly belligerent attitude. If we can determine the fundamental causes of this state of mind to which both management and labor were prey, we may possibly arrive at some conclusions that will be of value in labor disputes generally.

CAUSES OF THE STRIKE

The wage cut, itself, can hardly be considered the cause of the strike. It merely furnished the immediate stimulus to action. Howard Mayhew, secretary of the Union, advanced this idea in an interview with the Boston *Sunday Advertiser,* and others supported his testimony. He spoke of the wage cut and then continued, "But I can say that if a little tact and consideration had been shown at the proper time there is every likelihood that the strike never would have taken place and . . . the workers would have accepted it quietly."[3] Throughout the published matter on the strike there is the recurrent theme of justice, equity, and courtesy — not justice before the law, but the justice and equity that exists between friends.

Another inconsistency also points toward an underlying cause of unrest — the complaint of "intolerable conditions." Actual working conditions at Waltham were excellent. The employees worked a 48-hour week, which was not unusual for that time. The work was clean. The light and air in the shops were good. On the other hand, overtime was paid for at only the regular rates. The work in some cases was fine, requiring close concentration. The working pace had been increased, and rest periods abolished. Some of these conditions are grounds for complaint, but they are hardly of a character to justify the use of the word *intolerable*. Yet I believe that labor leaders were sincere in the use of the term. To them the conditions seemed intolerable, not because the management was using sweatshop methods, for they did not do so, but because the trade of watchmaking had suffered a severe decline in earning power and in social prestige.

Here, then, are two possible causes for labor unrest at Waltham:

the decline of watchmaking as a trade, and the presence of unnecessary friction in the relations between management and labor.

DECLINE OF THE WATCHMAKER

In the days of Robbins the Waltham Company resembled a watchmakers' gild, and the gild spirit prevailed in the relations between the master and his craftsmen. They collaborated in all matters pertaining to the production of watches and agreed as to standards of workmanship and wages. The Gild, if we may use that term for the Company, was the center of social activity and recreation. It was a moving political force in the community. And for many years it was the fountainhead of technical knowledge for the watch industry of the world.

The wage situation was satisfactory to management. In 1868 beginners were paid as little as 50 cents per day, and some of the less skilled workers received $1.25 per day. Skilled craftsmen, on the other hand, received $3.00 to $5.00 per day; foremen, $6.00 per day and better. Wages, however, were not a critical factor in the production of watches at that date. The use of machinery had so greatly increased the efficiency of the plant over that of competitive manufacturers that Robbins could afford to pay the going rate of wages for the best workers in any category. He chose native New England types, men and women of intelligence and energy.

The average worker, also, was well pleased with the wage scale at the watch factory. He made a good living, as far as the essentials of life were concerned. His food was cheap and of good quality, for Waltham was still a rural town of less than 10,000 inhabitants. Room and board for a man cost $4.50 per week and for women only $3.00 per week.[4] The worker's clothing requirements were simple and his taste not expensive. He could live in an excellent environment adjacent to the factory and might own his house if he chose. The Company had a hand in all this and was careful to see that good living accommodations were available at reasonable prices. The day-to-day problems of Waltham workers were not of a pressing nature.

Present blessings were made doubly enjoyable by the confident expectation of a secure and prosperous future. The opportunity for promotion to the aristocracy of skilled craftsmen was well assured. The rapid expansion of the business was continually creating new vacancies, and the prospect of better wages and higher social standing always seemed very near and real. Such promotions were occurring frequently. It had always been so in the past, and until the end of the World War there was no apparent cause for watch-factory workers to doubt the certainty of a thoroughly satisfactory future.

As the watch industry grew to maturity, the position of labor was weakened. Increasing competition among domestic and foreign watch producers and the declining secular trend brought heavy pressure to bear upon wages. The slower rate of industrial growth curtailed the opportunities for promotion, and there was an increasing tendency to follow the seniority rule. While the fortunes of the watchmaker were declining, the opportunities for wage earners in general were improving, and the wage differential which had given the watchmaker economic superiority and social distinction began to disappear.

As competition grew, other influences changed the setting of the watch-factory community. The industrial development of New England, the pressure of immigration, and the effects of World War I did much to alter the satisfactions of life at Waltham. The remote and delightful village became a crowded industrial town of 30,000 inhabitants, on the outskirts of Metropolitan Boston. Rural life and standards gave way before the haste and tension of the postwar urban pace. The food, imported from surrounding counties and sold in the stores, was neither so good nor so cheap as the farm produce of the earlier period. The physical surroundings of the plant also changed. A large section of Robbins Park was made into a parking lot for employees' automobiles, and a gas station made its appearance on the opposite corner. The natural beauty of the site was largely lost, and the spirited social life of the factory community ebbed away. Aaron Dennison, had he lived to see the change, would hardly have recognized the location as the one he had chosen and developed.

Ezra Fitch must have felt the change, for he did his best to maintain the old tradition of expansion in business and to preserve on a postwar scale the social cohesion of his workers. We have already seen the terrific price he paid for expansion, and a parallel condition developed in the field of labor relations.

On the bank of the river near the plant was the Riverside Club, maintained by the Waltham Company for its employees. Fitch tried to build up the Club activities as a substitute for the simpler social affairs that had previously been such a conspicuous part of watch-factory life.

When the girls' dormitory (the Adams House) was being maintained by the Company, a serious student and commentator said:[5]

> Bevies of girls were seen everywhere. They sang, they romped, they thrummed the piano, they played games, and a few took sidelong glances at the visitor who gazed with interest upon them. Some of them went out a-visiting or a-shopping. Some went to "sociables," public or private, some attended the grand and dress reception to invited guests in our big parlor; two or three more may have attended prayer-meeting; a half dozen struck into a walking match on the highway; some gathered in gossiping groups, while others, I was told, stayed in their rooms to stitch, or to read or write. Soon after nine o'clock they begin to retire, and by ten all is quiet in the house.

In this earlier period there had been a variety of small clubs devoted to special interests — cycling, canoeing, literature, and others — but the Riverside Club, after the World War, catered to the growing desire for organization, bigness, and lavish expenditures. Company outings drew crowds of as many as 4,000 people. The club grounds, which were extensive, had cost the Company approximately $30,000. The club building was equipped with a gymnasium and a large swimming-pool. In the matter of food, Fitch lived up to the tradition of a "varied and abundant, or rather superabundant"[6] table. The lavish style may be inferred from the expenditure of $82,649.59 on the cafeteria in eight months of 1921. Of this total only $29,647.24 was paid by the employees; all the remaining expense was borne by the Company.[7]

Fitch provided other modern luxuries that tended to compensate the employees for the disadvantages that attend industrial growth. There was a physician in attendance at the plant; also an optician and two nurses. Seventy-five hundred dollars was spent for a day nursery. There was a woman in charge of welfare work; an editor to supervise the publication of the employees' house organ, *Minutes;* and a banker to manage the Credit Union which received the employees' savings and made small loans. There were athletic teams and a Watch Factory Band. In 1917, in line with the trend of the period, leisure was provided by reducing the hours of work to fifty per week. And, in addition to all the official largess, there was a system of concession and privilege, extending to petty pilfering, that made a further contribution to real wages.

Through these devices Fitch maintained the Waltham employees in an industrial paradise which they were no longer earning. They might work as hard as ever and do as good work, but they no longer made an exclusive and unique contribution to the watch industry. Other producers made watches which were approximately as good and made them on machinery which was highly efficient. The Waltham staff of that period (1917) had failed to maintain, through technical and mechanical improvements, the outstanding leadership in the watch industry that Dennison had established.

Equally unfortunate for Waltham employees was the decreasing demand for master watchmakers, men of broad experience and superlative skill. The improvements in automatic machinery and the specialization of labor had shifted the demand from skilled to unskilled labor. Great skill was still required in individual operations, but a single skill often could be acquired rather quickly. Unskilled workers could be trained at the bench in the precise methods that the management considered most suitable. After a period of instruction of three to nine months, they could be placed at piecework where constant repetition rapidly developed a high degree of dexterity. Real craft skill was still employed at Waltham for certain tasks, but there was a smaller demand for such skill in the routine work of watch production. The premium paid for craft skill in 1917 was a diminishing proportion of the total Waltham payroll.

Fundamental changes in industry come slowly and gradually exert increasing pressure on the established social order. If adjustment to new conditions is delayed by a reactionary attitude or by lack of foresight, the eventual realignment may be very painful. It was long delayed at Waltham, and it was both painful and violent.

The first major effort at readjustment that affected the employees was undertaken by a firm of industrial engineers retained by Harry L. Brown. This was in 1921, and by then the Company's affairs were in a desperate position. Brown had been recently appointed general manager to succeed Conover Fitch.

Brown had been treasurer, and he owed his promotion to the hope that a financial man would succeed as the chief operating executive. Aware of his deficiencies as a factory manager, Brown looked to outside assistance for the details of a plan to reorganize the production departments. The engineers arrived in May, 1921, and remained approximately a year. With their arrival began the story of diplomacy, or the lack of it, in Waltham labor relations. From that time until the strike in 1924, trouble was constantly in the offing.

DIPLOMACY IN WALTHAM LABOR RELATIONS

The proper use of diplomacy in labor relations is a matter of opinion; there is no comprehensive science covering the subject. Techniques vary from gentle persuasion to unconcerned indifference, and on down the scale to coercion and intimidation. Each technique doubtless has its merits, and the circumstances attending any specific case will determine the choice of methods. It is hardly practical to lay down any general rules on this score or to attempt a detailed criticism of a particular incident — the theory and practice of personnel management is not yet sufficiently developed to permit such assurance. There are, however, certain well-defined reactions on the part of labor that appear repeatedly in the records of labor disputes, and these phenomena have come to be accepted as a relatively dependable basis for a few simple principles. Our discussion of this subject will attempt to avoid controversial ground and merely call attention to policies or practices that appear to have an undesirable effect on labor relations.

The consulting industrial engineer (he generally does not like to be called an "efficiency man") has a provocative effect on labor and, no matter what his methods may be, his mere presence is likely to cause unrest. Workers associate the industrial engineer with four practices that are highly objectionable to labor: the speed-up, the stretch-out, wage cuts, and interference with habitual methods of work. At Waltham the outside engineers made major use of these practices.

There was a great effort made to speed up production. This was managed in several ways. Some piece rates were reduced, thus necessitating faster work if the former weekly pay check was to be maintained — this is the most hated form of the speed-up. In addition, various day-rate jobs were put on a piece-rate basis, the intention here being to force an increase in production for the same weekly wage. The third form of speed-up attempted by the industrial engineers was the line method of production combined with the system of group wages. This is the method made famous by the automobile industry where all the employees work at a fixed rate, the faster workers urging the slower ones to keep up the pace. Wages are paid to the group on a piece-rate basis for the output of the department. The group wage is then divided among the workers in fixed percentages according to their skill. The magnitude of the rate-setting part of the task is apparent when we consider that there were over 32,000 piece rates at Waltham and that ten departments were put on the group-wage system.

The speed-up program of the industrial engineers was far too large and complex for completion in a year's time; as a result, the wage system of the plant was badly disrupted. The group-wage system was later abandoned in eight of the departments, but there remained throughout the plant a seriously unbalanced wage structure which was inherited by Dumaine in 1923. Some wages were too high. In other cases, there was insufficient recognition of such factors as quality, skill, and years of service. On the average, however, labor costs were higher than the Company believed it could bear.

The second feature of a typical efficiency campaign — the stretch-out — was not important at Waltham. The stretch-out usually requires machine operators to tend an increasing number of machines, but watchmaking machinery does not lend itself well to this practice. Much of it is purely automatic, while other types require the complete attention of the operator.

The 10 per cent wage cut that went into effect on August 1, 1921, was not primarily the work of the industrial engineers, but they undoubtedly received the credit for it in the eyes of labor. The direct cause of the cut was the depression of 1921, combined with a general reaction from the rapid rise of wages during the War and the postwar boom. The reduction of wages was in line with a 15 per cent decline in the cost of living from 1920 to 1921. Such economic facts are not apparent to workers, but the presence of the industrial engineer is conspicuous, and he tends to become the butt of every animosity and prejudice that the workers may be harboring. As a result, the unpleasant but necessary corrections imposed by the industrial engineer may take on undue significance merely because this so-called interloper from the realm of theory bulks so large on the worker's horizon.

Interference with working habits is a necessary part of the industrial engineer's work, but it is particularly annoying to the worker. Any real increase in efficiency involves a change in established techniques and these changes are normally received by labor with good grace, provided that they arise from obvious necessity and do not follow each other in too rapid succession. The objections to such changes, when they originate with outsiders, are three. First, the changes originate outside the business and therefore may not be strictly applicable under the circumstances peculiar to that business. Second, the need for the change is not apparent to the worker and he tends to regard it as an invasion of his rights, an encroachment upon his liberty, and an opening wedge leading to unbearable petty tyranny. Third, changes often follow each other so quickly that they outstrip the worker's capacity for adjustment. These objections relate, not to the changes themselves, but to the manner in which they are presented. The issue is not one of fact; it is one of diplomacy in presentation.

Under the circumstances that existed at Waltham in 1921, the use of adequate diplomacy was extremely difficult. There was not sufficient time available for a careful explanation of every move and for the allowance of an adequate period of adjustment between moves. There was too much to be done. The need for corrective action had been accumulating for over twenty years, and the emergency was immediate and pressing. A year was not time enough in which to effect so many changes. At the end of that period much had been attempted, but it appears that little had been thoroughly completed. In consequence, there were many maladjustments, misunderstandings, and tensions. The temper of the workers had become so unsettled that such diplomacy as was possible had lost much of its quieting effect.

With the arrival of Simonds as manager, and the departure of the industrial engineers, there were more changes; but there was little improvement in the relations between labor and management. Simonds was accustomed to heavy industry and had little sympathy with the jewelers' customs and traditions that still survived at Waltham. His action, previously mentioned, in depriving the workers in one department of their jewelers' magnifying glasses is a case in point. The magnifier may, or may not, be necessary to the best performance of the job; but it is most necessary to the self-esteem of the worker. It sets him apart from the mechanical and unskilled workmen. To deprive a worker of his watchmaker's glass is likely to be a blow to his pride that he will be slow to forgive. Simonds incurred further ill will by eliminating rest periods that were customary on fine work.

Diplomacy under Dumaine took a very different turn. Dumaine had been operating a cotton mill. He was accustomed to the management of a large working force of about 14,000 employees. These cotton-mill hands had been organized into unions to combat the reduction in their standards of living resulting from competition. Many of the workers were of recent foreign derivation. Few of them understood that the cause of their troubles lay in competition from cheap labor in the southern States and in foreign countries, and they fixed the responsibility for their plight upon the management of the Company. Class distinctions were sharp and class animosity pronounced. Under these conditions Dumaine had developed a form of diplomacy in his relations with labor which was radically different from any that the Waltham workers had previously known.

The characteristics of Dumaine's labor relations policy were the logical result of his cotton-mill experience. The general tone had a military quality — strict discipline was the first consideration. The military form was also followed in other respects. Contacts with the rank and file of the workers were almost exclusively through subordinates. The easy accessibility of the commander-in-chief was maintained as a principle, but it was not much followed as a practice. Any show of insubordination was met with instant and severe repressive measures. Great care was exercised to avoid any action on the part of management that would be construed as weakness.

The value of the military type of organization and the merits of military discipline are too well known to need comment here, but the abuses of the military manner are worth some mention. The most serious departures from the norm of good diplomacy frequently occur where they do the most damage — that is, among the lowest ranks of subordinates who are in direct contact with labor. Crisp, military precision on the part of senior officers quite frequently shows up in a foreman as a "hard-boiled" attitude that can be extremely irritating. The following incident, told by Howard Mayhew, secretary of the Waltham Union, and supported by subsequent testimony before the State Board of Conciliation, illustrates the point.

Dumaine had given a week's notice of the wage cut which took effect on August 11, 1924. The cut was announced by the foremen in person. One of them told the workers in his department, "There is going to be a wage cut. The management don't expect you to talk it over in groups. If you don't like it, you can get out and hunt a new job." [8] We are left with the impression that this was an unusual and extreme case of military bad manners, but that it did reflect a general attitude adopted by management to offset the rising tide of insubordination.

There is a temptation, perhaps, to put too much emphasis on this modern notion of courtesy in labor relations. After all, it is the opportunity to work, the wages paid, and the working conditions that are of vital importance to labor. But even if we charge off diplomatic friction to imaginary troubles, there were plenty of real ones left.

Beginning in 1921, the effect of serious economic difficulties was felt by Waltham employees. Work became scarce and pay checks grew smaller. What appeared at first to be the pinch of depression turned out to be a permanent shrinkage in employment. Welfare activities were cut more and more as the available funds became smaller and the spirit of coöperation weakened. The doctor and optician were released; pensions were cut or discontinued; and the program of social festivities was greatly curtailed. The lack of security in employment was increased by the frequent changes of management, Conover Fitch, Brown, Simonds, and Boucher serving in succession as general manager over a period of three years. The result was confusion and dissension; nobody's job was safe under the frequent shifting of plans and changing authority. The effect of such difficulties on employee morale was very apparent to Loring. In a letter of May 10, 1922, he wrote to William B. Mayo of the Ford Company outlining conditions at the plant. After describing the financial errors of the old régime, he went on to say:

> In the meanwhile, through unwise management there is a great disloyalty through the factory. A lot was done in the way of welfare work and prosperously started. Then the activities were suddenly shut down, at the same time that wages were reduced and employment made more strenuous. The result being great dissatisfaction among our people.

DUMAINE'S WAGE POLICY

When Dumaine arrived at Waltham, there was a good deal of dissatisfaction about wages. There were two complaints: the workers thought that wages were too low because they had not been raised from the depression level of 1921; they were also much disturbed by the piece rates which had been established by the industrial engineers — some workmen with relatively little skill earned higher weekly wages than others with longer experience. The traditional hierarchy of skill had been upset and there was much heartburning and jealousy.

The management was equally disturbed about the wage situation. Many workers were drawing more wages than they were worth to the firm, for they could easily be replaced by unskilled labor, after a brief period of training. Since both parties were dissatisfied, a prompt revision of piece rates seemed advisable; in April, 1923, the task of adjustment was begun.

Caution was necessary. The wholesale reduction of staff in the office suggested the possibility of a similar curtailment of factory personnel, and the workers in the plant were awaiting their turn with little patience. They had always been famous for their spirit. When John Swinton, the labor reformer, made his investigation at the plant, a townsman told him, "You won't find a more independent set anywhere in creation."[9] At this point all of them were uneasy and expectant; many of them were defiant, believing that their services were indispensable. The management had always boasted of the superlative skill of the workers, and some of the workers believed that they held the power of life and death over the business. That had been true at one time; and to a limited degree it was still true in the spring of 1923, for business was brisk and there was a shortage of skilled labor. Furthermore, the new management had been in office only two months and there was the greatest need for coöperation in the first months of readjustment. Dumaine knew that he could not afford a strike at that time.

The plan was carefully laid. Wage adjustment would be made in one department at a time. Only rates which were badly out of line were to be reduced. Any semblance of a general wage cut was to be avoided. A key department was chosen for the start — one of the assembly departments. The assemblers received the highest wages and had the most prestige; if the revision was accepted by them, the remaining departments would fall into line more readily. Unfortunately, when the cut was made, the department immediately struck.

Other departments joined in sympathy, and a dangerous outbreak was imminent.

The plans were immediately changed. Committees were appointed; conferences were held; differences were adjusted and the whole affair ironed out in a very few days. Boucher was in Europe at the time, and the affair was handled in very creditable fashion by Freistadter, the factory superintendent, under the direction of Dumaine himself. Operations were resumed on a regular schedule, but it cost the Company an increase in wages of approximately 10 per cent.

The disturbance of 1923 is regarded by the management as a minor episode — a mere family tiff — but there is evidence that suggests a more serious view of the affair. Ezra Fitch reported to Boucher on May 31, "We are having no more trouble with the people and do not expect to have. I attended several of the meetings with the Committee of operatives and was impressed with the good feeling displayed on both sides." This letter seems a trifle optimistic when viewed in the light of the events leading up to the strike in August, 1924. At that time Boucher refused to talk to his workers at their request, but his refusal is not hard to understand when we read the statement of the president of the union: "He [Boucher] told us that his office was open and invited us to call on him when we so desired but we felt that it would be proper for him to come to us once to show a proper attitude toward us."[10] And another union official is quoted as saying, "We've got him [Boucher] in the hollow of our hand, if he has anything to say, let him come to us."[11] It seems reasonable to attribute the blithe confidence and the contentious manner of the employees to their easy victory in 1923. Dumaine and Boucher, on the other hand, may have been driven to greater severity, in both action and manner, by this expensive preliminary skirmish. It seems quite probable that the 1923 dispute served seriously to aggravate the later outbreak and to delay the final settlement of the 1924 strike.

THE 1924 WAGE CUT

In the summer of 1924 the condition of general business favored a wage cut. Business activity had been dropping rapidly for a period of several months. A headline in the *New York Times Annalist* of July 7 reads, "Factory Unemployment at a Critical Stage. . . . Loss of $200,000,000 Monthly Buying Power by a Quarter of the Population an Energetic Business Depressant." The article continues, "Between the peak of May and June, 1923, and March, 1924, [workers'] income fell, though by no means as decisively as employment. The chief reason for this is that wage rates ruling in industry were on the whole strongly sustained by the influence of labor organizations coupled with competitive demand from non-factory industries such as construction." By midsummer, however, the wage structure could no longer be maintained by the unions, and wage reductions became common throughout the country.

The financial community looked on the reduction of wages as a sound business move. In September, when the movement had about completed its course, the *Chronicle* said, "What seems to be taking place is the beginning of a wide industrial readjustment, through wage cuts and much sharpened competition."[12] And after a month's further thought, the editor added that these fundamental readjustments were "sanatative, economically wholesome, and to our definite advantage."[13] The basis for this reasoning is illustrated by the figures for real wages calculated from data compiled by the National Industrial Conference Board.

	Cost of Living	*Average Weekly Earnings*	*Real Wages*
1914[a]	100	100	100
1920[a]	198	235	118
1924 (Jan.)	165	215	130
1924 (Aug.)	164	201	122

[a] Monthly average.

SOURCE: *Survey of Current Business*, Nov., 1924.

If one is willing to grant that real wages at 130 per cent of the 1914 level were excessive, then the wage cuts tended to correct the maladjustment.

In New England the fall of wages was particularly severe. The shoe workers at Lynn and Brockton were cut 20 per cent. Cuts in the textile industry, beginning in the South, spread to New England where they usually amounted to 10 per cent. The wages of common labor dropped from 60 cents an hour in March to 42 cents in August; again, the figures are for New England.

It was Dumaine's theory that wages at the plant should be the same as those paid by his domestic competitors. If Waltham wages were appreciably higher, he believed that the business would fail. Since conditions were favorable, he attempted to put this theory into practice by reducing wages in every case where the management considered them to be too high. The reductions ranged from nothing to 40 per cent, with an average drop of 9.04 per cent. The theory was simple and the application was logical, but a number of difficulties developed in the practical enforcement.

It was difficult to prove to the employees that wages were too high. The mathematical averages or a minute examination of piece rates might prove the point; on the other hand, there was the fact that the minimum wage for women at one competitor's plant was $3.00 per day,[14] while at Waltham it was about $2.00 per day. Under these circumstances it was hard to plead convincingly for a competitive standard. It appeared that the principle of adjusting wages to competition was applied only in reducing wages and not in raising them.

Another serious difficulty resulted from the fact that skilled labor bore the brunt of the cut. Many tasks which formerly had required considerable skill could be performed, under improved conditions, by workers with much less skill. In some cases the high wage rates were simply an error in rate-setting; regardless of the cause, however, the heavy end of the cut fell very largely on the highly skilled workers. Those who received the maximum reduction of 40 per cent would be forced to make a radical change in their standard of living, and they would suffer a consequent decline in social position. The extreme hardship fell on comparatively few, but there was a tendency to throw the burden on those best able to resist the action, and to irritate the class which was best qualified to undertake the leadership of a strike. The complaint of discrimination was heard very frequently in many forms. It appeared in the Waltham *News Tribune* the day after the strike had begun. A striker was quoted as saying, "If the cut was justified, there should have been a split on a more reasonable basis."

Looking back over the history of labor relations at Waltham, we raise the question: Could the strike have been avoided? The answer of the management is "No," and I am inclined to agree. The independent character of the employees, combined with their long enjoyment of a monopoly of watchmaking skill, had developed strong habits of life and thought. When the time came that the monopoly no longer existed and the watchmakers of Waltham were forced to accept the normal wages of skilled factory workers, the readjustment was too great for quiet acceptance. A certain amount of violence seems inevitable where the adjustment to new conditions must be so great.

COURSE OF THE STRIKE

The affair at Waltham was more than a strike—it was a spontaneous revolt. There was a martial spirit about the whole proceeding. An ultimatum was delivered; the workers demanded that Boucher appear before them and account for his actions in cutting wages. Boucher declined but offered to meet a committee. There was a disagreement as to the size of the committee, and then without warning the assemblers were marching out. All this happened early in the morning of August 11, 1924.

The workers of each department left their benches in a body, like volunteers enlisting in a glorious cause. As they appeared at the factory doors, the waiting throng cheered madly and soon there were bugle calls and marching and singing. Women were marching, as many as the men, laughing and singing, "We Ain't Gonna Work No More, No More." Who could resist it? Such confidence of success, such assurance of victory. Who would want to be known as a deserter when these stalwarts returned at the request of a chastened management? Two hundred, fifteen hundred, twenty-seven hundred, and finally all but a handful had joined the marching, milling crowds or, hoping that they might soon return without loss of caste among their fellows, had slipped quietly away.

Such was the beginning of the strike as described in the bold headlines and the long columns of copy in current newspapers. Some of the fine frenzy may be credited to romantic journalism, for I could discover nothing of that enthusiasm and bravado among the veterans from whom I sought some further light on the subject. There was a universal disinclination to talk about the strike, as though both the enthusiasm and the bitterness had been forgotten—and only the cost remained to burden the memory.

When the strike started, there was no labor union at Waltham, but one was soon organized and demands were presented to Boucher. They were substantially as follows:

1. Recognition of the union and the right of collective bargaining.
2. Reëmployment of union agitators who had been discharged.
3. Reëmployment of every operator who was on the payrolls on August 11, 1924.
4. Arbitration of all future cases of discharge of employees.
5. Restoration of the "idle time" allowance for machine operators.
6. Payment of time and a quarter for overtime, and time and a half for Saturday afternoons.
7. Arbitration of all wage reduction.
8. Settlement of the strike on the basis of the wage scale in effect before August 11.

The Company replied with a formal statement of its position. The major points were as follows:

> The management desires to make permanent the manufacture of watches in Waltham if it can be done creditably and profitably.
>
> Owing to the interruption in operation it may be impossible to re-establish full operation at once.
>
> Employment to competent applicants will be supplied without prejudice as fast as balanced output can be established.
>
> Upon investigation should it be developed Waltham rates differ from those prevailing in competitive establishments they will without delay be equalized.

Conferences were arranged under the auspices of Charles G. Wood, United States Commissioner of Conciliation, although he did not attend the meetings himself. The employees proposed a modification of the wage cut of August 11 by restricting it to men receiving more than $40 per week and women receiving more than $20 per week. This was equivalent to a cut of 4.03 per cent on the factory payroll. The saving was not sufficient to accomplish Dumaine's purpose, but he was willing to meet the employees halfway and a counter-offer was made to the men. Dumaine reported the results of these conferences to Wood in a letter dated October 6, which reads in part:

> The factory has not operated profitably for years. The present management upon assuming control proceeded at once to try and make it profitable. Every apparent unnecessary expenditure was discontinued and every economy, short of lowering wages, was instituted. The result has shown that even with these economies the Company was not able to compete profitably.

Wages were the last thing the Company desired to change, but lower rates prevailing elsewhere in the industry made this adjustment compulsory.

Although the Company could ill afford it, yet to show a desire to make some concession for the sake of bringing about peace promptly and future harmony, a 25% reduction in the original cut was offered.

This offer was promptly rejected by the employees. It is no longer open. The company returns to its original position which it now adheres to.

Charles G. Wood in his letter to the president of the union upheld Dumaine's position. He wrote that the rejection of the compromise proposal by the strikers and the "riotous action of certain strikers augmented by the disorder of irresponsible persons were reasons that justified the employer in . . . cancelling the offer of wage concession."[15] The employees and their sympathizers, however, were bitter in their denunciation of Dumaine's stand. He was branded a reactionary of the darkest hue, and many a worse epithet was thrown his way.

From the stalemate of early October until the strike was settled in January, 1925, it was a matter of endurance. Workers came straggling back, as sober thought or dire necessity impelled them, and new help was hired until some 600 people were at work. This was not an adequate staff even for emergency operation, but it was sufficient to keep about 250 watches per day passing through the finishing stages of production.

The strike was settled on the Company's terms, on January 7, 1925. As an indication of sincerity on the question of competitive wages, the Company agreed to send a committee to the Elgin factory to investigate wages there. This Committee was to consist of one representative for the strikers, one for the Company, and one for the State.

RESULTS OF THE STRIKE

The losses which attended the strike at the watch factory were serious. Fifteen weeks' wages, or approximately $600,000, were lost to the employees and to the business of the community. Production was crippled for about five months. Many experienced employees left the community, and the Company was forced to bear the expense of training new help. This is the familiar tally against almost every strike, but there were advantages also.

The good effects which were claimed for the strike were of real importance. The wage scale was reduced to a sound, competitive level at which a well-managed business could show adequate profits. The wage structure was adjusted so that wages more nearly reflected the skill, intelligence, and effort required for each job. The independent spirit of the employees was brought within the bounds of reason. The practice of restricting output which had been much used by workers before the strike was largely curbed. The Company, on its part, recognized the principles of collective bargaining and arbitration in its relations with labor. In general, the groundwork was laid for the development of a new era of stablity and gradual improvement in industrial relations at Waltham.

Some years later, Dumaine answered a question about employee morale by writing:[16]

> As to the help at Waltham, you must be aware the strike was brought on by irresponsible operatives and not by the old tried competent workmen. When the factory returned to work, all of the older and best workmen returned and are now working steadily and contentedly.
>
> Of course it is human nature to want to earn higher wages, but watches, like other manufacturing products, have to be sold in the market against competitors and no concern can continue long to exist if its product costs more than they bring in the open market.

CHAPTER XII

DUMAINE'S BUSINESS POLICIES

Major Policies in Finance

After the strike had been settled, prosperity returned to the Waltham Company. Substantial improvements were made in all departments, the most notable changes occurring in finance.

The first step in the program of financial reform was the liquidation of inventory. At the time of the reorganization the inventory was valued on the books of the new company at $4,000,000. Eleven months later it was reduced to $2,568,912, partly through liquidation and by reduction of the remainder to market value.[1] For the next five years the reduction of inventory continued at a more moderate rate, reaching $1,029,953 at the close of 1928. At this figure the inventory was only large enough to fill incoming orders for 53 days.

The second measure on Dumaine's financial program was the deflation of the capital structure. The Kidder, Peabody reorganization had reduced the capitalization from $18,000,000 to $13,000,000, but it was still far in excess of the true value of the Company's assets. Dumaine was not pleased with this state of affairs, but the details of the reorganization had been completed while he was in Europe, and it was too late to change them when he returned to Boston.[2] Under these circumstances the simplest remedy was to reduce the funded debt and the outstanding shares of stock by purchase and retirement of the Company's securities. By this means a sound capitalization could be achieved.

Reduction of the funded debt was accomplished by the use of about $3,000,000 in cash obtained by liquidating excess inventory, and further purchases of senior securities were made from earnings. In the first year (1923) Dumaine used $1,000,000 for the purchase of debentures, and more were purchased as funds became available and prices attractive. In this fashion the funded debt was reduced from $6,000,000 in 1923 to $1,145,000 in 1938. The cash balance carried during this period was ample. The figures, including short-term investments, ranged from $400,000 to well over $2,000,000. The debt-retirement policy was not allowed to jeopardize the cash position of the Company.

Deflation of the capital structure by the purchase of stock began in 1926, with the purchase of 971 shares of Prior Preference stock, 1,857 shares of Preferred, and 5,726 shares of "B" Common. The policy was continued in 1927 and 1928. In the latter year the investment bankers sold, at market prices, 10,000 shares of Preferred stock and 7,000 shares of "B" Common to the Company. Other purchases of Waltham securities were also made for the treasury in that year. Total stock purchases from 1923 to 1928, inclusive, were:

7% Prior Preference stock	5,299 shares
6% Preferred stock	18,071 shares
Class B Common stock	26,797 shares
Class A Common stock	40 shares

These securities cost the Company $2,526,002.

Purchases of the Company's own stock for the treasury after 1928 were small, amounting to approximately $150,000. In 1936, however, the Company offered to exchange 1¼ shares of 6 per cent Preferred stock and $3.00 in cash for every share of 7 per cent Prior Preference which was surrendered by stockholders.[3] Five thousand sixty-four shares of Prior Preference stock were exchanged on this basis. The net result of purchase and exchange is shown in Table 18.

TABLE 18

OUTSTANDING SECURITIES, 1923 AND 1943

WALTHAM WATCH COMPANY

	Feb. 9, 1923	July 2, 1943
6% Bonds	$ 3,000,000	$ 0
6% Debentures	$ 3,000,000	$ 0
7% Prior Preference stock	17,000 shares	2,777 shares
6% Preferred stock	50,000 shares	33,843 shares
Class B Common stock	70,000 shares	41,869 shares
Class A Common stock	25,000 shares	25,000 shares

SOURCE: Stewart, Watts & Bollong, *Waltham Watch Company, Reconciliation of Changes in Net Working Capital, Profit and Loss Statement, and Analysis of Surplus, February 9, 1923, to July 2, 1943.* (Boston, 1943.)

As the outstanding liabilities were reduced, the assets were correspondingly deflated. The major changes are given in Table 19.

TABLE 19

BOOK VALUE OF SELECTED ASSETS, 1923 AND 1943
WALTHAM WATCH COMPANY

	Feb. 9, 1923	July 2, 1943	Decrease
Inventory	$ 4,000,000	$ 923,632	$ 3,076,368
Fixed assets, net	4,338,860	1,175,215	3,163,645
Trade-marks & patents, etc.	2,790,090	1,350,000	1,440,090
Total of all assets	20,400,000	8,607,113	11,792,887

SOURCE: Stewart, Watts & Bollong, *Reconciliation of Changes.* (Boston, 1943.)

The figure for total decrease includes the reduction of assets by writing down their value and by liquidation.

The reduction of debt and the retirement of the Prior Preference stocks, in the twenty-year period, 1923–43, reduced the fixed charges by $452,559, as shown in Table 20.

TABLE 20

YEARLY FIXED CHARGES, 1923 AND 1943
WALTHAM WATCH COMPANY

	Feb., 1923	July, 1943	Decrease
Interest on Funded Debt	$360,000	$ 0	$360,000
Cumulative Dividends	119,000	26,441	92,559
Total	$479,000	$26,441	$452,559

SOURCE: Stewart, Watts & Bollong, *Reconciliation of Changes.* (Boston, 1943.)

The policy of retiring the Company's securities greatly strengthened the stock that remained outstanding. The increase in equity, combined with the splendid earnings record and the bull market of 1928, carried the price of Waltham stocks to a very high level, as illustrated in Table 21.

TABLE 21

PRICE RANGE, 1924 AND 1928
WALTHAM WATCH COMPANY STOCKS

	1924	1928
7% Prior Preference	62–73	101–106½
6% Preferred	14–23½	82–99
Class B Common	6½–10½	60–90

The stocks were listed on the Boston Stock Exchange, and in 1928 trading was active. In the following year the Company was less prosperous — public interest in the stocks subsided, and prices declined. After the general crash in 1929, the decline in price continued and the turnover decreased to less than two thousand shares per year. In 1935 the stocks were withdrawn from the Exchange list.

Questions put to Robert Winsor, partner in Kidder, Peabody & Company, in the Abbot trial suggested that the new Waltham Company was deliberately overcapitalized in order to fatten the firm's commissions. Winsor replied:[4]

> I don't remember the details, but of course this Company had to have proper working capital when it started, and we ultimately brought out a plan which *we* thought was safe to pay its debts and leave it with proper working capital.

As it turned out, a much smaller capitalization would have been adequate, but this fortunate circumstance was the result of the liquidation of inventory and a prompt resumption of profitable operations. When the Kidder, Peabody plan was formulated late in 1922, there were no trustworthy data for estimating the value and marketability of the inventories. Furthermore, the working-capital requirements depended on the speed with which Dumaine could adapt his manufacturing experience to an entirely new field, one which he admitted was "unusually complicated and delicate."[5] Robert Winsor chose to disregard these indeterminate sources of funds in his formal estimate of capital requirements.

The dividend policy has been conservative; there has been no tendency to milk the Company through extravagant disbursements.

No dividends were paid during the period 1923–26. In the period 1926–42, the total of dividends paid on all classes of stock amounted to $3,305,481, distributed as shown in Table 22.

TABLE 22

DIVIDENDS, 1926–42
WALTHAM WATCH COMPANY

Year ending Dec. 31	Prior Preference 7%	Preferred 6%	A Common	B Common
1926	$ 113,629	$ none	$ none	$
1927	308,800	none	none	
1928	81,797	191,088	174,450	
1929	81,827	191,185	161,135	
1930	81,844	191,230	131,712	
1931	61,388	63,752	35,229	
1936	203,046	287,068	55,778	
1937	30,072	204,361	129,649	83,648
1938	560[a]	202,733	133,784	
1939	none	none	none	
1940	27,293	none	none	
1941	53,123	none	none	
1942	26,418	none	none	
Total	$1,068,677	$1,331,417	$821,739[b]	$83,648

[a] Refund of dividends on stock held in treasury.
[b] Totals were taken before rounding off.

SOURCE: Stewart, Watts & Bollong, *Reconciliation of Changes.* (Boston, 1943.)

The sales for the period 1923–42, inclusive, amounted to $104,660,269. Net earnings for the period were $6,573,236, or 6.28 per cent of sales.[6] Half of earnings was distributed as dividends.

Since the accounting methods used were ultraconservative, the above account of Dumaine's stewardship hardly does him justice. The true earnings from the business may be derived from the other expenditures for the 1923–42 period, given in Table 23.

Earnings of $16,325,436 over a period of twenty years gave a return of 11.4 per cent per year on the 1940 capitalized value of $7,041,116. This is an excellent return for an industry well past its maturity and for a company having a capitalization that still contained substantial intangible assets.

TABLE 23

SELECTED EXPENDITURES, 1923–42
WALTHAM WATCH COMPANY

For retirement of Company securities	$ 8,475,132
Dividends paid	3,305,481
Purchase of new machinery	1,288,330
Reorganization expense	92,613
Expenses of the Old Company	588,599
Interest and discount on bonds and notes	2,575,281
	$16,325,436

SOURCE: Stewart, Watts & Bollong, *Reconciliation of Changes*. (Boston, 1943.)

The financial administration under Dumaine's direction was in the interest of the stockholders. All those stockholders who sold their securities back to the Company in the prosperous years, 1926–28, were very handsomely paid for their equity. Those who retained their holdings have now a far greater equity than they had immediately after the reorganization. Stockholders who were astute enough to sell in 1928 and buy in 1932 reaped a double profit.

A further indication of the conservative and meticulous financial procedure that Dumaine introduced at Waltham was the fact that the new Company paid its bills promptly. No accounts payable were permitted to accumulate on the Company's books, as had been the case before 1923. In financial matters the new Company stood squarely on its own feet. Its credit was good, but rarely used; Dumaine preferred to be a lender rather than a borrower.[7]

One other serious financial problem should receive mention at this point. Local taxation at Waltham has been very burdensome. The tax rate is high, $36 per thousand in 1941, and it has been important to strike a proper balance between the interests of the community and the Company. The total local tax bill for the years 1923 to 1940, inclusive, amounted to $1,538,443. Federal and State taxes brought the total to $3,520,301.

The rise in local taxes had been rapid. In 1906 the city tax levy was $52,000, and in 1925 it was $152,000. In the Annual Report for 1925, Dumaine characterized the tax as an "appalling sum" and stated that "Suit has been brought by the Company to determine whether or not the City of Waltham is entitled to put such a burden upon it." The report continued, "Few industries can bear so heavy a handicap, and it is safe to say that no enterprise which must compete in world markets can long endure so constant and so costly a drain upon its resources." A long campaign against excessive taxation followed. Appeals were made to the local board of assessors and other city officials, to the Tax Appeals Board, and to the courts. The refunds and abatements granted as a result of this campaign are listed by Stewart, Watts & Bollong in their report of January 22, 1938, the total amounting to $461,929.08.

MAJOR PRODUCTION POLICIES

Dumaine's general attitude toward production and distribution problems is summed up in a letter to Boucher. In 1925 he wrote, "The whole difficulty seems to be with factory production and it is as true of watches as it is of speedometers. If we could obtain production and obtain it right, there wouldn't be any trouble about business."[8] He did not mention costs in this letter, for they already had been reduced to a satisfactory level by reorganization, reduction of personnel, and reduction of wages. The matters that concerned him most — that gave him the most trouble — were the volume and quality of production. Problems relating to the volume and quality of production are common to all industry, but these factors were particularly important at Waltham. This was the result of an insistent market demand for new and better products.

One of the most important methods of increasing production and reducing costs was the elimination of a large proportion of the grades of watches that had been manufactured under the Fitch régime. In 1921 the number of grades produced was 180, and the firm of consulting engineers retained by Brown recommended a reduction to 37 standard grades. Dumaine reports that 145 were still being produced at the time of the reorganization (1923), and he made further drastic reductions. In 1926 there were 39 grades, including two eight-day clocks.

The difficulties encountered in attempting to increase production did not arise from lack of plant capacity; they pertained chiefly to labor. The factory was large enough, having over eleven acres of floor space, and the possible output of the machinery was estimated at 750,000 movements a year, or about 50 per cent more than the output in 1923. The problems involved related to the procurement and training of labor and to the willingness of employees to produce.

The volume of production was limited by three factors: the time required to design new movements and produce the tools for their manufacture; the willful restriction of output by the workers; and the lack of cheap, unskilled labor of good character.

Dumaine's objective was to change 70 per cent of the production of the plant from pocket watches to wrist watches in the least possible time; this was a slow task at best. Depending on circumstances, it required from eight months to three years to design a new model and get it into production.[9] The task of designing a number of new models with the normal staff was tremendous; congestion and delay were inevitable. The designing groups felt the loss of Freistadter, who had been made factory superintendent in 1923, and competent designers were hard to find. Good watch designers were available in Switzerland, but the difficulties in recruiting them from a distant country and the obstacles to the immigration of skilled labor into the United States greatly delayed this phase of the work.

Another curb on production was the restriction of output by the workers. Restriction of output is sometimes a reasonable protective measure adopted by workers to prevent the faster employees from setting a pace that the slower ones cannot keep, but the records for the period of the strike revealed the fact that there had been an abuse of the practice at Waltham. While the strike was still under way, Dumaine wrote to Freistadter, "If we have learned anything from this strike it is we have not been putting out anything like a [maximum] possible product."[10] The point was illustrated by one worker, who stepped up his rate of production just enough to compensate for the 15 per cent reduction in the piece rate.[11] After the settlement of the strike and the acceptance of the lower rates, the increased rate of production indicated that the practice of restricting output had been reduced. The management states the belief that it has been negligible since the strike.

Production was limited also by the availability of satisfactory labor. In the Annual Report of March 26, 1925, addressed to the stockholders, Dumaine states, "It is a pleasure to tell you that the work is proceeding once again normally, although not as yet at capacity. Some 1,650 people are at work today, and as more work is being started daily more will be employed. This will be continued as fast as possible and as justified by the market demand." But apparently there was not sufficient labor available in all categories. In July of the same year, advertisements appeared in the small-town papers in Maine, seeking women to learn watch assembling. Learners were offered 25 cents per hour for a training period estimated at three to five months. It has been the policy of the Company, when labor has not been available locally, to obtain recruits from the rural districts in the territory northeast of Boston, going as far afield as Canada if necessary. The descendants of old watchmaking families in Waltham are given preference; since in many instances, however, members of the present generation have entered the professions or taken up other lines of business, the recruiting of labor outside the community has been necessary.

The volume of production has been a matter of concern, but the maintenance of high quality has been a more elusive problem. Dumaine published his creed in the first Annual Report, dated December 31, 1923. It reads, "The quality of the work may have suffered during the time when the old company was in difficulties, but the aim and single purpose of the new management from the beginning, has been to maintain the Waltham standard, and it is believed the quality and excellence of the output today are as good, if not better, than ever before."

The "Waltham standard" was a notable one. In 1863, Robbins referred to the Waltham product as the "best watches of the world,"[12] and the statement was more than an idle boast. The Company had been a consistent winner at the exhibitions since 1857, when the American Institute of New York awarded a medal for the first level escapement model produced at Waltham. Further success at various exhibitions in the United States were followed by the highest awards at the Philadelphia World's Fair in 1876 and at the Exposition Universelle de Paris in 1878. This period, about 1863 to 1878, was the heyday of Waltham supremacy. In 1876 Favre-Ferret, Swiss member of the International Jury on watches at the Centennial Exhibition at Philadelphia, discussed the merits of Waltham watches in a speech to a group of his countrymen at Chaux-de-Fonds, Switzerland. The following quotation from the speech was used by Waltham in its advertising over twenty years later:[13]

Gentlemen, here is what I have seen. I asked from the manager of the Waltham Company a watch of a certain quality. He opened before me a big chest. I picked out a watch at random and fixed it to my chain. The manager asked me to leave the watch with them for three or four days, that they might regulate it. On the contrary, I said to him, I want to keep it just as it is to get an exact idea of your workmanship. On arriving at Locle I showed this watch to one of our first adjusters . . . who took it apart. At the end of several days he came to me and said literally, "I am astonished; the result is incredible. You do not find a watch to compare with that in 50,000 of our make."

This lavish praise may be in part an expression of his native enthusiasm, but the spirit of the quotation is in line with others of a similar nature, and it illustrates the remarkable position that the Waltham trade-mark enjoyed in that period. This reputation for superlative excellence has been one of Waltham's greatest assets, and it has also set up a most difficult standard of performance.

The extent to which Dumaine maintained the Waltham standard is indicated by the increase in sales that was obtained after the reorganization. For the period 1926–30, sales volume was maintained about one-third higher than the best prewar figure. A specific example of the reversal of the trend against Waltham came from Brockton, Massachusetts. Comparative figures were given by a local dealer, who said in a letter dated April 3, 1924, that Waltham sales had dropped from 97 per cent to 48 per cent of the total. But, "under Mr. Boucher's rule" Waltham popularity increased substantially. "Sales for the last few months" were:

	Waltham	*Domestic Competitors*	*Swiss*
Ladies' Watches	67%	5%	28%
Gentlemen's Watches	71%	27%	2%

The improvement in Waltham's standing with the dealers was not universal, however. Some dealers took an indifferent attitude, stating that the quality of the products of the principal domestic watch manufacturers was approximately equal. Others were strong in their disapproval of Waltham quality as compared with that of other domestic producers. Criticisms covered a wide range of topics: poor workmanship; poor adjustment; rush work; and competition on a price basis, with quality neglected. Such criticism was sometimes associated with prejudice against the new management, and one is inclined to suspect that the animosity left over from the strike may have had a large influence, particularly in the territory adjacent to the factory. But the issue is in doubt. There is even a question that any general loss of prestige ever existed, for on October 20, 1923, Boucher wrote to Dumaine, after a survey of the market, "The writer is glad to be able to say that most of the jewelers and watchmakers he has personally come in contact with make him feel that Waltham actually produces the best watch made."

The reputation that the Waltham watch enjoys with the public and the trade is not necessarily a final criterion of quality. Goodwill is developed from a composite of quality, service, and advertising, and it does not measure the actual merits of the product. For that purpose, evidence from within the Company is a somewhat better guide.

Waltham had always produced an accurate timepiece, and Dumaine had no serious difficulty in keeping up with that tradition. The Company had been founded by inventors and staffed with good mechanical designers. They had made and kept the Waltham reputation for accuracy, for accuracy is primarily a matter of good design.

In 1922, seventy years after Dennison had organized the first group of designing engineers, the Technical Engineering Department at Waltham was still the strongest and the best-paid unit in the factory. The department dominated the business and kept the Company years behind the fashion, but it never failed to design watches that gave commendable accuracy in each price class. Dumaine conserved this engineering talent by assigning each man to the task best suited to his abilities; the department as such was broken up, however, and its reactionary influence on Company policy was destroyed. These changes, plus the formation of a Watchmakers' Advisory Committee, increased the number of employees who were directly interested in mechanical design and thereby improved the probability of continued success in the production of accurate timepieces.

Quality is very often judged by the appearance of the product. On this score, Waltham policy has been somewhat mixed. The design and finish of the movements have been carefully planned to express the inward merits of the product. But in regard to cases, Waltham in the past has been content to purchase the best that the open market offered. There has been no attempt since 1890 to manufacture cases.

The organization apparently was never in a position to achieve the same superlative performance in the manufacture of cases that was obtained in the production of movements. Whether this condition represented a lack of skill in the technical problems of case manufacture, or a lack of appreciation for the element of beauty in cases, is not clear.

Waltham produced a few cases in the early days, but in 1890 the manufacture of cases was abandoned. The process of manufacture was relatively simple, and there were many producers in the field. Under these conditions there was strong competition for the Waltham watch-case orders, and the cases available on the open market were satisfactory as to quality and price. The Waltham Company preferred to sell watch movements and let the dealers mount them in cases.[14] The sale of cases was in the nature of a service to dealers who preferred to buy complete watches.

Criticism of the policy of purchasing watch cases has been rare, but a few instances are found in the records. For example, Frank Jenks wrote to E. C. Fitch in 1917, "I must say that it seems to me that for beauty of dial and hands the foreign watch is superior."[15] And two years later, Charles L. Depollier, who played a large part in the Waltham selling program from 1917 to 1920, complained that the old watch-case makers had died or lost their skill while working at war trades. He suggested that the Company manufacture cases in Switzerland from his designs. These two comments are the exception. The absence of other complaints points to a ready acceptance of Waltham movements, mounted in such cases as the market offered. The demand has been for variety in ornamentation to suit local and national tastes.[16] The advisability of developing superlative skill in the design and execution of watch cases has not appeared in the records as a debatable issue. There seems to be a disposition to regard the production of watch cases as unworthy of the same attention given to the manufacture of the mechanism, but the wisdom of this attitude is open to serious question.

The production policies established by Dumaine at Waltham were based on a financial approach to production problems. Dumaine was not especially concerned with merchandising and price, except to be sure that they met the requirements fixed by the demand of the market and the character of the competition. His policies followed the principle that the essential variable in manufacturing for profit is the cost of production. In other respects it is sufficient to meet competitive standards, but the cost of production is a constant object of attack. The continual evolution of process and design might be taken as an exception to the policy emphasizing routine production, but this evolution is primarily a part of the drive for lower production costs.[17]

Dumaine was keenly interested in pioneering developments and fundamental research, but efforts in that direction were not notably successful. The policy of economy and the desire for prompt results prevented the inauguration of lengthy and expensive research projects, and instead attempts were made to pick the winners from the field of free-lance inventors. Such efforts often fail — for example, Fitch failed to purchase the patents on the electric clock which were offered to him by Henry E. Warren of "Telechron" fame.

MAJOR DISTRIBUTION POLICIES

In the field of distribution Dumaine took a conservative position. In the domestic territory he followed Waltham precedent by confining sales effort to the conventional channels of distribution. Selected wholesalers were used as outlets for all products except speedometers and automobile clocks. Distribution in foreign markets was simplified by closing all foreign offices and by selling through exclusive foreign agents, each of whom assumed all the risks and expenses of the business in his territory. The foreign agents were permitted to sell Waltham products only to wholesalers.

The sales program under the new régime was more than conservative; by comparison with current practice in similar lines, it was distinctly reactionary. It consisted of the barest fundamentals of selling technique, for it rested on the theory that a competent salesman can always dispose of a good product when it is offered at a competitive price. All the frills and frippery that fill the endless volumes of modern sales literature were discarded. Missionary salesmen, advertising of assorted styles, promotion schemes, publicity — all were set aside as unnecessary to the plain business of selling Waltham watches. Each salesman received a photograph book, a catalogue, and instructions to produce results; or else — !

Dumaine's simplified sales program was successful because the Company had all the prerequisites that the theory assumed, namely a good product, a tremendous backlog of consumer preference, and competent sales personnel. Dumaine watched over the quality of the product and set a competitive price. The sales department, with Boucher as pacemaker, maintained the sales volume at five to seven million dollars per year from 1923 until the second year of the depression of the 'thirties. Rudimentary sales tactics were well suited to this period of general prosperity and low sales resistance; they were also appropriate to the limited capacity of the plant to produce the small wrist watches that were then in demand.

The development of an efficient salesforce was achieved by the process of elimination. As we have mentioned, there were many changes in the auxiliary and executive branches of the Sales Department, and these branches continued for a considerable period in a state of flux. These changes made a great difference in the department as a whole, but they had little effect on the backbone of the salesforce — the men who did the actual selling. After the excess personnel had been discharged, there remained a group of thoroughly competent salesmen. Replacements in this basic group were relatively few.

Dumaine's sales program is open to criticism. Had he used so-called modern methods, a larger sales volume might have been obtained; but there is room for doubt on that score. Aggressive selling methods might on the contrary have led to a competitive race that would have reduced profits for all participants. With a relatively inflexible demand and few domestic competitors, there was much advantage in maintaining an orderly market. From 1923 to 1929, general business was good, and there was volume enough in the market to butter everybody's bread, if no one took more than his share.

The sales program at Waltham was in no sense a fixture; it has been modified at various times. New missionary salesmen reëstablished the direct contact between the factory and the retailer. Experiments in advertising were tried, and although they were not highly successful, Dumaine continued to have a limited and skeptical interest in new advertising techniques. Still greater changes in the sales program were proposed, but Dumaine did not attempt to cover any weakness in his competitive position by an extravagant outlay for high-pressure selling.

It would be convenient to have a summary of Dumaine's policies in a few concise phrases, but the secret of successful business administration cannot be isolated and compressed in any such fashion. It may be in order, however, to mention some of the outstanding characteristics that influenced his plan of action during his early years at Waltham.

1. Independence. The spirit of independence pervaded the entire structure of Dumaine's policy. He preserved, as far as he could, a complete freedom of action. Every association that might impair that freedom was carefully avoided. He was independent of the bankers. He was independent of the unions.[18] He avoided publicity so that he might be independent of the press and the public. He was largely independent of the stockholders and the directors.
2. Simplicity. Dumaine believed in simplicity. He dealt in essentials, and chose, as his subordinates, men who could carry on the work in that fashion. Boucher reflected the spirit of the whole organization when he said, "I don't believe in systems, I believe in men." Subordinates enjoyed ample authority and were held strictly accountable for results.
3. Profits. It is the object of all business concerns to earn a profit, but Dumaine applied this principle to the individual parts of the business. Every function, every department, every individual worker had a dollar value to the business. Intangible returns were acceptable, but they were not a part of any man's claim to a Waltham pay check. The dollar-value of each worker, whether he was at the bench or at the desk, usually appeared somewhere on the accounts of the Company. The accounts might not do complete justice to every individual, but their normal accuracy was sufficient for the purpose.
4. Completeness of coördination. It is obvious that profitable operations require a close coördination of the parts of a business with each other and with the current markets — the market for the product and for the elements that go to produce it: raw materials, labor, and capital. The difficulty of assembling and correlating the mass of information required for this coördination is great. Few executives adequately cover all the important elements. Dumaine was one of the few. He devoted his energies impartially to every phase of the business, and no department was too obscure to receive his attention. Problems, once solved, were periodically reopened, and the solutions revised. Dumaine did not solve all the problems of coördination himself, but he prevented their neglect by others.

CHAPTER XIII

DEPRESSION AND RECOVERY, 1929 TO 1935

Employment and Inventory

The watch factory at Waltham did not share in the feverish industrial activity that characterized the boom year of 1929, but the plant was busy and prosperous. Steady work was provided for the normal force of twenty-three hundred employees; and the customary wages, averaging 50.1 cents per hour, were paid. Sales for the year 1929 increased 6 per cent above the figure for the previous years; although the drop of 8 per cent in earnings was disappointing, it was not alarming. Operations were remarkably stable; neither the industrial boom of the spring and summer nor the stock-market crash of the closing months of the year seemed seriously to affect the Company's business. This satisfactory position was further reinforced by the fact that the inventory was not burdensome, since at the current rate of sales the entire stocks of finished goods[1] could have been sold in a period of less than one month. Other items of the inventory, work in process and raw materials, represented minimum requirements for immediate needs. The prospect for continued steady operation was reasonably good.

Optimism on the part of the Waltham employees was justified, for the spring of 1930 brought a perceptible increase in the production schedule. The year opened with a normal payroll carrying 2,392 names and employment began to increase in the first week in February, reaching a peak in the third week in May. This spurt of activity at Waltham reflected the cheerful sentiment that was current after the first drastic deflation of security prices, and it coincided very closely with a speculative movement in the stock market. Stock prices collapsed again in June and the factory was closed, ostensibly for the annual two weeks' holiday. When operations were resumed about three weeks later, only 1,559 workers were recalled. The record suggests that a change of policy was made about January 1, 1930. Before that date, operations were maintained on an even keel, the rate corresponding to average sales. After that date, Dumaine avoided the risks of carrying unnecessary inventory. During 1930, manufacturing operations rose and fell according to the requirements of the market.[2]

THE WAGE-PRICE STRUCTURE

Depressions usually bear heavily on the producers of luxuries, and Waltham executives have been driven to strong measures in almost every instance of severe cyclical decline from 1857 to 1930. During the panic of 1857, Robbins cut wages by 50 per cent and kept the factory running full time, dumping the product on the market at auction. When the Civil War brought the Company its second depression, Robbins changed his tactics. "There was," he said, "little hope of finding a market for the factory output, unless it should be so reduced in quantity as to be manufactured at a loss. It was therefore decided to reduce expenditures to the lowest point, but to keep the factory in operation to such an extent as to hold the leading operatives."[3] In subsequent depressions, reductions were made in both employment and wages in whatever proportions seemed necessary under the circumstances. In every case, labor and capital divided the burden between them, and the emergency passed without tragic consequences to either party.

In the depression of 1930 to 1934, Dumaine followed the Waltham precedent, with some additions of his own.

Reduction in the number of employees took place promptly, as we have seen, but the reduction of wages was long delayed; it was not until February 8, 1932, that a cut was made. When the decision had been reached, the action was drastic — the cut amounted to 30 per cent. In the meantime an effort had been made to maintain prices and wages, in accordance with the theories of President Hoover, but the results had been disappointing. Instead of acting as a support to business activity, the inflexible price and wage structure seemed only to discourage such spirit as remained in the market. Interest faded, the volume of orders dwindled, and the schedule of operations at Waltham was curtailed more and more to keep pace with the falling demand. Finally, in the first weeks of 1932, the payroll was reduced to a mere handful of workers. In the week of January 30 there were only 311 employees remaining; the plant was practically closed.

A change from the policy of maintaining wages and prices was inevitable, and the Company was well prepared to make it. Employment in 1931 had been reduced more rapidly than the decline of sales had required, and as a result the finished goods inventory on December 31 had been cut to $184,687,[4] or approximately twenty-one days' supply. The sale of inventory and the practice of rigid economy had brought the cash account up to $2,201,544 from $738,637 for the previous year. The Company's affairs were in order and ready for a new line of action.

The old policy of high wages and prices had resulted in the closing of the plant, and Dumaine believed that a reduction in *both* wages and prices would make it possible to open the plant and keep it open. He tried that course of action and found it successful. The deficit for 1932 was less than half that of the previous year, and employment in total hours was increased 8 per cent above the 1931 figure. Total wages, however, fell 24 per cent. These figures cover operations in the blackest year of the depression, and a comparison with average figures for the nation leads me to the conclusion that Dumaine not only avoided the catastrophe of a prolonged shutdown of the plant but actually contributed to the recovery movement. Production rose from a virtual standstill in the early months of 1932 to a rate that was better than the national average. Comparisons are given in Table 24.

TABLE 24

INDICES OF EMPLOYMENT, PAYROLLS, AND PROFITS, 1931–1932
(1931 — 100)

	1931	1932
Waltham Employment[a]	100	92
U. S. Factory Employment[a]	100	85
Waltham Payroll	100	76
U. S. Factory Payrolls	100	69
Waltham Profits	— 100[b]	— 45[b]
Corporation Profits	100	— 29[b]

[a] Number of employees.
[b] Deficit.

SOURCE: *Survey of Current Business*, 1936 Supplement, and Waltham Watch Company records.

DEVELOPMENT OF CUTTHROAT COMPETITION

The Waltham Company's fight for a share of the 1932 market for watches was a sharp struggle. The depression was only part of the difficulty, for the intensity of competition had reached new heights. The expansion of productive facilities both at home and abroad had gone so far that unrestricted competition inevitably led to the liquidation of marginal producers.[5] Survival could be assured in some cases by a rapid adjustment to depressed markets and the faster competitive pace. For the industry as a whole, however, protection could be obtained only by the control of competition.

The capacity of the American watch industry as reported by the trade association was far too great for the demand. In a memorandum prepared in 1929 for presentation to the Finance Committee of the United States Senate, the capacity of the domestic industry was estimated at 3,700,000 movements; actual production in 1928 was 1,741,495 movements, and in 1932 it was 434,941[6] movements. Capacity estimates are likely to be higher than the normal efficient operating rate; but, where the discrepancy between estimated capacity and actual production is so great, we may assume with reasonable assurance that overcapacity exists to a highly undesirable extent.

Overcapacity also existed in Switzerland; although figures to prove the point apparently are not available, the fact is well established by the action of the Swiss Government in "prohibiting the opening of new enterprises in the watchmaking industry, or enlargement, transformation, or transfer of existing properties without the authorization of the Department of Public Economy."[7] Competition from Swiss imports was kept partially in check by the Smoot-Hawley Tariff Act of 1930, but the Swiss manufacturers continued to get the lion's share of the United States market.[8]

Although the threat of overcapacity in the watch industry was a source of much concern, there were two new factors in the competitive situation that were far more dangerous: the smuggling of Swiss movements into the United States and the assembling of foreign watch parts in American factories.[9]

GROWTH OF WATCH-SMUGGLING

After the passage of the Smoot-Hawley Tariff Act of 1930, smuggling developed rapidly and, according to press reports, the practice soon reached the proportions of a thriving industry. A headline in the Boston *Transcript* of October 24, 1932, reads, "Uncover Wide Swiss Watch Smuggling. . . . Twenty-two bales of rabbit skins, each containing at its center from 1,000 to 1,500 Swiss watch movements were seized today by Federal investigators in a stable at 305 West 26th Street." The following January, the master-mind of the smuggling ring was arrested, convicted, and sentenced for this, his second, offense to serve four years in the penitentiary and pay a fine of $10,000. But smuggling of watches had become a well-established criminal racket, and it continued to prosper in spite of the federal agents. The chief baker on a German liner used his huge girth to camouflage a belt containing 780 17-jewel movements.[10] Ships' officers were involved in the traffic. Professional smugglers acquired descriptive titles, such as the *Candy Kid,* proclaiming the bearer's achievements in using shipments of Swiss chocolate as a cover for his operations. The situation became so bad that on May 1, 1933, Dumaine wrote to Senator Walsh, "These [federal] investigations have repeatedly disclosed an organized conspiracy between Swiss watch manufacturers and their agents in the United States and Canada. . . ."[11] The letter continues with a summary of the principal convictions for smuggling since 1930; it estimates that the loss of revenue to the government was from two million to five million dollars per year and the lost sales of American watches from one million to two million movements per year.

Enforcement of the Tariff Act was difficult. The reaction of the Swiss manufacturers to smuggling operations is given in a letter printed in *Le Moment,* which claims that "The initial cause of this state of things is the Tariff Act of 1930 . . . which contains, for the Swiss watch industry fantastical increases in comparison with the old tariff. The duties levied at the present time often exceed the value of the movement only."[12] The Swiss Government seemed more concerned with the problem of increasing exports from Switzerland than of censoring the ethics of manufacturers of that country.[13] In the United States enforcement was hampered by the violent objections of the watch industry to the practice of selling at auction the watches seized from smugglers. H. Morgenthau, Jr., Secretary of the Treasury, wrote to Gen. Hugh Johnson, "Our enforcement of the tariff on watch movements is dependent on our ability to get the coöperation of outsiders having information concerning specific shipments about to come in. Since these individuals cannot be paid for their services except from the sale of a particular lot of watch movements seized as a result of the information which they give, the suspension of the sale of seized watch movements is having the effect of paralyzing our enforcement of the tariff on watch movements."[14]

Under these circumstances the domestic watch industry suffered no matter how the affair was handled. When the tariff was low, the competition from the Swiss tended to drive the remaining American watch manufacturers out of the business.[15] A high tariff induced smuggling, which the government seemed unable to check[16] even when it contributed to the evils of competition by auctioning off the seized watches. A satisfactory solution of the dilemma within the conventional framework of American tariff practice seemed impossible, and Dumaine proposed the following six-point program for the limitation of imports:[17]

1. "Limit importation of watch movements to the present volume, 432,000, plus such percentage of increase as the domestic production and sales may increase under the N.I.R.A. so that at no time the import volume shall exceed the total volume of the domestic production of the previous year."
2. License all importers of watches.
3. Require consecutive, unduplicated numbers on imported watches.
4. Item 3 to apply to the stock of licensed importers.
5. Require a certificate of legal importation for each watch.
6. Destroy all confiscated watches. Reclaim the precious metals for the United States Treasury.

Unfortunately for the American watch industry, President Franklin D. Roosevelt had quite different ideas about tariffs and foreign trade. After much petitioning and a public hearing before the Tariff Commission, a trade agreement was made with Switzerland. Among the concessions granted to Switzerland was an average reduction of 34 per cent in the tariffs on jeweled watch movements.[18]

The tariff remains one of the major hazards in the development of the watch industry. In view of the conflicts of opinion and interest which occur in this field, there is no assurance that an equitable solution of the problem can be achieved, and little hope that any *one* national policy will be consistently followed. Thus watch manufacturers are driven to protect their interests by any legitimate political means at their command. They are forced to maintain a competitive position among the various political pressure groups that influence administrative and legislative tariff action. Dumaine was well aware of the requirements of the case and thoroughly familiar with the rules of political practice, but that knowledge is no guarantee of success in the attempt to limit and stabilize foreign competition. In spite of the best efforts of the American manufacturers, the industry may be called upon to meet, without the aid of adequate tariff protection, any competitive prices and practices that Swiss producers find it expedient to use.

ASSEMBLING IMPORTED PARTS IN THE UNITED STATES

It has always been the practice of American watch manufacturers to buy a few parts of watches abroad. When Dennison started the Waltham enterprise, he went to England to find suppliers for jewels, enamel, and such other parts as could not be produced efficiently by the new organization. For all practical purposes, however, Waltham watches were wholly manufactured in America, and Waltham officials claimed that this was still true in 1938.[19]

This appears to have been the general practice until about 1918; after that date the importation of movements and parts for assembly in American factories was common. The magnitude of the change may be inferred from Table 25 and from comments in the Swiss trade papers.[20]

In the heyday of Waltham prosperity, foreign watch manufacturers had little advantage over American producers. It was true then, as it is now, that foreign labor was much cheaper than American labor, and that foreign watchmakers had skill of a high order. These advantages were outweighed, however, by the efficiency of American methods and machinery and by the standardization of dimensions and quality that were obtained in American factories. The arguments for American superiority were stated in an advertisement in *Harper's Weekly*, in 1868, which claimed that:

> The beauty, precision, the greater cheapness, the uniform excellence of a watch constructed by machinery so exquisite that the mere spectacle of its operation is poetic, gradually give the American watches a public preference that will not be deceived.

TABLE 25

WATCHES, MOVEMENTS, AND MATERIALS IMPORTED INTO THE UNITED STATES, 1912–1926
(Value in Dollars)

Year	Completed Watches	Watch Movements	Cases and Parts	Total
1912/13	......	......	......	2,615,744
1919	3,542,033	6,520,129	2,584,563	12,646,725
1920	3,938,980	8,147,876	3,601,377	15,688,233
1921	1,864,951	4,461,051	2,842,603	9,168,605
1922	7,122,783		2,204,576	9,327,359
1923	6,740,822		3,312,864	10,053,686
1924	4,761,678		5,977,233	10,738,911
1925	7,269,706		3,060,663	10,330,369
1926	10,416,582		1,414,656	11,831,238

As foreign producers adopted American machine methods of production, and gradually substituted the factory system for the practice of "putting out" work to independent craftsmen, the preference for American watches became less marked. In the course of years, the Swiss, in particular, became highly skilled in the construction of watchmaking tools and in the production of standardized, interchangeable watch parts. The extent of the improvement of Swiss methods is indicated by the following excerpt from a government publication:[21]

> There is no prejudice [in the Brazilian market] against watches and clocks of American manufacture on the score of quality, since American goods and high quality are practically synonymous. However, no one doubts the quality of high grade Swiss watches, and since they are usually cheaper in price than the American high grade watches, the latter are at a serious disadvantage even when the usually thicker, heavier construction of the American watch is not considered.

In spite of the progressively lower cost of foreign watch movements and parts, the growth of assembling plants in the United States was kept in check for some years by the tariff. The rate on watch parts in 1913 was 30 per cent ad valorem, and in 1932 it was increased to 45 per cent,[22] but these high rates were not sufficient to prevent the growth of companies that devoted much of their effort to the assembling of foreign parts in American plants.

It should not be supposed, however, that cheap labor was the only support of foreign competition. Companies that operated assembling plants frequently were conspicuous for aggressive sales-promotion methods, notably the development of small wrist watches, magazine and radio advertising, and the use of installment credit at the retail level. It is even claimed by proponents of these selling methods that they have created a new market for watches to the advantage of the industry as a whole.

A further element in the competitive situation during the postwar period was the organization of the Swiss watch industry on a national scale. Excellent horological schools were maintained by the government, which provided technical training of a theoretical and practical nature; both the manufacture and the design of timepieces were taught. The Swiss watch industry as a whole was organized into two divisions, the "Trust" and the "Superholding" Company. The Trust was reported to consist of the stronger organizations of the industry, while the Superholding Company included the smaller units.[23] With the aid of these two organizations, the Swiss government avoided destructive competition, maintained minimum prices and gross margins, prevented overexpansion, and otherwise encouraged stability in the export market. It would be presumptuous to estimate the effect of Swiss organization on price competition in the United States without more complete data, but the potential influence was obviously great. The Swiss contend that government control was exercised in the interest of an orderly and freely competitive market, but American producers complained that Swiss competition was ruinous.

Such were the competitive conditions that faced Dumaine in 1932: an overexpanded domestic industry, organized foreign competition, cheap foreign labor, unsatisfactory tariff protection, smuggling, the auction of smuggled goods by the federal government, and aggressive selling tactics by importers of complete watches and domestic assemblers of Swiss parts. This competitive pressure was brought to bear on a domestic market which was undergoing a rapid and extreme contraction. Dumaine met the situation by simple and decisive action. He fought for his share of the market on a price basis. He also produced two new models, small, rectangular baguette watches; one of them, the #400, was advertised as the smallest watch made in America.

The lower prices for Waltham watches did not bring an immediate increase in business, but the effectiveness of the move is suggested by a quotation from a letter written by an American wholesaler to a Swiss manufacturer. The letter contains this sentence, "We are not interested at all in buying, for the moment, Swiss watches, because the Waltham Watch Company has reduced its prices in so radical a manner that the difference between the price of Swiss movements and those of that firm is almost null."[24] It is worth noting that this wholesaler preferred Waltham watches to those of Swiss manufacture, if the former were offered at competitive prices.

The effect of the lower prices and wages[25] on employment is somewhat in doubt. Employment did rise in a most reassuring fashion, but the rise was due in part to philanthropy. Dumaine said in 1933:[26]

> We are employing about 50 per cent of our normal number of people. The management felt that since the company owes no money it should give as much work as possible to employees. We have been running about this number of people since early in December, but their production of watches has largely gone into the warehouse in hopes that it may be sold . . . . Our sales of watches this year have been 62 per cent below those of last year up to this time and have had a value of $160,000, as against $280,000.

The hope that the watches would be sold was justified, for the inventory at the year end was maintained at minimum figures. The inference is that the price cut was a major force in maintaining sales volume and employment.

MERCHANDISING FOR A DEPRESSION MARKET

The two new baguette models, #400 and #450, were well received by the public, and the yearly sales soon reached 15,000 to 20,000 movements. The #400 model appeared in 1931 and was priced at $30 to $100 to the consumer.[27] This offering served to meet the demand for modern styling at a medium price, and sales rose consistently even through the worst of the depression. The #450 model appeared in 1933. It was slightly larger than the #400 and less expensive, being offered in both 17- and 15-jewel grades at a minimum price of approximately $18 to the consumer. This model also was popular, as Table 26 shows.

TABLE 26

SALES OF BAGUETTE WATCHES #400, #450, 1931–1936
WALTHAM WATCH COMPANY
(In number of movements)

	#400	#450
1931	1,447	.....
1932	6,129	.....
1933	12,443	216[a]
1934	15,127	5,064
1935	15,080	17,875
1936	16,839	20,341

[a] Produced.

Merchandising for depression conditions and business growth was not confined to watches. The production of speedometers in 1935 was more than thirteen times as great as the 1927 output. This splendid increase in sales, at a time when it was most urgently needed, was an accomplishment worthy of special note. Waltham had been making speedometers since the early days of the motor car, but the sale of that product had lost its original impetus. The revival of the department during the depression years was of major assistance in maintaining employment and in minimizing losses.

The manufacture of electric clocks was also a feature of the program of diversification which helped to combat the effects of the depression. Production of electric clocks was begun in 1927, but the department did not show much growth until 1931. From 1931 to 1935 the output showed a very satisfactory increase, but this work did not constitute a major branch of the business. In fact, the gain in the sales of electric clocks was less than the loss in eight-day clocks, and the Clock Department as a whole suffered considerably from the combined effect of the depression and changes in the market. Table 27 gives the number of electric and eight-day clocks, as well as the number of pocket and wrist watches, produced in 1926–35.

TABLE 27

PRODUCTION OF MOVEMENTS, 1926–1935
WALTHAM WATCH COMPANY

	Pocket Watches	Wrist Watches	Electric Clocks	8-day Clocks
1926	271,919	189,215	.....	91,837
1927	165,628	301,426	1,214	124,301
1928	130,140	276,774	498	12,151
1929	172,931	263,991	952	70,823
1930	99,111	314,081	504	23,025
1931	33,666	82,868	5,234	24,546
1932	34,040	130,346	10,471	12,412
1933	36,159	121,044	15,300	6,245
1934	29,430	231,708	22,202	21,415
1935	26,363	332,374	33,515	6,800

THE NATIONAL RECOVERY ADMINISTRATION

The policy of maintaining low wages and prices came to an end with the passage of the National Industrial Recovery Act and the adoption of codes regulating wages, hours, and competitive practice. The Act was signed by President Franklin D. Roosevelt on June 16, 1933, and on August 7 Waltham wages were raised 20 per cent or more. Every worker received the basic increase of 20 per cent. For many employees, however, this substantial increase was not enough to bring their wages up to the minimum of $14 per week; such employees were given the additional sum required by the code. The net result was an increase in the Waltham wage scale of 28 per cent.[28]

Dumaine gave the NRA his unstinted support. In view of the character of foreign competition, and the success which attended his own diametrically opposite policy, it is a matter of some surprise that he should have accepted the radical program of the NRA with apparent satisfaction. If his personal views differed from those of President Roosevelt and his advisers, the records do not disclose it. On the contrary, the assistant administrator of the NRA, R. W. Lea, was much pleased with the turn of affairs at Waltham and sent a letter to Dumaine expressing his satisfaction. Lea wrote, "I have read the statement of the Waltham Watch Company to its employees[29] dated March 22 with great interest and much satisfaction. . . . It shows a sound understanding of the National Recovery Act and also indicates that a very satisfactory mutual feeling exists between that company and its employees." [30]

After the adoption of the NRA watch code [31] there was considerable confusion in labor relations. There was rivalry between the American Federation of Labor and the local union for the support of the employees. There were attempts by management to foster good relations with both unions and with the government; the reason for a conciliatory policy is apparent. The Roosevelt administration was openly partial to labor and hostile to big business. The survival of the watch industry depended on the high tariff which the administration might lower in an effort to stimulate foreign trade. The administration was not likely to be sympathetic toward a company which, in the past, had been branded by the press as a member of the "watch trust." Under these circumstances, labor became an invaluable political ally to a business which was dominated by political considerations.

Dumaine was not satisfied with merely avoiding labor disturbances; he went much further than that and took steps to foster fundamentally sound labor relations. During this period we find an increase in social and recreational activities for the employees. The Old Timers of the Dial Department Association held a reunion dinner.[32] The foremen were guests of the executives for supper and a subsequent conference to discuss factory problems and the more interesting topic of watch-smuggling. The famous employee picnics, which had been discontinued at the time of the postwar crisis in 1921, were revived after thirteen years, and some 1,500 people attended.[33] The baseball season was opened with due formality — and at all the major affairs of this sort some member of the Dumaine family usually was present.[34] The management's goodwill also took a more tangible form of expression in an offer to provide group insurance for employees in return for a pledge that employees would organize a campaign to reduce the waste of materials. In this labor relations policy we seem to see the old dispensation of Robbins and Fitch, the New Democracy of the left under Roosevelt, and the fine calculations of business and finance, all converging on common ground. It may be coincidence or mere expedient, but the circumstance suggests that the relation between employer and employee at Waltham was becoming broader and more stable.

An important milestone in Waltham labor relations was the signing of an agreement with both unions on June 6, 1934.[35] The significant clause of the agreement was the one that made arbitration binding on both capital and labor. The agreement was put to the test in January, 1935. The case related to the discharge of an employee of twelve years' service for lack of attention to his duties.

The union charged that the Company was discriminating against the employee for union activities, and the case was tried before an arbitration committee.[36] The evidence indicated that the employee had been used by the Company as a labor leader but that he had subsequently transferred the use of his talents as a leader to the union cause. Political interests may have caused him to neglect his work, for the specific accusation brought by the Company was one of gross carelessness in a matter of considerable importance.[37] The verdict of the committee was in favor of the Company, since the charge of discrimination was not proved, but the committee recommended that the employee be replaced on the payroll "at a wage commensurate with his admittedly demonstrated ability."[38]

RETURN TO THE PREDEPRESSION WAGE SCALE

The Waltham Company was free from labor troubles during the critical recovery period, 1933–38, and this state of affairs was no mere accident but the result of a carefully planned program, modified as conditions required. The program was liberal, but the timing was conservative. The best modern precedents were followed, but action was postponed until sound business judgment demanded a change. The Waltham enterprise is a business — not a philanthropy — but Dumaine knew, as well as anyone, that profits are the result of successful human relations in the factory, the industry, and the trade. He knew that the human factors are of increasing importance, and he acted accordingly — when the time was ripe. An illustration of precise timing of executive action is given by the wage increase of March 16, 1934.

On March 10, an article in the Waltham paper reported that the president of the Employees Association would receive a statement of the wage rates paid at Elgin from the superintendent of the Elgin plant. The account goes on to say, "It is a point of great interest to Waltham workers as the Elgin shop has been reported [to be] paying higher wages but that question is much in doubt."[39] As a matter of fact, Elgin wages averaged 7 cents an hour higher than Waltham wages, and there was trouble ahead.[40] Accordingly, six days later (March 16), the papers carried the headline, "Boost in Wages Comes as Great Surprise When Envelopes Are Given Out." The text of the article states, "The present action of the Waltham Watch Company has been taken independently of other leaders in the industry, no consultations have been held with them in regard to the local concern's move."[41] The official statement by the Company read, "The Waltham Watch Company, endeavoring to conform with the spirit of the times, surprised its employees yesterday by increasing their pay 10%."[42] This brought the average rate at Waltham to approximately 50 cents per hour, which was the wage level before the depression.

By the end of 1934, the normal force of approximately 2,500 workers was employed for the full week of forty working hours. The operating statement for the year showed a large loss, $315,350, owing almost entirely to the fact that the percentage increase in wages was double the increase in sales. (See Table 28.) But the outlook was not

TABLE 28

SALES AND WAGES, 1933–1934
WALTHAM WATCH COMPANY

Year	Sales	Wages
1933	$2,284,921	$1,108,644
1934	3,346,839	2,122,566
Increase 1934 over 1933	46%	91%

without hope, and Dumaine wrote in the annual report, "If, as is generally conceded, the great depression is showing signs of breaking, it should not be necessary further to encroach upon surplus if watch smuggling is prevented and the Government tariff changes are not serious."[43] This forecast was correct, and operations for the following year produced a profit.

UNIONIZATION UNDER THE WAGNER ACT

From 1938 to 1941 the relations between labor and management at Waltham were comparatively uneventful. In 1940 there was some difficulty in adjusting the wages of matchers and finishers during the change-over to the group incentive or "unit" system of production, but that issue was discussed and settled in conferences extending over a period of six months. The records kept by the Company show that a moderate attitude was adopted by both parties, that the finishers were patient and the Company officials open to reason.

In 1940 there seemed little likelihood that the local independent union could be displaced by a more militant group, but in 1941 the plant was organized in seven weeks by the American Federation of Labor.

The Waltham *News Tribune* of February 8 carried an announcement of a drive to organize a local of the International Watch and Jewelry Workers Union. The first meeting was held on February 11 with an estimated two hundred fifty workers attending. The second meeting, a week later, was attended by some four hundred persons, and the following day the membership of the new union was reported to be 980. Approximately two weeks after the drive for members began, the union approached the company asking for recognition and the abolishment of the unit system. At the end of the third week of the drive the union claimed 1,400 members, and three days later an appeal was made to the National Labor Relations Board for the right to represent all the workers of the Waltham Watch Company. An election was scheduled for March 25. On March 18 the union announced that it would seek a 30 per cent increase in wages and also gave notice of an increase in the initiation fee from $2 to $20, effective after the election. The election was held as scheduled and the union received 1,510 votes of a total of 2,006.

The demands of the union as given in the Waltham *News Tribune* were as follows:

> Two weeks' vacation with pay.
> Closed shop.
> Ten-minute rest period in the forenoon.
> $25 Christmas bonus.
> Wage increase of 30 per cent.

Negotiations resulted in an agreement between the Company and the union effective May 9, 1941, to April 30, 1942. The principal provisions of the agreement are given under the numbers which they bear in the printed pamphlet distributed by the Company.

4. A wage increase of 2½ cents per hour was granted. A Wage Board was established to make "equitable readjustments" in wage rates. A limit of $225,000 was set for the total of all wage increases including those incurred for vacations with pay (9).
5. A working week of 40 hours and the 8-hour day were specified, with time and a half for overtime in excess of 40 hours.
7. A 10 per cent premium wage was required for night work.
8. All work on Sundays or holidays was considered overtime.
9. Vacations with pay varied according to length of service to a maximum of two weeks.
10. "Reasonable rest periods" were to be allowed by foremen.
11. Arbitration of disputes was compulsory, and decisions of the Board of Arbitration were final and binding upon both parties.
20. Strikes and lockouts were prohibited.

The agreement was signed by I. E. Boucher, manager for the Company, and by Walter W. Cenerazzo, president and business agent for the union. The agreement was "underwritten" for the American Federation of Labor by Leon Williams, president of the International Jewelry Workers Union.

CHAPTER XIV

PROBLEMS IN PRODUCTION

Patents and Secret Processes

The American watch industry was founded and developed without the aid of patents. It is said that the essentials of watch design have not changed materially in two hundred years, and the spectacular development of watchmaking machinery has not been along patentable lines. Keith reports in 1854, "The Boston Watch Company [as the Waltham firm was then called] had no patents on the watch nor on machinery; and it was not until sixteen years after that company began that Mr. Howard took out a patent for improvements in the construction of watches."[1] To be sure, the records at Waltham list some 63 patents, granted to 17 inventors and assigned or leased to the Company, but these patents deal almost exclusively with minor points of design or construction. Of these 63 patents, 38 relate to watches, 7 to time fuses, 6 to clocks, and 12 to other matters. Some of them, in particular those concerned with the design of speedometers, have undoubtedly been of value; but Waltham executives do not consider that any of the patents dealing with watches have been of great significance in the development of the industry.

The absence of patents seems to represent a real lack of new ideas, for the records do not suggest that secrecy has been practised. Correspondence over a long period of years indicates that a relatively free exchange of data has been the rule and that reciprocal visits of inspection have been common, both at home and abroad. There have been exceptions to this rule, as in the case of the English watch manufacturers in 1850 and the strained relations in the domestic industry that followed the antitrust activities of the federal government in 1907, but they are rare. Secrets in the design of the product are impossible, since competitive models are carefully examined as soon as they reach the retailer. Secrets in the design of machinery, or in processes, have been discouraged by the frequent shifting of employees from one company to another. Trade secrets doubtless have existed, but their importance appears to be slight.

No monopoly of process or equipment has been maintained for any great length of time at Waltham. Even Dennison's ideas were taken from the common knowledge of his time, and they were copied as soon as their merits had been well established. It was not originality that made for success at Waltham, but rather the constant attention applied to the mechanical details of production. It was the continuous fall of production costs achieved through increasing mechanization that put Waltham at the head of the industry. It was the same attention to detail and the strict enforcement of economy that produced profits at Waltham under Dumaine's management.

THE PLANT LAYOUT

Dennison's new ideas were translated into action slowly, and with great difficulty. To make matters worse, Dennison was sometimes erratic in his notions. For example, "The benches in the factory [at Roxbury] were of mahogany. The wings of the building were divided into small rooms or stalls by partitions 8 feet in height, each of these rooms having a swinging blind door opening into the main aisle down the center. The reason for this arrangement was that Dennison thought European workmen, who had been accustomed to work in their own homes, would be better satisfied to have separate rooms and thus in a measure overcome the jealousy which would exist among them."[2] In contrast to this reactionary practice, which was soon discontinued, is the model plant built of pasteboard which showed the use of a belt conveyor "passing along in front of the workmen to transfer the work from one to another."[3] The theory of line production had been visualized by Dennison in this model before the industry was founded, but the principle has not yet been generally applied to the production of watches. Progress in the watch industry has been rapid in regard to essential details, but exceedingly slow in the matter of principles.

The Roxbury plant with its individual workrooms was a mechanized version of the established European practice, just as the first Ford car was a mechanized model of a carriage. According to Howard, "A brick building was built on East Street, Roxbury, Mass. [now a part of Boston] expressly designed for the business, as near as we could guess what the business required. The whole internal arrangement was torn out within one or two years and rearranged."[4] The second layout was better but on the whole very unsatisfactory, and it was decided to build a complete new plant.

After a total of three years' use at Roxbury, the building was abandoned and a third plant layout was made — this time at Waltham. There were some radical improvements. "The building was in the form of an open square, 100 feet each way. Each wing was 25 feet wide, the center or main building being 40 feet square, and all two stories in height. . . ."[5] This plan was dominated by two ideas: the watch *parts* were to be precisely accurate in dimensions, and they were to be made in large quantities at a low unit cost. The plant at Waltham was designed to meet those two requirements. Interest centered on the production by machinery of individual parts; the assembling of the parts into a watch movement remained a hand operation, essentially the same as it had been in Nuremberg in the sixteenth century. In so far as the principles of plant layout and the routing of production were concerned, the Waltham plant was not a *watch* factory but a factory for the production of a multiplicity of individual watch parts. For its time it was probably an excellent example of factory design; by present standards it was little more than a group of workshops.

Standard workshop design was used with long rows of benches facing the light. The necessity for good illumination on such fine work and the use of overhead line shafts for the distribution of power were the governing technical factors in determining the layout. A steam engine supplied the power for the whole plant, but with that exception the individual departments were practically independent.

The plant at Waltham was begun in 1854, and by 1861 the unsatisfactory character of the planning was very apparent. Confusion reigned. The president of that date severely criticized Dennison's abilities as a production manager; he wrote, "Our factory was a labyrinth and at almost every turn there was a section where some one of the multiplied departments of our work could be found with a 'boss' workman at its head."[6] Friction between Dennison and the president increased, and in 1861 Dennison was replaced as superintendent — his successors, however, did little better on the score of factory planning. Fifty years later, the layout was subject to the same criticism that had applied in 1861. In that interval the plant had been entirely

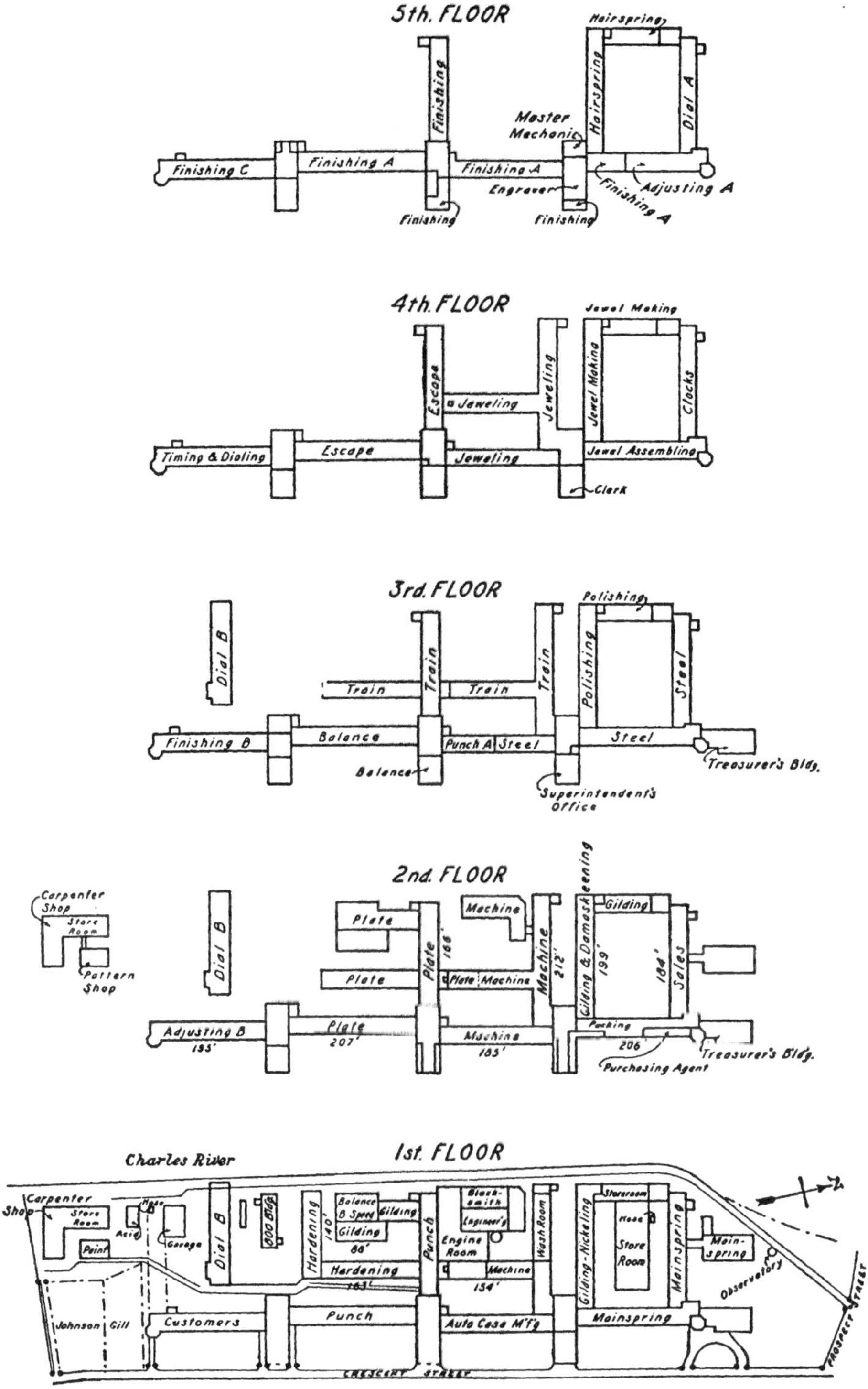

CHART I. 1913 Floor Plan

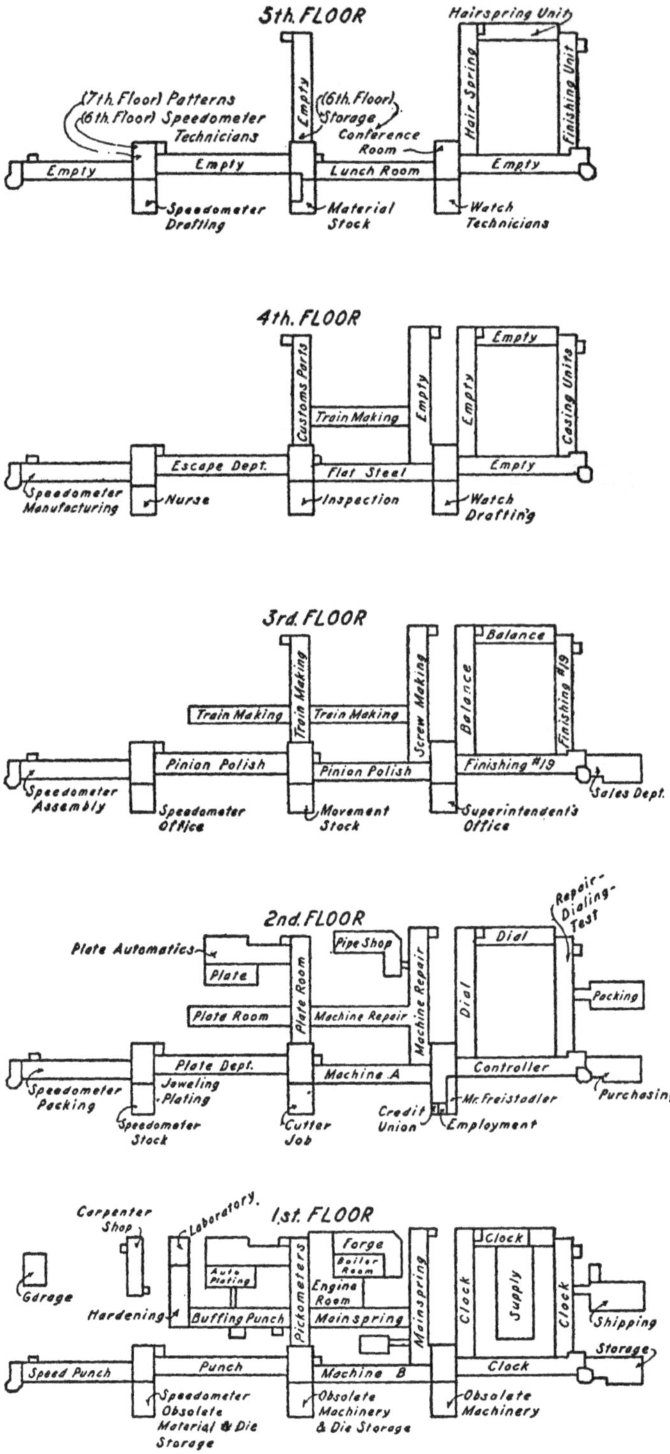

CHART II. 1938 Floor Plan

rebuilt (the last wing of the original "concrete" structure had been demolished in 1879), and the factory much enlarged; in 1881 an elaborate building for the executive offices had been constructed. When this ambitious program had been completed, the twenty-two departments were arranged as shown in the 1913 floor plan.

By 1913, some progress had been made toward systematic arrangement. Although it was by no means consistent, and far from ideal in principle and in execution, there had been a definite attempt to combine the units into an orderly arrangement. The structure was five stories high, and production began on the ground floor. Here the raw materials were received and the first operations performed. Since these first operations were carried out on heavy punch presses, solid foundations were required. The succeeding steps were performed on the upper floors, with final processes on the top floor. The goods were then sent to the second floor to be packed and shipped. Unfortunately, the plan was not followed consistently. Work on dials was distributed over all five floors. Adjusting was done on the second and fourth floors at opposite ends of the factory, and other departures from the plan are apparent. Confusion was more in evidence than order.

In 1923, the confused condition still existed. All of the factory floor space was in use, and operations were going on in the passageways. Although the *form* of integration had been incorporated into the plans, the activities of the various departments showed little coördination, as was mentioned in discussing the 1923 reorganization. Sweeping changes were necessary and Dumaine took the opportunity to revise the whole flow of production.

The factory buildings in 1938, as in 1913, were composed of 56 major sections of floor space. Six sections on the upper floors were vacant, owing to a reduction in the number of lines produced and probably also to more efficient operation throughout the plant. Of the remaining 50 wings, about 30 were put to a different use from that which they had served in 1913. The rearrangement was very thorough.

In the 1938 plan the factory was organized in three divisions, each producing a separate line of products: watches, clocks, and speedometers, respectively. The plan of production is different for each division.

The Clock Division has been segregated in one small section of the plant, where it is operated on an experimental basis. A highly superior electrical clock mechanism has been developed, but competition in the market for electric clocks has been too keen to warrant a major expansion of this department. Modernization of production methods had not been attempted in the Clock Division in 1938.

The manufacture of speedometers has lent itself to line-production methods in part. In this division the heavy punch work is done on the ground floor. The parts are then taken to the fourth floor for the light manufacturing steps. The finished parts are assembled in the third-floor section immediately below, and the finished speedometers are packed and stored on the second floor. Shipping is done from the storeroom which opens on the second-floor street level. The production plan in the Speedometer Division follows the gravity flow system, after the first heavy operation has been performed.

Some students of the subject question whether the Watch Division still lags in technical progress. The major development in watch construction has been the production of smaller and smaller sizes, thereby increasing the problems involved in mechanizing the operations. The problems have increased almost as rapidly as solutions for them have been developed and, as a result, the production of some of the smaller parts and almost all of the assembly work have remained in the stage of laborious hand operations.

The difficulty of producing the smaller watch parts by machine was noted by Howard. He wrote to Keith, "The interchangeability of parts, however, was found not to be practicable in the finer parts; never has been to this day [1863] and never will be. . . ."[7] In 1935, Boucher reported that the Swiss were approaching the ideal of producing completely interchangeable parts; he wrote, "They have succeeded wonderfully. Today they are producing enormous quantities of uniform material which is fast taking the skill out of watch manufacturing."[8] But Howard's forecast is still correct, in principle, and the need for meticulous handwork at various points in the manufacturing process makes it extremely difficult to apply the theory of line production to watchmaking.

The unit system of manufacture, which used mass-production principles and group incentive wages, was extensively tested in the period 1938–41, but was ultimately abandoned. Boucher reported in 1944 that watch parts were *not* truly interchangeable and always required a certain amount of fitting. These difficulties explain the objections of the employees and the union to the fixed operating rate of the unit system.

Experiments with improved methods of production have been under way for a number of years, and substantial advances in layout and technique are hoped for. In spite of difficulties, the flow of production in the Watch Division has been much improved. The heavy work is on the ground floor and the medium work is on the second, as in the 1913 plan, but light manufacturing has been rearranged for gravity flow. Beginning with the Hairspring Department on the fifth floor, the process continues progressively to the lower floors, with shipping at the lowest level.

EQUIPMENT AND EFFICIENCY

In some respects the manufacture of watchmaking machinery has overshadowed all other aspects of the watch business. The machinery has often been the controlling factor in both the quality and the cost of the product. When the industry was just starting, machine design was all-important, and it seems probable that the high cost of designing machinery was the underlying cause of the failure of Dennison, Howard & Davis in 1857. That conclusion is implied in Howard's account of the failure of the first machinery designed by Dennison and his statement that Dennison "was not a success in designing or making machinery."[9] It is more than possible, however, that Howard held Dennison responsible for errors that were not his fault; it is very rare indeed that the first attempts to design a radically new machine are successful.

As the Company developed, machine design continued to play an important part in Waltham production and profits. This was certainly true until the death of Duane Church in 1905, and the practice of depending on their own designers probably continued at Waltham until the reorganization in 1923.[10] After 1923, machinery was either designed at Waltham or was purchased from foreign or domestic sources, as seemed expedient. Substantial amounts of machinery were purchased from the Swiss, who have become famous for certain types of mass-production equipment.

For the entire period 1923 to 1943, inclusive, $1,288,330 was spent for new machinery, or 1.5 per cent per year, based on the book value of all machinery as shown on the balance sheet of February 9, 1923.[11] The available data do not warrant any conclusions as to the adequacy of this rate of replacement. The rate of obsolescence on watch-manufacturing equipment may be much lower than is the case for other industries. Visitors to the Waltham plant are shown equipment in operation which is reputed to have been designed fifty years ago by Church. The continued use of this equipment is a tribute to Church's genius, but it may also signify that further improvements in this old and highly developed industry are too difficult to be profitable. Where progress has been very rapid, it may be advisable to rest until the associated mechanical arts have made parallel advances. Table 29

TABLE 29

PRODUCTIVITY OF LABOR, 1790–1937

Date	Place	Man Days per Watch
1790	Geneva, Switzerland	28 days
1802	" "	14
1852	" "	less than 11 [a]
1876	Switzerland — hand methods	about 7½
1854	Waltham	21
1859	"	4
1862	"	3
1883	"	2.2
1905	"	1.5
1913	"	1.6
1922	"	1.7
1926	"	1.15
1930	"	1.32
1937	"	1.05 [b]

[a] This figure is based on the production of gold watches only; a considerable number of silver watches were probably also made. The correct figure is estimated to be about 8 days, or approximately the same as for 1876.

[b] Days of 10 hours.

SOURCES: 1790–1852 Pierre Dubois, *Lettres sur les fabriques d'horlogerie* (Paris: Saintin-Dauten-Pinard, 1853), pp. 18–20.
1876 *La Nationale Suisse*, Chaux-de-Fonds, Nov. 17, 1876.
1859–83 Old payroll and production figures.
1905–22 *Abbot* v. *Waltham Watch Company et al.*, vol. iv, p. 1739, including clocks and speedometers.
1926–37 Watches only. Miscellaneous reports.

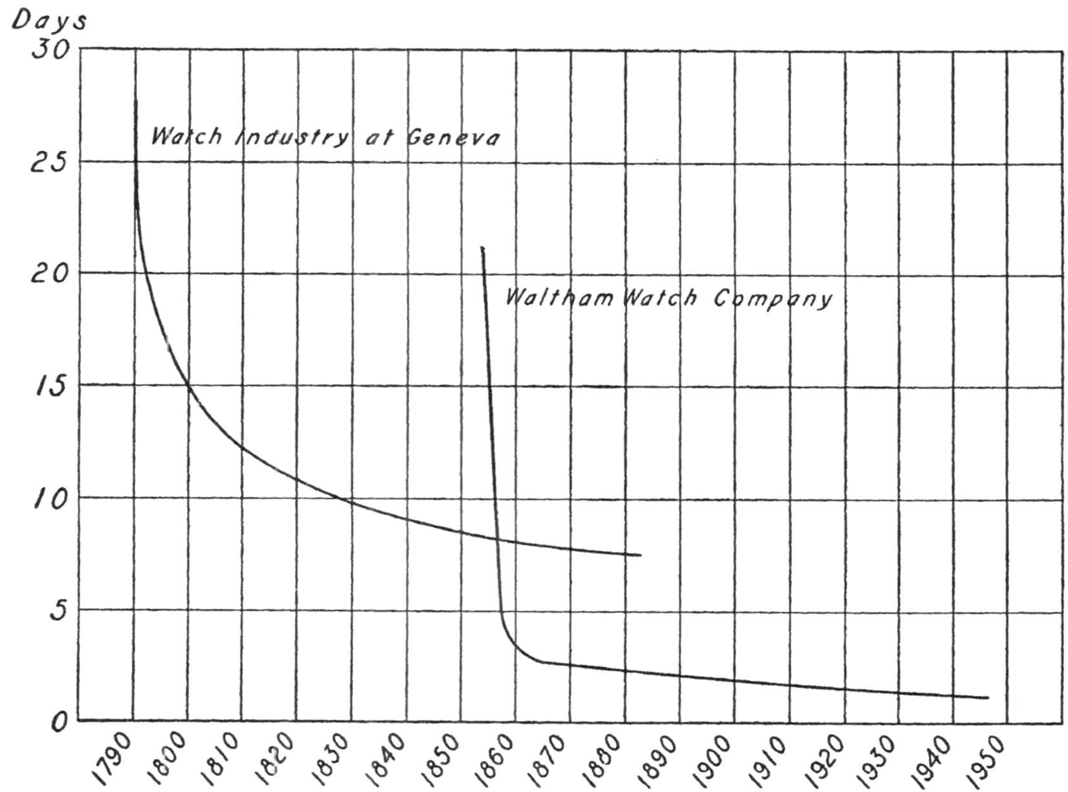

CHART III. Production of Watches — Time in Man-Days Required to Produce One Watch

and Chart III, showing the time required to produce a watch from 1790 to 1937, illustrate the great increase in efficiency resulting from mechanization. The data also support the suggestion that, unless a fundamentally new idea is introduced, further improvements will be difficult. Additional expenditures for new and improved machinery based on old ideas are less likely to yield a satisfactory return.

If we assume that the efficiency of the Swiss watch industry improved but little between 1854 and 1876, it is evident that Dennison, Howard & Davis operated for a period of five or six years at an efficiency below that of the Swiss industry. The curve also indicates that Dennison had reached the point where — if the panic of 1857 had not found him short of working capital — he could have provided successful competition to the Swiss industry.

Minor discrepancies in the production time curve may be explained as follows: the increase in the time required to produce a watch which occurs from 1905 to 1922 is probably a result of inefficient management in the latter part of the Fitch régime. The drop in production time in 1926 represents the results of reforms established by Dumaine. The increase in 1930 may be explained by the change from pocket watches to wrist watches, which require more time to produce. The drop in 1937 indicates that progress was still being made but that it was necessarily limited by the law of diminishing returns. Reports indicate that there was very little difference in efficiency of production between the Waltham Company and its competitors.[12]

QUALITY, WASTE, AND INSPECTION

High standards of accuracy and reliability have been claimed for Waltham watches ever since the founding of the Company, and actual maintenance of these standards has been a primary responsibility of every Waltham administration. The difficulties arising from the small size and delicate construction have been great, but even more perplexing has been the problem of adjusting size, accuracy, reliability, and cost to the varying requirements of the watch markets of the world.

Standards of quality have changed with the changing fashions in watches. In the days of Waltham's greatest fame, quality was precisely determined by the owner's daily check with the chronometer in the jeweler's window. Since the wrist watch came into popularity, quality has become an indefinite compromise between accuracy and size. As sizes have grown progressively smaller, there has been increasing difficulty in producing high and uniform quality. This difficulty is inherent in the small watch and constant vigilance is necessary if a reputation for quality is to be maintained.

The maintenance of Waltham quality stood first in Dumaine's industrial creed, as we have already seen. This policy was followed persistently, in spite of the fact that it was a very costly one. Quality control was Dumaine's sole extravagance at Waltham and perhaps his least successful field of effort.

Since the policy of maintaining quality influences expenditures in every department of the business, the total bill for all the factors that contribute to Waltham quality cannot be estimated with satisfactory accuracy. A rough measure of the cost in 1936 may be obtained, however, from the four major items:[13]

Inspection, 10% of the payroll	$247,200
Waste	500,000
Repairs, loss on operations of Repair Department	50,000
Machinery and tools, maintenance, 8% of the payroll	197,760
Total	$994,960

Again, it is not practical to estimate the proportion of this total that is directly chargeable to quality, nor is it feasible to determine accurately the possible economies in this part of the manufacturing process. But the total does reflect the cost of quality in a general way, and Waltham executives considered it excessive.

In spite of efforts to reduce the cost of quality, very little progress was made in that direction during the period 1923–38. The problem was not peculiar to the Dumaine management. In 1861, Robbins & Appleton, the selling agents in New York, wrote to the factory: "We have a good many complaints about the ladies' watch performance and particularly about the winding works. If there is any radical difficulty then it is of the utmost importance that it should be remedied thoroughly."[14] The problem appears to be inherent in the industry and it has proved very difficult to solve.

Most of the watches rejected by Dumaine's inspectors or returned by dealers showed poor workmanship. While some of the trouble may be attributed to worn tools or to mass-production methods, it seems reasonably clear that the chief cause of poor workmanship was low employee morale.

The general attitude of employees at Waltham appeared to be somewhat lacking in initiative; the intention was to produce a good day's work for a day's pay, but to avoid either excessive effort or original thought. This should be, however, no cause for surprise. Such an attitude is the normal one for the conditions existing at Waltham. The growth of the enterprise had ceased, and therefore the opportunities for promotion were limited. There was a restricted amount of research on new products, and therefore little prospect of broader horizons through new developments. (More will be said on research a little later.) Dumaine's vigorous and powerful personality tended to inhibit the development of initiative in the rank and file. Under such conditions the spirit of competition languished and there was little incentive for a workman to excel either in comparison with his fellow-workers or in relation to an established standard of quality. A quotation from a report by J. Freistadter gives a touch of realism to this generalization. The report reads in part, "There *must* be no more quibbling about tolerances on measurements or crying for larger tolerances. What we need *more than anything else* are smaller tolerances, strict adherence to *them,* and to the proved methods which are producing uniform parts. A man must *not* say, my machine will not repeat [at low tolerance] and rest content. He must roll up his sleeves and help determine why his machine will not repeat."[15]

In criticizing the morale of Waltham employees, there is no intention of discrediting either the employees or the Dumaine management. Emphasis has been placed on morale because the production of high-grade watches demands more voluntary coöperation between labor and management than is needed in the average manufacturing process. Waltham morale was probably better than existed in the average manufacturing plant, but Waltham urgently needed a superlatively high morale. From 1924 to 1944 progress in this direction was slow, but the total improvement was great.

RESEARCH AND ENGINEERING

The Waltham Company did not have a department devoted exclusively to research. There was, however, a Technical Engineering

ASSEMBLING OF WATCHES BY ONE OF THE SKILLED WORKERS

ASSEMBLING OF WATCH PARTS BY MANY HANDS

Department that attended to routine engineering work, designing, and drafting. There was a laboratory for testing materials. There was a Watchmakers' Committee that made suggestions for improvements and criticized suggestions from other sources. But there was no department that was primarily responsible for progress along scientific lines. This, again, is not an unusual state of affairs, but the public has grown to associate leadership in industry with publicized research activities, and the absence of formally organized research at Waltham requires an explanation.

When the Company was founded in 1850, it was purely a research organization. Dennison had an idea, $20,000, and the support of Edward Howard; but he had neither process nor equipment. It took about three years of continuous experimentation to produce the necessary machinery and start the flow of product — the first watches were marketed in 1853.[16] The new plant was built at Waltham in 1854, and production began in earnest. The erstwhile inventors took over the responsibility for production and also continued with their search for better equipment and methods. They were very successful, both as managers of production and as inventors, for total production increased and the time required to produce a watch was rapidly reduced.

Dennison left the Company in 1861, but it continued to be dominated by inventors: Ambrose Webster, Fogg, Vander Woerd, and others. This state of affairs continued until the promotion of Fitch to the position of general manager in 1883 brought a marked change in general policy; then the inventors, like the conservative financial men in the Company, had to subordinate their wishes to the dictates of the Sales Department. Notwithstanding the ascendancy of the Sales Department, the inventors remained in positions of authority in the factory and continued to exert a powerful influence on Company affairs.

About 1900 the Engineering Department was created, but it was not primarily a research organization. It appears to have been almost entirely a service department devoted to technical routine — drafting and the like. Duane Church, E. A. Marsh, and Olof Ohlson, the ranking research men of that time, were not included in the Engineering Department. The formation of this department probably reflects the increasing specialization in the field of engineering that was current at that period, but it does not imply any change in the approach to research problems, except in the execution of routine. Research, in 1900, was still a general function, a part of the duties of management.

During the period of lavish extravagance and overorganization which featured the closing years of the Fitch régime, a special Research Department was set up under Ohlson. Detailed records for that period are not available, and there is some question whether or not the change of title really involved the establishment of a department devoted entirely to original work. If so, it was a temporary departure which ended in 1923. Dumaine returned to the old system. He rechristened Ohlson's group the "Technical Engineering Department," and concentrated Waltham's engineering staff on the task of designing wrist watches and equipment for their production.

Under the plan in force since 1923, the superintendent is responsible for research and technical progress. He draws on the staff at large, and particularly on the Watchmakers' Committee, for suggestions and criticisms. He relies on the Technical Engineering Department and the Laboratory for the translation of ideas into practical results. This method of organizing research appears to be essentially the same as that employed by Dennison. The organization of the auxiliary services in the Watchmakers' Committee, the Engineering Department, and the Laboratory gives formal recognition to a division of labor which existed, to a very considerable degree, in the early stages of the development of the business; the diffusion of research throughout the staff remains the same.

If we refer to the curve of production time in Chart III, we observe that the research function as measured in terms of labor-saving was most effective from 1850 to 1860. From 1860 to 1870 the rate of improvement drops rapidly. After 1870 there is consistent improvement, but the rate is very slow. The curve is deceptive, however, for the brilliant research work done by Church came in the years 1882 to 1905. It is possible that research of equally high character and value has been done from 1923 to date but, if so, the results are not apparent. Church and his accomplishments were much publicized during the Fitch régime, but research has not been featured in advertising since 1923. It is not clear whether this represents a change in performance in the field of research or a change in policy in the field of advertising.

PERSONNEL POLICY

It frequently happens that the character of the chief executive is strongly reflected throughout the organization of a business enterprise. Such an organization is likely to function smoothly and to carry out effectively the instructions of the chief. Such an organization extends and perpetuates the genius of its leader, and it may also duplicate his shortcomings and his prejudices. The Waltham organization has some of these characteristics, and they are the result of a well-developed procedure in securing new employees.

The procedure is simple. Vacancies in upper brackets are filled by promotion and there are few exceptions to this rule. Each executive, whether of major or of subordinate rank, has an understudy. The turnover of executive personnel is low, and the line of promotion is defined well in advance of necessary changes.

New personnel comes into the organization at the bottom. Prospective employees are chosen from the applicant file; they are interviewed, and selections are made on the basis of character as judged by the interested executives. There are no tests for aptitude, skill, or intelligence. Experience and education are not usually important, for skill is acquired on the job. There are three prerequisites for employment at Waltham: an expressed desire to work for the Waltham Company, a personnel record indicating a normal degree of stability, and a satisfactory general demeanor.

Formal training is not usually provided at Waltham, and experience is the only teacher. There is one exception to this rule: applicants for technical work require specialized training: this applies to engineers and watchmakers. Watchmakers are trained in Waltham's own school of watchmaking, which provides nine months' training at beginners' wages. Watch designers, on the other hand, were obtained chiefly from the government horological schools of Switzerland, and eight such designers work in the Technical Engineering Department. Technical men, like the rank and file of production labor, are usually selected from a list of applicants. It is considered by the management at Waltham that the best results are obtained when the initiative comes from the person to be employed.

Out of a total payroll in 1938 of approximately 2,500 workers, 37, or 1.5 per cent, had received some collegiate technical training; and 13, or 0.5 per cent, had received degrees of Bachelor of Science from American colleges and universities. There were no technical employees with higher degrees. Of the 13 employees who held college degrees, 7 were from a coöperative school, the students of which divide their time between study and work in the neighboring industrial plants.

Judging from the personnel records, I should say that Dumaine was partial to students who have found it impossible to complete their collegiate work and to those who have completed it under difficulties. Many employers have followed that policy, notably Henry Ford and Thomas Edison. The net result of the policy depends in a large measure on the shrewdness of the executive in his appraisal of human nature, and on his ability to lead his men in the branches of their work that require bold and independent thought. Where such leadership is lacking, this personnel policy tends to produce an efficient and dependable organization, but an organization incapable of enough creative work to raise it above the level of price-cutting competition.

A deviation from established precedent was attempted in the early 'forties when specially qualified research talent was employed. Dumaine apparently suspected that his personnel policy was having a depressing effect on the Company's research work and he completely reversed his position by obtaining the services of development engineers of the highest professional standing. Rapid progress was expected, but the results were disappointing and the experiment was eventually abandoned. Similar experiments were made in the field of modern personnel management with similar results.

An important part of the personnel policy in recent years has been the payment of a bonus to employees. The first payment of $25 each was made on December 16, 1936, and subsequent distributions have raised the total to $524,856. In some years two bonuses have been paid, one at Christmas and the other just before the annual vacation during the early summer. The bonus was administered as a profit-sharing plan and was discontinued in 1938 when the Company showed a loss for the year. Payments were resumed in 1939 at a lower rate, anticipating the modest profits which were earned in that year. A summary of bonus payments is as follows:

Date	Total to All Employees
Dec. 16, 1936	$ 63,325
June 30, 1937	124,019
Dec. 31, 1937	158,049
June 30, 1939	35,693
Dec. 31, 1939	50,457
June 30, 1940	41,248
Dec. 24, 1940	52,065
Dec. 21, 1941	64,975
Dec. 19, 1942	72,450
TOTAL	$662,281 [a]

[a] Not including wages paid for vacation periods in 1941–42.

to absorb the increased output. When the Waltham plant began to turn out 100 watches a month, new customers were needed.

When this emergency arose, Dennison turned the management of the factory over to Howard and went out on the road to get new outlets for the product. Dennison was a good salesman and succeeded in inducing additional retailers to stock Waltham watches, but the business recession of 1856 developed into the panic of '57 and there was need for still more customers and also need for more capital. The New York firm of Fellows & Shell agreed to supply both; they advanced capital to keep the business afloat, and in return they received the exclusive agency for Waltham watches.[2] This arrangement set the pattern for Waltham distribution for the following fifty-three years. The policy of dealing largely or wholly through a selling agent was followed by Robbins and Fitch until 1911, when the Company paid $200,000 for the cancellation of the exclusive agency contract with Robbins & Appleton.

The agency agreement with Fellows & Shell indicated the direction of progress in watch distribution, but the arrangement lapsed with the bankruptcy of the Company in 1857. The change of methods actually took place slowly, in the following manner. At first, the reorganized Company sold to all wholesalers including Robbins & Appleton, of New York, at 20 per cent discount from list prices. An occasional account bearing no discount, or 10 per cent discount, indicates that sales to retailers were not prohibited.[3] In the following October, Tracy and Baker gave up their active interest in the project and Robbins undertook the management of the plant. At the same time, he established a separate selling agency in his own name. During the next sixteen years, this agency (R. E. Robbins) gradually took over the sale of all Waltham watches, except to a few favored accounts, and it was not until January, 1871, that the agency was given to the firm of Robbins & Appleton. No precise date can be set for the change of method, for it appears that the selling agency was originally set up to parallel the efforts of the factory salesforce. The old method of distribution was not dropped until the new one had developed ample strength.

The use of an exclusive selling agent was an improvement over previous methods. The infant industry was too small to maintain a salesforce adequate for a national market, and the specialized services of an agent were much more effective than the sketchy selling methods originally used by Dennison and Howard. At first the agent's commission amounted to approximately 20 per cent of the list price — the price to wholesalers — but in later years the rate was greatly reduced. In 1910, when the use of a selling agent was discontinued, the commission had been cut to 6 per cent. The estimated cost of distributing through Robbins & Appleton, as of the year 1871, is given in Table 31.

TABLE 31

DISTRIBUTION OF WATCHES THROUGH AN EXCLUSIVE AGENT, 1871
WALTHAM WATCH COMPANY

	Cost Index	Gross Margin (Per cent of selling price)
Cost of Manufacture	100	0[a]
Cost to the Selling Agent	100	20
" " " Wholesaler	125	22
" " " Retailer	161	40
" " " Consumer	268	..
Index of the Cost of Distribution (268 — 100)	168	

[a] Selling expense of the manufacturer.

In 1910 the Company returned to the use of a factory salesforce, against the strong opposition of the Robbins family — R. E. Robbins had died in 1902. Members of the family contended that a manufacturing company was not properly situated to carry the credit risk involved in the large number of wholesale accounts, many of which were maintained on a "shoe string."[4] To this avowed objection it is probably safe to add that the Robbins group did not believe that the factory executives were competent to manage sales activities. Whatever their reasons, the three members of the Robbins family ceased to be active in the Company's affairs soon after the contract with the selling agency had been canceled. Francis R. Appleton also resigned as vice-president, but remained as a member of the board of directors. Fitch was then, for the first time, unhampered in his command of the sales policies of the Company.

The cost of distribution, when using a selling organization managed by the factory, is estimated in Table 32.

TABLE 32

COST OF DISTRIBUTION, 1913 — SELLING AGENT ELIMINATED
WALTHAM WATCH COMPANY

	Cost Index	Gross Margin (Per cent)
Cost of Manufacture	100	9[a]
Cost to the Wholesaler	110	22
" " " Retailer	141	40
" " " Consumer	235	..
Index of the Cost of Distribution (235 − 100)	135	

[a] Selling expense of the manufacturer.

This plan of distribution through a factory salesforce, wholesalers, and retailers was followed at Waltham after 1910; sales by the factory to retailers were prohibited. The method was improved during the period 1930 to 1935, by reducing the number of wholesalers by 76 per cent. Wholesale territories were then much larger than before, and the Waltham wholesale franchise was therefore more desirable. This move strengthened the loyalty of the remaining wholesalers and gave the Company better control over both the wholesale and the retail functions. Under prewar conditions, wholesalers were likely to coöperate with the Company in any feasible measures proposed for stabilizing prices and for promoting fair trade practices.

Figures are not available on which to estimate the cost of direct distribution from factory to retailer. It seems probable, however, that the wholesaler is worth his commission where intensive retail distribution is maintained. On the other hand, selected retail distribution would make it practical for the factory to take over the wholesaler's function. If at some future date it should become advantageous for Waltham to sell directly to a selected group of retailers, it would then be feasible to expand the present sales organization for the purpose.

The difficulties mentioned above are good reasons for the use of caution, but they are poor arguments for the *status quo*. A comparison

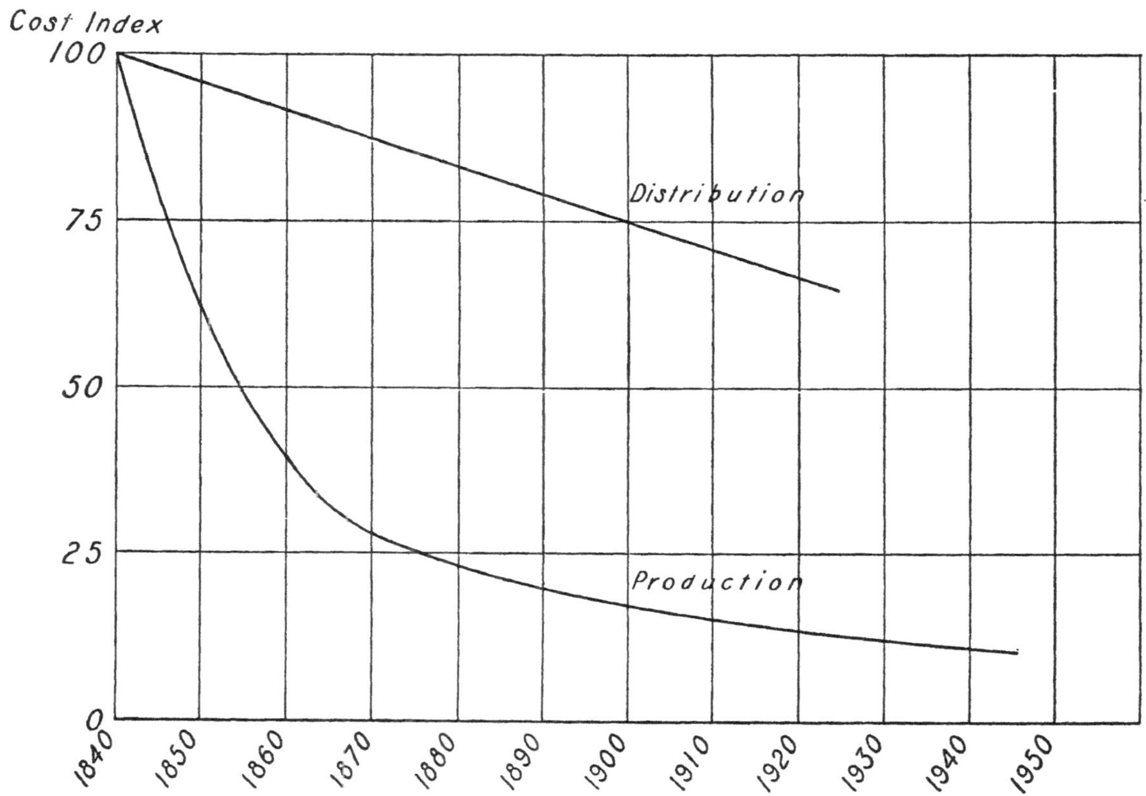

CHART IV. Production and Distribution of Watches — Cost Index Numbers

of the relative improvement in production and distribution indicates that progress in the latter field is likely to be easier and more profitable than improvements in production. Table 33 and Chart IV illustrate the point. The curve representing the cost of production suggests that Dennison's original idea has been exploited nearly to the limit, while the curve of the cost of distribution promises continued important improvements in this field. Theoretical generalizations on distribution are not applicable to particular cases except as they agree with the dictates of practical experience, but the historical facts represented by the table and the curves are very much a part of the practical experience of the watch industry. The historical data given in Table 33 suggest that the cost of distribution can be substantially reduced.

TABLE 33

INDEX OF ESTIMATED PRODUCTION AND DISTRIBUTION COSTS [a]

1840 — 100

	Index of Production Costs [a]			Index of Distribution Costs
1840	Switzerland	100	100	Manufacturer, Exporter, Importer, Wholesaler, Retailer, 1840
1871	Waltham	28	79	Selling Agent, Wholesaler, Retailer, 1857–1910, Waltham
1911 to 1922	Waltham	18	63	Manufacturer, Wholesaler, Retailer, 1910–1939, Waltham
1937	Waltham	12	[b]	Manufacturer, Retailer

[a] Cost of production as approximately determined by the labor in hours. It is estimated that 85 per cent of the cost of production is labor. All figures are approximate.
[b] Absolute figures not available.

EXPERIMENTS IN DISTRIBUTION

There have been radical experiments in the distribution of watches in the past, one of the most interesting of which was undertaken by Robert H. Ingersoll.[5] He came to New York from a Michigan farm, earned $160, and set up a business selling rubber stamps and novelties. The first venture being successful, he branched out into the chain-store and mail-order field. In 1892, Ingersoll conceived the idea of accomplishing, in the *distribution* of watches, what Dennison had done in their production. He started by listing the Ingersoll Watch, purchased from the Waterbury Clock Co., in his mail-order catalogues. The test proved successful and the business expanded.

Ingersoll achieved his goal of quantity distribution, but like Dennison he lacked financial shrewdness. After Ingersoll had become well established in the distribution of watches purchased from the Waterbury Clock Company, he attempted to do some of his own manufacturing — mostly of higher-priced watches. He overextended his resources during World War I and failed in the postwar depression.[6]

Ingersoll's experience illustrates how successful a radical innovation in distribution can be. The simplicity of the undertaking is startling—it is also deceptive. An established firm selling a medium or high-priced product is situated differently; the opportunities for a quick success are very limited. Many factors militate against it. For example, consumers normally rely upon the retail jeweler for advice in the purchase of a watch, and a boycott by retailers would be a catastrophe to the manufacturer. If a manufacturer attempted to operate his own retail stores, the need for variety in the watches displayed and the low frequency of sale would entail a tremendous investment in retail inventories.[7] Furthermore, the difficulties of managing factory-owned, nation-wide retail outlets are staggering.

In spite of the dangers involved, Waltham did permit distribution through the great mail-order houses in the period 1907–09. Minimum retail prices were set, and other control measures were taken; but the independent retailers objected to the competition of the mail-order companies. Although the mail-order companies tried hard to maintain relations with Waltham, the Company found it necessary to prevent supplies from reaching them.[8] Dumaine was convinced that it was impossible to deal with the ordinary retailers and the mail-order houses simultaneously. Of the two types of outlet, the independent retailers were considered more valuable to the Company.

Experience at Waltham has emphasized the dangers of tinkering with the distribution methods. Progress in distribution doubtless can and should be made, but specific measures need to be accurately adjusted to five other factors:

1. Invention or other monopoly.
2. Merchandising achievements.

3. Advertising methods.
4. Consumer buying habits.
5. Current retailing techniques.

CHANGES IN DISTRIBUTION UNDER DUMAINE

Although the general structure of Waltham's system of distribution has not been altered since Dumaine took over the management, there have been many secondary changes: the drastic contraction of sales activity in 1923 was followed by a very slight reëxpansion, new branch offices were opened in Cincinnati and Atlanta, missionary salesmen were added to the staff to maintain contact with the retail trade, and the ban on advertising was substantially relaxed. With these exceptions, the development of the sales organization was toward greater efficiency within the scope originally prescribed.

One important change was made in the method of compensation of the selling staff. Salaries for salesmen and branch managers were discontinued and compensation was placed on a commission basis, Tokyo excepted. The immediate stimulus of commission payments was re-inforced by the long-term incentive afforded by the privilege of buying Class A (management) stock, at a nominal figure. Commissions paid to the various branches in 1935 were variable, ranging from 0.59 per cent to 1.93 per cent of sales.

The net result of these changes is somewhat in doubt. The total sales volume and the decline in selling expense, under Dumaine's management, led to the conclusion that the work of the Sales Department had been highly effective and thoroughly efficient. Any decline in sales from 1930 to 1937 may be attributed to the severe depression of that period. If, however, we examine the sales volume obtained by the individual branch offices, the results are found to be quite inconsistent. Some offices have done very well, others very poorly indeed. This discrepancy may result from a variety of causes. Among the conditions that might give rise to such variation are the following:

1. Changes in demand may affect some territories more than others.
2. Changes in competition may not occur uniformly.
3. A variation in the timing of cyclical movements of purchasing power or business confidence may exist.
4. Local changes in taste or in methods of doing business may occur.

5. Lack of ability on the part of salesmen or branch managers may be important.
6. Inadequate compensation, or other factors, may produce low morale in some offices and not in others.

Variations in performance among branch offices are usually associated with problems in personnel or compensation. In this instance territorial lines were not observed in making sales, a circumstance which adds further confusion to a complex problem.[9] The variations in branch-office performance are given in Table 34.

TABLE 34

INDEX OF SALES BY TERRITORIES, 1927–1937
(1927 — 100)
WALTHAM WATCH COMPANY

Year	Cincinnati	Chicago	Pacific Coast	North-eastern	New York	Total [a]
1927	100	100	100	100	100	100
1928	128	101	77	77	92	85
1929	181	123	77	66	100	90
1930	151	127	59	61	68	74
1931	67	45	29	40	36	45
1932	51	40	22	23	28	31
1933	7	47	13	13	29	33
1934	38	67	24	28	42	48
1935	53	103	27	29	60	64
1936	..	..	..	..	..	81
1937	..	..	..	..	..	84

[a] Including foreign sales.
SOURCE: Waltham records.

The most significant comment on the achievements of the Sales Department under the management of Dumaine and Boucher is a comparison of the figures for selling expense for 1922, the year of Simonds' management, with 1937.

	Sales	*Selling Expense*	
1922	$5,459,905	$879,459	16.1%
1937	5,800,040	271,066	4.7

SELLING TO FOREIGN MARKETS

Up to the beginning of the second World War the method of distributing Waltham watches to foreign markets was very simple: the small volume of sales (7 per cent) did not justify an elaborate or expensive organization. Simplicity and economy were obtained by passing the responsibility to foreign agents. In Great Britain and Japan the agent dealt in Waltham watches only, but in other cases a general agent is used. The present organization of the foreign sales work was the result of experiment rather than theory, the London office being used as a field laboratory. The experiments have been expensive and have matured slowly, but a highly successful arrangement has been developed. Even the negative experiments are of interest in illustrating some of the major hazards of selling in foreign markets.

At the time of the reorganization, Dumaine went to England to look over the situation. After a preliminary survey, he returned to the States and sent Boucher and H. E. Melzar to London to revamp the whole arrangement. At that date, 1923, the English subsidiary (The Waltham Watch Company, Ltd.) was owned equally by the Waltham Company and the Dennison Watch Case Company, of Birmingham, England.[10] The active management of Waltham, Ltd., was in the hands of Major Gilbert Dennison, grandson of Aaron Dennison. Gilbert's father, Franklin, was then president of the Dennison Watch Case Company and a director in Waltham, Ltd., but he had no precise knowledge of affairs at the London office. These affairs, as a matter of fact, had gone so badly that Boucher decided to demand an immediate change in the management.

Several very serious criticisms were made of Gilbert Dennison's stewardship of Waltham, Ltd. The operations, according to figures prepared by accountants brought from America, resulted in a loss of £1,820 2s. 2d. for the period March 1 to June 1, 1923, and in an accumulated deficit of £28,242 18s. 11d. on the latter date.[11] Additional criticism arose on the grounds that the Dennison Company had received prompt payment for cases, while accounts payable for Waltham movements had been allowed to stand on the books. Any such preferential treatment of the Dennison Company was contrary to the agreement made when Waltham, Ltd., had been established. Boucher also was opposed to the English marketing program: Gilbert Dennison operated a large London office, employing 32 people in an unsuccessful attempt to deal directly with the retailers instead of through wholesalers.[12] The result of this program was to alienate the support of some eighteen wholesalers who concentrated their efforts on selling competitive goods.

When Boucher told Gilbert's father of these and other difficulties in the London office, he won the older man's support for a change of management. Since Franklin Dennison's vote gave the Waltham interests a majority of the directors of the English subsidiary, it became possible to effect an immediate reorganization, and a new régime was established forthwith. Accordingly the London staff was reduced to about half a dozen employees, the office was moved to smaller and less expensive quarters, and the distribution of watches to the retail trade was returned to the wholesalers. Subsequently, accounts between the Waltham and Dennison interests were settled by vesting complete ownership of Waltham, Ltd., in the parent company plus a payment by the Dennison interests of £5,502 4s. 1d.

The new manager for the London office was carefully selected. Dumaine knew him personally and had great confidence in his ability. To guide him during the first year, Dumaine called from retirement a former London manager, A. R. Harmon. Harmon had been highly successful in London and had enjoyed a long residence there; he knew the country well. In 1915 he had written to Ezra Fitch, "This morning there are reports that an air raid has been made on the 'hoopskirts' of London and that we may now be prepared to have a visit from them each morning before breakfast. Nobody seems to be very much frightened although of course it will be a serious matter, as there will surely be loss of property and lives before the thing is disposed of." Such an old hand should have been an excellent guide for the new manager, but perhaps the difference in age and experience was too great, for friction between them was reported. At any rate, the new manager did not prove successful, and in 1925 H. A. Hudson, the bookkeeper during Gilbert Dennison's régime, was appointed as head of the London office.

The appointment of an English-born manager appeared to be a step in the right direction, but in 1926 the sales in England fell below 17 per cent of the previous year's volume. Dumaine decided to make a personal investigation and set out on a tour of the English trade. He found that the market had been demoralized by the importation of Waltham watches through unauthorized channels and by the sale at cut prices of movements so imported. This confirmed the cable previously received from Gilbert Dennison, which said, "It is imperative you take drastic steps to prevent importation movements [into] England otherwise nothing can prevent disaster." The situation was further complicated by price-cutting on the part of a few English wholesalers, and the practice of applying Waltham dials to Swiss movements was suspected. The situation was very serious and there was need for a strong hand in the London office — a man who was a diplomat, a politician, and a power among the English wholesalers. Such a man was found in C. A. Schierwater, of the firm of wholesale jewelers, Schierwater & Lloyd.

In 1929, Schierwater signed an agreement by which he was to organize and wholly own the English subsidiary, subject to control by the main office at Waltham. The agreement was highly advantageous to the Waltham Company, for it passed to the agent the credit risk, the responsibilities of management, and the risk of incurring an operating loss, at the same time limiting the resale prices and profit margins. But the contract was by no means one-sided, for Waltham provided the stock in trade and carried the burden of obsolescence. As a result, the agent was required to put up very little capital, merely enough to take care of rent, payroll, and similar operating expenses.[13]

Schierwater had unusual qualifications for the enterprise. A native Englishman and senior partner in a well-known firm of wholesale jewelers, he had the experience and standing in the country so necessary to success. At the same time, his knowledge of American business practice and his sympathy with American temperament assured an easy understanding between the home office and the foreign branch. His interest in American affairs extended beyond the area of business, for shortly after the Waltham agreement had been signed he married the daughter of an American banker.

Other foreign selling has been managed by agents of foreign birth. The formation of a separate subsidiary has not been advisable, except in England, by reason of the smaller volume of business elsewhere; the general principles of the Schierwater agreement have been followed, however, as far as has been practical in each individual case.

The Tokyo office was a notable exception to the rule. That office was operated, in 1935, as a branch under the management of the Sales Department at Waltham. Compensation was by salary instead of commission. Selling expenses for the Tokyo branch were substantially higher than for the domestic branches or for the London agency, but that cannot be attributed solely to the methods of management which were employed.[14] The Tokyo branch was small in proportion to the others, which tended to result in higher expenses; and conditions peculiar to Japanese trade in recent years may have been the governing factors. Details are not available.

In spite of the skillful management shown in the handling of foreign sales, Waltham has not been successful in greatly stimulating foreign business: approximately 7 per cent of production has been sold in foreign markets in recent peacetime years. It is interesting, though perhaps unfair, to compare the present volume with Waltham's export sales in 1877. Robbins said in his report for that year, "Our foreign trade is now fully a quarter of our total business and seems to be growing in all directions."[15] This success may be explained by the fact that the Swiss had not fully adopted the American principles of watch manufacture.

MERCHANDISING FOR COMPETITIVE ADVANTAGE

The problems of merchandising are closely related to production, but in this chapter we shall consider only those factors which bear on distribution. The chief issues are:

1. What kind of watches will consumers buy?
2. What qualities are required?
3. What prices will consumers pay?
4. What section of the demand can Waltham serve to best advantage?
5. Can Waltham develop latent demands by offering new kinds of watches and show a profit on the undertaking?

The answers to these questions given by Waltham officials have gone to wide extremes according to the temper of the executives and the circumstances of each period. Merchandising policy at Waltham has been a very important and highly debatable issue.

When Dennison began the manufacture of watches, he stuck very closely to the well-defined standards of the day — with the glaring exception of the 8-day movement. But Dennison kept this conservative attitude toward merchandising only long enough to solve the fundamental manufacturing problems. As soon as the factory was running in a reasonably satisfactory manner, he turned his attention to the design of new and different watches in order to extend the scope of Waltham's market and to increase the volume of sales.

Until December, 1857, Waltham manufactured one movement, which was identified simply as a lever movement. At that time a less expensive model, the *C. T. Parker,* was put on the market. The old lever movement was sold for $23; the new *Parker,* for $15. This was followed by the *P. S. Bartlett,* in January, 1858, which sold for $12. In December, 1858, a new movement called a *Chronodrometer*—presumably a stop watch—appeared on the books at $30. Such a complete reversal of policy in a single year speaks well for Dennison's fertile mind and for Robbins' courage as an entrepreneur. But there was an end to Robbins' enthusiasm, and when Dennison proposed another model at a still lower price for the use of Civil War soldiers, Robbins balked —Dennison resigned.

The conservative attitude toward merchandising did not last long. Under the stimulus of the war boom it soon gave way to a very aggressive policy.[16] By 1865, the inexpensive watch for the army, the *Ellery,* was selling at the rate of nearly 3,000 per month; and ladies' watches were being made in both *Parker* and *Appleton Tracy & Co.* models. After the war the policy continued to be aggressive, but competitors copied each new development so quickly that it was difficult to keep an advantage for any considerable period. As aggressive merchandising became more expensive and less profitable, the policy lost favor and was gradually dropped.

During the first World War and the postwar boom, Waltham dropped far behind, and merchandising leadership passed to the Swiss. This was the state of affairs when Dumaine took command at Waltham. For the next twenty years, the abilities of Dumaine's designing staff were taxed to keep pace with the developments in Switzerland. The Swiss made rapid strides in the design of very small, reasonably accurate movements, and Waltham followed their example, carefully avoiding extremes of fashion and mere novelties. But Waltham, under Dumaine, only followed; there was no aggressive merchandising

ADVERTISEMENT, 1940

of Waltham Watches after the *Premier Maximus* appeared in 1911.[17] There were few distinctive Waltham improvements, no really distinguishing Waltham features.

In the early part of Dumaine's régime, attention was concentrated on the problems of production and finance, with eminently successful results. From 1927 to 1938, however, it became increasingly evident that greater effort outside the fields of production and finance would be required to maintain Waltham permanently in a position of leadership in the industry. Dumaine recognized the necessity for action on a wider front, but tradition and custom — in the trade, the industry, and the Company — are highly resistant to change in new directions. In spite of the obvious difficulties, in 1927 Dumaine was ready for an experiment in aggressive merchandising. The first step was taken in August of 1927, when Page Browne was appointed sales and advertising manager and Boucher turned all his attention to production. Browne was a man of broad experience, a former army officer, trained in practical advertising and selling methods by his work with the Curtis Publishing Company. He was a disciple of the new faith which shapes both policy and action to the needs and susceptibilities of the ultimate consumer. Browne's plan was to cater to the buying public and to appeal directly to the consumer in the national magazines. There was nothing radical about the plan, and there was ample precedent for it in the successful merchandising methods used by the importers of Swiss movements.

Browne had two years of good business, 1928 and 1929, in which to prove the merits of his plan, but two years were hardly enough to apply and test a major change in policy. After 1929, retrenchment was the order of the day, and in 1931 Browne resigned.

After 1931, Dumaine's merchandising policy was cautious rather than aggressive, and caution may have had more than a little merit in a period characterized by business instability. The line for 1938 consisted of 45 models, most of them cased at the factory. These cased models were built up from 6 sizes of wrist-watch and 4 pocket-watch movements. The movements contained from 9 to 23 jewels, 34 of the models using 17 jewels. Prices to the consumer ranged from $17.50 to $200, with most of the wrist watches selling between $25 and $45.

All models in the line were branded *Waltham Premier,* which carried the inference that they were all of the same high quality, the *Premier Maximus* being the Waltham masterpiece of an earlier day. This device smacks strongly of trading down[18] the *Premier* brand, but brand policy at Waltham has often been one of expedient. The usual practice has been to attach a new brand to each new or improved movement and to trade down on this top brand when it was replaced by something still newer. It is difficult to be convincingly critical of a practice that has been attended by so much success over a long period of years,[19] but the advisability of using the brand *Premier* on a 9-jewel movement is open to question.

Quality emphasis has also varied throughout the lifetime of the Company. Dennison started with no high-flown notions of quality. "The Roxbury watch appeared like a good common English watch. The movement had rather an English look . . . with English and French construction combined. . . ."[20]

Beginning in 1857 less expensive watches were produced at Waltham, and, from the time of the Civil War until World War I, Waltham watches were offered in a wide range of jeweled grades.[21] After the World War, Fitch devoted almost all effort to the production of the high-grade watches so much in demand during the hostilities and let the machinery for producing less expensive watches stand idle. Dumaine in 1923 threw the emphasis to the 7-jewel grades; after 1931, however, he had difficulty in meeting competition from Elgin and the Swiss producers. With the Hamilton Company well established in the high-grade brackets, the best opportunity appeared to be in the *middle* range, and since 1931 the Waltham Company has been putting its chief effort into that field.

In brief, Dumaine's merchandising policies at Waltham appear to have been sound from a conservative financial viewpoint. The limited line of products permitted efficient manufacturing schedules and simplified selling problems. On the other hand, the policies were not aggressive and did not offer much prospect of a better-than-average increase in sales for the predictable future. They did not contribute any appreciable competitive advantage.

ADVERTISING AND ITS LIMITATIONS

Waltham advertising in the 'thirties fell into three categories, each addressed to a different objective:

To the dealer.
To the consumer, for the dealer.
To the consumer, for Waltham.

Advertising directed to the dealer consisted chiefly of catalogues, window displays, and other dealer helps. This type of advertising was the first consideration at Waltham, and it dovetailed nicely with the policy of depending on the dealers, both wholesale and retail, for the real work of distribution. It was a primary necessity in good times and bad.

Advertising directed to the consumer, for the dealer, consisted of newspaper advertising, the expenses being shared by the retailer and the Company. This advertising was supposed to purchase retailer good-will, to bring customers into the retailer's store, and to produce in some small degree a consumer preference for Waltham watches. If we may judge from the frequent comment in the records, this form of advertising attracted customers to the retailer, who then sometimes attempted to switch the customer to a watch of Swiss manufacture which carried a higher retail profit. The continued use of coöperative newspaper advertising suggests that the results were satisfactory in the majority of cases, but the criticism stands — the practice of advertising well-known American brands and switching to Swiss products robs this phase of the advertising campaign of much of its value. There is also the objection that the use of newspaper space in this fashion involves a great deal of duplication. This form of advertising does not dovetail to good advantage with the policy of intensive retail distribution.

Advertising to the consumer, for the benefit of the Waltham brand, took the form of space advertising in the national magazines, point-of-sale leaflets for jewelers' counters, and the *Waltham Watch* display signs used in jewelers' windows. The value of this type of advertising depends on a number of variables that have changed radically during the lifetime of the Company. A review of the records of consumer advertising at Waltham will throw some light on the practice of recent years.

Both Dennison and Robbins believed in advertising. In 1857 there were few buyers for Waltham watches, but American watches were *news* and Robbins set aside $2,500 (4½ per cent of the total assets of the Company) for advertising. The total advertising expenditure from 1854 to 1859 was $4,559.36. The value of most advertising is open to debate, but at this stage of the development of the industry, and for many years afterward, the Company had something of importance to tell the public; it had a story with real news value. The probability of profitable returns was high.

The advertising used in the heyday of Waltham success and continued up to the time of the reorganization was "prestige" advertising, directed at both the dealer and the consumer. The tone was dignified, some of it distinctly Victorian in its heavy formality and high moral tone. Nevertheless, much of it was good, hard-hitting copy — straightforward and convincing.[22] Expenditures varied from $15,000 in 1916 to $275,000 in 1921.

The copy included three major appeals: claims of superior quality, a defense of the dealer against the mail-order houses, and disparagement of Swiss watches. The copy, the paper, and the printing all helped to sustain the concept of Waltham quality. For a considerable part of this period (1865 to 1917) Waltham enjoyed a reputation for superlative quality, which gave specific support and value to the consumer advertising campaign. During World War I, Waltham prestige suffered heavily because of the neglect of the watch business resulting from participation in the production of time fuses for the War Department. This loss of prestige threw Waltham performance out of mesh with Waltham advertising, and some readjustment was in order at the time of the reorganization in 1923.

Dumaine made drastic changes in Waltham's advertising policy, changes in volume, quality, and character. Practically all advertising was suspended at the time of the reorganization; when it was resumed on a small scale, the character or tone had been altered. The stifling rectitude was gone — and that was a blessing — but with it had departed some of the dignity and prestige that the older copy had carried so convincingly. The copy had been modernized, but not in the best manner. It had been "jazzed up," but much of the sincere, hard-hitting quality was gone. These deficiencies were largely corrected in later efforts, and the resort to cheap paper and printing was abandoned; in spite of improvement, however, Dumaine did not achieve an advertising technique equivalent to the 1895 standard.[23] It is only fair to add that the task of modernizing an antiquated ad-

REPRODUCTION OF AN ADVERTISEMENT SHOWING STYLES OF WATCHES, 1941

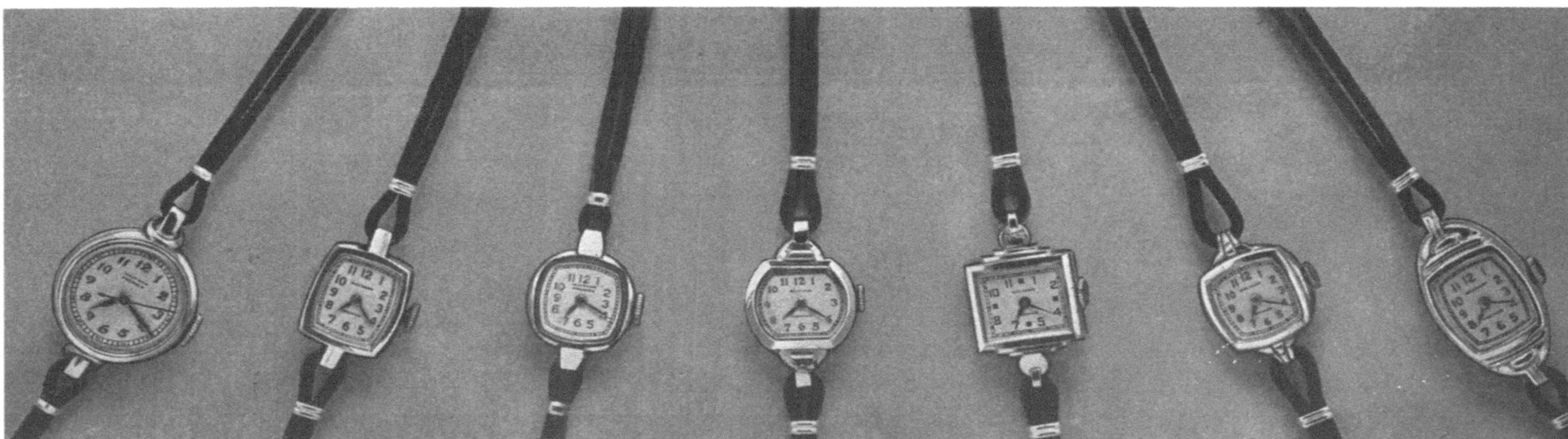

vertising technique on a small budget is beset with almost insuperable difficulties.

The use of *Waltham Watch* signs on the rear windows of automobiles was another moot question. These decalcomania signs were a simple, dignified device, a trifle smaller than a doctor's "shingle," with gold lettering on a black background.[24] The signs were originally made for use in jewelers' show windows to identify Waltham dealers. Subsequently, about 1932, the idea of placing them on the rear windows of automobiles was conceived and, in six years' time, 934,187 had been distributed. It is assumed that most of them were actually installed, since men were hired to place them on cars at 10 cents each, reporting the license number and owner of the car to the Company. At one time the management considered this a very effective form of advertising, and this opinion has been reflected in editorial comment in local papers.[25] The signs provided publicity undoubtedly, but the effect of that publicity was always open to question. About 1940 Dumaine reversed his appraisal of the distribution of decalcomania signs to motorists and the practice was stopped.

In one respect Dumaine followed early precedents in Waltham advertising, that is, by participating in the large industrial exhibitions. Although Waltham displays of that period were less lavish than some of the earlier ones, Dumaine had the advantage of being able to show a very fine collection of antique watches. This collection, valued at $250,000, was bequeathed to the Waltham Company in 1934 by Franklin Dennison, son of Aaron Dennison, the founder of the Waltham enterprise. Items in the collection date back to the early sixteenth century.

The value of advertising in national magazines was questioned by Dumaine. A flexible allotment of from 7 to 10 per cent of the 1938 advertising appropriation was set aside for this purpose, but without any very real enthusiasm or conviction that the expenditure would return a profit.[26] This hesitation is quite logical. In the absence of advertising copy having genuine news value, the probability of a return on the investment is reduced. Until such a time as renewed research or aggressive merchandising provides items having news value to consumers, there is limited justification for making large appropriations for space advertising.

CHAPTER XVI

FINANCE AND MANAGEMENT

THE WALTHAM WATCH COMPANY started in a corner of Howard's clock shop in Roxbury and grew to be a $22,000,000 concern. The speed and extent of this growth was phenomenal, for $22,000,000 is a large amount of capital to concentrate in a single company of a relatively minor industry. How was it done? From what sources was this capital derived? What promises of profit were necessary to persuade the owners of these funds to invest them in Waltham securities? How well were those promises fulfilled? The Waltham records provide definite answers to some of these questions, as well as much of the essential background of business sentiment during the critical periods in the past ninety years. Both the facts and the sentiments are necessary to a realistic view of the process of financial growth.

THE EXPERIMENTAL PHASE, 1850–1857

The Watch Company began as an experimental enterprise, based on the theory that watches could be manufactured by the same mass-production methods that were used for rifles at the Springfield Arsenal. The analogy was not apparent to prospective stockholders, but Dennison won acceptance for this eccentric notion by his dominating personality. He was a promoter of ardent persuasiveness and great driving force. Tracy said of him, "Mr. Dennison was always sanguine and could make more figures showing [profitable] results than any other man I ever met." And again, "Dennison, like the man in the Scriptures, kept writing and coming to Philadelphia, importuning us and multiplying figures on the greatness of the American watch."[1] Dennison had the restless enthusiasm and the contagious optimism of a visionary; at the same time he displayed a confidence and poise that was magnificent. Any period since the Industrial Revolution would have afforded sufficient scope for Dennison's talents, but he was particularly fortunate in launching the Waltham enterprise — the most difficult of his many ventures — in the early part of a speculative boom.

Prosperity had begun in 1845, and by 1850 speculation had acquired considerable momentum. Hunt's *Merchants' Magazine* of January, 1850, reported, "The position and prospects of cotton are flattering; for nearly a year, the market has been on the rise . . . and prices now range from 60 to 100 per cent over those current one year ago."[2] And in the same issue, "The arrivals [of gold] from California at the Philadelphia Mint, up to the close of November, had reached $3,800,000, and the arrival of the Crescent City has supplied a further sum of $1,218,000, to various firms. . . . Under all these circumstances favoring the continued abundance of money, there is a growing disposition to speculate; real estate, and stocks particularly, are showing such results as must necessarily promote confidence in them as investments."[3] This optimism was not merely the result of gold inflation and speculation in commodities, for it had a firm basis in the growth of production and trade. Hunt's *Merchants' Magazine* says on this this point, "The United States manufacturers have taken 50 per cent more cotton this year than for the corresponding season last year."[4] And, too, business showed greater seasonal stability. "The business of the fall usually ceases with the closing of the canals, which took place this year on the 5th of December. Of late, however, the use of the telegraph and the increase of railway communication, has served to prolong transactions throughout the year. . . ."[5]

Under these favorable conditions, Dennison succeeded in obtaining funds for the Roxbury plant from men who were poorly prepared for the venture. The project was a radical departure for which no precedent existed, and none of the men connected with the original enterprise, not even Dennison, had had any experience in the actual manufacture of watches. They were small industrial capitalists of limited means, each successful in his own restricted field. They were induced to invest in this extremely risky enterprise by Dennison's eloquence, by their own ignorance of the obstacles in the way of success, and by the speculative fever that was current at the time.

The plant was built and the business prospered — that is to say, good watches were produced cheaply by machinery — but the early machines were obsolete before the product had reached the market. There were no profits, but only ever increasing expenditures for the design and construction of equipment. After three years' experience in manufacturing, expenditure still exceeded income, and it became apparent that the financial requirements of the enterprise had been underestimated. The resources of the original investors were already severely taxed, and the failure to pay dividends made it extremely difficult to attract new investors of the original type. In this emergency it was necessary to draw funds from a new class of capitalist, and small speculators offered the most promising source.

In view of the poor record at Roxbury, speculators had little confidence in the future of the Watch Company. Profits, if any, were likely to be tremendous — Dennison had no difficulty in demonstrating that proposition — but the risk of total failure was correspondingly high. It was necessary to give the project greater stability, and Dennison achieved this end by combining watchmaking with land speculation. Land gave the venture an element of residual value, even if the watch factory failed completely, and the watch factory increased the speculative value of the land. The financial devices for accomplishing this *tour de force* were simple but effective. In principle they closely resemble the methods used by Kidder, Peabody & Company at a much later date.

The reorganization of the Watch Company was completed in the spring of 1854. Under the stimulus of Dennison's oratory, a land company was formed and christened the Waltham Improvement Company. Land speculation was already under way in Waltham, and small investors were eager to share in the large profits that were being reaped in this field.[6] One hundred shares of stock in the Improvement Company were offered to the public at $1,000 par value per share, and in ten days all the stock had been subscribed.[7]

The details of the financing were arranged with considerable skill. More working capital was wrung from the original partners in the Watch Company on the threat of losing their previous investments; the great speculative risk continued to be borne by them. The stockholders of the Improvement Company supplied the site for a new watch plant, subject to a mortgage; and they provided funds for erecting the buildings, in exchange for demand notes.[8] But advances of cash by the Improvement Company to the Watch Company were largely offset, in the long run, by the payment of cash assessments on the 25 shares of Improvement Company stock held by the Watch

Company. The net effect of this intricate arrangement was to provide a new plant for the Watch Company from the funds of small speculators, under arrangements which appeared to entail a minimum of risk for the latter. As a final appeal, the subscriber for a share of stock in the Improvement Company was required to pay only $50 down and the balance in installments of $50 semiannually.[9] It was a very attractive offer.

The new Company had difficulty in obtaining a charter. An act of the State Legislature was required, and strong opposition was encountered in both House and Senate. Popular prejudice against land companies ran high, and the situation was complicated by the fact that a local politician was also speculating in Waltham land.[10] Fortunately, the Improvement Company was not without friends. The Chairman of the House Committee on Corporations was a stockholder, and support was not lacking in the Senate. After a lively and heated campaign, the charter was granted.

State control of corporate enterprise in this period — like federal control today — was directed against speculative excesses and the business reactions which followed them. In this period of sustained prosperity, 1845 to 1857, there was every temptation to indulge in wild-cat speculation of fraudulent or merely injudicious types, and some degree of public control seems altogether logical. The Massachusetts statutes dealing with the subject undoubtedly exercised a salutary influence in restraining unwarranted optimism, but they fell far short of the purpose for which they were conceived. Their effect, in the case of the watch companies, was temporarily to impede the flow of capital into a new industry without safeguarding the project from future difficulty. The failure of the Watch Company in 1857, and again in 1922, did not result from an excess of speculative enterprise but rather from a deficiency of working capital. So long as the capital structure of corporations deviates from sound and adequate standards, no amount of government regulation is likely to prevent periodical liquidation.

About a year before the failure of the Watch Company in 1857, Dennison made a third attempt to raise money, this time along new lines. In his first campaign he had obtained funds in amounts of $10,000 to $20,000 from industrial capitalists who were plungers for their time and place. The second campaign drew capital from small speculators, chiefly residents of Waltham, in amounts from $350 to $700.[11] In this third attempt he used little discrimination as to the persons approached — every possible source of funds was tapped. The banks lent money against deposits of finished goods. Charles Rice advanced funds on a chattel mortgage. Various companies provided materials on long credits. Fellows & Shell, the New York jobbers, offered $20,000 in exchange for watches and the exclusive Waltham agency. The partners raised as much as they could; Samuel Curtis, according to Crossman, "had by this venture and other unsuccessful investments, whitened his hair with care and brought himself down, in his closing years, to the verge of bankruptcy."[12] A considerable sum was raised, probably exceeding $35,000, but to no avail. The plant was auctioned off at a sheriff's sale in the spring of 1857.

The settlement of the Watch Company's affairs was a heavy blow to the original entrepreneurs. They lost their entire investment, which was estimated at $150,000.[13] The proceeds of the sale, about $44,000, were prorated among the general creditors. The mortgages were assumed by the new owner of the plant.

MANAGEMENT IN THE EXPERIMENTAL PHASE

During this first period in the Company's history, 1850 to 1857, the major functions of finance and management appear to have belonged to Dennison. There is, however, some evidence to the contrary. In the first place, Edward Howard was treasurer, and the title often carried the authority of chief executive in New England concerns of that period. Dennison says of him, "I do not think there were seven times in the seven years we were together that we had money enough to pay all our employees at the time their wages were due. Very often we found ourselves without any cash on hand, but Mr. Howard would manage some way to produce enough to tide over with."[14] W. H. Keith also gives Howard much of the credit for management of the enterprise,[15] and Crossman says, "The practical details of the business of the company, however, were in large part left to Mr. Edward Howard. . . ."[16] In spite of the evidence that Howard was the manager of the firm, the context of the records strongly suggests that Dennison had the greater share of executive responsibility. In the loose organization which they seem to have used, he probably held the final authority by reason of his dominating personality. At a later period we find Dennison, as an employee, at loggerheads with the management of the Company, and it is not likely that he would have tolerated a subordinate position in the original venture.

There is also some question in regard to the capital contributed by Dennison. The records show that he was the holder of four shares of stock in the Waltham Improvement Company in 1853, but they do not mention that he contributed financially to the Watch Company proper. In any event, it seems certain that his influence on the management was far greater than his financial interest in the venture justified.

Although the records are incomplete and contradictory, they give considerable support to the theory that diffusion of ownership led to injudicious management and financial failure. It is interesting to note that Dennison was successful in at least three ventures which he both owned and managed: the jewelry business in Boston; the early stages of the Dennison Manufacturing Company; and the Dennison Watch Case Company, of Birmingham, England. He failed in the Waltham Watch Company, the Tremont Watch Company, and in two similar ventures where he was responsible for the management of capital which was not his own.[17]

When Dennison was faced with bankruptcy, in the spring of 1857, he embarked on a fourth attempt to raise money for the Waltham enterprise. This time he succeeded in interesting the firm of Tracy & Baker, creditors of the Waltham Company to the amount of approximately $8,000. Influenced partly by the desire to recover the credits advanced, and partly by Dennison's confident forecast of large profits, Tracy and Baker agreed to put up $7,500 each, and persuaded Royal E. Robbins to join them. Robbins agreed to provide $35,000 as a silent partner.[18] From the chain of circumstances previously mentioned, it is clear that Dennison was the moving force until Robbins became infected with Dennison's optimism; from that point forward, Robbins unquestionably dominated the field.

At this point the character of the ownership and management changed. The new capitalists were New Yorkers, men of mercantile pursuits. Robbins' experience had been entirely in trade, chiefly in watches. The firm of Tracy & Baker had been devoted largely to the importation of watches, although the partners also operated a watch-case factory in Philadelphia. Baker was also speculating in western land. He was an office man, a fine penman as one may see in the opening entries of the surviving cashbook. The advent of these men into the watch industry marks the beginning of the ascendancy of the market place and the countinghouse over the workshop and the factory. They brought to Waltham a stiffening of business discipline; they were responsible for the slow transition of emphasis from production to distribution, to finance, that was to continue to the time of writing, 1944.

NEW MANAGEMENT AND NEW SOURCES OF CAPITAL

After the sale in bankruptcy, changes in management were rapid. The interest that Tracy and Baker took in the enterprise soon waned, probably as a result of the panic which occurred a few months after they had embarked on the undertaking. Baker sold his share to Robbins for $6,000; Tracy, although he retained his financial interest, took no active part in the Company's affairs. Dennison remained with the new Company as mechanical superintendent, a subordinate position which he apparently did not relish. These changes left Robbins virtually the sole owner, with complete command of the business — a circumstance which he had not anticipated.

The panic of 1857 put the reorganized Company to a severe test. Robbins could not supply the capital needed to keep the business going, and he sought outside assistance. Two Boston merchants supplied funds against finished watches deposited in State Street banks, "at the moderate rate of 18%."[19] Watches were sold at auction in outlying cities such as Providence and Portland. Most important, however, was an entirely new source of capital so far as Waltham was concerned — that is, *labor*. Faced with the alternative of complete unemployment, the workers voluntarily contributed one-half of their wages in order to keep the business afloat. This expedient for obtaining working capital from labor was used by Robbins in 1857 and again in 1860.[20]

The year 1858 brought a brisk recovery and Robbins, his finances somewhat strained by the panic of 1857, protected his position by consolidating the Land Company with the Watch Company. Robbins traded a half-interest in the Watch Company for a half-interest in the Land Company and a $20,000 bonus in cash. He also purchased for himself, or for the accounts of friends in New York, 28 shares in the original Land Company. This gave Robbins a majority ownership and absolute control of the consolidated Company. By this maneuver the small investors were involved, more deeply than in 1854, in the speculative venture of watchmaking; and Robbins reduced his risk by diversification in the less hazardous business of land speculation. The most significant phase of this transfer is the development of a body of minority stockholders, many of them new ones, who did not have any effective voice in management. These investors had every confidence in Robbins' executive ability, and they were content to be silent partners in his enterprise.

The Civil War brought prosperity and a new source of capital—earnings. For the next twenty-five years, 1860 to 1884, the outstanding capital stock was increased from $200,000 to $1,500,000. Of this amount only $350,000 represented new investment, the remaining $950,000 being earnings re-invested in the business. In later years, 1885 to 1906, new capital amounting to $2,500,000 was obtained, and $1,500,000 of this sum came from earnings.[21] On one occasion a stock dividend of 150 per cent was issued. At other times cash dividends, as high as 66⅔ per cent, were paid at dates coinciding with the issue of new stock in like amounts.

In spite of the lavish additions of capital through new investment and the re-investment of earnings, the amounts obtained were not sufficient for the requirements of the business. The Company resorted to borrowing. Bank loans and the sale of commercial paper had been sources of *seasonal* working capital from the beginning of the enterprise; since 1884, however, funds from these sources formed an increasingly large part of the Company's permanent capital. By 1921 the Company's commercial paper had become unsalable, and bank loans stood at $8,000,000.

Still another device for obtaining capital was used in 1906, namely the capitalization of earning power. During the period from 1900 to 1906 the corporations of the country enjoyed a remarkable prosperity, which in some cases resulted from the formation of trusts and trade agreements. Waltham profits for that period reached unprecedented heights, about four times the usual figure. In 1906 the directors took advantage of this good fortune by issuing common stock to the amount of $7,000,000 par value. Of this amount $3,300,000 was covered by earnings retained in the business, and the remainder represented a capitalization of earning power. Since the stock was distributed as a dividend, the capitalization of earning power did not bring capital into the business; the stock dividend was, however, a source of capital to those who sold the stock before the temporary earning power disappeared.

SECOND PHASE OF FINANCIAL DEVELOPMENT, 1857–1922

In 1857 the management at Waltham was typical of industrial capitalism at its best. Robbins owned and operated the business himself. Under his absolute rule the Company weathered its first and most dangerous depression, beginning with the panic of 1857. But this ideal simplicity of organization did not continue long. In 1858, Robbins shared his venture in watch manufacturing with the stockholders of the Waltham Improvement Company, but he kept a majority of the stock in his own hands. In 1862, because of the dilution of his interest through the sale of new shares to the public, he lost his majority by a small margin. In 1863 he recovered majority ownership, not in his own right, but as leader of a group consisting of eight members of the Robbins family and his associate, D. F. Appleton. Robbins continued to control the Company by virtue of this closely related group until 1866, when his holdings declined to 29 per cent of the total. This date marks the end of control through personal or family ownership of a majority of the stock.[22]

The loss of majority ownership did not, however, mean the loss of control of the stockholders' meetings. Until his death in 1902, Robbins could always muster enough votes to carry any measures that he advocated. In 1901 the Robbins group, consisting of 16 persons or firms, owned 32 per cent of the outstanding stock — more than the total number of votes cast at the stockholders' meeting of that year.[23]

Although Robbins retained a nominal control over the stockholders' meetings throughout his lifetime, the effective control of management began to pass from his hands about 1883. Before that date, Robbins, as treasurer, had been chief executive in the fullest sense of the word, the office of president carrying only nominal responsibilities.[24] After 1883 he shared the burden of executive duties with Fitch, who became general manager in that year and president in 1886. Ten years later, Robbins' health was seriously impaired and he leaned more heavily on his son Royal, who was being trained to succeed him as treasurer, and on Fitch. After Robbins' death, both ownership and management gradually passed from the Robbins group, and in 1911 Royal Robbins and Francis R. Appleton resigned as treasurer and vice-president, respectively, leaving a free field to the new owners of the business.

With the decline of the Robbins group, the balance of power was transferred to a new class of investor, consisting chiefly of lawyers and bankers. These men, such as Augustus P. Loring and George P. Gardner, derived their influence not only from their own holdings but largely by virtue of the stock which they controlled as executors, trustees, or financial agents.[25] Individually or collectively they dominated the board of directors and participated fitfully and ineffectively in the actual management of the Company. They knew that Fitch's management was not satisfactory, but they were unable greatly to improve it. Divided among themselves as regards the nature and scope of the corrective measures to be applied, they were ill equipped to harmonize the conflicting forces that were undermining the efficiency of the organization. The concentration of power necessary for decisive action was lacking, and their good intentions were hampered by the necessity for compromise.[26]

The investment bankers made an appearance at this same period, but there is nothing to suggest that they exercised any influence on the management of the Company. J. P. Morgan was a comparatively large stockholder as early as 1901, when he held 1,334 shares in his own name and 200 shares for J. P. Morgan & Company. In 1910 Kidder, Peabody & Company held 786 shares of Preferred stock, and H. C. Wainwright & Company owned 1,660 shares. The Wainwright Company, with several others, was active in trading in the Company's securities.

The responsibility for the management of the Company, from Robbins' death until the collapse in 1921, rested almost entirely on Ezra Fitch; yet it hardly is fair to condemn him, without reservation, for the financial disaster that occurred under his leadership. At no time, as far as the available records show, did Fitch own enough stock to give him control of the stockholders' meetings. And he not only failed to control the board of directors but was unable even to gain their confidence, if we may judge from their frequent attempts to interfere in executive matters. Fitch was the titular head of a system rather than a dominant leader. He personified the accumulated precedent of Waltham's era of growth and prosperity; under his régime the old forms of management were preserved, but the substance of authority had departed. The management was sustained by momentum, and it followed the path of least resistance. There was no force in the Company strong enough to drive it in a new direction.

FINANCIAL DEVELOPMENT — THIRD PHASE, 1923–1938

The depression of 1921 precipitated a financial crisis at Waltham that had been long in the making. New capital was urgently required to replace the funds that had been squandered through waste and inefficiency, but the Company's credit was gone and no further funds could be obtained from the familiar sources. The sale of securities was not feasible, for the Company was already overcapitalized. The market for Waltham's commercial paper had been saturated early in 1921, and since that date Waltham had relied on the commercial banks for both permanent and working capital.[27] The commercial banks had been induced to supply funds in 1921 to protect their previous commitments, but in 1922 they refused to carry the load any longer and demanded payment in full.

The uncompromising attitude of the commercial banks was the result of their unsuccessful venture at Waltham into the field of financial capitalism. When the banks supplied additional credits in 1921, they demanded that the management of the Company be turned over to them. The errors of the management from 1910 to 1921 had been so obvious that it seemed a comparatively simple matter to recoup the Company's losses by installing a competent industrial executive as president. This the banks did, but the results were not satisfactory. The nature and extent of the difficulties that confronted the chief executive at Waltham were far more serious than the banks had supposed, and they sought to transfer the responsibility and the risk to other shoulders.

RE-COMBINATION OF OWNERSHIP AND MANAGEMENT

At this juncture it was necessary to supply approximately $7,000,000 and a manager of exceptional force and ability. No individual capitalist could be found to undertake the venture; the only adequate source of funds lay with the small investors, and they lacked confidence in the current Waltham management. The first requirement was for a manager who was well known for his outstanding ability. The sec-

Pencil drawing made under the direction of Irvin Noyes Gould

THE PRESIDENT'S OFFICE, WALTHAM WATCH COMPANY

ond was for the surrender by the stockholders of a substantial part of their equity. The third was for the endorsement of the reorganized Company by a conservative firm of investment bankers, having a large clientele. The investment banking house of Kidder, Peabody & Company arranged to fulfill all these requirements. In brief, that firm supplied the Waltham Watch Company with sound management and endowed it with the confidence of the investing public.

For ten years following the reorganization, Kidder, Peabody & Company represented the investing public on the Waltham board of directors. Through the firm's close relations with the new president, F. C. Dumaine, they provided the connecting link between ownership and management.[28] Although the investment bankers were able to combine ownership and management only by proxy, there is every indication that the device was quite as effective as the actual combination of ownership and management in a single person. Under investment banker control, Waltham enjoyed the unity of purpose, the firmness of policy, and the promptness and precision of execution that are characteristic of a strong, centralized authority.

The control of Waltham affairs by the investment bankers was not, however, a permanent arrangement; when their services were no longer important to the Company, the control ceased. Kidder, Peabody & Company retained actual stock ownership in the Company only until 1928, but the firm continued to be represented on the Waltham board of directors until 1932. The extent of the control exercised by the investment bankers and the duration of their influence cannot be estimated with any considerable degree of accuracy. There was undoubtedly a gradual transition from the complete control exercised at the time of the reorganization to an entirely negligible influence after 1932.

SUMMARY

The history of the Waltham Company may be summed up in terms of the general development of capitalism.[29] The enterprise was founded at a time when the transition from mercantile capitalism to industrial capitalism was in full swing. The growth of the Company followed the common pattern of development of the times. A period of rapid expansion was followed by financial complications and the intervention of financial capitalism.

In 1850 the original organization was typical of the early stages of industrial capitalism. The partners in the enterprise were inventors, promoters, and manufacturing executives, each a specialist in his own line of endeavor. Both Howard and Dennison were promoters with an inventive turn of mind, and many of the employees of the new Company showed marked inventive talent. Howard, Davis, and Curtis were manufacturers; Charles Rice, who came to their assistance about 1856, was also interested in manufacturing. This group of specialists possessed a great deal of the technical skill and experience which was so necessary to the success of the enterprise, but the scope of the business was too great for them. Its scale exceeded the limits imposed by their financial resources, and the complex problems of management required a degree of coördination that was far greater than they were accustomed to employ. The procurement of supplies from foreign sources; the design of product, factory, and equipment; the sale of a new product in a nation-wide market; the raising of large amounts of capital — all these problems had to be solved simultaneously or the business could not succeed. In this respect the Company differed from the usual pattern. Most enterprises under early industrial capitalism began as small, specialized ventures, catering to a local or regional market; but the manufacture of watches was conceived as a mass-production industry and it could not succeed on any but a grand scale.

Bankruptcy proceedings in 1857 eliminated the small manufacturers from the business and brought in men with mercantile experience, R. E. Robbins and the Appletons. Dennison remained with the Company long enough to assist in the reorganization, but his departure in 1861 left the business entirely in Robbins' hands. This new arrangement was also typical of the early stages of industrial capitalism. Merchants, faced with the decline of profits in general trade, turned, as Robbins did, to dealing in special lines and to manufacturing. Some of them retired; others took up banking; others followed the example of John Jacob Astor, becoming landlords and land speculators. The talent for finance and the insistence on business discipline which these merchants brought to their new pursuits were frequently of great value. This was true at Waltham, and a liberal share of the credit for the rapid growth of the enterprise may be attributed to the influence of mercantile experience.

After 1883 the increase in competition became alarming and Waltham history, from that date to the present, tells of a series of moves intended to prevent competition from reaching destructive proportions. Various devices for curbing it were tried, some of them with great success, but the success was only temporary. No permanent advantage was gained until 1923, when the methods of financial capitalism were applied by Kidder, Peabody & Company and F. C. Dumaine. Dumaine raised the financial management of the Company to new levels of efficiency, partly by native skill and partly by the application of simple and precise methods of cost accounting. He also introduced new standards of industrial discipline and provided a sound basis for renewing the coöperation between labor and management which had been lost under the previous régime. Under his direction the varied activities of the business were balanced and coördinated.

There is some question about the recent status of the Company as regards its place in the categories of capitalism. From one point of view, the enterprise is still an example of organization along the lines of financial capitalism. The Dumaine management displayed many of the best qualities that are normally associated with the control of industry by financial leaders. On the other hand, the influence of financial *institutions* on Waltham policy appears to have been very slight, and the abuses of financial capitalism seem to have been entirely absent. There are grounds for the view that the Company returned to a state of industrial capitalism under the predominant ownership and the management of Dumaine.[30]

CHAPTER XVII

A CHANGE IN STRATEGY

Waltham Goes to War, 1942

War production under Dumaine reached its peak and perfection during the war years of 1942–44. The variety of products manufactured in support of the war effort is evidence of the marked versatility and skill of both management and labor.[1] The list of war items includes the following:

Aircraft clocks of four types.
Aircraft and camera tachometers.
Chronometers of several types.
Compasses.
Fuses: base detonating, percussion, and mechanical time fuses.
Pick counters.
Recording drift sights.
Remote-control cables.
Rifle parts.
Speedometers.
Springs, compensating precision.
Watches for navigation, fire-control, railroad, and general military service.
Precision parts in wide variety.

In quantity of war production the Waltham performance is outstanding. As of February 28, 1945, shipments of war goods totaled $28,458,000 and unfilled war orders stood at a peak of $9,688,000. The record for punctual delivery has also been exceptionally good, and no government contract has been canceled for failure to deliver as promised.

In the matter of quality, Waltham workers finally achieved a standard of excellence that was all that Dumaine could ask for. In 1943, the average government watch shipped from the factory gained or lost not more than 12 seconds per day and some were within plus or minus 3 seconds.[2] This performance is much better than the rigid government standards require.

This record — in such great contrast with Waltham performance in the first World War — was partly the outcome of sound management methods applied over a twenty-year period, and partly the result of special measures taken to offset the difficulties of war-time operation. When the disorganizing effect of war pressures began to be felt, Boucher made two changes in his production organization. He appointed Pierre Dumaine, better known as "Spike," to the position of Assistant Manager; and he set up a central factory office.

"Spike" has none of his father's fire and drive — these qualities are supplied by Boucher. Indeed, Spike is to be judged by other standards, for he makes his own distinctive contribution to the management team. He is friendly and quiet; he carries the calm assurance that eleven years of experience in the plant and his thorough grasp of factory operations justify. The men like him, and he enjoys Boucher's full confidence.

The use of a central factory office is based on a management principle that is often ignored — the principle that executive privacy impedes coördination. Privacy is the father of conferences, and conferences beget multiple offspring of debate, confusion, delay, and overhead. One can often measure the decay of a business organization by the growth of partitions in the offices. Indeed, one of Boucher's first moves when he came to Waltham in 1923 was to tear down the partitions in the general offices, and the establishment of a central factory office was one more step in the same direction.

The factory office consists of one large, well-lighted room. In the room are eleven desks for the use of the manager, his assistant, seven departmental superintendents, and two secretaries. Boucher still uses his formally appointed office next to that of the president for the entertainment of guests; but, from 7 A.M. to well after closing time, he is more often to be found in the factory office. Foremen do not use this office. In case of trouble, a foreman calls his superintendent into the department; the factory office is merely the coördination point for the top bracket of factory management. The last time the author visited the factory office Boucher apologized for the three superintendents who were seated at their desks. "They should all be out in the plant at this hour," he said.

Waltham's war production has received the official stamp of government approval, the Army-Navy E. In addition to this formal acknowledgment, Waltham files contain many letters of commendation from officials of the armed forces, among them letters from the Royal Canadian Air Force, the Air Technical Service Command (U. S.), the Boston Ordnance District, the Navy Department, and others. One of these, noteworthy for its brevity, reads as follows:

> Thanks for your kind letter of the 18th. The fact that [this Service] is buying quantities of these 16-jewel Waltham Hack Watches is in itself the highest sort of commendation because they have tested watches of various makes and Waltham rates highest.

MANAGEMENT AND LABOR, 1941–1945

To understand labor relations at Waltham you must be introduced to Walter W. Cenerazzo. He is president of the Waltham Watch Workers Union and also national president of the American Watch Workers Union, which includes the Waltham, Elgin, and Hamilton locals and the California Watch Workers Union. Born in Somerville, Cenerazzo was heir to the Boston political traditions and he has been active in political work as far back as he can remember. Although trained from infancy as an organizer, Cenerazzo is predominantly an administrator and economist. He is well aware of the fundamental fact that the union's first task is to promote the prosperity of the producing companies and that the second is to bargain for the greatest possible reward. He has a working knowledge of cost accounting, a ready flow of thought and speech, the zeal of a prophet, the tenacity of a bulldog, and the patience essential to a successful negotiator.

Cenerazzo organized the Waltham workers in 1941. He acted for the International Jewelry Workers Union, A. F. of L., but he had very little help from them. Cenerazzo personally borrowed money from a bank to finance the formation of the new union and was repaid on a commission basis of 50 cents per member. The whirlwind course of that campaign is characteristic of Cenerazzo's methods and success. His campaign plans are constructive, positive, and specific. His appeals are not lacking in emotional quality and he does not refrain from *criticizing* the Waltham Company when occasion warrants, but by his own

WAR PRODUCTS, WALTHAM WATCH COMPANY, 1945

statement he has never *attacked* the management. This moderation springs in part, no doubt, from his membership in the old, well-seasoned union of printers.

The Waltham local was at first affiliated with the International Jewelry Workers Union, which, in turn, was a member of the American Federation of Labor. This affiliation, however, proved a bar to joint action with the employees of other watch companies. Accordingly, the Waltham Local was disbanded and reorganized as an independent union. The ultimate goal was to make the union a power in the industry as a whole. The first issue of the independent union's official publication stated, "Our Organization is dedicated to bring about a uniform contract in the plants of the Elgin National Watch Company, the Hamilton Watch Company, and the Waltham Watch Company."

Cenerazzo carried his campaign at Waltham to a successful conclusion under the banner of high wages. The Waltham *News Tribune* of March 18, 1941, carried the headline, "Watch Workers To Seek 30 Per Cent Raise." At that date the union claimed 1,600 members, and a week later won the election by a 4 to 1 vote. The wage increase initially granted was approximately 2 per cent for men and 14 per cent for women, but the total increase since the union was organized has exceeded the union goal, as Table 35 figures show.

TABLE 35

AVERAGE WAGE RATES PER HOUR, 1940–1943[a]
WALTHAM WATCH COMPANY

	Male	Female	Combined
Jan. 13, 1940	$ .64	$.39	$.51
Dec. 15, 1940	.65	.42	.53
Apr. 19, 1941	.66	.48	.57
Apr. 4, 1942	.77	.49	.63
Feb. 6, 1943	.918	.589	.731
Nov. 6, 1943	1.00	.739	.842
Increase Dec. 15, 1940, to Nov. 6, 1943	.35	.319	.312
Per Cent	54	76	59

[a] Excluding overtime and bonus.

SOURCE: Records of the Waltham Watch Company.

Other gains for which the union may take a share of the credit are set forth in the contract which took effect October 30, 1943. In each job classification, seniority regulations protect the average worker from favoritism and from competition of younger or faster workers. Minimum hourly wage rates are set for day work and for piecework. The principle of equal pay for equal work by men and women is accepted. A premium of 10 per cent is agreed upon for night work. Vacations with pay are granted, an employee of at least two years' standing being entitled to a vacation of two weeks. A group-insurance plan has been established. A Joint Committee of labor and management has been set up "to discuss suggestions from employees, questions of working conditions and production (but not grievances not concerned with production) and to make such recommendations to the Employer in connection therewith as the Committee may agree upon."[3]

Relations between the union and management have been pretty much a matter of friendly coöperation. Demands for higher wages have been referred to the War Labor Board, where they have received sympathetic consideration and prompt action. The Company has not been involved in wage controversies. The specter of insecurity, which so frequently induces unexpected and irrational demands, has been laid effectively by the long list of good jobs open at high wages. And, perhaps most important of all, labor's aspirations for prestige have been met with courtesy and understanding on the part of management.

The mechanism for maintaining smooth industrial relations is simple and effective. Dumaine, Sr., took no part in the negotiations with union representatives. The burden fell on Boucher, who has shown an adaptability unusual in a man of strong convictions. He has laid aside whatever prejudice he may have acquired in previous clashes with labor unions and has maintained a uniformly coöperative demeanor. His superintendents have fought with Cenerazzo, as occasion has arisen, but Boucher has kept strictly clear of these more or less amicable altercations. Of course, the record has not been perfect. On at least one occasion Boucher was forced to appeal to Cenerazzo to bring his people into line with their contract, which Cenerazzo promptly did. Boucher says of him, "He's a straightforward, honest fellow with a big heart." The give and take of collective bargaining as Boucher and Cenerazzo practise it might well serve as a standard of excellence for both management and labor.

Cenerazzo has taken an active part in the industry's campaign to restrict the importation of Swiss watches. On April 23, 1943, he appeared before the Ways and Means Committee of the House of Representatives on behalf of the workers in the watch industry. His demands were much stronger than the petitions presented by the Company in previous years. He said in part:[4]

> We ask that this Congress keep within its hands the power to approve these [reciprocal] trade treaties; insist that no article, whether of farm or industry, be allowed to land in this country for one cent less than the cost of competitive American-made goods.
>
> Is there any good reason why products of workers in Switzerland should continue to control 50 to 80 per cent of the American watch market?

The cause for alarm is evident from the statistics on imports given in Table 36.

TABLE 36

IMPORTS OF SWISS WATCHES AND MOVEMENTS, 1934–1942

Year	Number of Watches and Movements	Foreign Declared Value
1934	920,393	$ 2,834,092
1935	1,201,986	3,668,645
1936	2,228,606	5,877,676
1937	3,127,274	8,183,117
1938	2,386,226	6,562,570
1939	2,919,147	8,057,789
1940	3,536,982	10,220,772
1941 [a]	4,400,000	13,700,000
1942 [a]	5,700,000	20,700,000

[a] The figures for these years are obviously not on the same basis as for the other years.

SOURCE: Boston *Traveler*, June 1, 1943. Cf. New York *Times* for May 22 and May 23, 1943.

DUMAINE'S FINANCIAL RECORD, 1923–1943

Late in 1943 the accounting firm of Stewart, Watts & Bollong drew up a summary of Dumaine's financial stewardship at Waltham, as shown in Appendix F. Briefly summarized, the figures tell us that

Dumaine took a plant valued at 4 million dollars and, by a shrewd management of finances, made it yield 24 million dollars over a period of twenty years. Of these 24 million dollars, 4½ millions went for taxes, 2½ millions were paid as interest to the owners of borrowed capital, and 17 millions accrued to the stockholders as dividends or as equity in the business. By July 2, 1943, 6 million dollars in bonds and debentures had been paid off and the outstanding prior preference stock had been reduced from $1,700,000 to $377,730. The Company was in sound financial condition. A considerable feat had been performed.

The uses to which Dumaine put the funds which he took from the business were conservative. The net increase in working capital was $4,262,052, of which $2,922,893 was in cash. Of the 17 millions available for distribution to the stockholders only $3,305,481 were paid as dividends; the remainder went to strengthen the financial position of the Company. This thrifty policy did not please some of the stockholders, who entered suit against the Company for the distribution of additional dividends. The suit was dismissed by the lower court but, on appeal to the Supreme Court of Massachusetts, the decision was reversed. The final decree awarded to the stockholders dividends on the Class A common and the 6 per cent preferred stock for the years 1939, 1940, and 1941.

The June, 1944, issue of the *American Watch Worker* carried an article announcing the sale of Dumaine's interest in the Waltham Watch Company to the Union Securities Trust Company of New York. The article goes on to say:

> Frederic C. Dumaine represents truly the significance of the name "New England Industry." He represents a school of thought that built America. His personal and business integrity is unquestioned by all who know him.

By the year 1944, Dumaine had reached his major objectives at Waltham. The task that he had set himself in 1923 was finished. The challenge had been met; the opportunity had been turned into profit. At Amoskeag and other textile mills he had sold off the remaining assets of a dying enterprise, but at Waltham he had shown the world that he could build a solid manufacturing establishment on the wreckage left by flagrant mismanagement. At the age of seventy-eight, with this and many other accomplishments behind him, he was more than a little weary and somewhat discouraged. Further effort at Waltham promised little in the way of new achievement for him, and so Dumaine accepted an offer for his interest in the Company and turned over the job of president to a younger man.

WALTHAM GOES ON THE AIR

On October 11, 1944, the Waltham Watch Company began a series of broadcasts on the Mutual Network. To anyone familiar with Waltham policy, as expressed by Dumaine, this broadcast revealed great changes in the making on the banks of the Charles. The scene of Aaron Dennison's industrial idyl had gradually lost its Arcadian beauty until the still waters reflected only the brick walls of the watch plant, the sagging verandas of what was once the Riverside Club, and the black reaches of a railroad siding. From these drab surroundings the flow of wages and profits continued in reassuring volume, but there was nothing there to stir the spirit or lift the heart. Today (in 1945) it is different, for Waltham is animated by a new personality, the atmosphere is charged with a new spirit, and action is spurred by a new hope.

Ira Guilden, who succeeded Dumaine as president of the Waltham Watch Company, bears a superficial resemblance to the typical successful American executive, but if you test his mettle you will find a new alloy cast in the old mold. The pattern is traditional: Ira, at the age of ten, helping his widowed mother in the little candy store in Brooklyn; Ira, at the age of seventeen, leaving a commercial high school to travel for a small jewelry-manufacturing firm, selling jewelry and imported watches; Mr. Guilden, aged twenty-six, buying the decadent Knickerbocker Watch Company and building it from a one-man firm to an organization with national distribution; Mr. Guilden, aged thirty-two, vice-president and director of the Bulova Watch Company; and, at forty-eight, president of Waltham. In addition, Guilden found time to serve as director and chairman of the Board of Trade Bank and Trust Company of New York City, and, in recent years, as business consultant and adviser to the Longines-Wittnauer Company.

Some executives kill two birds with one stone — Ira Guilden uses a shotgun and bags the limit. Take the matter of the Waltham Bond Rally. This affair was Guilden's formal introduction to his fellow-workers and to the community. It was staged in the grand manner, but the limelight was shared with the generous courtesy that is so characteristic of his dealings at Waltham. The guests of honor were Leverett Saltonstall, Governor of Massachusetts and U. S. Senator-elect; Maurice J. Tobin, Mayor of Boston and Governor-elect; and Robert F. Bradford, Lieutenant-governor. Sumner Welles gave his regular nation-wide radio broadcast under Waltham sponsorship, while the others were confined to a local station. The union acted as hosts and sponsors for the rally, although the Company defrayed all expenses. Boucher was one of the speakers and Michael J. Kelleher, Chairman of the Greater Boston United War Fund, was master of ceremonies. The rally was held in the Embassy Theatre and opened with a first-run movie. The occasion was an unqualified success.

Guilden's speech was reported in full in the January, 1945, issue of the *American Watch Worker*. He spoke briefly and simply of his plans for Waltham and the basic tenets of his business creed. He paid tribute to Boucher and "Spike" Dumaine and Cenerazzo, and then continued:

> Now let me tell you of the new management's hopes and plans for Waltham and for the after-war prosperity for Waltham Watch workers. When I came to Waltham, I burnt all my bridges behind me. I am in the American watch business *only* and in it right up to my neck, — and don't let anyone tell you different. My allegiance is to America and American industry. As President of this Company I tell you we shall have the finest machinery, install the latest devices and shall have working conditions second to none in the industry. . . . I believe we have more skill, more genius, more "know how" here than anywhere else and . . . with your help we can make Waltham the first American watch in every sense.

These remarks might have been taken for platitudes, had they not been followed up instantly with specific plans, already well begun, as everyone knew.

> Let me elaborate. More styling is needed in the Waltham Watch of the future. We shall have the best. . . . To assure us a market for our product, a forceful advertising campaign had to be undertaken, — a campaign that could successfully compete with and be superior to our competitors'. . . . But first, and above all else, we need a good product, — good Waltham movements. That is where *YOU* come in. . . . We must give the American public a Waltham of superior time-keeping quality. Waltham Watches must function accurately and with dependability, and *that is your responsibility.*

IRA GUILDEN

President of the Waltham Watch Company, 1944–

Guilden also spoke of increasing production and a thousand additional employees, and of how that end was to be achieved through the ultimate buyer's pride of ownership. He spoke of the stability of the organization and of the management's personal interest in the workers and their families, and then closed with this paragraph:

> An old friend of mine, whose judgment I respect, said to me a long time ago, "Show me activity and I will show you opportunity," which means, as I interpret it, wherever there is action there is change. If you give me action, I will do the same for you and we shall both — you and I — have opportunity — opportunity that will assure a full measure of prosperity to Waltham when peace is with us again.

Guilden's address at the Bond Rally was a bold prophecy and a direct challenge. He promised an abundance of those two great spiritual commodities, *security* and *opportunity*. In return, he demanded faithful and intelligent coöperation. That is a fair bargain for both parties, and there is good evidence that both of them can and will deliver as promised.

THE ART OF MERCHANDISING

The business of selling jeweled watches is a traffic in ideas. It is not only the watch itself that counts — watches are not bought on specifications or performance — it is the emotional satisfaction of the consumer that is paramount. High standards of dependability and accuracy are essential — so also are adequate profit margins — but the critical variable in the watch business is merchandising, and Guilden is an expert merchandiser.

The first consideration in watch merchandising is style. Guilden knows from his experience, both here and abroad, how powerful is the appeal of style. He knows from years of selling in every one of our own forty-eight States what are the aesthetic standards of the country's watch buyers. To what use he can put his experience and aptitude at Waltham, of course, remains to be seen.

We are all born with a desire for prestige, but envy and advertising give specific direction to our instinctive yearnings. Advertising, therefore, is the mill or factory where prestige is manufactured for distribution with each watch that goes across the counter. To sell prestige one must have prestige, and the advertising must be geared to that purpose. It must be appealing, continuous, and superior; anything less than that is a drain on the reservoir of consumer preference. Guilden's use of these principles is already fully evident at Waltham.

The past, however, is no exact measure of Guilden's future; he has set new standards and new objectives. Among the ambitious and socially valuable plans for Waltham publicity is the Air Time Research Institute, a non-profit organization financed by the Waltham Watch Company and governed by a distinguished board of trustees.

The excursions into advertising and public relations which have been mentioned here are only the highlights of preliminary undertakings. The complete campaign promises to be of large proportions, designed for the long perspective.

The new merchandising plans at Waltham call for higher quality (watches of 17 jewels or more) and for larger volume. The result should be better values for consumers, higher margins for dealers, and adequate profits for the Company. Distribution policies have not been announced as this volume goes to press, but Guilden's experience has proved that the effective use of advertising as a selling tool can expand a market manyfold.

RECEMENTING THE ORGANIZATION

"Production," says Guilden, "is just people at work." This is no casual epigram as Guilden uses it; it is a mature philosophy, meticulously applied to practice.

Guilden wants the best machinery available for war production and postwar watches, and so "Spike" Dumaine was flown to Switzerland in an Army plane to get the types not available in this country. He wants the best industrial manager in the industry, whom he believes he has in Boucher, and so he has doubled his salary. He wants the best technical man in the field and he knows how to get him. He buys on the same philosophy that he sells — on the belief that premium quality is worth much more than it costs.

But Guilden does not try to buy his way blindly into perfection; many other considerations bind his people to him and ensure the best use of their talents in his service. He knows the value of courtesy and personal consideration. He sets the working pace and personally leads his organization toward the goals he has set, but he shares both the responsibilities and the honors with his associates. Whatever the place or the company, he is always at ease and interested in his surroundings, and that simple confidence in the present and the future is as contagious as laughter.

Where personal leadership is strong there is often a lack of sound organization, but that does not seem to be true of the new management at Waltham. No chart is necessary, for there is a simple line organization as follows:

Ira Guilden, President
I. E. Boucher, First Vice-President and Manager
Leo Kamion, Vice-President for Sales and Merchandising
Pierre Dumaine, Assistant Manager

It is an inflexible rule that every executive and supervisor shall have a competent assistant, so that the Company cannot be crippled by the unexpected loss of a key man. Guilden says, "I'll set the policies and give it the impetus, then it's got to function without me."

Guilden's selection of Leo Kamion as Vice-President for Sales and Merchandising is worthy of note. Kamion brings to Waltham a knowledge of watch cases and watch distribution. He was General Manager of the Kamion Watch Case Company and more recently President of his own enterprise, the American Perfit Crystal Corporation. He and sales promotion, and a reputation for straightforward honesty. was chosen for the Waltham post because of his combination of professional standing as an executive specialist in style, development, That reputation will be an asset in the proposed expansion of Waltham's dealer organization.

FINANCIAL CHANGES

Guilden first approached Dumaine about the purchase of the Waltham Watch Company in 1939, shortly after his resignation from the Bulova Company, but the negotiations were not completed until 1944. At that time Guilden, with the support of his investment bankers, agreed to purchase Dumaine's interest at $11 per share of B stock. The market price was $8. The agreement specified that the Guilden interests would offer to buy the stock of all stockholders willing to sell at the same price. The other stockholders were not in a selling mood, and the market value of the B stock climbed to a peak of $30 per share.[5] From these events it is evident that Guilden is no novice in financial matters. On the contrary, in matters affecting the financial requirements of his companies, he has acted as financial manager for his firm on previous occasions with success. The investing public seems to have confidence in his ability.

The details of Waltham's new financing are set forth in the Registration Statement filed with the Securities and Exchange Commission. If the plan is accepted by the stockholders, the new capital structure will consist simply of 5% Income Debentures and Class B common stock. The 7% Prior Preference stock will be called and purchased for cash. Shares of 6% Preferred stock will be exchanged for $120 of Income Debentures per share of Preferred. Class A common will be exchanged on the basis of 5 shares of Class B stock for each share of Class A. The debentures have been protected against inflation by making them convertible into Class B common stock at the ratio of 4 shares of Class B stock for each hundred dollars of debentures.[6] It is planned to list the stock on the New York Stock Exchange.

BUSINESS LEADERSHIP

Leadership at any given stage in the development of capitalism requires all the old skills and at least *one* new one. Guilden meets these requirements. He emphasizes craftsmanship as the foundation of all business. He is a trader and a merchant; at home or abroad, in watches or platinum or cotton or machinery, he is a master in the art of marketing, whether it be sale or barter. He is a natural financier because he thinks in terms of money *at work*, in terms of values produced and services rendered. But beyond these things he has the soaring imagination, the precise appraisal of ultimate values, and the concentration on detail that mark our outstanding leaders in the field of national capitalism.

The major difference between the national capitalist and his immediate predecessors lies in his sense of values. The industrial capitalist was chiefly concerned with his machines and their product; the financial capitalist, with the interlocking mechanism of markets, men, and accounting systems. But the national capitalist does not deal primarily in tangibles; his thinking and his action cut through to the ultimate sales appeals, to the fundamental human incentives. He deals in those final satisfactions for which men and women promptly pay their money in prices, dues, or taxes, and for which they will pay their blood if threatened by a predatory power. This is the bright thread that runs through all of Guilden's speech and action.

And now, we come back to our general theme — the history of a business unit. The Waltham Watch Company has changed its name many times. It has seen its workers and its executives come and go. It has experienced various vicissitudes of fortune, and it has passed through, or reflected, the chief phases of business development of its century of existence — petty, industrial, financial, and national capitalism. It has been kept alive and useful to society for these many years by the coöperation of various groups and many persons.

While the mortality of business at times appears to be heavy, we find some concerns that are capable of meeting their recurring problems with success. Such companies give stability and continuity to our business and social life. They can do this fundamentally because they continue to serve society well. Down at the bottom of the success, as of the failure, are the policy and management of the executives. Property is not the fruit of labor, as some commentators have thoughtlessly asserted; rather is it the fruit of management, labor, investment, and government, at times working at cross purposes but generally in effective unison. Not a few of us will watch the fortunes of Waltham with more than passing interest; and in this preoccupation it is hoped the present volume will be helpful.

APPENDIX A

PARTNERS AND OFFICERS OF THE WALTHAM WATCH COMPANY AND ANTECEDENTS[a]

THE CHANGING FORTUNES of the Waltham Watch Company have depended very largely on the policies, ability, and temperament shown by each succeeding group of administrators. External factors in the nation and in the watch industry have been of vital importance, but the action of the story is best reflected in the contrasting personalities of the chief executives and their immediate satellites. The following list of officers summarizes material that is spread throughout the text:

PARTNERS

Aaron L. Dennison	1850–57	American Horologe Co.
Edward Howard	1850–57	Warren Manufacturing Co.
David P. Davis	1850–57	Boston Watch Co.
Samuel Curtis	1850–57	
Royal E. Robbins	1857	Tracy Baker & Co.
Eliashib Tracy	1857	
Theodore W. Baker	1857	
Royal E. Robbins	1857–58	Appleton, Tracy & Co.
Daniel F. Appleton[b]	1857–58	
James W. Appleton, Jr.[b]	1857–58	

PRESIDENTS

Horatio Adams	1854–60	resigned
William H. Keith	1861–66	resigned
Isaac W. Mulliken	1867–73	died
Frank M. Stone	1874–77	resigned
Horatio Moore	1878–83	died
Ezra C. Fitch	1886–1921	was elected vice-president
Gifford K. Simonds	1922	resigned
Frederic C. Dumaine	1923–44	resigned
Ira Guilden	1944–	incumbent, 1945

[a] See page 12, Chapter 1, for successive names used by the Company.

[b] The records do not state whether one or both of the Appletons were partners. James W. Appleton, Jr., was active at Waltham for a brief period; D. F. Appleton was a partner in Robbins & Appleton, exclusive agents for the Waltham Watch Co. until 1910.

TREASURERS [c]

William H. Keith	1854–56	not reëlected
Samuel B. Whitney	1857	not reëlected
William H. Keith	1858	was elected president
Royal E. Robbins	1859–1902	died
Royal Robbins [d]	1903–10	resigned
Harry L. Brown	1911–22	resigned
Frederic C. Dumaine	1923–44	resigned
Ira Guilden	1944–	incumbent, 1945

VICE-PRESIDENTS [e]

Francis R. Appleton	1899–1910	
William L. Putnam	1911	
Conover Fitch [f]	1912–22	
Ezra C. Fitch [g]	1923–32	honorary office
Elmer E. Silver, Jr.	1923	temporary, during the reorganization
I. E. Boucher	1944–	
Leo Kamion	1945–	

SUPERINTENDENTS [h]

Aaron L. Dennison	1857–61	Ezra C. Fitch	1883–1903
Charles W. Fogg	1862–? [i]	E. A. Marsh	1904–10 [i]
Charles Vander Woerd	1876–82		

GENERAL MANAGERS [h]

William L. Putnam	1911	Gifford K. Simonds	1922
Conover Fitch	1912–20	I. E. Boucher [j]	1923–
H. L. Brown	1921		

[c] The treasurer was the chief executive from 1859 to 1902. The treasurer and president shared authority from 1903 to 1910. The treasurer was purely a fiscal officer from 1854 to 1858, and from 1911 to 1920. The offices of treasurer and general manager were combined in 1921. The offices of president and treasurer have been combined since 1923.

[d] Royal Robbins was a son of Royal E. Robbins.

[e] The office of vice-president was created in 1899, abolished in 1932, and re-created in 1944.

[f] Conover Fitch was a son of Ezra C. Fitch.

[g] E. C. Fitch acted in an advisory capacity from 1923 until his death in 1932.

[h] The terms *superintendent, general superintendent,* and *general manager* are not clearly differentiated in the records.

[i] The end of the term has not been established definitely. Conflicting aspirations have sometimes made it appear necessary to use a loose and informal organization where two or more men shared the authority and responsibility usually allocated to a single executive.

[j] Vice-president and general manager, 1944–.

APPENDIX B

DIRECTORS OF THE WALTHAM WATCH COMPANY AND ANTECEDENTS

Directors	*Term*	*Occupation*[a]
Reuben P. Davis	1854–56	
James Brown	1854	Little & Brown, publishers
Samuel Curtis	1854	Manufacturer of mirrors
Edward Howard	1854–56	Manufacturer of clocks
William B. Fessenden	1854–57	Jeweler
Frederick M. Stone	1855–58, 1869–73	Politician
Horatio Moore	1855–57	Politician
Josiah Rutter	1857–63	Lawyer and politician
Isaac R. Scott	1857	
Samuel B. Whitney	1858, 1861–67	
Isaac W. Mulliken	1858–66	Doctor
William H. Keith	1859–60	Watchmaker and clerk
George Lawton	1859–75	
Henry A. Robbins[b]	1864–75, 1878–83	Watch merchant
B. F. D. Adams	1867	
Henry Martyn	1868–71	Clerk
Percival L. Everett	1872–90	
William H. Titcomb	1874–77	Clerk
William Roberts	1876	
Joshua V. Kettell	1877–96	
Charles W. Hersey	1877–78	
Benjamin F. Brown	1878–1908	
Charles W. Fogg[c]	1879–91, 1893	Mechanic
Ezra C. Fitch	1884–86, 1904–22	Watchmaker, salesman
Irving Smith	1887–91	
Benjamin F. Stevens	1891–93	

[a] Descendants of Waltham officials are listed as "second generation."

[b] Henry A. Robbins was a brother of Royal E. Robbins.

[c] The records do not show Fogg as a director in 1892; only four directors are listed for that year.

Directors	*Term*	*Occupation*
A. Lawrence Edmands	1892–1905	
Daniel F. Appleton (N. Y.)	1894–1903	Watch merchant
George H. Shirley	1894–1900	Mechanic
Augustus K. Sloan (N. Y.)	1897–1909	Wholesale jeweler
Harry P. Robbins (N. Y.)	1900–10	Second generation
Reginald C. Robbins [d]	1901–05, 1907–09	Second generation
Francis R. Appleton	1904–11, 1913–19	Second generation
James W. Appleton	1904–09, 1912	Second generation
William G. Thompson [e]	1906	Lawyer
William L. Putnam	1906–22	Lawyer, trustee
I. Tucker Burr [f]	1907–11, 1913–21	Stockbroker
Royal Robbins [d]	1906–10	Second generation
Conover Fitch [g]	1906–22	Second generation
Romney Spring [e]	1906	Lawyer
Edward A. Marsh	1909, 1911	Mechanic
Augustus P. Loring	1910–22	Lawyer, trustee
Horace E. Hildreth	1910–22	Manufacturer
Charles W. Leonard	1910–20	Manufacturer of textiles
Arthur Lyman	1910–22	Lawyer, trustee
Thomas B. Gannett [f]	1912	Stockbroker
Harry L. Brown	1911–22	Hotel manager
W. B. H. Dowse	1912–22	Manufacturer of silverware
Gifford K. Simonds	1922	Manufacturer of saws
Charles Francis Adams	1923–29, 1933–44	Lawyer and banker
Philip Dexter	1923–35	Lawyer
F. C. Dumaine	1923–44	Manufacturer of textiles
F. C. Dumaine, Jr.	1923–44	Second generation
Allan Forbes	1923–	Banker
George P. Gardner, Jr.	1923–	Stockbroker
James L. Richards	1923–44	Public utilities
Robert Winsor	1923–29	Investment banker
Louis K. Liggett	1923–25	Drug merchant
William Dexter	1926–43	Lawyer, trustee
Alexander Winsor	1926–31	Investment banker
Robert G. Stone	1926–44	Investment banker

[d] Reginald C. Robbins and Royal Robbins were sons of R. E. Robbins.
[e] Of Matthews, Thompson & Spring.
[f] Of the firm of Parkinson & Burr.
[g] Conover Fitch was a son of E. C. Fitch.

Directors	Term	Occupation
Norton Wigglesworth	1926–44	Real estate
Robert Amory	1930–31	Manufacturer of textiles
John P. Chase	1930–	Investment counsel
Ronald T. Lyman	1933–44	Manufacturer of textiles
Chandler Hovey	1939–	Investment banker
Roger Amory	1944–	Trustee
O. Kelley Anderson	1944–	Investments
Henry C. Breck	1944–	Investment banker
Ira Guilden	1944–	Watch trade and industry
Carroll L. Cheverie	1945–	Investments

Directors Who Served Temporarily During the Reorganization of 1923

Arthur P. Brown, treasurer
Warren Motley
Eugene Darling
F. W. Busk
F. R. Boyd, lawyer
William B. Snow, Jr.
H. C. Robbins
Dunbar F. Carpenter
Elmer E. Silver, Jr., vice-president
John C. Rice, lawyer
Ray Henry

Number of Directors Constituting the Board

1854–99	Five directors, not including officers.
1900–03	Six directors, not including officers.
1904–05	Eight directors, including president and vice-president
1906–22	Eleven directors, including president, vice-president and treasurer
1923	Twelve directors, including the president-treasurer
1924–25	Nine directors, including the president-treasurer
1926–44	Twelve directors, including the president-treasurer
1944–	Eight directors, including the president-treasurer

APPENDIX C

SOURCES OF CAPITAL OF THE WALTHAM WATCH COMPANY

THE SOURCES OF CAPITAL used by the Company indicate the changing structure of the financial organization of the country. The first source of funds was found among the small industrial capitalists, but it was soon necessary to tap the larger supply held by suburban petty capitalists. After the failure in 1857, new capital was obtained chiefly from a mercantile source, R. E. Robbins, but in 1858 the petty capitalists of Waltham made another substantial contribution. After the Civil War and until 1906, new capital came largely from earnings. After 1906, public interest in corporate securities gave encouragement to the practice of capitalizing temporary earning power. In 1923 the procurement of capital fell entirely under the control of the investment banking system. The approximate amounts of capital raised and the dates are shown in the following table:

	Source	New Capital	Total Issued
1848	Samuel Curtis	$ 20,000	
1850	" "	10,000	
to	Howard & Davis	10,000	
1854	Dennison, doubtful		
	Other Persons	20,000	
	TOTAL AT ROXBURY	$ 60,000	
1854	Original partners, amount unknown		
to	Charles Rice on chattel mtg., amt. unknown		
1857	Boston banks on watch cases, amt. unknown		
	Waltham Improvement Co.		
	Cash	$ 7,000	
	Land	7,000	
	Notes of Boston Watch gtd. by W. I. Co. later sold to Wm. T. Cook	7,000	

	Source		New Capital	Total Issued
	Fellows & Shell, of N.Y., agents		$ 20,000	
	Tracy Baker & Co., cases on credit E. Tracy		8,000	
	Other Sources (estimated)		41,000	
1848 to April 1857	GRAND TOTAL		$ 150,000	
1858	R. E. Robbins		$ 35,000	
May	E. Tracy		7,500	
	T. W. Baker		7,500	
	Waltham Improvement Co.		7,380	
1857 } 1858 }	R. E. Robbins or Earnings (estimated)		55,000	
	TOTAL 1857 to 1858		$ 112,380	
1857	TEMPORARY LOANS			
	Banks 2% per month			
	Boston Financiers 18% per annum			
1858	Consolidation of Watch Co. with the Land Co.			
	Stockholders of the W. I. Co.		$ 72,000	
	Stock issued to Robbins		100,000	
	Robbins purchased 28 shares from the W. I. Co.		28,000	
	Total Stock issued			$ 200,000
1859	Bills Payable		$ 37,263.17	
	Stock Issued			200,000
	" Paid up	$182,110		
1860	" " "	200,000		
1860	Cash for new stock		100,000	300,000
1865	Stock dividend 150%		450,000	750,000
1870	Cash dividend 16⅔%		500,000	1,250,000
1873	Cash for new stock		250,000	1,500,000
1885	Cash for new stock		500,000	2,000,000
1889	Cash dividend 50%		1,000,000	3,000,000
1899	" " 16⅔%		500,000	
1899	" for new stock		500,000	4,000,000
1906	New Company	Pfd.		4,000,000
"		Common		7,000,000
"	Earnings re-invested		3,000,000	
	Capitalization of earning power		4,000,000	

	Source		New Capital	Total Issued
1907	Cash for new stock	Pfd.	$ 500,000	$4,500,000
1910	" " " "	Pfd.	500,000	5,000,000
	CAPITAL FROM LOANS, as shown on the balance sheets.			
1859 to 1885	Bills Payable range from		13,000	
	to		270,000	
1884 to 1900	" " range from		234,000	
	to		800,000	
1919	Note Issue — Coupon		3,000,000	
1921	Notes Payable		5,216,000	
	TOTAL NOTES			$8,216,000
				TOTAL SECURITIES
1923	Bonds and Debenture Cash less Disc.		$6,000,000	
	Prior Preferred Stock		1,700,000	$7,700,000
	Common B Stock — Capitalization of expected earning power		70,000 [a]	
	Preferred, cap. of earning power		50,000 [a]	
1937	Capital — Securities outstanding			
	Bonds			$1,145,000
	Prior Pref. Stock			478,800
	Preferred Stock			34,119 [a]
	Common A Stock			25,000 [a]
	" B Stock			41,868 [a]
1943	Capital — Securities outstanding			
	Bonds			None
	Prior Pref. Stock			$377,330
	Preferred Stock			33,843 [a]
	Common A Stock			25,000 [a]
	Common B Stock			41,868 [a]

[a] Shares.

SOURCES: Marsh, Early Watchmaking.
Keith, A Family Tale.
Brearley, *Time Telling through the Ages.*

APPENDIX D

TYPES OF STOCKHOLDERS IN THE WALTHAM WATCH COMPANY

DATA ON THE OWNERSHIP of stock, shown on page 300, help to trace the diffusion of ownership and the transfer of voting power from strong to weak hands. The figures also indicate the importance of the trustee system in corporate management. Records of the stockholders are not available after 1910.

Frequency Distribution of Holdings by Types of Stockholders, 1859–1910
Waltham Watch Company

Number of Stockholders and Shares Held	1859	1865	1870	1880	1890	1900	Com. 1906	Pfd. 1906	Com. 1910	Pfd. 1910
Total no. stockholders	37	49	125	357	364	553	730	667	778	1,017
Shares held	2,000	3,000	7,500	15,000	30,000	40,000	70,000	40,000	70,000	50,000
Women	2	17	23	54	155	248	335	319	364	463
Shares held	20	351	756	1,126	4,819	8,349	16,387	9,411	18,448	13,620
Trustees[a]	0	3	5	14	40	65	108	115	115	256
Shares held	0	24	54	566	3,078	4,501	15,319[b]	10,425[b]	10,336	14,688

Frequency Distribution of Stockholders by Size of Holdings

Shares	1859	1865	1870	1880	1890	1900	Com. 1906	Pfd. 1906	Com. 1910	Pfd. 1910
0–10	18	22	51	212	179	233	242	320	257	454
11–100	18	23	61	121	140	250	371	284	393	467
101–200	0	0	6	16	22	46	54	37	58	57
201–500	0	3	3	6	15	12	46	16	49	29
501–1,000	0	0	3	1	3	7	8	6	12	7
Over 1,000	1	1	1	1	5	5	9	4	9	3

[a] Trustees and charitable organizations.

[b] Includes 6,091 shares of common stock and 4,777 shares of preferred held by the estate of R. E. Robbins.

APPENDIX E

A PARTIAL LIST OF WATCH MANUFACTURERS IN THE UNITED STATES IN CHRONOLOGICAL ORDER

THE FOLLOWING LIST has been compiled chiefly from J. Freistadter, "Development of the Watch Industry in the United States," *Northwestern Jeweler*, Aug., 1939. Other sources consulted were:

H. C. Brearley, *Time Telling through the Ages* (New York, 1919), Appendix C.

Poor's Manual of Investments.

Thomas' Register, 1939.

Marvyn Scudder Manual of Extinct or Obsolete Companies (New York, 1926–34), vols. i–iv.

Sundry original sources.

No attempt has been made to check the list for completeness or accuracy. Manufacturers of various grades of watches are included. Certain manufacturers having a considerable interest in the importation of Swiss movements or parts have been omitted from the list.

APPENDIX E

Watch Manufacturers

1809–15	Luther Goddard	Shrewsbury, Mass.	Five hundred movements were produced. Repeal of the Jefferson Embargo in 1815 deprived Goddard of protection against foreign competition.
1812	(name unknown)	Worcester, Mass.	
1837 1841	Henry & J. F. Pitkin	East Hartford, Conn. New York	A thousand movements were produced. The project was abandoned shortly after 1841.
1840–45	Jacob D. Custer	Norristown, Penna.	A dozen movements were produced.
1850	Waltham Watch Co.		
1857–81	E. Howard Watch & Clock Co.		The company practically failed and was reorganized in 1863, and again in 1881. Howard retired in 1882. The Howard trade-mark is now in possession of the Hamilton Watch Co.
1859–62	Nashua Watch Co.	Nashua, N. H.	A thousand movements were produced. The concern failed and was purchased by the Waltham Watch Co.
1863–70	Newark Watch Co.	Newark, N. J.	Sold to the Cornell Watch Co.
1863–72	U. S. Watch Co.	Marion, N. J.	Operated briefly after 1872 as the Marion Watch Co., then the machinery was sold to E. F. Bowman of Lancaster, Penna.

			Bowman sold the machinery to the J. P. Stevens Watch Co. of Atlanta, Ga., in 1882.[a]
1864	National Watch Co. Elgin National Watch Co.	Elgin, Ill.	
1864–66	Tremont Watch Co.	Melrose, Mass., and Zurich, Switzerland	A. L. Dennison managed the factory in Zurich. The machinery was later operated by Dennison for the Anglo-American Watch Company of Birmingham, England. The latter company was subsequently known as the English Watch Co.
1864–70	New York Watch Co.	Springfield, Mass.	The company was reorganized after virtual failure in 1866. It was reorganized again as the New York Watch Mfg. Co. in 1870 and as the Hampden Watch Co. in 1877. Purchase by the Dueber Watch Case Mfg. Co. of Canton, Ohio, followed about 1889.
1867–71	Mozart Watch Co.	Ann Arbor, Mich.	The business was sold to the Rock Island Watch Co. of Rock Island, Ill.
1869–1927	Illinois Springfield Watch Co.	Springfield, Ill.	The company was reorganized as follows: 1875 as the Illinois Springfield Watch Co., and in 1879 as the Springfield Illinois Watch Co. The name was later changed

[a] Freistadter (*op. cit.*, p. 7) also reports that the machinery was sold to the Auburndale Watch Co. in 1879.

			to the Illinois Watch Co., of Springfield, Illinois. The business was sold to the Hamilton Watch Co. in 1927.
1870–74	Cornell Watch Co.	Chicago, Ill.	The business was reorganized as the Cornell Watch Co., of San Francisco, Calif., in 1874. The company was reorganized again as the California Watch Co. and sold to the Independent Watch Co., of Fredonia, N. Y., in 1877. The latter company was sold in 1885 to the Peoria Watch Co., which soon failed.
1871	Rock Island Watch Co.	Rock Island, Ill.	The company failed without producing any watches.
1872	The Marion Watch Co.	Marion, N. J.	See United States Watch Co., 1863.
1872–74	Washington Watch Co.	Washington, D. C.	
1873–1915	Rockford Watch Co.	Rockford, Ill.	The company failed in 1896 and was operated by receivers until 1901, when it was reorganized as the Rockford Watch Co., Ltd.
1874	Adams & Perry Watch Mfg. Co.	Lancaster, Penna.	The original company failed in 1876 without producing any watches. The project was reorganized under a syndicate in 1877 as the Lancaster Pennsylvania Watch Co. It was reorganized again as the Lancaster Pennsylvania Watch Co.,

			Ltd. In 1884 the company came under the control of Abram Bitzner, and Oppenheimer Bros. & Veith, selling agents in New York City. The latter group used the trade-mark *Keystone Watch Company*. Failure in 1890 resulted in the sale of the property to the Hamilton Watch Co. in 1892.
1874–75	Freeport Watch Manufacturing Co.	Freeport, Ill.	The company produced no watches. The property was destroyed by fire in 1875.
1874–77	Cornell Watch Co.	San Francisco, Calif.	See Cornell Watch Co., of Chicago, 1870.
1875	Fitchburg Watch Co.	Fitchburg, Mass.	The company failed after a few years for lack of funds. No watches were produced.
1877–1927	Hampden Watch Co.	Springfield, Mass.	See the New York Watch Co., 1864. The Hampden Company was purchased by the Dueber Watch Case Mfg. Co. and moved to Canton, Ohio, about 1889. Dueber failed in 1890 but reorganized the company in 1891.
1877–85	Independent Watch Co.	Fredonia, N. Y.	See Cornell Watch Co., of Chicago.
1879–83	Auburndale Watch Co.	Auburndale, Mass.	The Auburndale Co. purchased the equipment of the United States Watch Co., of Marion, N. J.[b]

[b] Freistadter's statements (*op. cit.*, pp. 7–8) on the disposal of machinery of the United States Watch Co. appear to conflict.

APPENDIX E (*continued*)

1880	Waterbury Watch Co.	Waterbury, Conn.	The name was changed to the New England Watch Co. in 1898. The company failed in 1912 and was bought by Robert H. Ingersoll & Bro. in 1914. In 1922 the Waterbury Clock Co. acquired the bankrupt Ingersoll firm.
1880	E. Ingraham Co.	Bristol, Conn.	Founded in 1835, incorporated in 1880, acquired the Bannatyne Watch Co., of Waterbury, Conn., in 1912.
1880	Western Watch Co.	Chicago, Ill.	Failed in the same year without producing any watches. The machinery was sold to the Illinois Watch Co.
1882–1903	Columbus Watch Co.	Columbus, Ohio	The company "was the outgrowth of a private enterprise started in 1876 by D. Gruen and W. J. Savage."[c] The business was purchased in 1903 by the South Bend Watch Co.
1882–87	J. P. Stevens Watch Co.	Atlanta, Ga.	The company failed in 1887. See United States Watch Co., of Marion, N. J., 1863.
1883–1907	New Haven Watch Co.	New Haven, Conn.	The business was moved to Chambersburg, N. J., in 1886 and the name was changed to the Trenton Watch Co. It failed in 1907 and was purchased by Robert H. Ingersoll & Bro. in 1908.

[c] Freistadter, *op. cit.*, p. 26.

1883	Manhattan Watch Co.	New York, N. Y.	The company "was organized but discontinued after a very short time." [c]
1883	Cheshire Watch Co.	Cheshire, Conn.	The company "continued in business for about ten years." [c]
1883–86	Aurora Watch Co.	Aurora, Ill.	The company failed in 1886, and the machinery was purchased by the Hamilton Co. in 1892.
1884–1914	Seth Thomas Clock Co.	Thomaston, Conn.	The Seth Thomas Co. was founded in 1813 but did not manufacture watches until 1884. The company discontinued its watch department in 1914.
1884	United States Watch Co.	Waltham, Mass.	The company was founded by Charles Vander Woerd, formerly general superintendent of the Waltham Company. The venture failed and the plant was purchased by the Keystone Watch Case Co. It was operated as the Howard Watch Co.
1885–1902	New York Standard Watch Co.	Jersey City, N. J.	Purchased by the Keystone Watch Case Co. in 1902.
1885	Peoria Watch Co.	Peoria, Ill.	See Cornell Watch Co., 1870. The Peoria Co. soon failed.
1887	Wichita Watch Co.	Wichita, Kan.	The company operated for "only a few years." [c]

[c] Freistadter, *op. cit.*, p. 26.

1888	Western Clock Manufacturing Co.	Peru, Ill., factory La Salle, Ill., office	The manufacture of watches was begun in 1895. The company uses the brands *Big Ben* and *Pocket Ben*.
1892	Hamilton Watch Co.	Lancaster, Penna.	See Adams & Perry Watch Mfg. Co., 1874.
1893–1922	Robert H. Ingersoll & Bro.	Waterbury, Conn., factory Trenton, N. J., " New York, N. Y., office	See Waterbury Watch Co., 1880. Failure of the Ingersoll firm in 1922 was caused by overexpansion during the World War.
1894	Webb C. Ball Co.	Cleveland, Ohio	The company was founded in 1879, incorporated in 1891, and began to make watches in 1894.
1899	Keystone Watch Case Co.	Philadelphia, Penna.	The company, known after 1927 as the Keystone Watch Corporation, controlled the following: Howard Watch Co., Waltham, Mass.; New York Standard Watch Co., Jersey City, N. J.; Crescent Watch Case Co., Inc., Newark, N. J.; Philadelphia Watch Case Co., Riverside, N. J., and other subsidiaries.
1902–33	South Bend Watch Co.	South Bend, Ind.	The enterprise was incorporated under the name American National Watch Co., but changed to the South Bend Watch Co. at once. The company went into voluntary liquidation in 1933. See Columbus Watch Co., 1882.
1904	Ansonia Clock Co.	Brooklyn, N. Y.	Incorporated in 1873, this company began the manufacture of inexpensive watches in 1904.

APPENDIX F

FINANCIAL RECORD OF PRESIDENT DUMAINE

THE ACCOUNTS of the Company for the past twenty years have been summarized in terms of the cash which has been taken in over the counter and rung up in the till. The flow of cash in the opposite direction has also been summarized, indicating those expenditures that are essential to operations, and other disbursements. The opening and closing balance sheets and the flow of cash are as follows:

WALTHAM WATCH COMPANY

FEBRUARY 9, 1923, TO JULY 2, 1943

(CASH TRANSACTIONS)

Cash on hand 2-9-23			$ 574,522.19
Received from:			
Customers	$110,932,187.22		
Sale of Own Securities	249,900.00		
Sale of Real Estate	67,753.20		
Sale of Machinery	44,764.53		
Other Income	1,091,592.41		
Total		$112,386,197.36	
Less Expenditures for Operations			
Labor, Materials, etc.	$ 88,351,503.18		
Taxes	4,441,892.78		
Interest paid	2,357,998.18		
		95,151,394.14	
Cash after Operating Expenditures		$ 17,234,803.22	
Less Non-Operating Disbursements			
Dividends	$ 3,305,481.32		
Purchase of Own Securities	8,516,221.04		
Additions to Plant	1,294,330.27		
U. S. Securities	367,000.00		
Notes and Loans	74,029.22		
Expenses of Predecessor Co.	588,599.25		
Organization Expense	92,613.30		
Investments	8,500.00		
Prepaid Items & Deposits	65,135.34		
Total		14,311,909.74	
Balance, Cash Increment			2,922,893.48
Cash on Hand 7-2-43			$3,497,415.67

Reducing these figures to a minimum of words, we may say (as we have said in Chapter XVII) that Dumaine took a plant valued at 4 million dollars and made it yield 24 million dollars over a period of twenty years. Of these 24 million dollars, 4½ millions went for taxes, 2½ millions were paid as interest to the owners of borrowed capital, and 17 millions accrued to the stockholders as dividends, or as equity in the business.

COMPARISON OF BALANCE SHEETS

	February 9, 1923	July 2, 1943
ASSETS		
Cash	$ 574,522.19	$3,497,415.67
Other Quick Assets	249,900.00	369,109.42
Accounts Receivable	1,446,627.81	1,133,301.66
Inventory	4,000,000.00	923,632.26
Total Current Assets	$ 6,271,050.00	$5,923,459.01
Fixed Assets	4,338,860.00	1,175,215.48
Patents, Trade-marks, etc.	2,790,090.00	1,350,000.00
Other Assets	....	158,438.07
Total Assets	$13,400,000.00	$8,607,112.56
LIABILITIES		
Accrued Payroll and Accounts Payable	$ 239,936.98	$ 377,119.78
Taxes	....	1,253,174.55
Total Current Liabilities	$ 239,936.98	$1,630,294.33
Debentures	3,000,000.00	....
Bonds	3,000,000.00	....
7% Prior Preference Stock	1,700,000.00	377,730.00
6% Preferred Stock	5,000,000.00	3,384,285.00
Common Stock and Surplus	200,000.00	2,795,730.24
Other Liabilities	260,063.02	419,072.99
Total Liabilities	$13,400,000.00	$8,607,112.56

NOTES AND REFERENCES

CHAPTER I

1. Thomas P. Martin, History of the Dennison Manufacturing Company (manuscript, Framingham, 1922), pp. 1 ff.

2. Charles S. Crossman, A Complete History of Watch and Clockmaking in America (manuscript, about 1883), pp. 10–11.

3. E. W. to Col. Andrew Dennison, Bangor, Maine, Dec. 21, 1843. "This makes my saying true 'that if you could content yourself to sit on your bench for a period longer or shorter, it would clear you from the cursed thraldom [of debt] that has ever encompassed you and embittered your existence.' "

4. Martin, *op. cit.*, p. 13.

5. *Ibid.*, p. 6.

6. A. L. to E. W. Dennison, Boston, June 29, 1834, in the collection of letters at the Dennison Mfg. Co., Framingham, Mass. (Hereafter this source will be referred to as Dennison Coll.) "Charlotte" probably refers to Charlotte Foster, who married Aaron Dennison, Jan. 15, 1840, after he was established in business for himself in Boston. See Martin, *op. cit.*, p. 17, and Crossman, *op. cit.*, p. 11.

7. Crossman, *op. cit.*, p. 11.

8. *Ibid.* Harry Chase Brearley, *Time Telling through the Ages* (N. Y., 1919), pp. 161–162. W. H. Keith, A Family Tale (manuscript, Waltham, about 1883), p. 246. Watches had been produced in America before 1809, but Goddard's scale of operation was larger than that of his predecessors.

9. Crossman, *op. cit.*, p. 11. Dennison apparently had several reasons for going to New York. His brother Benjamin wrote to Eliphalet:

> Aaron went to New York yesterday not going any farther at present for the reason is he couldn't raise the *dosh* on the notes, but one — this he got of R. L. Page $1,000 enclosed I send the other notes and deed. . . .
>
> Aaron calculates to carry on a sort of wholesale trade between here and New York. . . .

B. G. to E. W. Dennison, Boston, Nov. 27, 1838. Dennison coll.

10. Martin, *op. cit.*, pp. 30–38. The partners were Dennison, George E. Adams, and J. C. Farnsworth.

11. *Loc. cit.*

12. A. L. to Col. Andrew Dennison, Mar. 19, 1836. Dennison Coll.

13. Col. Andrew to A. L. Dennison, Brunswick, Dec. 18, 1848. Dennison Coll.

14. *Ibid.*, Dec. 12, 1854.

15. Martin, *op. cit.*, p. 75.

16. A. L. to B. G. Dennison, Liverpool, July 4, 1857, Dennison Coll.; and A. L. Dennison to A. O. Bigelow, Zurich, Mar. 8, 1866, Bigelow, Kennard & Co. Collection, Baker Library, Harvard University. The latter contains the following estimate of funds required by A. L. Dennison, presumably for a period of six months:

To Mr. Philbrick say	$ 5,000
Tremont Watch Co. accts.	2,500
Mass. Bank	3,750
Due I think on New Roger's note	1,500
Life Policy about	450 [a]
{ Charles Swift, Gardiner, Me. a remittance on acct. this was put down before 300–]	250
John P. Fellows, New York on acct.	400
A. Dennison, Brunswick, &. (My Father) for a note and interest say	300
for my use on this side	1,000
	$15,150

[[a] Set down in former memo at $400.]

From which the Dividend now due on A. W. Co. stock — 200 shares — is to be deducted and the balance to be raised by a new loan.
If the amt could all be obtained from the Mass. or another Bank on note to run 6 mo. with privilege of renewing any amt which may not be covered by the semi annual Dividends that would seem to be the nicest way to provide for it.

17. The Dennison Manufacturing Co., of Framingham, Massachusetts, is famous as the makers of boxes, tags, and paper novelties. The Dennison Watch Case Manufacturing Co. was founded in Handsworth, near Birmingham, England, about 1874. Arthur Tremayne, *One Hundred Years After* (Birmingham, 1912).

18. Crossman, *op. cit.*, p. 12.

19. Penrose R. Hoopes, *Connecticut Clockmakers of the Eighteenth Century* (N. Y., 1930), p. 22.

20. Manuscript in Dennison Coll.

21. E. A. Marsh, History of Early Watchmaking in America (manuscript, Waltham, about 1890), p. 3. According to Brearley, *op. cit.*, p. 178, financing was arranged in 1848.

22. Orra L. Stone, *History of Massachusetts Industries* (Boston, 1930), vol. i, p. 945.

23. Marsh, Early Watchmaking, p. 3; Crossman, *op. cit.*, p. 13; A. L. to E. W. Dennison, Sept. 19, 1850, Dennison Coll.

24. E. Tracy to C. N. Thorpe, Bryn Mawr, Nov. 25, 1886, Waltham Watch Co. Collection. The main sources of Waltham data are listed in the Author's Preface to the present volume, page xxvi; hereafter the sources will be referred to generally as Waltham Coll., although occasionally the reference will be slightly more specific.

25. A. L. to E. W. Dennison, Handsworth, Apr. 17, 1873, Dennison Coll. Edward Howard gave Aaron Dennison financial assistance at this critical period in Dennison's affairs (1873).

26. See Appendix C, Sources of Capital.

27. Dennison Coll.

28. The arrangement may have been similar to the one between Dennison and the Anglo-American Watch Co., of Birmingham, in 1872. In the latter case the agreement was as follows: at the end of five years, Dennison was to receive an interest in the concern and a share of the excess profits if they exceeded 5 per cent for the first year, 10 per cent for the second, 15 per cent for the third, 20 per cent for the fourth, and 25 per cent for the fifth year.

Dennison's services as manager were retained, subject to dismissal on three months' notice, for £350 per year. The agreement was complicated by the fact that Dennison had an equity in the tools and equipment which had been previously used in Switzerland. Copies of the articles of agreement, dated Jan. 1, 1872, are in the Dennison Coll.

29. This letter is signed "Howard and Davis" and dated Boston, Aug. 6, 1850. The records rarely mention Davis, and the evidence indicates that he was an inactive partner.

30. From an address by E. C. Fitch dated May 11, 1925, Waltham Watch Co. historical files.

31. Keith, *op. cit.*, p. 68. Waltham Coll.

32. Marsh, Early Watchmaking, p. 5.

33. Henry G. Abbott, *History of the American Waltham Watch Company*, reprinted from *The Watch Factories of America* (Chicago, 1905), pp. 14–15, 51. The firm of H. & J. F. Pitkin, 1836 to 1841, used crude machinery to manufacture watches at their plant in East Hartford, Conn. The total output of the firm for the five years of its life was about 800 watches.

34. *Ibid.*, pp. 52–53.

35. E. W. to Col. Andrew Dennison, Boston, Oct. 11, 1850, Dennison Coll.

36. Martin, *op. cit.*, p. 156.

CHAPTER II

1. Rates of interest on commercial paper are from the tables prepared by Leonard P. Ayres for the Cleveland Trust Co., *Business Activity and Four Price Series*, 8th edition, 1938.

2. Anonymous manuscript, History [of the Waltham Watch Co.], undated (about 1900), p. 9.

3. Chauncey Depew, editor, *One Hundred Years of American Commerce* (N. Y., 1895), p. 542.

4. *Loc. cit.*

5. Marsh, Early Watchmaking, pp. 8–9. The beauty of this part of the Charles River has been preserved by converting both banks of the stream from Waltham to Newton Lower Falls into a natural park.

6. E. Tracy to C. N. Thorpe, Bryn Mawr, Nov. 25, 1886. Waltham Coll.

7. *Ibid.*
8. A. L. to B. G. Dennison, Liverpool, July 4, 1857. Dennison Coll.

CHAPTER III

1. E. Tracy to C. N. Thorpe, Bryn Mawr, Nov. 25, 1886; a copy is attached to Marsh, Early Watchmaking.
2. N. P. Stratton to A. L. Dennison, July 2, 1857, Dennison Coll.
3. Tracy to Thorpe, Nov. 25, 1886.
4. The opening entries in the books of Tracy Baker & Co. are:

Dr.	*Cash*	
1857		
May 21	To Royal E. Robbins pd into concern	35,000.00
" "	" Eliashib Tracy " " "	7,500.00
" "	" Theodore W. Baker " " "	7,500.00
" "	" Merchandise, change found in [illegible]	.35
		50,000.35

5. Tracy to Thorpe, Nov. 25, 1886. Tracy reports that Robbins retired because of ill health, but this statement was not confirmed by his son, R. C. Robbins.
6. R. E. Robbins' Cash & Journal book contains these entries:

1857		
Feb. 2	H. A. Robbins & D. F. Appleton on a/c of my interest in the business of Robbins Bros. & Co.	50,000.
9	Do	2,000.
13	H. A. Robbins & D. F. Appleton on a/c	1,000.
17	Do	1,000.
Mar. 3	H. A. Robbins & D. F. Appleton pd. H. D. Clapp	105.
	Do their notes opposite	6,584.
4	Do their notes January 31 8 mos.	2,861.
9	Personal Estate my bala in the business of Robbins Bros. & Co. as chgd opposite	69,572.
		$133,122.

Tracy to Thorpe, Nov. 25, 1886, estimates Robbins' fortune at $150,000.

7. It has not been definitely established that R. E. Robbins had a controlling interest in Robbins & Appleton at this date, but his investment of $50,000 probably was sufficient for that purpose.
8. Tracy Baker & Co., cashbook:

1857			
May	By Real Estate	Factory & grounds	8,500.00
"		Machinery & tools	33,000.00

May	Expense a/c	Insurance	37.50
"	Merchandise	Material & work not finished	2,359.82
" 21	Expense a/c	Insurance	300.00
" "	Expense a/c	Dennison's trip to England	355.00
" 22	Merchandise	Coin silver for cases 165 oz.	202.12
" 23	Manuf. charges	Pd. hands to date	822.90
" 23	Merchandise	Pd. Lynch for jewels	8.58
		Balance	4,414.43
			$50,000.35

9. Keith, A Family Tale. The friction between Dennison and Keith is given in detail in various parts of the manuscript.

10. R. E. Robbins' accounts mention C. G. Robbins as a member of the family, but the relationship is not disclosed. The accounts also mention G. S. Robbins & Son, and Rev. Royal Robbins, who was R. E. Robbins' father.

11. The Watch Factory Foremen's Association was founded in 1883.

12. John Swinton, *A Model Factory in a Model City* (N. Y., 1888), p. 7. "The workshops are filled by young men and women of the soil, almost wholly of New England lineage."

Comparative Wages in Waltham
in August, 1859

Boston Manufacturing Co.	524 workers average $0.765 per day
American Watch Co.	124 workers average $1.546 per day

Source: Payroll books of the respective companies. The Boston Mfg. Co. produced cotton textiles.

13. Swinton, *op. cit.*, p. 16.

14. Anonymous History, pp. 22–23. The operating schedule may be inferred from approximate figures for the payroll. Payroll does not necessarily indicate employment for the month since payments were sometimes curtailed for lack of cash. The figures are estimated from the cashbook of Tracy Baker & Co.:

1857		*1858*	
July	$2,575	Feb.	$2,257
Aug.	3,728	Mar.	3,499
Sept.	3,190	Apr.	2,817
Oct.	417	May	3,570
Nov.	1,316 [a]	June	6,171
Dec.	2,713	July	none [b]
		Aug.	3,183
1858		Sept.	3,506 [c]
Jan.	$2,552		

[a] For 3 weeks: 50% wage cut.
[b] No cash available for payroll.
[c] Balance due workers by old company.

15. The original books of account show that Robbins began his activities as selling agent on Oct. 22, 1857, when he sold a large bill of goods to Fellows & Co., of New York. Robbins apparently "dumped" these goods in order to bring in cash. He received a discount from the company of 40% and 2½%, instead of the usual 20% given to wholesalers. The next sale recorded in Robbins' name is on Feb. 23, 1858, when he began to sell to the general trade, the firm of Robbins & Appleton being one of his customers. In May, J. A. Stoddard, of Philadelphia, became a heavy dealer — probably exclusive agent for the southeastern territory — and Robbins & Appleton held a similar position in New York. In Sept., 1858, there is evidence of a Boston office as well as a sales office in Waltham. The next salesbook in the Harvard collection of Waltham records is dated 1865, and at that time all accounts were sold by Robbins & Appleton except a few small transactions under the heading "Sales at Factory." Beginning Jan. 1, 1871, the firm of Robbins & Appleton acted as exclusive selling agent without exception. This arrangement continued until 1911, at which date a sales department was set up at the Waltham factory.

16. The cash outlay for Sept., 1857, was $5,057.67 plus $2,500.00, which was withdrawn from the business by Robbins, presumably to meet other calls for cash incident to the panic.

17. The sale to Fellows & Co. amounted to $2,136.08 net to the Watch Co.

18. The *Parker* movement sold for a list price of $16. The original Waltham model had been selling at $23.50 list. The first movement, #1001, was sold to Robbins & Appleton, Dec. 11, 1857.

19. Sales — Tracy Baker & Co.

1857		*1858*		*1858*	
June	$ 789.20	Jan.	$2,041.28	July	$ 6,332.11
July	1,959.00	Feb.	2,278.70	Aug.	11,616.34
Aug.	4,436.92	Mar.	7,894.28	Sept.	11,487.90
Sept.	5,286.27	Apr.	7,658.64	Oct.	9,437.91
Oct.	3,084.35	May	8,700.43	Nov.	14,649.60
Nov.	167.90	June	5,852.66	Dec.	17,138.59 [a]
Dec.	3,515.69				

20. Keith, *op. cit.*, p. 137. The Charles River is navigable by small sailboats from the dam at Waltham to Riverside, Mass.

21. Marsh, Early Watchmaking, p. 12.

22. A. L. to E. W. Dennison, Handsworth, England, April 28, 1874. Dennison Coll.

23. Col. Andrew to Aaron Dennison, Dec. 30, 1857:

> I shall be much pleased if you can bring the thing about that you mention in your letter if the new Co. do not do by you as they ought. If the 4 you name had about 5,000 each of spare capital to put into such a concern I see no reason why it might not work to a charm but you must be very careful not to make a wrong move.
>
> Will Mr. Keith take hold of the concern and go heart and hand with you?

[a] Not including $31,056.36 sales of stocks by the old Company to the new Company.

24. Figures relating to the sale are from the minutes of the directors' meetings.

25. Anonymous History, p. 24:

An examination of the minutes of the directors' meetings and the books of account provides a clearer understanding of the consolidation of the two companies. The major events are given below in their chronological order.

1858.

May 17. The board of directors authorized the appointment of a committee to "confer with Mr. Robbins on the purchase by this company of the Watch Factory Estate."

June 17. The board voted "that the Treasurer be a committee to inform Mr. Robbins of the action [acceptance] of the Directors in regard to the purchase of the Watch Establishment—and on his assent thereto to solicit from the stockholders of the Improvement Company their assent to assess the shares to the amount $1,000. the present year." The assessment up to that date had been only $387.50 per share.

June 28. "The Board will agree to sell Mr. Robbins fifteen shares of Stock recently purchased by the Company, for the sum of $350. per share." This agreement gave Robbins a majority of the stock in the new Company.

Aug. 16. Robbins was elected a director of the Land Co. [Waltham Improvement Co.]

Aug. 25. Horatio Moore, president of the Land Co., was authorized to receive the watch factory from Robbins.

Sept. 1. The cashbook shows that the operation of the plant was taken over by the new Company. Robbins at this date had an inventory of finished watches worth about $83,770.

Sept. 8. A credit entry in Robbins' cashbook reads:
"Appleton Tracy & Co bo't E Tracys interest 6500.
Interest on notes given 1170."
The corresponding debit entry is:
"Do [Bills Payable] my notes to E Tracy 7670."
Tracy must have been very poorly informed as to the conditions of the sale of the Company to relinquish his interest for less than his investment of $7,500.

Sept. 29. The board petitioned the General Court of Massachusetts to change the name of the Company to the American Watch Company. Robbins was elected treasurer of the new Company.

Oct. 11. The board agreed to Robbins' proposal that his salary should be "Nothing if the company do not declare ten per cent dividend. Fifteen hundred dollars if Company declares ten per cent and under fifteen per ¢; Three thousand dollars if Company declares fifteen pr cent or over." On Dec. 22 the basis of payment was changed from dividends to earnings.

Dec. 30. Robbins sold the remaining stock of finished watches to the new Company.

1859.

Jan. 1. The new Company took over the selling function. From Sept. 1, 1858, to Jan. 1, 1859, the new Company had been operating the plant and building up an inventory of finished watches. During this period, Robbins had been disposing of the inventory of watches which he had had on hand on September 1.

ROBBINS' INVESTMENT IN THE WATCH CO.

Robbins' original investment	$ 35,000.00
Baker's interest bought by Robbins	6,000.00
Tracy's interest bought by Robbins	6,500.00
Cash paid in by Robbins	74,580.51
Gross investment by Robbins	$122,080.51
Less cash taken out of the business by Robbins	15,868.98
Investment by Robbins, as of Sept. 1, 1858	106,211.53
Less sales to R. E. Robbins, June 1, 1857, to Sept. 1, 1858	38,285.34
Net Investment	$ 67,926.19 [a]

[a] Assuming that there was no balance due from Robbins to the Company on Sept. 1, 1858. A precise figure on Robbins' profit cannot be obtained from the existing records.

CHAPTER IV

1. In the treasurer's report of Mar. 29, 1860, Robbins wrote, "A dividend of $3.12½ per cent having been declared and credited to a certain portion of the stock in pursuance of agreements to which I need not now refer. . . ." No record of the "agreements" has come to light. There was no restriction on the dividend in the resolution of the board of directors except that it was payable only to stock on which all assessments had been paid.

2. Anonymous History, p. 27.

3. Keith, A Family Tale, p. 228.

4. Minutes of the directors' meetings, Sept. 29 and Oct. 11, 1858.

5. *Ibid.,* Nov. 8, 1858.

6. Keith, *op. cit.,* p. 188. Keith quotes the article in the Waltham *Record* of Apr. 6, 1883, and brings arguments to prove that undue credit is given to Dennison for the success of the Waltham Watch Co.

7. *Ibid.,* pp. 190–191.

8. A. L. to E. W. Dennison, Handsworth, Eng., May 16, 1874, Dennison Coll.

9. A. L. to B. G. Dennison, Aug. 10, 1863, Dennison Coll.

The minutes of the directors' meetings for Nov. 3, 1863, show that the resolution discharging Dennison was rescinded, but the payment is given as $4,000 instead of the $5,000 that Dennison expected.

Some years later when Aaron Dennison was in difficulties of a similar nature with the Anglo-American Watch Co., he received the following letter from Theophilus Parsons, the attorney who represented him in the dispute with the American (Waltham) Watch Co.:

> Cambridge, Mass.
> Feb. 3, 1874.
>
> My Dear Sir —
>
> I take pleasure in assuring you that at no time during your controversy with the Waltham Watch Factory & from no party — did I hear any intimation of any charge brought against you in respect to your skill — intelligence — integrity or fidelity to duty.
>
> As I understood the matter, you held opinions concerning some part of the business — different from those held by the large stockholders. As your views could not be reconciled, it was concluded to be best that you should leave the concern.
>
> Then a question arose as to the sum which should be paid you. Here also your views differed from theirs. After much negotiation in which you employed me professionally, a large sum was offered you — less than you claimed — and less than I thought your due, but more than was at first proposed; and it was finally agreed to by both parties.

10. A. L. to E. W. Dennison, Handsworth, Feb. 23, 1874, Dennison Coll. The passage reads:

> I do not take such a discouraging view as to the prospects at Waltham as you do for you know R E R fell in with an arrangement for me to come abroad as the Cos. agent after I left the Factory and the arrangement only fell through so far as I know from my claiming the privilege of furnishing England with goods at the same [time]. It is true I did not insist strongly and should have given away had not negotiations been broken off rather suddenly.

11. A. L. to Andrew Dennison, Birmingham, January, 1864, Dennison Coll.

> It is my purpose now to turn my engineering talent and experience with my means — for a few years — to the best account I can without much reference to the precise direction, but I by no means intend to abandon the idea of a good thing in my own country at no distant day if my life and health are spared.

12. E. W. to A. L. Dennison, Boston, Jan. 19, 1874, Dennison Coll.
13. *Ibid.*, Nov. 22, 1873, Dennison Coll.
14. *Ibid.*, Jan. 31, 1874.
15. See note 24.
16. A partial list of exhibitions of Waltham watches is as follows:

    1856 Massachusetts Charitable Mechanical Association
    1857 The American Institute at New York
    1858 Franklin Institute, Philadelphia
    1860 United States Agricultural Society
    1876 Centennial Exposition, Philadelphia
    1878 Exposition Universelle, Paris

1879 International Exposition, Sydney, Australia
1880 International Exposition, Melbourne, Australia
1880 Industrial Exposition, Cincinnati
1881 International Cotton Exposition, Atlanta
1884 Louisiana Industrial Exposition, New Orleans
1885 International Inventions Exposition, London, England
1886 International Exposition, Liverpool, England
1892 World's Columbian Exposition, Chicago
1894 Exposition Universelle, Antwerp, Belgium
1898 Trans Mississippi and International Exposition
1900 Exposition Universelle Internationale
1903 Canada Industrial Exposition, Toronto
1904 Louisiana Purchase Exposition
1904 Exposition Universelle, Liége, Belgium
1906 Expositione Internationale, Milan, Italy
1907 Jamestown Tercentennial Exposition
1909 Yukon Pacific Exposition, Seattle
1915 Panama Pacific International Exposition, San Francisco

17. Anonymous History, p. 49.

18. E. B. to A. L. Dennison, Aug. 1, 1874, Dennison Coll.

19. The treasurer's reports for 1863 and 1864 give employment and production in approximate figures as follows:

Year	*No. of Employees*	*Production Watches/Day*	*Production Man Days per Watch*
1859	200	50	4
1862	300	100	3
1863	429	150	2.86
1865	640 [a]	250 [a]	2.56

20. Abbott, *Hist. of the Amer. Waltham Watch Company,* p. 79.

21. Stone, *Hist. of Mass. Industries,* p. 946. Stone does not give the source of his information. The statement is reminiscent of the advertising copy of the period, but in any case it will serve to illustrate the point.

22. Treasurer's annual report, Waltham Watch Co., 1866.

23. An offer of an equivalent amount of new stock accompanied the cash dividend of 66⅔%, declared Aug. 3, 1870. The dividend has, therefore, been treated as a stock dividend.

24. The monetary conditions referred to are mentioned in the *Commercial and Financial Chronicle* as follows:

> Our debt is assuming stupendous proportions, and, as it will amount to at least three thousand million dollars, its annual charges will press heavily on our

[a] Estimated.

industry and must be felt severely by the masses of our people. (Aug. 19, 1865, p. 226.)

The amount of legal tender notes in circulation is about six hundred and eighty-five millions and the circulation of the banks, State and National, is about three hundred millions. . . . The circulation of the country is about three times greater than it was or ever had been before the suspension of specie payments. (Sept. 23, 1865, p. 385.)

25. Pierre Dubois, *Lettres sur les fabriques d'horlogerie* (Paris, 1853), p. 34:

> Hélas! la plupart de ces pauvres petits artistes marchent pied nus sur le sol pierreux de leurs montagnes, et quelques-uns d'entre eux n'ont pas toujours, pour se couvrier, ce vêtement si necessaire qui n'a pas de nom dans la langue anglaise.

26. Brearley, *Time Telling through the Ages,* p. 144.

27. The Tremont Watch Co. was headed by A. O. Bigelow of Bigelow & Kennard, of Boston, Mass. The company failed, and Dennison took the equipment to England, where he formed another company, the Anglo-American Watch Co. This project also went on the rocks.

28. Brearley, *op. cit.,* p. 242.

29. Nelson P. Stratton was assistant superintendent at Waltham at the time the Nashua Co. was formed. Belding Dart Bingham of Nashua, N. H., had been a maker of clocks and regulators before entering the employ of the Waltham Co. Charles S. Moseley was master-mechanic at Waltham in 1859. He later became general superintendent for the Elgin National Watch Co. Charles Vander Woerd, a native of Leyden, Holland, had marked ability as an inventor and machine designer. He was superintendent of the Waltham factory from 1876 to 1883.

30. Anonymous History, p. 30.

31. Both the treasurer's report dated 1863 and the Company's cashbook give the price of the Nashua factory as $23,000 ($23,009.48, Oct. 21, 1862, according to the cashbook). Marsh apparently is in error (Early Watchmaking, p. 17) in stating that the price was $53,000 "for the entire property."

32. Abbott, *op. cit.,* pp. 75–76.

33. *Keystone,* Aug., 1890.

34. *Ibid.*

35. The treasurer's report of 1886 gave the following list of watch manufacturers:

Howard Watch and Clock Co., Roxbury, Mass.
Elgin National Watch Co., Elgin, Ill.
Illinois Springfield Watch Co., Springfield, Ill.
Hampden Co., Springfield, Mass.
Rockford Co., Rockford, Ill.
Aurora Watch Co., Aurora, Ill.
Adams & Perry Watch Mfg. Co., Lancaster, Pa.
Fredonia Co., Fredonia, N. Y.
Columbus Watch Co., Columbus, O.
Waterbury Watch Co., Waterbury, Conn.

Cheshire Company of Connecticut
Seth Thomas Clock Co., Thomaston, Conn.
New Haven Watch Co., New Haven, Conn.
Manhattan Company of New York
United States Watch Co., Waltham, Mass.
Williamstown Company of Massachusetts
New York Standard Watch Co., Jersey City, N. J.

Robbins did not give complete titles and addresses, but where they are available from other sources they have been used.

CHAPTER V

1. For a discussion of the secular trend, see N. S. B. Gras, *Business and Capitalism* (New York, 1939), pp. 215–218, *et passim;* N. S. B. Gras and Henrietta M. Larson, *Casebook in American Business History* (New York, 1939), pp. 661–744; Joseph A. Schumpeter, *Business Cycles* (New York, 1939), vol. i, chap. iv, "The Contours of Economic Evolution." Schumpeter's analysis of the secular trend stresses innovation; Gras and Larson emphasize the development of business organization.

2. F. C. Dumaine wrote in a memorandum dated Jan. 9, 1939: "Since Waltham started manufacturing watches 90 years ago, there have been started about 60 other watch factories."

The three survivors (1941) are Waltham, Elgin, and Hamilton. (Sometimes Bulova is also regarded as a manufacturer, but for the purpose of the argument in the text is of little importance.) Companies alleged to be assembling Swiss parts are not included. For a partial list see Appendix E.

3. Treasurer's report, Mar. 25, 1875.

4. *Ibid.*, 1883.

5. Charles Vander Woerd was born in Leyden, Holland. He was a man of remarkable mechanical genius and had a fair knowledge of mathematics and astronomy. He modeled some of the Waltham watch movements, but his best work was in the field of machine design. Some of the screw machines in use at Waltham in 1939 were developed by Vander Woerd.

He was employed by the Waltham Co. sometime before 1857 and was general superintendent from 1876 to 1883. See Abbott, *Hist. of the American Waltham Watch Co.*, pp. 86–88; and Marsh, Early Watchmaking, p. 32.

6. Anonymous History, pp. 46–47; and Marsh, Early Watchmaking, p. 37. One of the means of obtaining coöperation within the plant and between the factory and the selling agents was the Watch Factory Foremen's Association. The association was founded early in 1883 and was used to promote the business efficiency and social compatibility of the members of the staff.

7. Ezra Charles Fitch was born in Germany of American seafaring parents. He was educated in the American public schools at Worcester, Mass., and also learned the trade of watchmaker in Worcester. He went to work for Bigelow & Kennard, Boston jewelers, and in 1867 was employed by Robbins & Appleton. He remained with the latter firm in the capacity of salesman and sales manager

until Robbins brought him to Waltham in 1883. Prior to that time, Fitch had been manager of the New York office of Robbins & Appleton and a partner in the firm.

8. Burton J. Hendrick, *Life of Andrew Carnegie* (N. Y., 1932), vol. i, p. 137.

9. Ida M. Tarbell, *The History of the Standard Oil Company* (N. Y., 1925), pp. 42–43; John D. Rockefeller, *Random Reminiscences of Men and Events* (N. Y., 1909), p. 85.

10. In this period, 1873–85, research work was not segregated either in the plant or in the accounts. Expenditures for this purpose are inferred from the results obtained.

11. Chicago *Tribune,* July 13, 1889.

12. Sales for the period ranged between three and four million dollars per year, the largest sales in the history of the Company up to that time. General business activity was above normal for every year of the period except 1883 and 1884.

13. Harrison John Thornton, *The History of the Quaker Oats Company* (Chicago, 1933), chaps. iii and ix.

14. Canton, Ohio, *Repository,* Sept. 21 or 22, 1891. *Jewelers' Circular,* under the date line Boston, Mass., Sept. 26 [1891]. The *Repository* quotes Robbins as follows:

> In all the revisions [of wages] which, like the present one, are due in great part to these improvements in the mechanical means of producing watches, the individual wages are seldom permanently reduced. Only the rate per piece is changed to conform to the changed conditions.

An examination of the payroll records confirms Robbins' statement that no sweeping reduction of day rates or of total wage payments took effect at this date.

15. *Jewelers' Circular* under the date line, Rockford, Illinois, Sept. 26 [1891].

16. Waltham Watch Co., treasurer's annual report, 1893.

17. Chicago *Tribune,* Feb. 15, 1889.

18. Undated clipping, probably Feb., 1889, Waltham Coll., Baker Library, vol. 1025, p. 28. The Missouri antitrust law of 1889 was declared unconstitutional in 1892.

19. Index of wholesale prices by Leonard P. Ayres, *Business Activity and Four Price Series.*

20. The theory of the secular trend assumes that prices rise and fall rhythmically, in accordance with psychological factors similar to those that are currently thought to govern the business cycle, but having a lower frequency of oscillation.

According to this theory monetary instability, political agitation, social unrest, and frequently recurring depressions are normal results of a downward secular trend. After a fixed period the psychological resistance to deflation results in inflationary actions, such as the discovery of gold, the increased employment of cheap labor, the exploitation of new inventions, the increase of administrative efficiency, the growth of industry, finance, and population, and finally the supreme inflationary measure, a war of conquest.

21. Figures from the 1894 report:

WALTHAM WATCH CO.

Assets	*Jan. 31, 1892*	*Jan. 31, 1898*	*Liquid Assets — Change*	*Slow Moving Assets — Change*
Finished goods	$1,062,847.20	$ 872,856.45	$ — 189,990.75	$ ......
Goods in process	1,189,422.43	1,653,807.82		464,385.39
Machinery	823,954.43	1,322,349.99		498,395.56
Factory	467,955.38	521,490.70		53,555.32
Accounts receivable	358,831.68	49,464.97	— 309,366.71	
Cash	80,407.39	65,578.99 [a]	— 14,826.40	
Gold — watch cases and bullion	339,231.80		— 339,231.80	
Supplies	538,563.46	366,800.74	— 171,762.72	
Other assets	254,628.38	261,791.85		7,163.47
Total assets	$5,115,842.15	$5,114,141.51		
Liabilities				
Capital stock	$3,000,000.00	$3,000,000.00		
Accounts payable [b]	677,131.06	810,206.58		
Surplus and reserves	1,438,711.09	1,303,934.93		
Total liabilities	$5,115,842.15	$5,114,141.51		

22. Minutes of the directors' meetings, Apr. 18, 1889.

23. Internal records do not check with the annual reports on the subject of profits. For example:

	Profit as per cent of Sales, from annual reports	*Unit Gross Margin per cent of Sales, from internal records*
1891	9.4	12.2
1892	8.3	10.7
1893	missing	missing
1894	12.3	9.0
1895	12.8	16.9
1896	10.8	10.6
1897	12.8	D
1898	12.8	11.3
1899	11.0	19.9

D = deficit.

24. *Commercial and Financial Chronicle*, Jan. 5, 1901, p. 6.

25. *Ibid.*, Jan. 4, 1902, p. 6.

26. See Table 11. Figures are for the fiscal year.

[a] Balance January wages unpaid, $22,241.33, has been deducted from cash.
[b] Including notes and bills.

27. Telegram from F. C. Beckwith of Feb. 3, 1932, on the death of Ezra Fitch, Waltham Watch Co. files.

28. Chicago *Journal*, Apr. 7, 1907.

29. "The United States Supreme Court declared the Illinois Anti-Trust law unconstitutional because of the provision exempting agricultural products and live stock from its operation." The *Chronicle*, Jan. 3, 1903, p. 10.

30. *Ibid.*, p. 6.

31. *Ibid.*, Jan. 2, 1904, p. 6.

32. *Loc. cit.*

33. See Table 10.

34. *Com. and Fin. Chronicle*, Jan. 5, 1907, pp. 6–7.

CHAPTER VI

1. Henry S. Dennison and J. K. Galbraith, *Modern Competition and Business Policy* (N. Y., Oxford Univ. Press, 1938), p. 71. "Where stock ownership is widely dispersed, the *de facto* control of the modern corporation rests partly with the operating heads of the business and partly with a banker or investment house group or groups."

2. See Table 10.

3. Robert S. Gorham to J. B. Warner, June 23, 1910. Records of Loring, Coolidge, Noble & Boyd, Boston.

4. Dennison and Galbraith, *op. cit.*, p. 69.

5. H. P. Robbins, a director of the Waltham Watch Co., was the son of H. A. Robbins and a nephew of R. E. Robbins. H. A. Robbins was the second largest stockholder, Ezra Fitch being the largest.

6. H. P. Robbins to A. P. Loring, June 13, 1910. Records of Loring *et al.*

7. Minutes of the directors' meeting of May 20, 1910.

8. *Ibid.*, June 3, 1910.

9. For the number of small stockholders, see Appendix D.

10. The stockholders' meeting of June 10, 1910, was attended by forty stockholders representing 93,656 shares of stock, including proxies. Source: Minutes of the stockholders' meeting.

11. Bills payable Apr. 1, 1910, amounted to $425,000. Source: Trial balance book (Baker Library).

12. Stock owned or controlled by the directors who were chosen to represent the outside stockholders in 1910.

	Shares owned	*Shares in trust* [a]
I. Tucker Burr	100	1,074
Horace E. Hildreth	43	666
C. W. Leonard	660	482
A. P. Loring	0	577
Arthur Lyman	0	338

[a] Including shares held by persons of the same surname.

13. Number of stockholders, Waltham Watch Co.:

	No. of stockholders		*Capitalization*	
	Preferred	*Common*	*Preferred*	*Common*
1899	none	389	none	$3,000,000
1910	1,017	778	$4,000,000	$7,000,000

See also Chapter v.

14. See Table 10.

15. Dennison and Galbraith, *op. cit.*, p. 116. "We must recognize that the directorate of our larger corporate enterprises is actually in a fiduciary capacity for security holders."

16. E. C. Fitch, evidence in *Abbot* v. *Waltham*, vol. ii, p. 476.

17. *The Plymouth Cordage Company, 1624–1899* (Cambridge, 1900), p. 54.

18. A. P. Loring to W. L. Putnam, Nov. 17, 1910. Loring acted as investment banker for the sale of treasury stock of the Union Twist Drill Co. in the amount of $470,000. Records of Loring *et al.*

19. Royal Robbins tendered his resignation on Aug. 2, 1910. It became effective Jan. 2, 1911.

20. A. P. Loring to C. W. Leonard, Oct. 31, 1911. Records of Loring *et al.*

21. *Loc. cit.*

22. *Loc. cit.*

23. *Loc. cit.*

24. *Ibid.*, July 18, 1911.

25. A. P. Loring to H. L. Brown, Oct. 11, 1913. Records of Loring *et al.*

26. *Ibid.*, June 25, 1913.

27. Gras, *Business and Capitalism*, p. 298.

28. See Table 13.

29. Income tax data belonging to the Bureau of Internal Revenue, Washington, D. C. This contract was amended after the Armistice, June 3, 1919, to require 200,000 fuses with complete delivery on or before Jan. 1, 1921. The price specified was $8 each.

30. Income tax data belonging to the Bureau of Internal Revenue, Washington, D. C.

INCOME, MISCELLANEOUS
Waltham Watch Company

#900 Dept. (fuse mfg.)	1918		$ 12,744.
" "	1919		10,546.
#800 Dept. (casing and shipping)	1920		295,510.
" "	1921		86,960.
		Total	$405,760.

31. C. L. Depollier was president of the Dubois Watch Case Co. He had an exclusive agency for the sale of Waltham movements in Dubois patented cases.

The agreement ran from July 16, 1915, until it was discontinued by F. C. Dumaine in 1923.

32. The payroll during the peak of the postwar boom exceeded 5,000 workers.

33. Treasurer's reports show that the average cost of movements made by Waltham was:

1913[a]	*1914*[a]	*1918*[b]	*1919*[b]
$3.75	$3.90	$5.56	$7.05

34. According to Day & Zimmerman, *Report 1870 on Inventory of the Waltham Watch Company*, earnings, 1911–14, were:

1911[a]	*1912*[a]	*1913*[a]	*1914*[a]
$150,478	$251,126	$473,092	$439,480

35. A. P. Loring to Loring G. Peede, Nov. 4, 1912. Records of Loring *et al.*

36. Minutes of the directors' meeting of Apr. 20, 1920.

37. *Abbot* v. *Waltham Watch Company et al.*, vol. iii, pp. 1448–1449.

38. H. B. Dowse, evidence, *ibid.*, vol. ii, p. 840.

39. Conover Fitch to the foremen, Sept. 12, 1917. Company files at Waltham, Mass.

40. E. C. Fitch, evidence, *Abbot* v. *Waltham Watch Company et al.*, vol. ii, pp. 462, 510.

41. James A. Faust, evidence, *ibid.*, vol. iv, p. 1717.

42. *Ibid.*, p. 1725.

43. A. P. Loring, evidence, *ibid.*, vol. iii, p. 1478.

44. Treasurer's report of Mar. 8, 1881.

45. Carl Snyder to E. C. Fitch, Oct. 28, 1920. Company files at Waltham, Mass.

CHAPTER VII

1. *Poor's Manual*, 1913, p. 371.

2. *Who's Who in New England* (Chicago, 1938), vol. iii, p. 1152. G. K. Simonds, 1880–1941.

3. *Poor's Manual*, 1912, p. 2501; 1922, p. 396.

4. Women of the Simonds family have served as both directors and officers of the company.

5. *Poor's Manual*, 1912, p. 396.

6. G. K. Simonds, evidence, *Abbot* v. *Waltham*, vol. iii, p. 1251.

7. G. K. Simonds, interview, Jan. 23, 1939.

8. H. L. Brown to A. P. Loring, Nov. 26, 1921, files of Loring *et al.*

9. *Ibid.*

10. Simonds, *Abbot* v. *Waltham*, vol. iii, p. 987.

11. *Ibid.*, p. 1032.

12. *Ibid.*, pp. 976–977.

[a] Year ending Mar. 31.
[b] 8 months ending Nov. 30.

13. *Ibid.*, p. 983.
14. Conover Fitch, *ibid.*, vol. i, p. 195.
15. H. L. Brown to A. P. Loring, Mar. 14, 1922, files of Loring *et al.*
16. A. P. Loring, *Abbot* v. *Waltham*, vol. iii, p. 1359.
17. The body of theory on personnel management—and on human relations in general—is attaining impressive proportions. The theory is being applied to practice by many progressive companies, but, compared to the physical sciences, the science of human relations is very little used.
18. H. L. Brown, *Abbot* v. *Waltham*, vol. i, pp. 108, 115.
19. *Loc. cit.*
20. Rufus L. Wilbor, *ibid.*, vol. iv, pp. 2035, 2036.
21. G. K. Simonds, *ibid.*, vol. iii, p. 948.
22. *Ibid.*, p. 949.
23. Wilbor, *ibid.*, vol. iv, p. 2035.
24. *Ibid.*, vol. iii, p. 1454.
25. O'Grady, *ibid.*, vol. i, p. 283.
26. *Ibid.*, p. 288.

CHAPTER VIII

1. Evidence, *Abbot* v. *Waltham*, vol. iv, p. 2044.
2. Bill of Complaint, *ibid.*, Aug. 9, 1923.
3. $2,710,011,386 in 1920, *Commercial and Financial Chronicle*, Jan. 27, pp. 343–345.
4. *Statistical Abstract of the United States*, 1936, p. 242; 1915—$18,965,700,000; 1920—$37,268,100,000.
5. *New York Times Annalist*, Dec. 29, 1913, p. 815; Jan. 3, 1921, p. 38.
6. *Ibid.*, pp. 435–436.
7. Inventory—$11,411,186; Loans—$8,240,500. Report of the directors to the stockholders, dated Oct. 16, 1922.
8. See pages 105–109.
9. *Abbot* v. *Waltham*, vol. iii, p. 1476.
10. *Ibid.*, vol. i, p. 188.
11. *Loc. cit.*
12. *Ibid.*, vol. iii, p. 1475.
13. F. C. Dumaine, interview, July 11, 1938.
14. Day & Zimmerman, *Report No. 1870*, attached memo as of Dec., 1922.
15. $124,101 reserve for depreciation of inventories is shown in the treasurer's report of Mar., 1920.
16. Jan. 5, 1920, p. 7.
17. W. P. G. Harding, governor of the Federal Reserve Board, to Senator Reed Smoot, July 11, 1921. *Federal Reserve Bulletin*, Aug., 1921, p. 896.
18. Total earning assets of the Federal Reserve banks: Nov. 5, 1920—$3,400,000,000; July 26, 1922—$1,076,927,000. Source: *Federal Reserve Bulletin*.
19. Letter from C. L. Depollier to E. C. Fitch, quoting Dietrich Gruen, dated Mar. 8, 1919.

20. John Miller to E. C. Fitch, Oct. 16, 1920.
21. G. K. Simonds, *Abbot* v. *Waltham*, vol. iii, p. 1237.
22. See page 132 for a summary of inflationary factors.
23. Letter by the Waltham Co. board of directors to the stockholders, dated Oct. 16, 1922.
24. *Abbot* v. *Waltham*, vol. iii, p. 1483.
25. *Ibid.*, p. 1451.
26. *Ibid.*, p. 1485.
27. *Ibid.*, p. 1452.
28. Henrietta M. Larson, *Jay Cooke, Banker* (Cambridge: Harvard University Press, 1936), p. 119.
29. Bill of Complaint, *Abbot* v. *Waltham*, p. 3.
30. *Abbot* v. *Waltham*, vol. iii, p. 1184.
31. *Survey of Current Business*, 1936, Supplement, p. 63.
32. *The Boston News Bureau* of May 31, 1941, reports a statement by F. C. Dumaine as to the salary received by him, as follows:
"July 1, 1927 to Oct. 1, 1931, $50,000 annually; Oct. 1, 1931 to June 1, 1932, $45,000 annnually; June 1, 1932 to Dec. 1, 1937, $25,000 annually; Dec. 1, 1937 to Jan. 1, 1939, $16,666.67; Jan. 1, 1939 to date, $25,000 annually."
33. Based on data supplied by Kidder, Peabody & Co. and other records.

CHAPTER IX

1. From an address by E. C. Fitch, dated May 11, 1925, to the Associated Group of Visiting Manufacturers at Waltham.
2. Brearley, *Time Telling through the Ages*, p. 167.
3. E. C. Fitch, address cited in note 1 above.
4. Marsh, Early Watchmaking, pp. 8–9.
5. *Ibid.*, p. 10.
6. Stone, *Hist. of Mass. Industries*, vol. i, p. 945.
7. E. Tracy, letter to C. N. Thorpe, Nov. 25, 1886.

* * *

This being a summary chapter, the details appear elsewhere. Citations of original materials consulted would be too voluminous; direct quotations are mentioned in the footnotes.

CHAPTER X

1. *The President's Report to the Stockholders*, as of Dec. 31, 1923.
2. F. C. Dumaine to Miss R. B. Cary, Roxbury, Mass., dated Boston, Sept. 27, 1923.
3. Same as note 1. Dumaine received no salary during the years 1923–26, but in 1927—after the Company earnings had exceeded $1,000,000 per year for two years—he was paid $75,000 compensation for the 1923–26 period.

4. Letter of Apr. 23, 1923.

5. C. L. Depollier to E. C. Fitch, Brooklyn, N. Y., Mar. 3, 1919.

6. Walter J. Barr to E. C. Fitch, Toronto, Canada, Dec. 13, 1920.

7. F. C. Dumaine, interview of June 20, 1938.

8. Conover Fitch, *Abbot* v. *Waltham,* vol. i, p. 252.

9. DeForest L. Bachman of John Wanamaker to F. Depollier, dated Philadelphia, May 13, 1920.

10. Day & Zimmerman, *Report No. 1870,* p. 17a.

11. Letter dated Boston, Mar. 10, 1924.

12. F. C. Dumaine to Hulburd of Elgin, dated Boston, Mar. 10, 1924.

CHAPTER XI

1. This account of the strike has been compiled from Waltham and Boston newspaper clippings. Dumaine discounted the newspaper stories and stated that the mob was noisy but good-natured.

2. Howard N. Mayhew, secretary, Watchmakers' Protective Association, in an open letter to the American Federation of Labor membership, dated Dec., 1924.

3. Interview published Aug. 31, 1924.

4. Swinton, *Model Factory,* p. 12.

5. *Ibid.,* pp. 11–12.

6. *Ibid.,* p. 11.

7. It is reported "by a usually reliable source" that one of the directors insisted on serving a balanced ration to workers, and maintained a check on operations by auditing the purchases of the cafeteria on a dietetic basis. The cafeteria, it is said, purchased according to dietetic balance, sold what the workers wanted to eat, and disposed of the residue as convenient.

8. Boston *Sunday Advertiser,* Aug. 31, 1924.

9. Swinton, *op. cit.,* p. 6.

10. Address by Ernest Faulkner quoted in the Waltham *News Tribune* of Aug. 20, 1924.

11. Waltham *News Tribune,* Sept. 5, 1924.

12. *New York Times Annalist,* Sept. 22, 1924, p. 281.

13. *Ibid.,* Oct. 13, 1924, p. 361.

14. Report by Carlstrom dated Sept. 10, *Report on Western Activities.*

15. Charles G. Wood to Ernest Faulkner, dated Oct. 3, 1924.

16. F. C. Dumaine to C. Fitch, Apr. 10, 1924, and attached draft of a letter to Samuel Triebe.

CHAPTER XII

1. Dumaine wrote in his first annual report of Dec. 31, 1923: "When the present company was formed the best information available indicated a value [for inventory] of $4,000,000. This has been found to include a large quantity of material not adapted to the styles now manufactured and a considerable amount

of partially manufactured articles for which there was little or no demand. A large part of these superseded articles have been sold; what remains is of small value." The amount written off in reducing the inventory to market value does not appear in the records examined to date.

Much worthless inventory was scrapped or destroyed. For example, one lot of obsolete watch hands, estimated at more than 1,000,000 pieces, was thrown into the boiler.

2. Dumaine said (1939): "Foolishly, I went away. When I came back I found we were loaded with $3,000,000 in bonds and $3,000,000 in stock [debentures]."

3. The exchange of Prior Preference stock for Preferred stock and cash had a double purpose. It was a part of the policy of reducing the amount of outstanding senior securities and the accompanying fixed charges. It also relieved the Company of the necessity of paying $28.75 accrued dividends per share of Prior Preference stock. This was a boon to holders of the management or Class A Common stock, for it permitted a resumption of dividends to them. Preferred and Class B Common shareholders also profited, but not in the same degree, since the retirement of Prior Preference stock was offset by the distribution of Preferred stock from the shares in the Company's treasury.

4. *Abbot* v. *Waltham*, vol. iv, p. 1959.

5. Treasurer's report, Dec. 31, 1923.

6. Stewart, Watts & Bollong, *Reconciliation of Changes in Net Working Capital, Profit and Loss Statement, and Analysis of Surplus, February 9, 1923, to December 31, 1940* (Boston, 1941): "The total of profits as taken from the annual reports for 1923–40 is $4,647,229. Subsequent adjustment raised the figure to $5,557,771."

7. Stewart, Watts & Bollong, in their report, *Waltham Watch Company, Review of Progress of Company since Reorganization*, dated Jan. 22, 1938, make this statement: "The Company enjoys excellent credit and although money has been borrowed from banks on a few occasions, it was borrowed and still may be borrowed on a very favorable basis."

8. F. C. Dumaine to I. E. Boucher, July 13, 1925.

9. Reports from a competitor indicate that a minimum period of 8 months is required to design a watch and place it in production, provided that routine manufacturing and maintenance operations do not cause delays, but under ordinary conditions it may take as much as three years.

10. F. C. Dumaine to J. Freistadter, Oct. 10, 1924.

11. Earnings of one worker, a 12-size watchmaker, averaged $1.198 per hour before the 15 per cent wage cut and $1.173 afterwards.

12. Waltham Watch Co., treasurer's report, dated Mar. 26, 1863.

13. From a translation used by the Waltham Co. for advertising purposes. The translation has been checked for accuracy against a facsimile of the original speech as published in *La Nationale Suisse*, Chaux-de-Fonds, Switzerland, Nov. 17, 1876, no. 275.

14. In 1925 only 15% of Waltham movements were sold in cases. Source: I. E. Boucher in a statement to the Associated Group of Visiting Manufacturers.

15. Frank Jenks to E. C. Fitch, Aug. 4, 1917.

16. The catalogues of the late nineteenth century offer numerous ornate designs calculated to please American, English, and Latin-American buyers. The photograph book used by domestic missionary salesmen, after 1910, shows more restraint in the use of ornament and reflects a predominant taste for severe simplicity. More recent designs follow the current trend toward ornament by embellishing the functional lines of the case.

17. Dumaine forced the adoption of several changes in design and process that were not approved by the Watchmakers' Committee. These changes were usually successful, and their success was subsequently acknowledged by the Committee.

18. Until 1941 the Waltham Watch Co. operated an open shop. Approximately one-third of the employees belonged to a union which had no affiliations outside the plant.

CHAPTER XIII

1. "Finished goods" includes stock charged to the Sales Department, movement stock, and movements in the process of adjusting.

2. The following table gives a comparison of employment at Waltham with the prices of industrial stocks. The table illustrates the policy of adjusting production to market conditions, but it is not intended to imply that company policy was based on stock-market gyrations.

Employment vs. *Market Conditions, 1930*

Week Ending	*Employment W. W. Co.*	*Price Ind. Stocks*[a] *High*	*Low*
January 4	2,392	294	273
February 1	2,416	314	295
April 19	2,571	358	349 (peak)
May 24	2,655 (peak)	293	258
June 28	factory closed	272	253
July 19	1,559	293	277
August 9	2,442	294	267
September 27	2,138	280	259
October 11	562	259	240
December 20	750	217	196

3. Anonymous History, p. 27.

4. See note 1, above.

5. The South Bend Watch Co. went into voluntary liquidation in 1933.

6. Primary source, Amer. Jeweled Watch Mfrs.' Assoc., quoted by the U. S. Tariff Commission, *Concessions Granted by the United States in the Trade Agreement with Switzerland* (Washington, 1936), p. 51. Figures for capacity and pro-

[a] *New York Times Annalist,* weekly range of 25 industrial stocks.

duction are exclusive of the companies alleged to be assembling watches from Swiss parts.

7. Decree of Mar. 12, 1934. The quotation is from the U. S. Tariff Commission publication, *Concessions Granted Switzerland*, p. 63.

8. Jeweled Watch Movements. Domestic Apparent Consumption, and Imports in Number of Movements and Per Cent of the Consumers' Market:

Year	*Apparent Consumption No. Movements*	*Imports No. Movements*	*Imports Per Cent*
1929	5,088,434	3,400,315	66.8
1930	3,610,707	2,300,029	63.7
1931	1,416,967	815,208	57.5
1932	854,241	421,781	49.4
1933	821,240	432,005	52.6
1934[a]	1,266,666	610,183	48.2

9. A letter from F. C. Dumaine to President F. D. Roosevelt dated Oct. 10, 1933, gives the following figures:

	Domestic Consumption	*Swiss Imports*	*Smuggled*
1926	4,500,000 watches	65%	
1929	5,500,000 watches	75%	
1932	1,935,000 watches	432,000 [22%]	1,000,000 [52%]

SOURCE: Waltham *News Tribune*, Oct. 13, 1933.

There is a considerable discrepancy between the figures for apparent consumption given above, and those issued by the government given in note 8, above.

10. New York *Herald Tribune*, Apr. 5, 1934.

11. Waltham *News Tribune*, May 12, 1933.

12. From a translation of a letter printed in *Le Moment*, Geneva, Jan. 16, 1934.

13. A statement by Samuel Dinerstein, chairman of the Executive Committee of the Waltham Watch Employees' Association, reads in part, "No action has been taken by the Swiss Government to assist the United States Government in enforcing its customs laws or in stamping out this criminal practice." Waltham *News Tribune*, Dec. 14, 1934.

14. *Ibid.*, Oct. 19, 1934.

15. "Since 1914 twelve watch companies have gone out of business, leaving only three members of this Association [American Jeweled Watch Manufacturers' Association] — Elgin, Hamilton, and Waltham," F. C. Dumaine to President Roosevelt, Oct. 10, 1933. Dumaine did not include alleged assemblers of Swiss parts.

16. "Intense activity on the part of the Treasury Department soon reduced or eliminated one form of illegal entry, namely, the fraudulent entry of watches

[a] 10 months. *Concessions Granted Switzerland*, p. 51.

through customs. But there were many indications that the watches continued to be smuggled into the United States which had been purchased from Switzerland by agents in intermediate countries and smuggled from those countries into the United States, the movements eventually coming across the Mexican or Canadian border." U. S. Tariff Commission, *op. cit.*, p. 71.

17. Waltham *News Tribune,* Oct. 13, 1933. F. C. Dumaine to President Roosevelt, Oct. 10, 1933.

18. *Concessions Granted Switzerland,* p. 49.

19. An advertisement in the Waltham *Times* of Sept. 28, 1934, reads: "Waltham Watches are entirely American made (jewels only are imported). Made by American workmen for Americans. . . . Everything is made in one factory with concentrated responsibility assuring uniformity of product."

20. Dr. F. Scheurer, professor of the University of Neufchatel, *Zeitschrift für Sweizerische Statistik,* vol. 64 (1928), p. 503:

"Quant aux Etas Unis, nous y exportons aussi principalement des mouvements de montre-bracelets, mais cette exportation ne s'est pas faite au détriment de la montre complète. Elle nous a permis au contraire d'augmenter considérablement le commerce avec ce pays qui, avant la guerre, n'occupait que le 7e rang, alors que maintenant il est au premier."

21. Jeannette M. Calvin, *International Trade in Clocks and Watches,* Bureau of Foreign and Domestic Commerce (Washington, 1928), p. 62.

22. U. S. Tariff Commission, *Concessions Granted Switzerland,* p. 91.

23. Available information on the "Trust" is limited. Waltham records report that it has a capital of 10,000,000 francs Swiss and that the government formed the organization through the purchase of a 60% interest in the individual concerns during the depression. On p. 63 of *Concessions Granted Switzerland* is a reference to an organization of Swiss watch producers who export to the United States, but no details are given.

The "Superholding" Company, the popular name for the Société Générale de l'Horlogerie Suisse, S. A., was capitalized at 50,000,000 francs Swiss. Of this amount, 20,000,000 francs were subscribed by the interested banks, 20,000,000 francs by the industry, and 6,000,000 francs by the government. Additional funds, amounting to 7,500,000 francs, were loaned to Superholding without interest. *Ibid.*

24. From a translation of an open letter from a Swiss manufacturer of watches to *Le Moment,* Geneva, Switzerland, published in the issue of Jan. 16, 1934.

25. Wages were reduced about 30 per cent in 1932.

26. Waltham *News Tribune,* Mar. 21, 1933.

27. Boston *Transcript,* Nov. 16, 1931, advertisement by Bigelow Kennard Co.

28. The Waltham Summary Pay Roll shows an increase from 31.5 cents per hour for the week ending July 29, 1933, to 40.4 cents per hour for the week ending Aug. 5. The increase which was announced in the newspapers Aug. 7 was retroactive to Aug. 1. (See the Waltham *News Tribune* of Aug. 7, 1933.) *The News Tribune* of Mar. 16, 1934, reported that the wage increase of Aug. 7, 1933, amounted to 38 per cent but the figure appears to be an error. The average wage did rise gradually from 40.4 cents to approximately 45 cents per hour, but it has not been established whether this rise was due to changes in

rates, changes from unskilled to skilled work, or to an increase in the rate of production by pieceworkers.

The following editorial appeared in the Waltham *Courier*, Aug. 7, 1933:

> The Courier has heard [many], yes, too many, disturbing stories of our Waltham Watch Company regarding wages and hours of employment. Possibly many of these stories were true, and we think the management is as familiar with the story as the Courier. . . . [As a consequence of low wages] the company went out among the trade and got orders for its product at a price making it possible to keep the plant in operation. As a result the company is in much stronger financial and physical condition than any of its competitors, and the city and employees are the gainers. Let us pull together for Waltham and all its industries.

29. The Company's statement was made after the employees' election, which showed a majority in favor of representation by the Amalgamated Watchmakers' Union, an affiliate of the American Federation of Labor. The statement announced that the Company would recognize the rights of employees to bargain collectively through the American Federation of Labor union, the Waltham Watch Employees' Association, or individually. Although the National Recovery Administration was satisfied with this statement at the time, this attitude was later considered by the NLRB to be a violation of the spirit of collective bargaining and it was ruled that the union selected by the majority must bargain for all employees. Waltham *News Tribune*, Sept. 5, 1934; Mar. 21, 1934.

30. Waltham *News Tribune*, Apr. 10, 1934.

31. The NRA code for the watch industry had the following provisions: minimum wages 35 cents per hour, or $14 for a 40-hour week. A 48-hour week was permitted in the rush season, but the average for the year must not exceed 40 hours per week.

The minimum wage for learners was 80% of minimum for workers. Office boys and runners were paid the same wage as learners. Learners must be paid workers' wages after three months' training, or discharged.

32. Waltham *News Tribune*, Apr. 23, 1934.

33. *Ibid.*, May 12, 1934.

34. *Ibid.*, May 8, 1934.

35. The terms of the agreement, in brief, are as follows:

1. Workers pledge observation of the agreement and promise to furnish "efficient, competent, and capable workers."
2. The company is pledged not to discriminate against workers for union connections or activities, but the open shop is preserved.
3. Where qualifications are equal, hiring and firing shall be done with regard to the seniority and the number of dependents of employees.
4. Employees of each department shall elect two representatives from the membership of Local No. 80, Amalgamated Watchmakers' Union. (See note 37.)

5. }
6. } Grievances are to be settled according to a routine procedure.
7. }

8. The final resort for grievances is the Arbitration Committee whose decision is binding on both parties.

9. No strikes or lockouts are permitted, but the Company shall not be forced to operate the plant at a loss.

The agreement was subject to cancellation on any January first upon one month's notice. Waltham *News Tribune,* June 6, 1934.

36. The Arbitration Committee consisted of
Professor Sumner H. Slichter, Harvard Graduate School of Business Administration, Chairman
Judge Patrick Duane, for the Company
Attorney Francis P. Fenton, for the union

37. For details see the Waltham *News Tribune,* Jan. 7 and 16, 1935.

38. *Ibid.,* Jan. 16, 1935.

39. *Ibid.,* Mar. 10, 1934.

40. Report dated Aug. 16, 1933, by J. Freistatder.

41. Waltham *News Tribune,* Mar. 16, 1934.

42. *Ibid.*

43. Waltham Watch Co., Annual Report, Mar. 25, 1935.

CHAPTER XIV

1. Keith, A Family Tale, p. 265.

2. Crossman, *Hist. of Watch and Clock Making,* p. 15.

3. *Ibid.,* p. 12.

4. Keith, *op. cit.,* p. 68.

5. Crossman, *op. cit.,* p. 23.

6. Keith, *op. cit.,* p. 210.

7. *Ibid.,* p. 68.

8. Reports covering the period Jan. 18 to Mar. 15, 1935, by I. E. Boucher and J. Freistadter. Waltham Watch Co. records.

9. Keith, *op. cit.,* p. 71.

10. Cf. E. A. Marsh, *The Evolution of Automatic* [*Watchmaking*] *Machinery* (Chicago, 1896).

11. Stewart, Watts & Bollong, *Review of Progress,* p. 3, and *Reconciliation,* Oct., 1943, p. 2.

12. "Apparently during 1929, A—— consumed a fraction over nine hours labor per watch. During the same year watches produced by us [Waltham] consumed just a fraction of an hour more time than A." From a report by J. Freistadter dated Aug. 16, 1935.

13. Estimates by Waltham officials calculated as of 1936.

14. Keith, *op. cit.,* p. 249.

15. Reports covering the period Jan. 18 to Mar. 15, 1935, by I. E. Boucher and J. Freistadter. Waltham Watch Co. records.

16. Stone, *Hist. of Mass. Industries,* vol. i, p. 945.

CHAPTER XV

1. The cost of distributing Swiss watches to French consumers in 1852 was much less than the cost of distribution to United States consumers, even when duty, freight, and insurance were omitted from the comparison.

2. A letter from E. Tracy to C. N. Thorpe, Bryn Mawr, Nov. 25, 1886.

3. Sales books of the Waltham Watch Co. predecessors, 1857 to 1872.

4. Reginald C. Robbins in an interview, Oct. 14, 1938.

5. Brearley, *Time Telling through the Ages*, pp. 196–205.

6. New York *Times*, Apr. 30, May 19, and June 7, 1921; Jan. 6 and Mar. 10, 1922.

7. According to an advertisement by Elgin in the *Saturday Evening Post*, appearing in the first six months of 1928, there were at that time 14,418 retail jewelers in the United States and all but 12 of them were Elgin dealers.

8. Waltham *Free Press-Tribune*, Dec., 1909. Also exhibits relating to lawsuits brought by Waltham against mail-order houses. Waltham Records, Baker Library, Harvard University.

9. A complete discussion of the data on branch office sales cannot be undertaken, since it would involve current policies which are beyond the scope of this work.

10. A. L. Dennison founded the Dennison Watch Case Co. in Birmingham, England, in 1874. In 1923 it was operated by his descendants.

11. Operating figures are from records submitted by F. C. Dumaine on Aug. 12, 1941. A letter from George Gradon, accountant, to I. E. Boucher dated May 18, 1923, reports an operating loss of £8,479 19s. 6d. for the year ending Feb. 28, 1923. A duty refund made it appear, however, that a profit of £2,544 12s. 9d. had resulted.

These results are in sharp contrast to a letter from Conover Fitch to the London manager, dated Aug. 28, 1922. One paragraph reads, "Mr. Hillyer and I are very much pleased with reports which you are sending and we seem to be making steady progress along the right lines in our London office. . . ."

12. I. E. Boucher in an interview on June 22, 1938.

13. A digest of the agreement between C. A. Schierwater and the Waltham Watch Co. is as follows:

(1) Schierwater to be sole representative of Waltham in Great Britain and Ireland.
(2) Commission to Schierwater to be 5% of the domestic (United States) price.
(3) Uniform price to be charged equal to the domestic price plus duty, plus not more than 5% of the duty.
(4) Schierwater to guarantee all sales.
(5) Stocks to be shipped from Waltham on consignment.
(6) Payment by Schierwater to be in cash. Schierwater to be responsible for the consignments.
(7) Consignments to remain the property of the Waltham Co. until sold by Schierwater.

(8) Accounts to be audited by a Waltham representative.
(9) Schierwater to pay all duties.
(10) Schierwater to remit for sales within 60 days.
(11) All expenses of doing business in Great Britain and Ireland to be borne by Schierwater.
(12) Agreement to remain in force for 5 years, but may be terminated by death or illness of Schierwater.
(13) Schierwater to organize the English company using the Waltham name. Schierwater to own all the stock. Waltham to have one of the two directors of which the board is to consist.
(14) After 5 years and upon 6 months' notice or the illness of Schierwater, Waltham may buy the English company for the subscribed capital or £1,000, whichever is less.
(15) Stock in the English company is assignable to Waltham only.
(16) Both parties intend to renew the agreement for five years if it is successful.
(17) Schierwater may levy on his customers not more than 2½ per cent for publicity and Waltham will pay an equal amount. "Documents," Boston Office File, 1923–29, Waltham Watch Co., Waltham, Mass.

14. The Tokyo office showed a sales expense of 8.6% of net sales in 1935, as compared with the average of 1.6% for the domestic offices and Tokyo.

15. Waltham Watch Co., treasurer's report, Feb., 1877, also dated Mar. 29, 1877.

16. By "aggressive merchandising" is meant the policy of attempting to develop latent consumer needs or preferences into active demands for new models or products.

17. Minutes of the stockholders' meeting, May 22, 1911.

18. "Trading down" refers to the practice of attaching a brand to a high-priced product and later using the brand on a product of lower price. A variety of similar devices for converting goodwill into cash also come under the term.

19. Waltham brand policy. When the Company was founded the product was branded with the name of *Samuel Curtis,* and for many years afterwards the names of various individuals were used. The use of the Company name (then Appleton Tracy & Co.) was begun in 1857 and was placed on the highest-grade watch that was produced at Waltham. During the Civil War a cheap watch, the *Ellery,* was put out, and about that time the brand *American Watch Company* was placed on a new model which sold at wholesale for the high price of $175. After the war, a medium-grade movement carried the brand *Waltham Watch Company.* The brand *Waltham* appears in 1871 on a watch of medium grade. About 1872 the streets adjoining the factory began to be used for brand names, and the *Crescent Street* and *Park Road* models were at the top of the line. In 1879 the *American Watch Company* brand was back at the head of the list, a first-quality movement constructed of nickel selling at $250, wholesale. The catalogues for 1895 show the old brands and *Waltham* on the dial, but about 1910 the dial carried only the *Waltham* brand, while the old brands appeared on

the movement. By 1910 new brands had been added and the old ones reshuffled again, the *American Watch Company* brand appearing near the bottom of the list.

20. Keith, A Family Tale, p. 266.

21. The very cheap watches without jewels are technically pocket clocks. The Ingersoll Watch is reported to have been conceived as a clock reduced in size but of essentially the same construction. See Brearley, *op. cit.*, pp. 200–202.

22. The contrast in advertising copy between 1897 and 1931 is shown by the following quotations, which relate to the same incident:

A. An extract from a leaflet printed in 1897 illustrates the old style:

> The American Watch Was Right
>
> The idea of the owner of an American Watch using his timepiece to correct the Royal Observatory at Greenwich may seem absurd to an Englishman, but that was done recently. One day Thomas Wheate of No. 26 Ormiston Road, Westcombe Park, London, S. E., noticed that the time-ball which falls accurately at 1 o'clock P. M. each day, was, according to his Waltham Watch, a few seconds fast. . . .
>
> "In answer to your letter of yesterday, the Astronomer Royal requests me to inform you that on Thursday last the time-ball was, through an accident, dropped about 18 seconds before 1 o'clock." — New York *Tribune*

The advertising leaflet from which these two passages were taken was composed of a newspaper clipping and a letter which were quoted verbatim with no attempt to write additional copy into the advertisement.

B. A newspaper clipping dated Nov. 28, 1931, carries the following advertisement:

> Waltham Gives You "Time Peace"
>
> A man detected an error of a few seconds in the Greenwich Time signal by his Waltham Watch and was thanked by the Astronomer Royal. This almost uncanny accuracy is Waltham's great claim to fame. There need be no losing of trains, no missing of appointments, no anxieties about time for the owner of a Waltham watch. That is what we mean by "time-peace." Get a Waltham, it is one of the few constant things in a changeable world.

Another comparison follows:

A. An announcement to the trade dated 1897 reads:

> We beg to announce the issue of the following new grade of 12 size movement:
>
> 12 SIZE 3/4 PLATE S. W. MOVEMENTS
> PENDANT SETTING
>
> Hunting or Open Face
>
> No. 250 Nickel:
>
> 17 Fine Ruby Jewels; Gold Settings, Double Roller Escapement; Exposed Pallets; Patent Micrometric Regulation, Compensation Balance, Adjusted to temperature and position; Patent Breguet Hairspring, Hardened and Tempered in Form. $17.50
>
> Robbins & Appleton

B. Extracts from the opening page of the 1938 catalogue read as follows:

> The Premier, this catalog illustrates, is Waltham's latest and best contribution to the Watch World.
>
> Combining all improvements developed during nearly a century of continuous watch making, it has every last element for a perfect time-keeper.
>
> American Made, its purpose is to offer the American public a timepiece equal to any produced in the world at a comparable price.

23. The comments on the subject of advertising are the writer's personal opinions based on the examination of a limited number of samples. Single opinions do not measure the merits of an advertising campaign or the pulling power of advertising copy. The reader may render his own verdict from the samples of copy quoted in note 22.

24. The decalcomania signs were $1\frac{13}{16} \times 8\frac{13}{16}$ inches. The lettering was $\frac{9}{16}$ inches high. A decorative border in gold was used.

25. Boston *Transcript,* Aug. 7, 1933; Dedham *Transcript,* Mar. 24, 1933.

26. The advertising appropriation for 1938 was scheduled for the following distribution:

Catalog and dealers' helps		$70,000
Coöperative Newspaper Advertising		50,000
National Magazines	$10,000 —	15,000
Misc., including Decalcomania signs	10,000 —	5,000
Total Advertising Appropriation		$140,000

CHAPTER XVI

1. A letter from E. Tracy to C. N. Thorpe, Bryn Mawr, Nov. 25, 1886.
2. Hunt's *Merchants' Magazine,* vol. xxii, pp. 80–81.
3. *Ibid.,* pp. 78–79.
4. *Ibid.,* p. 81.
5. *Ibid.,* p. 80.
6. Keith, A Family Tale, pp. 91–92. One 5-acre piece in the Waltham Improvement Company's holdings cost $330 in 1841 and was sold to the Company for $5,000 in 1853.
7. Crossman, Hist. of Watch and Clockmaking, p. 21.
8. Waltham Improvement Co., *Minutes of the Directors' Meeting,* May 29, 1854. "Voted that the treasurer be authorized and instructed to pay over from time to time such balances of Cash as may be in the treasury, (reserving a sufficient sum to meet the expenses and obligations of the Corporation), to the Boston Watch Company, or to their treasurer, upon receiving a promissory note on interest, payable on demand, from the Boston Watch Co. . . ." The money was to be used for the construction of the plant, and the order was to stand until rescinded. The order was rescinded at the directors' meeting of May 21, 1855.
9. Crossman, *op. cit.,* p. 24.

10. Keith, *op. cit.*, pp. 102–103.

11. *Ibid.*, p. 97, and Waltham Improvement Company Cashbook.

Of the original partners, only Samuel Curtis is listed in Abner Forbes, *Rich Men of Massachusetts* (Boston, 1852).

"Curtis, Samuel $150,000
"Started poor. Looking-glass manufacturer."

Of the stockholders of the Waltham Improvement Co. in 1854, Forbes lists the following:

Waltham

"Hobbs, Ebenezer $100,000

"Started poor. Superintendent of a cotton factory. A worthy man. Has given large sums for the benefit of literary institutions in the town."

"Plympton, Thomas $50,000

"Commenced without a copper except what he earned. Figured for a while as watch repairer and general tinkering of articles in that line. Came to Waltham, bought real estate — a good investment, — prospered in his enterprises, and became rich. Has now partially retired to take care of his property."

Boston

"Brown, James $200,000

"Of the firm of Little & Brown, publishers and booksellers. . . . He owns a country seat in Watertown. . . ." [Brown was the previous owner of the main parcel of land bought by the Waltham Improvement Co.]

"Emerson, Elijah $150,000

"Began poor. shoe dealer. Firm of Emerson, Cochran & Co."

S. P. Emerson was foreman of the machine shop of the Boston Mfg. Co. Abbott, *Hist. of Waltham Watch Co.*, p. 18.

In the cases of Curtis, Hobbs, Plympton, and Elijah Emerson, the evidence that the men listed by Forbes were stockholders in the Waltham Improvement Co. depends on the similarity of names.

From the Boston *Almanac* (Boston, 1854), we learn that George E. Porter was a manufacturer of chronometers at 7 Congress St., Boston. E. W. Fiske was deputy sheriff at Waltham. Both these names appear on the list of stockholders. The same source mentions that two jewelry firms in Boston have a partner whose name appears on the stockholders' list. Initials of the partners are not given in the Almanac, and therefore the identity is merely suggested as a logical possibility. The firms are Fessenden Brothers, and Lincoln & Foss.

Fifty-nine shareholders held 75 shares at $1,000 par value each. The remaining 25 shares were subscribed by the Boston Watch Co. The average subscription, not including the shares of the Boston Watch Co., was $1,271. Assessments totaling $387.50 per share were paid in the period 1854 to 1858. Forty of the shareholders were residents of Waltham, a village of about 5,000 inhabitants.

The above data seem to warrant the classification of the Waltham Improvement Co. stockholders as predominantly small investors, both in point of the size of their investments in the Company and of their probable total resources. The list of shareholders follows:

WALTHAM IMPROVEMENT CO. SHAREHOLDERS, 1853

Boston Watch Co. shares nos. 1–25, inclusive:	
Samuel Curtis	
Edward Howard	
A. L. Dennison	
Somerby & Rutter	26
John E. Tolman	27
R. W. Shattuck	28
R. P. Davis	30, 31
Brown Bro.	32
James P. Tolman	33
E. Barnes & Son	34
S. P. Emerson	35
Francis Buttrick	36
Thos. J. Marsh	37
Pope & Whitney	38
F. N. Stone	39
J. & W. Pike	40
Wm. Gibbs	41
E. W. Fiske	42
Josiah Beard	43
J. W. Milliken	44
W. Simonds, Jr.	45
Elijah Emerson	46
Upham & Clark	47
Geo. M. Thompson	48
Dr. Horatio Adams [State Representative]	49, 50
T. R. Plympton	51
Sam B. Whitney	52
Jonathan D. Fiske	53
James Brown	54, 55
Geo. M. Thompson, Trustee	56

J. W. Parmentier	58
Fred J. Foss	57
Josiah Hastings	59
W. A. Blaisdell	60
J. M. S. Williams	61
Eben Hobbs	62, 63
David P. Davis, Trustee [of Howard & Davis]	64
Ann L. Holden	65
Jonathan D. Fiske, Trustee	66, 67
Wm. H. Keith	68–72 inclusive
E. W. Dennison	73
Wm. Sparel [Sparrell]	74
Chas. D. Foster	75
Geo. E. Porter	76
Wm. B. Fessenden	77–79
Chas. M. Foss	80
D. W. Wilder	81
D. H. Rogers	82
B. G. Dennison	84
Matilda O. Dennison	85
A. L. Dennison	86–90
Geo. Hastings	91
John S. Moor	92
Oliver A. Richardson	93
Chas. S. Moseley	94
John Harris	95
Horatio Moore	96
M. L. Beckford	97
Steven C. Kendall	98
Wm. H. Keith, Trustee	99
Thos. J. Marsh, Jr.	100

12. Crossman, *op. cit.*, pp. 24–25.

13. Keith, *op. cit.*, p. 57.

14. Brearley, *Time Telling through the Ages*, p. 171.

15. Keith, *op. cit.*, pp. 70–75.

16. Crossman, *op. cit.*, p. 10.

17. *Ibid.*, p. 91; Stone, *Hist. of Mass. Industries*, vol. i, p. 945; Dennison correspondence. The evidence is pertinent, but not conclusive.

18. E. Tracy to C. N. Thorpe, Bryn Mawr, Nov. 25, 1886.

19. Anonymous History, pp. 22–23.

20. Keith, *op. cit.*, p. 176. Where wages are cut far below the general level for the time and place considered, it is equivalent to a contribution by labor to the working capital of the company.

21. Not including the common-stock issue of 70,000 shares in 1906.

22. Significant figures on the ownership of stock in the Waltham Watch Co. are given in the following tabulation:

Year	*Mo.*	*Owner*		*Total Shares Owned*	*Total Shares Issued*	*% of Total*	*Business Activity*[a]
1857	Oct.	R. E. Robbins		....	....	About 84	− 10.1
1859	Mar.	"		1,240	2,000	62	+ 0.3
1862	Feb.	"		1,050	2,841	37	− 7.3
1863	Feb.	"		1,238	3,000	41	+ 1.3
1865	Aug.	"		3,364	7,500	45	− 13.5
1866	Aug.	"		2,175	7,500	29	+ 9.2
1871	Feb.	"		1,683	12,500	13½	+ 0.4
1871	Aug.	"		2,600	12,500	21	+ 5.6
1873	Feb.	"		2,323	12,500	18½	+ 14.3
1873	Aug.	"		1,564	15,000	10½	+ 5.0
1874	Aug.	"		1,030	15,000	7	− 3.9
1875	Feb.	"		3,083	15,000	30½	− 6.8
1881	Feb.	"		4,837	15,000	32	+ 10.6
1883	Feb.	"		4,394	15,000	29	+ 6.9
1901	Aug.	"		3,111	40,000	8	+ 4.2
1906	Dec.	Estate of R. E. Robbins	PFD.	4,777	40,000	12	+ 11.8
1907	Dec.	" " "	COM.	6,091	70,000	8½	− 17.2
1909	Dec.	R. E. Robbins (ALL)	COM.	8,107	70,000	11½	+ 9.4
1910	Nov.	" "	PFD.	2,552	50,000	5	− 4.1
1909	Dec.	R. E. Robbins' Sons[b]	COM.	185	70,000	0.2	..
1910	Nov.	" "	PFD.	285	50,000	0.6	..
1901	Aug.	J. P. Morgan		1,334	40,000	3½	..
		J. P. Morgan & Co.		200	40,000	½	..
1906	Dec.	J. P. Morgan	PFD.	1,500	40,000	4	..
1910	Nov.	"	"	832	50,000	1½	..
1910	Nov.	Kidder, Peabody & Co.	"	786	50,000	1½	..
1883	Feb.	E. C. Fitch		165	15,000	1	..
1910	Nov.	"	PFD.	4,036	50,000	8	..
1909	Dec.	"	COM.	8,987	70,000	13	..
1923	Feb.	"	COM.	4,302[c]	70,000	6	..

[a] Ayres, *Business Activity and Four Price Series*, 1938.

[b] Royal Robbins and R. C. Robbins.

[c] *Abbot* v. *Waltham*, p. 457.

SOURCE: Dividend records of the Company.

23. Stockholdings of the Robbins group, Aug. 26, 1901, compiled from the Dividend records of the Waltham Watch Co.:

Shareholder	*No. of Shares*
R. E. Robbins	3,111
H. A. Robbins	2,925
Robbins Ex'r	200
Royal Robbins	16
R. C. Robbins	22
H. P. Robbins	75
Miss F. A. Robbins	200
Mrs. M. P. Robbins	36
Robbins & Appleton	4,560
Robbins Appleton & Co.	585
D. F. Appleton	399
D. F. Appleton, Atty.	3
Mrs. Susan C. Appleton	100
Francis R. Appleton	520
Mrs. Fanny Appleton	200
James W. Appleton	40
Total	12,992

Total shares outstanding, 40,000.
Owned by Robbins group, 32 per cent of the shares outstanding.
Total shares voted at the stockholders' meeting in 1901 = 12,567.

24. E. Tracy to C. N. Thorpe, Bryn Mawr, Nov. 25, 1886.

25. See Appendix D on stockholders.

26. The official records do not show that the board of directors lacked harmony, but the evidence in *Abbot* v. *Waltham* and the context of informal correspondence and comment suggest that any drastic or incisive measures would have met with great opposition.

27. Waltham Watch Co., *Report to Stockholders,* Oct. 16, 1922.

28. The relationship between F. C. Dumaine and Kidder, Peabody & Co. was based on Dumaine's friendship for Robert Winsor of that firm. For this reason the relationship is not subject to precise definition, but Dumaine's position may be considered as analogous to that of a silent partner.

29. See N. S. B. Gras, "Types of Capitalism," a monograph in *Facts and Factors in Economic History* (Cambridge, 1932), pp. 580–595.

30. F. C. Dumaine has been reputed to be the "owner" of the Waltham Watch Co. (that is, 1923–44). Indirect evidence, such as the personnel of the Board of Directors, lends some support to the popular belief. Statistics on the ownership of the Company's securities are not at hand. It is believed that Dumaine has owned a large minority block of the voting stock.

CHAPTER XVII

1. See illustration, War Products, opposite page 278.

2. Rudolph Bruce to C. W. Moore, Dec. 10, 1943.

3. On page 20 of the agreement by and between the Waltham Watch Company and the Waltham Watch Workers' Union. In effect: Oct. 30, 1943, to Apr. 30, 1944.

4. Waltham *News Tribune,* Apr. 24, 1943.

5. From an interview with Ira Guilden on March 22, 1945.

6. See the *Prospectus, Waltham Watch Company.* Securities and Exchange Commission, April 9, 1945.

INDEX